AN AGE OF TRANSITION?

An Age of Transition?

Economy and Society in England in the Later Middle Ages

CHRISTOPHER DYER

The Ford Lectures
delivered in the University of Oxford
in Hilary Term 2001

CLARENDON PRESS · OXFORD

OXFORD

UNIVERSITY PRESS

Great Clarendon Street, Oxford OX2 6DP

Oxford University Press is a department of the University of Oxford.
It furthers the University's objective of excellence in research, scholarship,
and education by publishing worldwide in

Oxford New York

Auckland Cape Town Dar es Salaam Hong Kong Karachi Kuala Lumpur
Madrid Melbourne Mexico City Nairobi New Delhi Shanghai Taipei
Toronto

With offices in

Argentina Austria Brazil Chile Czech Republic France Greece
Guatemala Hungary Italy Japan Poland Portugal
Singapore South Korea Switzerland Thailand Turkey Ukraine Vietnam

Published in the United States
by Oxford University Press Inc., New York

© Christopher Dyer 2005

British Library Cataloguing in Publication Data

Data available

Library of Congress Cataloging in Publication Data

Data available

ISBN 0-19-822166-5

1 3 5 7 9 10 8 6 4 2

Typeset by Kolam Information Services Pvt. Ltd, Pondicherry, India

Printed in Great Britain
on acid-free paper by
Biddles Ltd
King's Lynn, Norfolk

Preface

This book is based on the Ford Lectures which were delivered in the University of Oxford in the Hilary Term of 2001. In introducing his celebrated Ford Lectures in 1953, K. B. McFarlane reports that some of his students imagined that the lectures were funded by the Ford motor company. Their founder was in fact James Ford, the vicar of Navestock in Essex, who cannot have anticipated that his modest endowment would be so influential, not just through the lectures as delivered, but more widely in their published versions. I confess that when an Oxford friend at a seminar at All Souls in 1998 gave me the first hint that I might be asked to give these lectures—'Have you heard from the Ford?'—my immediate reaction, accustomed as I am to writing references for applicants for research grants, was to assume that he was referring to the Ford Foundation, and to think of another place in Essex, Dagenham. This lapse reveals me to be an outsider in Oxford, as I have not been a student or teacher there, with the exception of lectures over the years at Rewley House, the University's lively external studies department. As the result of the generous invitation from the Ford electors, and the good advice of Dr Paul Slack, the chair of the electors, I was able to spend six months living in Oxford. The fellows of St John's College elected me to their Senior Research Fellowship, which provided me with a house in the town, with easy access to the Bodleian Library and to local archives such as those of Magdalen College. The Oxford historians and archaeologists were very generous in their hospitality, and this gave me the opportunity to sample the cuisine, conversation, ambience, and variety of Latin graces in a dozen colleges.

A lecture is very different from a book chapter, and I have encountered the usual dilemmas in converting pieces of writing designed for oral delivery into the fuller and more formal prose appropriate for a book. My solution to the problem has been to preserve the original structure of the six lectures. The obvious difficulty derives from the fact that a text delivered within an hour is so brief that the volume resulting from six lectures, if it faithfully represented the oral version, would be very slim. In my case the script that I carried into the lecture room was much longer than could be accommodated within the allotted time. The text had been drastically shortened with ruthless pencil excisions, but in a process which was uncomfortable for the lecturer (but one hopes not too obvious to listeners), paraphrasing sometimes had to be done at the moment of delivery. The result of this risky strategy was that a full-length book has emerged naturally out of the lecture texts.

Dozens of people and organizations contributed to the development of the ideas and information that this book contains, and I hope that my selection of those to be acknowledged here causes no offence. My first thanks are to the British Academy, who generously funded the gathering of material and time to analyse it, well before these lectures were delivered. The Arts and Humanities Research Board helped by granting me under their research leave scheme an extra term for research. The University of Birmingham assisted my work by their policy of granting study leaves. The material on which the book depends has been gathered from more than thirty archives, record offices, and libraries, and I thank the staff of those institutions. I have already mentioned the help that I received from the Ford electors, Paul Slack, and St John's College, and I am very grateful to them. Rees Davies, the Chichele professor, gave good advice, and organized a seminar as an addition to the traditional lecture series, which gave an opportunity for dialogue between lecturer and some of those attending. Specific practical help, references to sources, and general encouragement were provided by Nat Alcock, Anne Baker, George Demidowicz, Geoff Egan, Harold Fox, Mark Gardiner, Evan Jones, Derek Keene, Hannes Kleineke, John Langdon, Jane Laughton, Maureen Mellor, Colin Richmond, Chris Thornton, Penny Upton, Jei Yang, and Margaret Yates. The typescript was prepared by Nancy Moore, and Andy Isham drew the maps and figures. Jenny Dyer helpfully commented on drafts. Barbara Harvey and John Langdon read the whole text and recommended improvements. At the Oxford University Press I was encouraged initially by Tony Morris, and then by the always patient and helpful Ruth Parr and Anne Gelling. Jeff New has been an observant and conscientious editor.

The success of a lecture series depends on those who attend the occasions. No one was under any obligation to take part, and the presence of the Oxford historians, and many visitors from Birmingham and elsewhere, maintained my morale, and led me to believe that the material merited the extra effort to produce this book. I should add that preparing and delivering these lectures changed my life in a number of ways. Working and living in Oxford provided an intense and enjoyable respite from the routines of teaching and administration of normal academic life. Within two months of the last lecture I had decided to accept an offer of a new post at the University of Leicester. The move inevitably took up some time, which delayed the writing of this book, but Leicester's generous treatment has also given me the opportunity to bring the lectures through the last stages for publication.

C.C.D.

April 2004

Contents

List of Maps and Figures

List of Tables

Abbreviations

AHEW	*Agrarian History of England and Wales*, ed. J. Thirsk; vol. 2, *1042–1350*, ed. H. E. Hallam (Cambridge, 1988); vol. 3, 1348–1500, ed. E. Miller (Cambridge, 1991)
Ag.HR	*Agricultural History Review*
CUHB	*Cambridge Urban History of Britain*, ed. P. Clark; vol. 1, *c.600–1540*, ed. D. Palliser (Cambridge, 2000); vol. 2, *1540–1840*, ed. P. Clark (Cambridge, 2000)
Ec.HR	*Economic History Review*
MA	*Medieval Archaeology*
P&P	*Past and Present*
TNA: PRO	*The National Archives: the Public Record Office*
VCH	*Victoria County History*

Introduction

The 'transition' in this book's title refers to an old historical dilemma, which goes back to the beginnings of scientific history in the nineteenth century. The post-Roman centuries have usually been divided between the medieval and the modern periods, with a line drawn around the year 1500. Characteristics of modernity include new forms of the state, religious diversity, and the spread of renaissance ideas. Those influenced by Marxist ideas prefer to think of feudalism being superseded by capitalism, which can be dated as late as the eighteenth century, but the decades around 1500, the age of the English enclosures and the voyages of discovery, can be seen as a significant turning point in that process. Those using the vocabulary and concepts of 'medieval' and 'modern', and those favouring 'feudal' and 'capitalist' recognize that changes did not occur overnight, and therefore expect to find a transitional phase, and this idea provided the starting point for this exploration of social and economic tendencies at the end of the middle ages.[1]

Here it will be shown that social structures and methods of production were remodelled in the long fifteenth century (1350–1520), reiterating the traditional view of the significance of that period. A number of the characteristics of the economy at the end of the middle ages, however, can be traced back to the thirteenth century. Those who promoted change included people below the ranks of the gentry, including the peasants who are sometimes seen as the victims.[2] This conclusion leads to an emphasis on the social basis of

[1] For the debate on the transition, R. H. Hilton (ed.), *The Transition from Feudalism to Capitalism* (London, 1976); R. J. Holton, *The Transition from Feudalism to Capitalism* (London, 1985).

[2] For the controversy on this issue, see T. H. Aston and C. H. E. Philpin (eds.), *The Brenner Debate: Agrarian Class Structure and Economic Development in Pre-Industrial Europe* (Cambridge, 1985); P. Glennie, 'In Search of Agrarian Capitalism: Manorial Land Markets and the Acquisition of Land in the Lea Valley *c.*1450–*c.*1560', *Continuity and Change*, 3 (1988), 11–40; R. W. Hoyle, 'Tenure and the Land Market in Early Modern England: Or a Late Contribution to the Brenner Debate', *Ec.HR*, 2nd ser., 43 (1990), 1–20; M. E. Mate, 'The East Sussex Land Market and Agrarian Class Structure in the Late Middle Ages', *P&P* 139 (1993), 46–65.

change, against a background of fluctuations in population, prices, wages, and rents.

Historians of economy and society have been offered in the 'transition from feudalism to capitalism' a framework for interpreting the past. According to Marx and his successors, a feudal society or mode of production was fundamentally agrarian and based on the extraction of rents and services from a dependent peasantry by a ruling aristocracy. This was replaced by capitalism, in which entrepreneurs who owned the means of production employed a class of wage-earners, and were governed in their economic activities by the forces of the market. This scheme of historical change now seems old-fashioned, with its use of such outmoded terms as 'class', yet as with many of these old questions, even if we use different words we cannot escape from the fundamental problem.

To use more conventional twenty-first-century language, England in 1150 had a mainly agricultural economy, with a numerous peasantry. Exchange was limited, so that there were relatively few towns, and industry was based on handicrafts in family workshops. A powerful aristocracy extracted wealth through rents and services from a subordinate peasantry. Custom, tradition, patronage, honour, service, and coercion played a large part in social relations. The church enjoyed great landed resources, controlled education, and influenced the whole of society though its teachings. All of these characteristics had changed considerably by 1550. Trade had become part of everyone's daily experience, towns had multiplied, England was one of the most industrialized countries in Europe, much land was worked in holdings so large that we doubt whether we should call their tenants peasants, and lords' economic influence had been weakened. The market had a more pervasive impact, and service in exchange for the tenure of land played little part in social relations. Private courts wielded reduced power, and many customs had lapsed. The church had been brought under closer control by the state. Much remained of the old conditions, and world trade, colonial expansion, large farms, factories, and secular education would not be fully established until the nineteenth century. Historians should be concerned with explaining how, when, and why these transformations came about.

The lectures which are the basis of this book examine a long chronology of economic and social change. They argue that many of the tendencies of the end of the middle ages had their roots in a much earlier period. The framework of units of landholding and the agrarian landscape had been created before 1200. The network of towns had largely formed by 1300. When the number of fields enclosed within hedges was controversially increased around 1500, much of the land in some districts had been lying in closes and crofts for centuries, and indeed there had been an earlier controversy over enclosure in the early thirteenth century. The advance of commercialization, as towns grew and markets multiplied in the thirteenth century, has led to doubts about whether the changes of the long fifteenth century were of much significance.[3]

We must accept that marketing and a commercial mentality grew before 1300, but not lose sight of the impressive developments after 1350. The initial burgeoning of the commercial economy took place in the period of rising population in the twelfth and thirteenth centuries, when numbers grew from perhaps $2\frac{1}{2}$ million in 1100 to 5 or 6 million in 1300. In the fourteenth century the population was halved. The decline began with the famine of 1315–17, continued with the slow erosion of the period 1320–48, and then accelerated with the epidemics of 1348–9 and 1361–2. In the long fifteenth century the population remained obstinately low, apparently hovering around $2\frac{1}{2}$ million until about 1540. Resources, and particularly land, were therefore concentrated in fewer hands, and the rewards of wage-earners were high. This period of relatively high individual incomes had a wide impact on the shape of the economy, because improved living standards resulted in new patterns of consumption, with demand for high-quality foodstuffs such as beef, and for textiles, housing, and other goods. At the same time, and of greater long-term significance, land was being brought together in larger holdings, and more land was being managed by tenants rather than by lords. Cloth-making, an industry which had satisfied a high proportion of home demand and no more in *c*.1300, had become a major exporter by 1500.

Just as the commercial growth of the thirteenth century prepared the way for the structural changes of the fifteenth, so developments before 1500 can be connected with the trends of the early modern period. The divergence in rural society between prosperous yeomen and labourers, innovations in farm-ing such as the use of leys, the growth in occupational specialization (so that by 1688 40 per cent of the population were employed in non-agricultural jobs), and the rise of a 'consumer society' were all continuing tendencies that are apparent in the fifteenth century.[4] Of course there were many novelties in the sixteenth and seventeenth centuries, including the long-term conse-quences of the Reformation, overseas expansion, new crops and industries,

[3] R. H. Britnell, 'Commerce and Capitalism in Late Medieval England: Problems of Description and Theory', *Journal of Historical Sociology*, 6 (1993), 359–76.

[4] R. H. Tawney, *The Agrarian Problem in the Sixteenth Century* (London, 1912); M. Spufford, *Contrasting Communities: English Villagers in the Sixteenth and Seventeenth Centuries* (Cambridge, 1974), 46–164; K. Wrightson, ' "Sorts of people" in Tudor and Stuart England', in J. Barry and C. Brooks (eds.), *The Middling Sort of People: Culture, Society and Politics in England, 1550–1800*; E. A. Wrigley, 'Country and Town: The Primary, Secondary and Tertiary Peopling of England in the Early Modern Period', in P. Slack and R. Ward (eds.), *The Peopling of Britain: The Shaping of a Human Landscape. The Linacre Lectures 1999* (Oxford, 2002), 225–6; J. Thirsk, *Economic Policy and Projects: The Development of a Consumer Society in Early Modern England* (Oxford, 1978).

inflation, and population growth, but it is hard to draw a sharp dividing line through the decades around 1500 and state that this marks the start of a new era.

How and why did these changes come about? Towns were not in themselves the sources of new ideas and structures, as they had been born out of traditional landed society. Of course the urban economy helped to change the orientation of the whole country, by encouraging agricultural specialization, for example, and creating numerous jobs in rural crafts and retail trade. The ups and downs in population, which had in turn a strong influence on long-term trends in prices and wages, provide the backdrop for economic activity, but do not in themselves explain structural change. For example, when people were scarce and land cheap, holdings increased in size. Making a profit from large acreages posed many problems, because corn was sold cheaply and labour hired at great cost. When population rose decisively again after 1540, and the demand for land grew, the holdings were not necessarily fragmented, but instead new generations of tenants cultivated them in different circumstances, with cheap labour and high prices for the crops.[5]

Social factors need to be used in interpreting these processes. The aristocracy mattered a great deal: they are best defined as all of those living on the profits of lordship, rents, and such revenues as court profits, which brings together the gentry (gentlemen, esquires, and knights) and the higher nobility (barons and earls). Because of their very similar position as controllers of landed estates, the higher ranks of the clergy and monastic houses must also be included. Competition among different members and groups within the aristocracy, and the shifting effectiveness with which they dominated the rest of society, stimulated change. Above all, their retreat from direct cultivation of the land, even among the gentry, gave opportunities for the peasants to take over a larger proportion of agricultural production. Peasants can be defined as small-scale cultivators, and plenty of them were still working holdings of 30 acres and below that figure in 1550. So many, however, had acquired large holdings with 60 acres and above that they were emerging out of the peasantry, and were called at the time yeomen, graziers, and farmers. Many initiatives came from the ranks of society below the gentry. The improvement in peasant conditions, including the disappearance of serfdom, the reduction in rents, and the general removal of impositions, were made possible by the scarcity of people, but were also demanded and secured by the actions of peasants themselves.[6] New techniques, and much of the investment

[5] J. Whittle, *The Development of Agrarian Capitalism: Land and Labour in Norfolk 1440–1580* (Oxford, 2000), esp. 5–27, 173–7.
[6] R. H. Hilton, *Bond Men Made Free: Medieval Peasant Movements and the English Rising of 1381* (London, 1973), 233–6; id., *Class Conflict and the Crisis of Feudalism* (London, 1985), esp. 216–26.

in enclosures, buildings, and mills originated with them rather than with the aristocracy. We become more aware of a minority of people who do not fall within the conventional social categories implied by such commonplace modern phrases as 'lords and peasants' or 'merchants and artisans', or the medieval notion that society consisted of warriors, clergy, and peasants. These groups included the managers of production, such as the farmers of land and clothiers, and the many middlemen, dealers, and mongers who organized sections of the market.

The context for all of these changes was provided by the centralized English state. Continental states have been credited with channelling and directing economic activity.[7] In England we can find monopolies and protection of special interests, but the country lacked the widespread enforcement of controls and exclusive rights. In spite of the legal disputes over property and outbreaks of violence, much of it aristocratic, the political regime in England, compared with those elsewhere, offered some protection for property rights and a secure environment for trade.

In the late fifteenth and early sixteenth century England can be depicted as a commercialized society, in which complex transactions, often involving credit, could be conducted, in which farmers were cultivating on a large scale, and in which towns offered a network of internal markets and access to the international trading system. Did the population of England have an individualistic, wealth-seeking outlook? Certainly, concepts of 'improvement' and profit were familiar, and we can see in the arrangement of settlements and houses a concern for maintaining personal privacy and the definition of property boundaries. On the other hand, family loyalties, though diminished, still survived, and individuals supported communities by, for example, contributing generously to the funds of their parish church.

This was not as expansive a society as we might expect. Trade grew after the 1460s, but until the great surge of inflation just before 1520 prices remained low. Population expansion in theory should have been encouraged by high wages, full employment, large landholdings, and profitable industries. It was held back, partly by high mortality, which tended to increase at the end of the fifteenth century, but also by the adoption of a custom of late marriage, and by the celibacy of a minority. Can England be described as a capitalist society in the early sixteenth century? For all of the movements in that direction, and the prevalence of wage labour, much work was carried out by smallholders employed for part of the year, and young people serving others at the

---

[7] T. Scott, *Freiburg and the Breisgau: Town–Country Relations in the Age of Reformation and Peasants' War* (Oxford, 1986); T. Scott, *Regional Identity and Economic Change: The Upper Rhine, 1450–1600* (Oxford, 1997); S. R. Epstein, *Freedom and Growth: The Rise of States and Markets in Europe, 1300–1750* (London, 2000).

beginning of their careers. Marx's proletariat, that is, a numerous workforce dependent entirely on wages in the long term, had still not emerged.

The sources used in this enquiry are necessarily varied. Those investigating the economic and social history of the thirteenth and fourteenth centuries are aided by the remarkable series of records generated by the manor: surveys, accounts made by reeves and bailiffs, and the rolls of the manor court and the court leet. These can be supplemented by the deeds recording the property transfers of free tenants, tax records, the judicial and administrative records of the state, the registers of bishops, and the archives of the towns. Some of these sources of information disappear or decline after 1400. This was not an administrative accident. Detailed surveys and accounts were not needed as lords ceased to manage their demesnes directly, or use labour services. The manor courts lost power and functions. Tax assessment was left to local communities to organize among themselves, out of sight of both the royal authority and the modern historian. A great deal of administration was conducted in a similar way, that is, informally, by word of mouth, and in consequence without documentation. Accordingly, as this investigation moves into the fifteenth century it takes note of manorial records, but makes use of the archives of new organizations such as fraternities and churchwardens, and the leases, letters, and wills which increase in number. Much information can be gleaned from the material evidence of buildings, artefacts, and the landscape. Historians have to follow the movement away from the lords to their former subordinates, but during that shift gaps appear, as the new economic leaders kept few records. For that reason we rely on indirect evidence, and must read between the lines of our sources. Inevitably, much remains uncertain, and some of the questions that we ask cannot receive a definite answer.

I

A New Middle Ages

Readers may find the title of this first chapter pretentious, but it claims no more than to provide an outline of 'a' new middle ages, a particular view of the period, and one of many alternative and valid perspectives. It has some slight connection with 'the' new middle ages of the cultural historians, which offers new insights based on the close analysis of texts. But it has nothing to do with 'the' New Middle Ages hailed as the next phase of history by a school of German philosophers who are expressing their frustrations with the impersonal and individualistic spirit of the modern age.[1] The choice of title is partly designed to attract the curiosity of non-specialists, as one of my concerns is to create links between medieval historians and those of the modern period. Indeed, one of my themes will be the similarities between the economic and social history of the middle ages and that of the centuries after 1500.

The medieval period which will be considered here runs from about 400 to about 1500, and the phases of that period on which I will be concentrating, the later middle ages, begins in the thirteenth century and is usually thought to have ended around 1500, but I will press forward into the first few decades of the sixteenth century.

My title refers to the way in which the approach to the economy and society of the middle ages has shifted radically in the last twenty years, and I hope that I am representing here not just my own views, but those of the small community of scholars who have reconceived and rewritten the economic and social history of the period.[2] I will emphasize more than is customary the ability of medieval people to overcome their problems, the

---

[1] O. G. Oexle, 'The Middle Ages Through Modern Eyes: A Historical Problem', *Transactions of the Royal Historical Society*, 6th ser., 9 (1999), 121–42.

[2] The two most influential works are R. H. Britnell, *The Commercialisation of English Society, 1100–1500* (Cambridge, 1993) and B. M. S. Campbell, *English Seigniorial Agriculture, 1250–1450* (Cambridge, 2000).

long-term themes that run through the period, such as the use of the market, the positive changes in the years 1350–1520, and the active role of the lower ranks of society.

Ways of Looking at Economic and Social History

The 'old middle ages', or rather the interpretation which was well established in the 1970s painted a picture of economic failure. The period can be divided into three distinct phases.[3] Growth is recorded up to about 1300—that is, an expansion in the number of people, in the number and size of settlements, in the area of land under agricultural exploitation, especially the area under the plough, and in overall output. The twelfth and thirteenth centuries saw an expanding commercial economy, with an increase in the number, size, and wealth of towns. The amount of money in circulation more than doubled between 1200 and 1300, and prices increased. The revenues of the great landed estates sometimes rose threefold. Then in the second phase came the crisis of the fourteenth century, associated with the Great Famine of 1315–17, and the plague epidemics, especially the Black Death of 1348–9, when most of the upward movements stopped or went into reverse. The third period, from the late fourteenth to the early sixteenth century, contains puzzling and contradictory trends, in one phrase 'both . . . a time of economic decline . . . and . . . the golden age of the English peasantry'; in the view of one commentator a period of economic growth, for others a time of urban decay.[4] The main tendencies on which everyone can agree include a contraction in population, settlement, and cultivated land. Grain prices and rents declined. The volume of production and the export trade in primary commodities such as wool were reduced. The period breaks down into a series of episodes, with turning points in about 1375, after which corn became cheap, in the 1430s, when a near famine combined with a slump in trade and a fall in lords' incomes, and in the 1460s, when trade showed signs of revival.[5] A French

---

[3] This is based on many general works interpreting the period, such as J. L. Bolton, *The Medieval English Economy 1150–1500* (London, 1980). For a similar continental perspective, P. Contamine et al., *L'Économie médiévale* (Paris, 1993).

[4] The quotation comes from M. M. Postan, *The Medieval Economy and Society: An Economic History of Britain 1100–1500* (London, 1972), 142; A. R. Bridbury, *Economic Growth: England in the Later Middle Ages* (London, 1962); A. Dyer, *Decline and Growth in English Towns 1400–1600* (Cambridge, 1995).

[5] On episodes within the period, C. Dyer, 'Did the Peasants Really Starve in Medieval England?', in M. Carlin and J. Rosenthal (eds.), *Food and Eating in Medieval Europe* (London, 1998), 70; A. Pollard, 'The North-Eastern Economy and the Agrarian Crisis of 1438–40', *Northern History*, 25 (1989), 88–105; J. Hatcher, 'The Great Slump of the Mid-Fifteenth Century', in R. Britnell and

historian has now employed the phrase 'the great medieval depression' to describe the whole of the fourteenth and fifteenth centuries, but he has also written about the 'crisis of feudalism', which implied that new developments emerged from the ruins of the old social system.[6]

This book is designed to counteract the view that these phases should be seen as frustrated by underdevelopment and constraints. It was once argued that population growth in the twelfth and thirteenth centuries, unchecked by major epidemic disease, frequent catastrophic crop failures, or other natural or man-made disasters, led to high densities of people seeking to make their living from limited amounts of land. An increasing proportion of the rural population were holding no more than a few acres, and depended for part of their living on thinly rewarded wage labour. Eventually poor land, which had been taken into cultivation under pressure for holdings and food production, proved to be infertile. The good corn-growing land, which was deprived of manure by the ploughing up of pasture and the restricted numbers of animals, was starved of nutrients. Cultivators did not make technical innovations to relieve these problems. Less productive land was gradually abandoned after 1300. Famine and disease took a terrible toll among the population, which was halved during the fourteenth century.[7]

For those who took a pessimistic view of the expansion of the twelfth and thirteenth centuries, it seemed to represent a false start, an illusory growth which made the years around 1300 a period of particular misery.[8] In addition to the overextension in the countryside, the larger towns also seem to have expanded too far. Some commentators emphasize the influx of poor immigrants, desperate for casual work or charitable handouts, with the consequence that the towns suffered from 'elephantiasis'.[9] Towns had as their principal function the supply of luxury goods to the elite, which inevitably limited their economic base. High rents and frequent taxes contributed to the

---

J. Hatcher (eds.), *Progress and Problems in Medieval England: Essays in Honour of Edward Miller* (Cambridge, 1996), 237–72; P. Spufford, *Money and its Use in Medieval Europe* (Cambridge, 1988), 339–77.

[6] G. Bois, *La Grande Dépression médiévale: XIVᵉ–XVᵉ siècles. Le précédent d'une crise systémique* (Paris, 2000); id., *The Crisis of Feudalism: Economy and Society in Eastern Normandy c.1300–1550* (Cambridge, 1984).

[7] This is a schematic summary of Postan's hypothesis, for which see Postan, *Medieval Economy*, and his chapter in M. M. Postan (ed.), *Cambridge Economic History of Europe*, Vol. I, *The Agrarian life of the Middle Ages*, 2nd edn. (Cambridge, 1966), 548–632; M. M. Postan, *Medieval Agriculture and General Problems of the Medieval Economy* (Cambridge, 1973). His views have been supported by others, e.g. J. Z. Titow, *English Rural Society 1200–1350* (London, 1969).

[8] *AHEW* ii. 772–9; M. Bailey, 'Peasant Welfare in England, 1290–1348', *Ec.HR* 51 (1998), 223–51.

[9] A. R. Bridbury, 'English Provincial Towns in the Later Middle Ages', *Ec.HR*, 2nd ser., 34 (1981), 3.

problems of the rural population. Lords did well from the sale of high-priced grain and wool, but put only a limited amount back into their estates by way of investment.[10]

If the problems around 1300 were caused mainly by large numbers of people dependent on limited resources, surely the halving of the population after 1349 would have removed the pressure, and made individuals more prosperous in the succeeding generations. This was the period, for historians emphasizing the economic failures, of the great depression in the middle of the fifteenth century, when overseas trade, rents, and prices all reached a low point.[11] The 'bullion famine' has been identified at the same time, when precious metals were in short supply, which is believed to have depressed prices and commerce.[12] The population was kept low until after 1500, even after 1530, it is said, mainly because of high levels of mortality, with epidemics frequent enough to cut back any population growth that might have been encouraged by good harvests and cheap food.[13] Faint rays of hope can be given a gloomy interpretation. Wages rose, and those in employment in the fifteenth century, even during the great depression, enjoyed a standard of living that was not to be attained again until the late nineteenth century.[14] However, earnings may not have risen as fast as wage rates. It is said that the feckless workers, if given more money, would work for a few days, take enough cash to satisfy their basic needs, and go off to enjoy themselves in the alehouse and to play wasteful games.[15] Productivity in agriculture, which was low before 1348, did not rise much in the period of labour scarcity. Workers may have increased their output per head, as few people were totally unemployed, but if measured in relation to the amount of land, then productivity tended to fall, partly because of the reduction in the labour applied to such time-consuming tasks as clod-breaking or weeding.[16] The amount harvested for each acre declined, and the weight of a sheep's fleece was reduced, partly because of adverse weather conditions.[17] Even the

[10] J. R. Maddicott, *The English Peasantry and the Demands of the Crown, 1294–1341*, *P&P* supplement, 1 (1975); R. H. Hilton, 'Rent and Capital Formation in Feudal Society', in id., *The English Peasantry in the Later Middle Ages* (Oxford, 1975), 174–214.

[11] Hatcher, 'Great Slump'.

[12] J. Day, *The Medieval Market Economy* (Oxford, 1987), 1–54; P. Nightingale, *A Medieval Mercantile Community: The Grocers' Company and the Politics and Trade of London 1000–1485* (New Haven and London, 1995), 463–89.

[13] J. Hatcher, 'Mortality in the Fifteenth Century: Some New Evidence', *Ec.HR*, 2nd ser., 39 (1986), 19–38; B. Harvey, *Living and Dying in England, 1100–1540* (Oxford, 1993), 112–45.

[14] C. Dyer, *Standards of Living in the Later Middle Ages: Social Change in England c.1200–1520*, revised edn. (Cambridge, 1998), 306–11.

[15] J. Hatcher, 'Labour, Leisure and Economic Thought Before the Nineteenth Century', *P&P* 160 (1998), 64–115.

[16] Campbell, *Seigniorial Agriculture*, 375–80.

[17] M. Stephenson, 'Wool Yields in the Medieval Economy', *Ec.HR*, 2nd ser., 41 (1988), 368–91.

advances of the period around 1500, when trade was climbing out of its earlier depressed state, may not have benefited many people: industry only expanded in 1450–1540 enough to employ another 1.3 per cent of the adult population, and the continued low levels of population prevented more growth.[18]

Like any historical interpretation, perceptions of the middle ages reflect our attitudes to our own times. Some historians take a very favourable view of modern progress, and consequently make a low assessment of medieval achievements. Writing on early modern towns can begin with a bleak picture of the urban scene around 1500, in which the market towns seem small and stunted, and lacking in amenities and civilization. They were particularly underdeveloped, it is said, in such regions as the north of England. All of this changed with the 'urban renaissance', the growth of the 'leisure town' and a general improvement in the size and importance of towns.[19] In fact the number of towns did not increase greatly in the three centuries after 1500, and many towns under Elizabeth were still returning to the size they had reached in the time of Edward I. Medieval towns were by no means lacking in social complexity or cultural activity. It is true that written sources become more abundant and informative after 1540, which accounts for some of the perceived differences. But sometimes we do not depend on documents, as in the case of buildings, for which the main evidence comes from the structures themselves. The belief that the overwhelming majority of surviving timber-framed houses belong to the 'Tudor' period, and to a late date within that period, has been corrected by scientific evidence showing that many were built between 1380 and 1530.[20]

Historians whose work is focused on the centuries before 1500 sometimes show low expectations of the period. They have used modern yardsticks to measure medieval performance, and point out that cereal yields per acre in the thirteenth century were a tenth of the figure in recent times. Such yield statistics help us to understand the scale of medieval farming, but so much has changed in the intervening centuries that a simple comparison has little meaning. Similarly, in industry and commerce communications seem slow, financial dealings clumsy, mechanization only haphazardly adopted, and work unspecialized.[21] Historians sometimes show disappointment that technical developments were not pressed forward, and had to wait until the

[18] R. H. Britnell, *The Closing of the Middle Ages? England, 1471–1519* (Oxford, 1997), 228–47; id., 'The English Economy and the Government, 1450–1550', in J. L. Watts (ed.), *The End of the Middle Ages? England in the Fifteenth and Sixteenth Centuries* (Stroud, 1998), 89–116.

[19] *CUHB* ii. 1–2, 111–31, 379–80.

[20] S. Pearson, 'The Chronological Distribution of Tree-ring Dates, 1980–2001: An Update', *Vernacular Architecture*, 32 (2001), 68–9.

[21] R. Britnell, 'Specialization of Work in England, 1100–1300', *Ec.HR* 54 (2001), 1–16.

eighteenth century. Meanwhile the real achievements of the middle ages are noted but underrated, as modern historians know that they came to nothing.

Let us look briefly at two examples which show how we are influenced by hindsight. It has always been a matter of pride for historians of Bristol, and indeed of England as a whole, that merchants from that town encouraged the voyages of John Cabot in 1497 and 1498 across the north Atlantic.[22] But there is also a sense of disappointment that these early exploratory ventures had no immediate result, and English settlement in America followed long after the conquests by Portugal and Spain. We know little about Cabot and his travels because they aroused limited interest among contemporaries. Another Bristolian of the fifteenth century enjoyed much more fame at the time: William Cannynges had a legendary reputation from his many ships, mercantile ventures, and charitable gifts.[23] In contrast to their failure to conquer the New World, medieval English people put a great deal of effort into such enterprises as rabbit-keeping. They invested time and trouble in encouraging these animals to live and breed in designated warrens, and even sometimes heaped up mounds of loose earth and built burrows for them. Warreners protected them from human and animal predators. These investments made good sense when rabbit meat was prized as a delicacy and their fur commanded a high price. The warrens were often sited in places, such as Dartmoor and the sandy Breckland of East Anglia, which were not capable of supporting a full range of conventional crops and animals, so they suggest an ingenious adaptation of production to make most profitable use of resources.[24] As we live in the modern world, we cannot avoid the perspectives derived from our own knowledge, which regards Cabot's voyage as a landmark and rabbit warrens as a quaint curiosity. But we should be conscious that our perception is distorting the past as it was lived and experienced.

A comparative approach helps us to form historical judgements, but we should not always use the modern period as our standard of comparison. The economy and society of *c*.1300 can, for example, be considered alongside that of about 850. The towns of the fourteenth century look small to us, with only fifty regional capitals and larger provincial centres containing between 4,000 and 20,000 people, with London alone resembling a large town of recent times, with its 80,000 people and built-up area covering more than a square mile.[25] The coinage had a limited volume, with only £1 million (about 240

[22] J. A. Williamson, *The Cabot Voyages and Bristol Discovery Under Henry VII*, Hakluyt Society, 2nd ser., 120 (1962).

[23] E. M. Carus-Wilson, *Medieval Merchant Venturers: Collected Studies* (London, 1954), 80–94.

[24] M. Bailey, 'The Rabbit and the Medieval East Anglian Economy', *Ag.HR* 36 (1988), 1–20; C. D. Linehan, 'Deserted Sites and Rabbit-Warrens on Dartmoor, Devon', *MA* 10 (1966), 113–44.

[25] *CUHB* i. 273–90.

million silver pennies) in circulation, with the result that a scarcity of coins caused problems for potential users.[26] The small scale of industry is suggested by the shallow coal-mines in a few locations, and iron was smelted in fourteenth-century bloomeries which each produced no more than 3 tons in a year.[27] In the mid-ninth century, however, there may have been no more than a dozen places with any claim to urban status, which contained less than 2 per cent of the population. The amount of cash in circulation has been estimated at less than a tenth of the figure for 1300, and money was apparently not much used in large parts of the country. Specialist metalworking crafts were practised by isolated, itinerant artisans, moving from patron to patron.[28] The economy of 1300 may look backward and small-scale from our point of view, but by the perspectives of *c*.850 it would have seemed complex and productive.

Late medieval England is more often judged alongside continental Europe. English towns seem small and thinly distributed if seen alongside heavily urbanized Flanders, Holland, Tuscany, and Lombardy. Like a modern colony, thirteenth-century England exported raw materials, such as wool and tin, and imported luxuries and manufactured goods. Trade to and from English ports was dominated by continental merchants. The English were no match for their sophisticated Italian contemporaries, who used partnerships, including companies with a number of investors, factors resident overseas, marine insurance, business textbooks, and advanced systems of accounting. In manufacture continental products were the brand leaders, from Ypres cloth to Limoges enamels. The most advanced agricultural methods were to be found in the intensively cultivated fields of the Low Countries, with their early development of fodder crops, or in the irrigated plains of Valencia, or the Sicilian sugar plantations.[29]

[26] N. J. Mayhew, 'Modelling Medieval Monetisation', in R. H. Britnell and B. M. S. Campbell (eds.), *A Commercialising Economy: England 1086–c.1300* (Manchester, 1995), 62–8, suggests a figure of *c*.£900,000 in *c*.1300, whereas M. Allen, 'The Volume of the English Currency, 1158–1470', *Ec.HR* 54 (2001), 595–611, argues for a figure of £1,100,000–£1,400,000 in 1299.

[27] J. Hatcher, *History of the British Coal Industry*, Vol. I, *Before 1700: Towards the Age of Coal* (Oxford 1993), 26–30, 72–7; H. R. Schubert, *History of the British Iron and Steel Industry from c.450 BC to AD 1775* (London, 1957), 139–41.

[28] *CUHB* i. 30–4; D. M. Metcalf, 'The Prosperity of North-Western Europe in the Eighth and Ninth Centuries', *Ec.HR*, 2nd ser., 20 (1967), 354–7; D. A. Hinton, *Archaeology, Economy and Society: England from the Fifth to the Fifteenth Century* (London, 1990), 64–9; D. M. Metcalf, 'The Monetary Economy of Ninth–Tenth Century England South of the Humber: A Topographical Analysis', in M. A. S. Blackburn and D. N. Dumville (eds.), *Kings, Currency and Alliances: History and Coinage of Southern England in the Ninth Century* (Woodbridge, 1998), 167–97.

[29] For examples of continental sophistication, P. Spufford, *Power and Profit: The Merchant in Medieval Europe* (London, 2002), 16–59, 116–29; M.-J. Tits-Dieuaide, *La Formation des prix céréalières en Brabant et en Flandre au XVe siècle* (Brussels, 1975); T. F. Glick, *Irrigation and Society in Medieval Valencia* (Cambridge, Mass., 1970); S. R. Epstein, *An Island for Itself: Economic Development and Social Change in Late Medieval Sicily* (Cambridge, 1992), 210–21.

Now we know that in the fourteenth and fifteenth centuries almost a fifth of the whole population of England lived in towns, a very similar proportion to that found over much of the continent, such as Castile, France, and the Empire.[30] England had no concentration of large towns comparable with Flanders, but London is now recognized as one of the ten largest towns in Christendom. Cloth was made in England throughout the period. It disappears from view during the early fourteenth century because little was exported, but it was still being sold in quantity in the domestic market.[31] After about 1300 English merchants came to play a stronger role in the export of wool, though, like merchants in northern Europe in general, they could not match the business methods of the Mediterranean world—and for example, they kept minimal written records. However, like traders in Venice or Marseilles they entered into partnerships of the *commenda* type, whereby one party contributed the capital and the other sold the goods.[32] English artisans could produce woollen cloths which were valued on the continent, such as Lincoln scarlets and 'stamfords' in the thirteenth century, and Stroud-waters in the fifteenth. Alabaster devotional statuary carved in the east midlands in the fifteenth century was carried all over Europe.[33] Agricultural methods varied from region to region, as on the continent, and intensive cultivation comparable with that of the Low Countries was practised in northeast Norfolk. The extensive farming methods of the midlands and south, with an increasing proportion of pasture after 1350, gave the peasants a reasonable standard of living, and maintained cheap food supplies to the rest of the population. With one exception, in the late 1430s, famine disappeared from England, while food crises persisted in parts of the continent.[34]

English inferiority to continental Europe and the rest of the world is commonly assumed in matters of technology. Inventions and new methods are often thought to have diffused across the continent to England, sometimes from an ultimate source in the east. This is probably the case for

[30] C. Dyer, 'How Urbanised was Medieval England?', in J.-M. Duvosquel and E. Thoen (eds.), *Peasants and Townsmen in Medieval Europe: Studies in Honorem Adriaan Verhulst* (Ghent, 1995), 169–83; S. R. Epstein (ed.), *Town and Country in Europe, 1300–1800* (Cambridge, 2001), 2–3. For an explicit comparison, R. H. Britnell, 'The Towns of England and Northern Italy in the Early Fourteenth Century', *Ec.HR* 44 (1991), 21–35.

[31] J. H. Munro, 'The "Industrial Crisis" of the English Textile Towns, c.1290–c.1330', *Thirteenth Century England*, 7 (1997), 103–42; E. Miller and J. Hatcher, *Medieval England: Towns, Commerce and Crafts 1086–1348* (Harlow, 1995), 121–7.

[32] W. Childs, 'The English Export Trade in Cloth in the Fourteenth Century', in Britnell and Hatcher (eds.), *Progress and Problems*, 122–31; M. Kowaleski, *Local Markets and Regional Trade in Medieval Exeter* (Cambridge, 1995), 207–12.

[33] N. Ramsay, 'Alabaster', in J. Blair and N. Ramsay (eds.), *English Medieval Industries: Craftsmen, Techniques, Products* (London, 1991), 29–40.

[34] On regional variations in agriculture, Campbell, *Seigniorial Agriculture*; on the retreat of famine, Dyer, 'Did the Peasants Really Starve?'

innovations in mining and smelting metals, in use of gunpowder, in ship-building, or in paper-making. But some new ideas could have originated in England, such as the windmill, which in the form that it appears in northern Europe was not brought from the east, but appeared simultaneously around the shores of the North Sea at the end of the twelfth century.[35] It could well have been devised by carpenters who were familiar with building both watermills and ships in Norfolk, Lincolnshire, or eastern Yorkshire. In the case of the more intensive methods of farming, in which fallows were eliminated through growing peas and beans as fodder crops, their appearance on the North Sea littoral in Norfolk and Flanders suggests parallel development in similar environments. Practical farmers, faced with growing population densities and strong urban influence, in different countries adapted similar techniques through trial and error.

The final comparative approach to be considered here concerns the parallels frequently drawn between medieval England or western Europe and the contemporary 'underdeveloped', 'less-developed', or 'developing' countries of the Third World. It was believed that much could be learned by direct comparison between thirteenth-century England and the Asia and Africa of the 1960s. Advice could be offered in 1962 by a distinguished economic historian to the Indian government on its next five-year plan on the basis of his interpretation of English agricultural development.[36] There has been a consistent interest in medieval and early modern English peasants and farmers among scholars from Russia since the late nineteenth century, and more recently from historians and social scientists based in Japan and China. The disappearance of the English peasantry seems very relevant to them. Comparison with developing countries allows us usefully to learn about such matters as family structures, co-operative management of assets, and the causes of famine. But that does not mean that medieval Europe and modern Asia and Africa can be regarded as living in the same circumstances. In the mid-twentieth century it was believed that the Third World was heading for demographic and ecological catastrophes similar to those experienced in northern Europe in 1315–17. This analogy helped to convince historians that Europe went through a Malthusian crisis in the fourteenth century. In the event the population of the Third World has increased dramatically, with

---

[35] R. Holt, *The Mills of Medieval England* (Oxford, 1988), 20–2; J. Langdon, 'Was England a Technological Backwater in the Middle Ages?', in G. G. Astill and J. Langdon (eds.), *Medieval Farming and Technology: The Impact of Agricultural Change in Northwest Europe* (Leiden, 1997), 275–91.

[36] M. M. Postan, 'Agricultural Problems of Under-Developed Countries in the Light of European Agrarian History', in *Second International Conference of Economic History, Aix en Provence, 1962* (Paris, 1965), 9–24.

many troubles, but without the universal disaster that had been predicted by followers of Malthus. The inevitable link between high population densities and starvation has been denied by Boserup, who, from an examination of historical and contemporary agricultural technology, showed that the abundant labour of a high population could be an asset. Intensive methods could raise productivity and feed the extra mouths.[37]

Meanwhile the developed world lived through a series of setbacks associated with scientific advance. After Chernobyl, BSE, and the threat of global warming we began to lose faith in the superiority of modern technology, and novelties such as genetically modified crops and cloned animals arouse widespread disquiet. At the beginning of the twenty-first century the fastest-growing agricultural sector in Britain uses organic methods, which follows older farming practices. Perhaps medieval farmers were right sometimes to resist change? A supposed improvement of the medieval period, the change from a two-field to a three-field system, increased the cropped area by 33 per cent. In fact the change was rarely made at the time when it would seem to have been most necessary, in the thirteenth century.[38] This decision may not have been the result of ignorance and conservatism, but demonstrates a reasoned response to a change which would have forced peasants to cut back on their number of animals, as part of the fallow grazing came under the plough, and could have threatened yields per acre by reducing the amount of manure spread on the arable, and giving the land less rest between crops.

Historians should seek to explain the attitudes and circumstances that led to change or resistance to change. Just as it is mistaken to dismiss peasants as ignorant, we should also beware of patronizing attitudes towards aristocrats whose actions need to be understood in their political and cultural environment. Lavish entertainment in large, expensive households, for example, won them political support, which ultimately could have been rewarded with great profits. This represented better returns than could have been gained by investment in their estates.

Archaeologists can teach historians lessons in their more tolerant approach to people in the past, and their appreciation of their achievements. They study mundane examples of early technology, such as joints in timber buildings, and point out that they display accomplishments in the use of the material, and a flexible approach to solving problems. Physical remains also reveal the complexity of early societies, as structures and objects cannot simply be regarded as the functional solutions to practical problems, but are

---

[37] E. Boserup, *The Conditions of Agricultural Growth* (London, 1965).

[38] H. S. A. Fox, 'The Alleged Transformation from Two-Field to Three-Field Systems in Medieval England', *Ec.HR*, 2nd ser., 39 (1986), 526–48.

also expressive of social relationships. For example, the study of human bones reveals that individuals with congenital deformities, or who had suffered serious injuries, lived for many years, demonstrating the spirit of charity and strong family and community loyalties which took responsibility for the care of the sick and disabled.[39]

A Modern Interpretation of the Middle Ages

I now propose to set aside as much as possible patronizing and superior attitudes, and establish some of the main characteristics of the late medieval economy and society. This will inevitably be a superficial survey, selecting those aspects that seem important. I will not be idealizing the period, avoiding the positive interpretations of a century ago which saw the middle ages as secure, communal, and giving dignity to the common man. We can assume certain crucial limitations, such as the low levels of productivity, the short span of life, and the extreme inequalities in access to power and wealth. But lest these dominate entirely our view of the period, here we will be setting out some of the features of the 'new middle ages' by looking briefly at frameworks, marketing, crisis, and social control.

Frameworks

Much of the fabric and the underlying foundations of the economy were established by 1300 and indeed by 1100. The majority of village territories which were the main units of land holding where agricultural production was organized, were established and named in the early middle ages.[40] Their boundaries, some of which are described in charters of the pre-Conquest period, and the great majority of which were fixed in their present positions by *c*.1200, were designed to define pieces of land which had an agrarian logic. They included where possible land best suited for cultivation, the grazing of animals, mowing grass for hay, growing underwood and larger trees for fuel and building timber, and moors or heaths for vegetation and raw materials for fodder, litter, building, and crafts. The territory of the small village of Lark Stoke (Gloucestershire historically, but now in Warwickshire) strad-dles the edge of the Cotswolds, and its boundaries were probably fixed by the

[39] W. J. White, *Skeletal Remains from the Cemetery of St. Nicholas Shambles, City of London*, London and Middlesex Archaeological Society, Special Paper 9 (1988), 49.

[40] M. Aston, *Interpreting the Landscape: Landscape Archaeology in Local Studies* (London, 1985), 39–43; D. Hooke, *The Landscape of Anglo-Saxon England* (London, 1998), 62–83.

tenth century. Its inhabitants were provided with lowland arable, meadow, a stream which could be dammed to power a mill, upland capable of being used as either pasture or for cultivation, and an area of woodland. (Figure 1.1)[41]

The main types of agrarian landscape, such as the champion country with its nucleated villages and open fields, and the woodlands with their hamlets strung out along lanes, interspersed with enclosed fields and patches of open field, were well established by the twelfth century. Their existence by 900–1150 is made clear by the topographical descriptions in charter boundaries, and the varied distributions of resources described in Domesday and early estate surveys.[42]

Not just the territorial boundaries and broad character of the landscapes were created in the earlier medieval centuries. Much of the fine detail of settlements and fields, such as the boundaries between house plots in the villages and towns, the line of hedges in the enclosed sections of the countryside, and the sites of isolated farms in the woodlands and uplands, again can be shown to have existed by the mid-thirteenth century. The enduring framework of the middle ages can be observed in the twenty-first century. We can walk now along the boundaries of the working farm at Lark Stoke, which follow closely the perimeter of the township established before Domesday, and we can measure the shop-fronts on the main streets of a market town and find that many of them are based on plots first set out in the twelfth century.[43]

This is not stated as a preface to the commonly expressed belief in the unchanging and enduring character of rural life. While it is true that much land has been in continuous agricultural use since later prehistoric times, the methods of production and the underlying social structures have undergone many changes. The settlements and landscapes which were to be so influential in the later middle ages inherited something from remote antiquity, but were also moulded by a revolutionary restructuring in the ninth, tenth, and eleventh centuries.[44]

The emphasis on the early medieval legacy is not meant to disparage or underrate the extension of cultivation and reclamation schemes of the twelfth

---

[41] This is based on an estate map of 1786 in the possession of Mr and Mrs Wilson of The Dingle, Admington, Warwickshire, and my own fieldwork observations.

[42] J. Thirsk (ed.), *The English Rural Landscape* (Oxford, 2000), 105, 79–81.

[43] On villages and smaller settlements, C. C. Taylor, *Village and Farmstead: A History of Rural Settlement in England* (London, 1983), 151–9, 175–200; on towns, T. Slater, 'Domesday Village to Medieval Town: The Topography of Medieval Stratford-upon-Avon', in R. Bearman (ed.), *The History of an English Borough: Stratford-upon-Avon 1196–1996* (Stroud, 1997), 30–42.

[44] C. Lewis, P. Mitchell-Fox, and C. Dyer, *Village, Hamlet and Field: Changing Medieval Settlements in Central England*, 2nd edn. (Macclesfield, 2001), 15–24.

Fig. 1.1. The township of Lark Stoke (Warwickshire, formerly Gloucestershire), (a) in *c.*1300 and (b) in the early modern period. (a) uses ridge and furrow from aerial photographs and field observation, pottery scatters, and other evidence to indicate the lay out of the settlement and fields in *c.*1300. The village territory lies across the edge of the Ilmington Hills (an outlier of the Cotswold Hills), so that it includes land used mainly as arable in open fields both in the valley to the north and on the hill to the south. Woodland and pasture lay mostly on the steeper slopes. The stream, running off the hill through an area of meadow, powered a mill. (b) is based on a map of 1786, and shows the field boundaries which were likely to be those established after the village was abandoned and the fields converted to pasture closes. Some of the enclosure hedges followed the lines of former headlands in the open fields. The field name 'The Town' marks the site of the deserted village.

Sources: see n. 41.

and thirteenth centuries, when perhaps a million acres of woodland, and similar quantities of moor, heath, and fen, were brought into more product- ive use as arable and improved grassland.[45] This internal colonization, however, was adding to an already high level of exploitation of resources. It perhaps brought the cultivated area up from 8 million acres in 1086 to 10 million acres in 1300. We should add to this quantitative growth the changes in the intensity of agriculture, which created the farming systems of the eastern coastal regions, such as north-eastern Norfolk, where by the thir- teenth century the arable was ploughed repeatedly, weeded intensively, thor- oughly manured, and cropped continuously, with only occasional fallow years or sometimes with no fallows at all.[46] Throughout the country valleys were flooded for fish ponds, garden plots enclosed for growing industrial crops such as flax, hemp, dye plants, fruit and vegetables, animals were housed in substantial buildings, and many other devices used to increase output.[47]

The story of the development of an already developed countryside is becoming well known. We have only recently become fully aware of the medieval origins of the urban network. Economists talk of the 'maturity of an urban system', meaning the process by which each town defined its hinterland from which country people came to buy and sell, and towns formed a hierarchy with larger towns ('higher order centres') performing a wider range of functions, satisfying the more affluent market for luxury and specialized goods, and serving a wider area than the small market towns.[48] The urban system lacked maturity for much of the twelfth and thirteenth centuries, as the number of urban centres increased by about 500 in England in those two centuries, and there was much jockeying for position, shifting of hinterland boundaries, and movement of towns up and down the hier- archy. The new foundations were designed to fill the gaps between existing centres, but in the fierce competition some new towns faltered, or apparently well-established older towns were ruined. Lords also set up 2,000 weekly markets, mostly in villages, and almost as many annual fairs, in the hope sometimes that the trading occasion would stimulate the growth of a new

[45] O. Rackham, *Ancient Woodland* (London, 1980), 134; Campbell, *Seigniorial Agriculture*, 387–8.

[46] B. M. S. Campbell, 'Agricultural Progress in Medieval England: Some Evidence from Eastern Norfolk', *Ec.HR*, 2nd ser., 36 (1983), 26–46.

[47] M. Aston (ed.), *Medieval Fish, Fisheries and Fishponds in England*, British Archaeological Reports, British Series, 182 (1988); C. Dyer, 'Gardens and Orchards in Medieval England', in id., *Everyday Life in Medieval England* (London, 1994), 113–31; C. Dyer, 'Sheepcotes: Evidence for Medieval Sheep Farming', *MA* 34 (1995), 136–64.

[48] J. Galloway (ed.), *Trade, Urban Hinterlands and Market Integration c.1300–1600*, Centre for Metropolitan History Working Papers Series, 3 (2000); C. Dyer, 'Market Towns and the Country- side in Late Medieval England', *Canadian Journal of History*, 31 (1996), 17–35.

town. They expected to gain revenue from tolls and benefits for rural estates on which peasants would be able conveniently to sell produce and pay rents in cash. Most country markets failed, either immediately or within a century or two.[49]

By about 1300 the first phase of this Darwinian struggle between commercial centres had ended, and the fittest towns which had emerged from the upheaval survived for the rest of the middle ages, and often into subsequent centuries. In Leicestershire, for example, the main market towns of Ashby de la Zouch, Hinckley, Loughborough, Lutterworth, Market Harborough, and Melton Mowbray by *c.*1300 formed a ring around Leicester itself. (Figure 1.2)[50] They have retained their role until the present day. An element of renewed instability came in the period after 1349, especially in the industrial districts like the Stour valley on the borders of Essex and Suffolk, or south Gloucestershire, resulting in the growth of new towns such as Boxford and Stroud. This new phase of urban growth, though it deserves emphasis because it is often overlooked in a period usually portrayed as one of decline and shrinkage, tended to be localized and small scale. Urban decline in the fifteenth century also affected many towns. In Leicestershire for example a place with some potential as a market town at Mountsorrel seems to have fallen out of contention as an urban centre.[51] The outright failures in the episode of urban decay may have been no more numerous than the casualties caused by ruthless competition in the thirteenth and early fourteenth centuries. Gains and losses tended to cancel one another, with the result that the total of English towns in the 1520s—about 650—was similar to the number that had formed by 1300. Indeed the estimate of about 850 towns in the seventeenth century suggests that many more urban centres emerged in the middle ages than were to be established in the subsequent phase of urbanization.[52]

Marketing

The establishment of a relatively mature urban system by about 1300, and its subsequent persistence, depended on a transport system that connected towns

---

[49] Britnell, *Commercialisation*, 81–90; J. Masschaele, *Peasants, Merchants, and Markets: Inland Trade in Medieval England, 1150–1350* (New York, 1997), 57–72; J. Masschaele, 'The Multiplicity of Medieval Markets Reconsidered', *Journal of Historical Geography*, 20 (1994), 255–71.

[50] J. Laughton, E. Jones, and C. Dyer, 'The Urban Hierarchy in the Later Middle Ages: A Study of the East Midlands', *Urban History*, 28 (2001), 331–57.

[51] C. Dyer, 'Small Places with Large Consequences: The Importance of Small Towns in England, 1000–1540', *Historical Research*, 75 (2002), 23; J. Patten, 'Village and Town: An Occupational Study', *Ag.HR* 20 (1972), 12–15; Laughton, Jones, and Dyer, 'Urban Hierarchy', 335–6.

[52] *CUHB* i. 506–8; ii. 466.

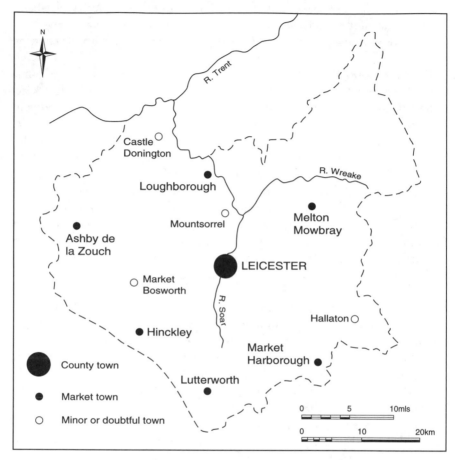

Fig. 1.2. Towns in Leicestershire in the fourteenth century.
Source: see n. 50.

with their rural surroundings, and which could ensure a flow of goods and people between towns, including the carriage of bulky and relatively cheap commodities such as grain, herring, fodder, fuel, and building materials. Some luxury goods were also carried as bulky loads, such as wine, which was hauled for many miles across country in barrels holding 120 or 240 gallons. The poor quality of roads before the industrial revolution has often been assumed, partly because of the complaints of mud and potholes made by travellers in the seventeenth and eighteenth centuries. The roads, however, deteriorated in that period because more and heavier vehicles were being brought into use on the traditional road system, and some of the criticisms belong to the rhetoric of improvement in the turnpike age to convince investors that a new road system was needed.[53]

In the middle ages roads were given metalled surfaces, and not just on the busiest routes near large towns. For example, a stretch of the road on the route from Okehampton in Devon to Launceston in Cornwall was paved to a standard comparable with that of its Roman predecessor.[54] New roads were built, not just for military purposes as in the construction of communication routes into north Wales by Edward I's armies in 1277, but also when roads were rerouted, whether for a few miles to bring traffic into a newly founded market town, or on a larger scale when the Great North Road in Huntingdonshire developed three alternative routes on the twelve-mile stretch between Alconbury and Wansford.[55] A great deal of effort was put into bridge-building, so that by the early sixteenth century, and in some cases by *c.*1300, there were as many bridges as in the early eighteenth century, on the eve of the industrial revolution. On the Severn, for example, between Preston Montford (on the upper reaches in Shropshire) and Gloucester there were eight bridges by *c.*1330, ten in *c.*1530, and still only ten in 1700. At the majority of points where a main road crossed an important river a bridge was built which, in a growing number of cases, was of stone construction and wide enough for the normal carts of the day, and in many cases a causeway was provided to make a safe and convenient approach to the bridge.[56]

Heavy and bulky goods were carried, wherever possible, by water. In the early sixteenth century, when the canons of St Paul's Cathedral were building a large London house at Aldermanbury and wished to use timber from their Essex woods at Navestock (later to be James Ford's parish), they took it by road to the wharf at Dagenham, and then brought it by water up the river to London.[57] Large parts of the country, however, were not served by nearby waterways, and therefore depended on the roads. In *c.*1300 the cost of carriage by road was quite high, at about $1\frac{1}{2}d.$ per ton per mile, which was affordable for high-value goods such as wine over long distances, but imposed economic limits on carrying building materials, cheap cereals, fuel, hay, and straw.[58]

---

[53] J. Chartres, *Internal Trade in England 1500–1700*, Economic History Society (1977), 39–41.

[54] P. J. Weddell and S. J. Reed, 'Observations at Sourton Down, Okehampton, 1986–1991: Roman Road, Deserted Medieval Hamlet and Other Landscape Features', *Devon Archaeological Society Proceedings*, 55 (1997), 70–8, 133–6.

[55] J. E. Morris, *The Welsh Wars of Edward I* (Oxford, 1901), 105, 130–1; C. Taylor, *Roads and Tracks of Britain* (London, 1979), 120–4, 134–6.

[56] D. F. Harrison, 'Bridges and Economic Development, 1300–1800', *Ec.HR* 45 (1992), 240–61.

[57] Guildhall Library, Corporation of London, Ms. 25304.

[58] The extent to which waterways were navigable is a matter for controversy, but clearly large parts of the country could not be reached by boat: E. Jones, 'River Navigation in Medieval England',

The full range of towns of every size and type has recently been fully recognized. The urban sector includes every place where the inhabitants pursued a variety of non-agricultural occupations, including small market towns with a few hundred inhabitants.[59] The definition, which avoids institutional characteristics and focuses attention on economies and functions, means that we can draw the line between towns and villages with a little more certainty, and therefore make some assessment of the importance of towns in relation to the countryside. It used to be said that that a tenth or an even smaller fraction of the late medieval population lived in towns, but in the poll taxes of 1377–81 or the subsidy lists of the early sixteenth century the proportion of town-dwellers from county to county varies between 15 per cent and 25 per cent, with a median near to 20 per cent.[60] A similar figure would be expected in *c.*1300, which is generally regarded as marking a high-water mark of urban growth. It can be rightly objected that the towns were not entirely based on trade, manufacture, and tertiary occupations (clergy, lawyers, etc.). Some townspeople held agricultural land, even the burgesses and citizens of the larger urban centres, and in any inventory of goods owned by townspeople grain and livestock figure prominently.[61] Clearly the towns were not entirely dependent on food supplies brought in by country producers. On the other hand, thousands among the rural population, especially the smallholders, gained all or most of their living from crafts and commerce, so the proportion of working time devoted to non-agricultural production can be estimated at well above a fifth.

The calculation that near to a fifth of the English population between 1300 and 1530 lived in towns, and yet more people worked in rural industries, makes the whole economy look complex, and diminishes the proportion of production that was intended for consumption by the producer's household. In other words, 'self-sufficiency' was not a totally dominant characteristic. The size of the urban and industrial sector has large implications for our understanding of the agricultural surplus, as the peasants and the other rural workers were evidently capable of producing grain, legumes, vegetables, cheese, and meat for their own needs, and enough to support the significant minority who were not employed mainly in food production. The suggestion

Journal of Historical Geography, 26 (2000), 60–75; J. Langdon, 'Inland Water Transport in Medieval England—The View From the Mill', *Journal of Historical Geography*, 26 (2000), 75–82. On roads, J. Masschaele, 'Transport Costs in Medieval England', *Ec.HR* 46 (1993), 266–79; their impact on trade is discussed in B. M. S. Campbell *et al.*, *A Medieval Capital and its Grain Supply: Agrarian Production and Distribution in the London Region c.1300*, Historical Geography Research Series, 30 (1993), 60–3.

[59] Dyer, 'Small Places', 1–24.
[60] Dyer, 'How Urbanised?'
[61] Britnell, 'Specialization of Work'.

has been made that a figure of 20 per cent of town-dwellers represents a maximum figure—it might be described as a ceiling—that could be attained without the technologies of the agricultural and industrial revolutions.[62] Now we know that this figure was reached, and in some localities exceeded, not on the eve of industrialization, but well before 1500.

A degree of compulsion lay behind some of the increase in volume and liveliness of the exchange of goods and services. Some historians would say that peasants were forced into the market-place because lords insisted that rents be paid in cash, and the state collected taxes in money. For example, in 1268–9 the hundred or so tenants of the Worcestershire manor of Fladbury were recorded paying annual rents in total of £22 to their lord. Seven years later the people with larger holdings living in the villages of the manor contributed to the royal lay subsidy, which yielded £16 16s.[63] For an individual like William Pule, who probably had a yardland of 30 acres, this meant finding 4s. per annum for his lord, and he was assessed to pay 5s. to the king in 1275. Each of these payments would have meant selling the crops from an acre of land, of which he sowed about 15 acres each year. But pressure from above does not wholly explain the peasants' involvement in selling produce, because they were also encouraged by the prospect of purchasing goods. Towns could grow in such number and the total urban population could only expand as it did by making and selling for a wide market, which included peasant consumers. English towns, unlike those in parts of the continent, or indeed in Scotland and Wales, had no power to compel those in the surrounding countryside to use their markets.

The urban artisans and small-scale traders stimulated the better-off peasants into expanding production, and the demand from peasants in turn encouraged an increase in the number of specialist artisans to make more cloth, utensils, and implements, and to prepare food and drink for consumption in both town and country. In the towns nearest to Fladbury in 1275, Evesham and Pershore, judging from the surnames of the taxpayers, bakers, braziers, tailors, smiths, tanners, cooks, and weavers were active, most of them dealing in relatively cheap commodities that country people like William Pule could occasionally afford to buy.[64] As there were four thousand

[62] E. A. Wrigley, 'Urban Growth and Agricultural Change: England and the Continent in the Early Modern Period', *Journal of Interdisciplinary History*, 15 (1985), 683–728.

[63] M. Hollings (ed.), *The Red Book of Worcester*, Worcestershire Historical Society (1934–50), 462; J. W. Willis Bund and J. Amphlett (eds.), *Lay Subsidy Roll for the County of Worcester circa 1280 [recte 1275]*, Worcestershire Historical Society (1893), 36–7.

[64] Willis Bund and Amphlett (eds.), *Lay Subsidy*, 89–91; R. H. Hilton, 'The Small Town and Urbanisation—Evesham in the Middle Ages', in id., *Class Conflict and the Crisis of Feudalism* (London, 1985), 187–93; Hilton, *English Peasantry*, 81–2, 90–1.

households resembling Pule's with a yardland or a half-yardland living within the trading hinterlands of the two towns, their cumulative purchasing power helped to sustain the urban economy. The market allowed a minority of peasants to expand their holdings, make more money, and add further to demand.

A remarkable insight into the lives of the peasant elite comes from documents relating to William Lene of Walsham-le-Willows in Suffolk, who died on 28 October 1329, probably in his forties, who for reasons which are not entirely clear had a list of his possessions and the expenses arising from his will entered on his lord's court roll.[65] He held 40 acres of land, and was therefore one of the wealthiest peasants in his village. He produced much more corn, dairy produce, and meat than his own family would have eaten, as is indicated by the corn in excess of 16 quarters that he had in store, and his fourteen cattle. At least half of his grain and most of his cheese would have been sold, and all of the wool from his flock of a hundred sheep. He paid a high rent charge, as his land was mainly held by customary tenure, but he had been able to buy brass pots worth more than £1; 10 yards of russet cloth valued at 9s.; items of clothing worth 13s.; linen towels, tablecloths, and sheets; a table, three benches, and a chair; and practical items necessary for the management of his household, such as wooden vessels for brewing and preparing dough for baking. The inventory does not list all of Lene's possessions, as many would individually have been judged too cheap to be worth including, but we know from other documents and archaeological excavations of peasant houses that he would have owned pottery vessels, wooden tableware, knives and other kitchen utensils, furnishings such as candleholders, metal buckles and brooches, iron farming tools, and horse harness and horseshoes. Lene indicated that his horizons extended far beyond his village by leaving money to the friars of Babwell, on the outskirts of Bury St Edmunds. Bury, 10 miles from Walsham, was the town where he would have made many of his sales and purchases. He could also have visited Botesdale and Stowmarket, which were within easy reach. For his funeral his executors bought salt, spices, and wax. The spices presumably were acquired from Bury traders, as imported goods were more likely to be found in a relatively large town. Lene incidentally demonstrated his even wider horizons, both in a geographical and political sense, by leaving money for a pilgrim to visit the London shrine of Thomas, earl of Lancaster, who had been accorded popular canonization after he was killed resisting the rule of Edward II seven years before Lene's death.

---

[65] R. Lock (ed.), *The Court Rolls of Walsham le Willows 1303–1350*, Suffolk Records Society, 41 (1998), 133–5.

We know that the stimulus of the market had a strong influence on the crops and techniques of the demesne. In north-east Norfolk the amount of wheat harvested per acre was comparable with productivity measured in the same way in the same county in the early eighteenth century.[66] An strong element in the economy of that county was the concentration of towns and demand for food. Great care was taken over decision-making. If those in charge of demesnes could make the estimation that one crop would fetch a better price than another, then they would increase their acreage, not just in the long term but even from year to year. By analysing such short-term changes on the bishop of Ely's demesne at Wisbech, it is possible to show that Martin Dousing, who was reeve in 1404–9, was a better manager than his immediate predecessor John Nevo.[67] These men were working for their lord, and would only profit indirectly (or through dishonesty) from their success.

Peasants took even more care in running their own holdings, on which their whole livelihood depended, both the feeding of their families and the sale of any surplus. We cannot trace the returns of a peasant holding from year to year, but we can notice the very great variations in their prosperity, for example, when they were assessed to contribute to the royal lay subsidy. The tax was supposed to be based on a valuation of moveable goods, but in practice each household's wealth was judged on the livestock and sometimes grain which were surplus to their subsistence requirements. This gives us a crude indication of the produce that they could have sold. To return to the example of Fladbury, most of the peasants who were expected to pay taxes resembled William Pule in having a standard holding of a yardland of 30 acres or a half-yardland of 15 acres. One might expect, therefore, to find that when they paid their taxes half of the assessments would be grouped around a sum of say 2s. (24d.), and the other half around 4s. (48d.) In fact they were spread over a dozen grades of assessment, from 1s. to 7s.[68] Clearly, although many peasants of Fladbury worked holdings approximately equal in size to those of many of their neighbours, they had very varied experiences in terms of luck and judgement, and some individuals were apparently seven times more successful than their less fortunate, capable, or ruthless neighbours. In contemporary East Anglia, where the land market was much more fluid, the more skilful and selfish tenants bought parcels of land from the

---

[66] B. M. S. Campbell and M. Overton, 'A New Perspective on Medieval and Early Modern Agriculture: Six Centuries of Norfolk Farming *c.*1250–*c.*1850', *P&P* 141 (1994), 69–75.

[67] D. Stone, 'Farm Management and Agricultural Mentalities on the Demesne of Wisbech Barton in the Fourteenth and Early Fifteenth Centuries', in Economic History Society, *New Researchers' Papers* (Oxford, 1999), 106–7.

[68] Willis Bund and Amphlett (eds.), *Lay Subsidy*, 36–7.

less able.[69] Some differences in wealth stemmed from variations in the size of families, or their position in their life-cycle. A peasant blessed with two strong teenage sons would have an advantage over a widow. Differences in skill in responding to the demand for produce, both by the male head of the household and his wife, who often had frequent contacts with the market through the sale of ale, dairy produce, and garden crops, would also have played a part in creating the hierarchy of wealth in the village.

Producers could react to the opportunities for sale by specialization, which in turn had a impact on technology. Different cultivators made their own assessments of the best combinations of crops and animals. On the bishopric of Worcester manor of Bishop's Cleeve, for example, in the 1390s the managers of the lord's demesne planted a great deal of wheat, on a third of the available land, partly to supply the bishop's household when it made its regular visits, but also for the sake of its sale price in nearby Gloucester, from which boats went down the Severn to Bristol (Table 1.1).[70] Quantities of barley and peas/beans were grown, the latter being used as animal feed, especially for sheep. A few acres of oats were intended to feed the lord's horses. The peasants who lived in Cleeve and the surrounding villages, whose tithe payments to the parish church are recorded in the same decade, also planted a sizeable acreage of wheat but only a small amount of peas and beans, suggesting that their flocks were not so well fed as the lord's. Barley accounted for more than a half of their harvest, partly for their own use and partly for sale. They were probably attracted to the crop by its relatively high yields, and the chances of local sales as a brewing corn. The crops produced on the small demesne of the rector of Cleeve, the glebe land, which because of the absenteeism of the wealthy clergyman was intended mainly for sale, fell

Table 1.1. Crops produced at Bishop's Cleeve, Gloucestershire, in the 1390s (%)

Source of data (date)	Wheat	Barley/dredge	Peas/beans	Oats	Total
Bishop of Worcester's demesne (1393–5)	31	43	21	5	100
Rectory demesne (1396–7)	37	48	15	0	100
Tithe corn (1396–7)	36	55	8	1	100

Sources: Worcestershire RO, ref. 009:1, BA 2636/162 92114; 193/92627 12/12; Corpus Christi College, Oxford, B14/2/3/6.

[69] R. M. Smith, 'Families and Their Land in an Area of Partible Inheritance: Redgrave, Suffolk 1260–1320', in id. (ed.), *Land, Kinship and Life-Cycle* (Cambridge, 1984), 135–95.

[70] D. Enright and M. Watts, *A Romano-British and Medieval Settlement Site at Stoke Road, Bishop's Cleeve, Gloucestershire*, Cotswold Archaeology: Bristol and Gloucestershire Archaeological Reports, 1 (2002), 70–4.

between those of the peasants and those of the bishops. The striking feature of these figures, which can be paralleled by other examples, is that they show the lord pursuing the strategy often associated with peasants, by growing crops for a variety of purposes, including his own consumption, and avoiding risk by planting different crops. Meanwhile the peasants seem more adapted to the needs of the market.

Improvements in technology can be linked to the increase in buying and selling. Peasants acquired horses and carts in the thirteenth century, partly in order to carry goods to market. They also sometimes hauled their ploughs with horses, as at Cuxham in Oxfordshire in the thirteenth century. They could buy the horses quite cheaply, and they were not expensive to feed, as they needed to work for only a few weeks in the year to cultivate a holding of about 12 acres. By another paradox in which the lords seem more conservative than the peasants, the steady, continuous work which the lord of Cuxham needed from his plough teams made the traditional ox a more suitable plough beast.[71]

The market was therefore playing an important role in the late medieval economy. Goods could be transported through a tolerably effective infrastructure. The urban sector provided a network of commercial opportunities. The market penetrated deeply into society, touching not just the affluent Lene and the substantial Pules, but also the half-yardlanders and cottagers. It stimulated mutually advantageous and wealth-creating exchange between town and country, rewarded the skills of those with talent (and cunning), and encouraged specialization in production and some technical changes.

Crisis

Economic historians focus on the fourteenth-century crisis as the defining and decisive episode of the whole middle ages. Between about 1310 and 1375 came the disasters of the famine, the Black Death and two further epidemics of the 1360s, the upheavals of the wars with Scotland and France, and the sometimes damaging financial measures designed to pay for them. Expansion had continued from the twelfth century, perhaps from the tenth, until *c*.1300, with population growth, rising prices of grain and livestock, higher rents, and increasing incomes for the large landed estates. The volume of trade increased until the first decades of the fourteenth century: wool exports, for example, reached their peak in 1304–5. Low wages reflected the surplus of

[71] J. Langdon, 'Horse Hauling: A Revolution in Vehicle Transport in Twelfth- and Thirteenth-Century England', in T. H. Aston (ed.), *Landlords, Peasants and Politics in Medieval England* (Cambridge, 1987), 33–64; J. Langdon, 'The Economics of Horses and Oxen in Medieval England', *Ag.HR* 30 (1982), 31–40.

labour caused by the high levels of population. After the famine of 1315–17 all of these tendencies went into reverse—initially the fall in grain prices, rents, and landed incomes, and the rise in wages were modest and gradual. The really decisive changes came after in 1375, from which date grain prices declined and generally remained low for 140 years. Population, which was falling before the first epidemics, reached a low level by the 1370s, and did not make a sustained recovery until the second quarter of the sixteenth century. Through most of the fifteenth century rents tended to fall, and aristocratic estates struggled against falling incomes from their manors. Towns had their problems, not just taking their share of the fall in population, but also experiencing shifts in trade, such as the decline in wool exports which impoverished the east-coast ports. Wage rates increased as workers were in such short supply, giving problems to those attempting to hire labour. The workers themselves enjoyed high real wages, as lower food prices enhanced their purchasing power.

We can no longer accept that these changes were precipitated by a Malthusian check. A direct and simple relationship between dense populations and poverty cannot be accepted, because labour would have been an asset for those using more intensive methods, and could be employed in both farming and industry.[72] The thirteenth century cannot be seen as a period of stagnant technology, because we can identify a number of innovations in husbandry, the mix of crops and their rotations, in draft animals, and in milling.[73] The extension of cultivation in the twelfth and thirteenth centuries over marginal land, such as fens, marshes, moors, heaths, and woods, which has been portrayed as a disastrous attempt to convert poor soils into corn fields, was combined with intelligent exploitation of the resources of these lands.[74] The maximum benefit was gained from assets such as the turf, reeds, sedge, fish, and waterfowl of the wetlands, and the pastures of the hills. The areas of 'marginal lands' often provided the right environment for industrial development, with their minerals and fuel (in the Forest of Dean, for example). Many potential workers lived there, who had time for extracting raw materials and manufacture as their work in pastoral agriculture did not keep them fully occupied. When the population declined after the Black Death, the 'marginal areas' often retained people while villages were shrinking and even being deserted on the better-quality arable lands of the midlands

[72] Campbell, 'Agricultural Progress'; J. R. Birrell, 'Peasant Craftsmen in the Medieval Forest', *Ag.HR* 17 (1969), 91–107; H. E. J. Le Patourel, 'Documentary Evidence and the Medieval Pottery Industry', *MA* 12 (1968), 101–26.

[73] Astill and Langdon (eds.), *Medieval Farming*, 193–223, 225–49, 275–91, 293–312.

[74] M. Bailey, *A Marginal Economy? East Anglian Breckland in the Later Middle Ages* (Cambridge, 1989), 97–199.

and on the limestone hills.[75] The ups and downs in population need not just be seen in cataclysmic terms of periodic rises in mortality, but rather as the result of early marriage and a high rate of marriage in the period of opportunity before 1300, and later marriage, less marriage, and reduced numbers of children when land and other sources of income became less available.[76] Above all, if the high mortality in the famine and the epidemics, which cut the population by more than half between 1310 and 1380, was a Malthusian check, it should have been followed by a demographic revival, as high wages and the acquisition of cheap land allowed young people to marry and have offspring. Instead, the population stagnated for more than century after the worst parts of the crisis had ended.

The crisis was too complex to be explained by a single influence or sequence of changes. External events undoubtedly gave the economy a shock, including the episodic bad weather of 1293–1375 and its worst catastrophe in 1315–17. Nor must the accident of the arrival of a new and virulent disease in 1348–9 be underestimated. To these must be added the man-made destruction and instability of large-scale and prolonged war, beginning in the mid-1290s, with its associated high taxes and monetary problems. The expense of trade ('transaction costs') in money, time, and anguish was raised by military threats and customs duties. The market eventually became glutted, as demand for traded and manufactured goods reached a ceiling. Through the thirteenth century urban and rural society had stimulated each other to increase production, but the point was reached when the country-dwellers could buy no more goods from the town, and town growth ceased.[77] In the case of London, a point was reached when local resources of wood fuel could only just keep the city supplied with the means to heat houses, cook food, and carry out industrial processes.[78] The growth in population may have had its own momentum, but it had been stimulated by the prospect of employment which commercial expansion encouraged. In the same way a downturn in trade discouraged marriage and depressed fertility.

The results of the crisis are more easily identified than its enigmatic causes. Its importance lies in its promotion of structural change. There was a degree

---

[75] C. Dyer, ' "The Retreat From Marginal Land": The Growth and Decline of Medieval Rural Settlements', in id., *Everyday Life*, 23–5.

[76] R. M. Smith, 'Human Resources', in G. Astill and A. Grant (eds.), *The Countryside of Medieval England* (Oxford, 1988), 202–11.

[77] D. M. Nicholas, 'Economic Reorientation and Social Change in Fourteenth-Century Flanders', *P&P* 70 (1976), 5–13; J. H. Munro, 'Industrial Transformation in the North-West European Textile Trades, *c.*1290–*c.*1340: Economic Progress or Economic Crisis?', in B. M. S. Campbell (ed.), *Before the Black Death* (Manchester, 1991), 110–48.

[78] J. A. Galloway, D. Keene, and M. Murphy, 'Fuelling the City: Production and Distribution of Firewood and Fuel in London's Region, 1290–1400', *Ec.HR* 49 (1996), 447–72.

of continuity, in the sense that some of the innovations of the period before 1300 persisted. Attitudes towards money had been permanently changed. Even when no coins were exchanged in a transaction—and coins, especially the most convenient silver currency, were in short supply for much of the fifteenth century—the goods or labour were still given a monetary value. When the fruit and vegetables in a garden were damaged or stolen, the owner would claim damages in cash, even when the produce would probably not enter the market but was intended for domestic consumption. Just as the apples which were lost by John Beneyt of Great Horwood (Buckinghamshire) in 1305 were valued at 3*d.*, so in 1415 the apples and fruit carried off from John Robyns' garden at Marham in Norfolk could (with the usual exaggeration) be said to have caused damage worth 5*s.*[79] On a rather larger canvas, we have already noticed the achievement of the thirteenth century in establishing a network of towns covering the whole country with a continuous chain of hinterlands, which continued to function, with modifications, for centuries.

The tendency for markets to encourage specialization continued, and may have intensified. Peasants realized in the decades after the end of high corn prices in 1375 the advantages of keeping more animals, and we find them turning part of their land permanently to pasture. They practised convertible husbandry, whereby the land was put down to grass for a number of years, which increased their capacity to feed livestock, and at the same time to gain some good corn crops from the grassland when it was eventually ploughed. In districts with enclosed land, such as the woodlands of the west midlands or parts of Devon, a few peasants converted all of their land to pasture.[80]

One of the most significant changes in post-Black Death England, the growth in cloth-making, especially in the countryside, had begun before 1348, but was promoted by changes following the crisis, such as rising demand at home and abroad for particular types of cloth. Labour became scarce in general after the plagues, but in pastoral localities some workers had spare time, and English cloth-makers could obtain their wool more cheaply than their overseas competitors because taxes were raised on exports.[81]

The changes affecting the different classes and groups can be seen in purely economic terms, and so the world was turned upside down because the aristocracy lost income, and the lower orders, especially the wage-earners, prospered. Within the peasantry more tenants gained larger holdings, so that relatively wealthy peasants resembling William Lene were less exceptional by

---

[79] New College, Oxford, MS. 3912; Norfolk Record Office, HARE 2199, 194 × 4.
[80] *AHEW* iii. 48–9, 75, 83–4, 134, 146–7, 156–8, 176–7, 223–7.
[81] E. Carus-Wilson, 'The Woollen Industry', in M. M. Postan and E. Miller (eds.), *The Cambridge Economic History of Europe*, vol. II, 2nd edn. (Cambridge, 1987), 674–90.

*c.*1500. The structural changes also altered the politics within society. The lords were weakened. Under pressure from the shortage of labour and tenants, and lower prices of the grain and wool on their estates, they abandoned direct management of agriculture, by leasing their demesnes. They also saw their jurisdictional power over peasants eroded, as serfdom withered away and private courts lost much power. On their side, peasants gained land both from the lords' demesnes and from their neighbours, as many villages halved in population. They became more assertive, not just in relation to the lords, but also in redefining relationships within their families and in their village communities. Both lords and peasants developed new positions within the state, which can be seen in many ways as providing a framework for property-holding very different from that prevailing before the crisis. The state expected villagers more than ever to run their own affairs in co-operation with the central government, and in the long term attempted to protect peasant tenures.[82]

A new physical environment emerged from the fourteenth-century crisis which was visible in shrunken villages and towns, and grassed-over deserted villages. Innovations included enclosed pastures which had once been open fields, new farmhouses, cottages on wastes and roadsides, and hamlets and small towns newly built, especially in the cloth-making districts.[83] These changes in the physical landscape reflected directly a transformation in society.

Social Control

Much of the evidence for economic activity takes the form of legislation, both national and local, long and detailed descriptions of tenants' obligations, regulations governing the members of guilds, and sermons and other exhortations. Historians have perhaps contributed to an impression of a controlled society by using terms such as 'system', in relation to fields and inheritance, for example.

The authorities sought to control behaviour, and their attempts at enforcement could be damaging to the economy. The lords' demands that serfs pay cash sums in tallage, recognition fines, common fines, and entry fines undoubtedly deprived a section of the peasantry of resources, limited their

---

[82] R. M. Smith, 'The English Peasantry 1250–1650', in T. Scott (ed.), *The Peasantries of Europe from the Fourteenth to the Eighteenth Centuries* (Harlow, 1998), 360–71; C. Dyer, 'The Political Life of the Fifteenth-Century English Village', *The Fifteenth Century*, 4 (2004), 135–57.

[83] C. Dyer, 'Peasants and Farmers: Rural Settlements in an Age of Transition', in D. Gaimster and P. Stamper (eds.), *The Age of Transition: The Archaeology of English Culture 1400–1600* (Oxford, 1997), 61–76.

capacity to invest, and in some circumstances caused real hardship. The policy of directing wool exports to the Calais staple discouraged mercantile enterprise. In building up our picture of the new middle ages, however, we should not allow restraints and controls to dominate our picture of medieval society.

If we take the most extreme case of restriction, serfdom or villeinage appears in the writings of thirteenth-century lords and lawyers as a denial of any individual independence or initiative. Servile or villein land belonged to their lords, and could be taken from them at any time. Lords propagated the idea that in the beginning they had settled peasants on the land, and had provided them with animals, farming equipment, and even household goods. The tenants owned no chattels or money, which belonged ultimately to the lord: if they fell foul of the church courts and incurred a financial penalty, their lord could punish them for wasting his money. A lord could take a tax in money from his serfs, or 'tallage them at will', so he could demand payment when he wished. Tallage, entry fines, marriage fines, payments for permission to leave the manor, and other dues could be levied 'high and low', that is, without financial limits. Servile widows could be married off at their lord's command, and unmarried servile men could be ordered to marry a widow and therefore take on her holding. In the course of disputes with serfs, a lord could state that serfdom or villeinage was a permanent condition, and that serfs owned 'nothing but their bellies'.[84]

In practice, however, servile tenants were scarcely ever evicted, and holdings passed through families by inheritance. Serfs accumulated money and bought goods which often made them wealthier than their free neighbours. They were able to acquire additional land, and their sons and daughters migrated without much interference from the lord. Their annual rents and services were defined, sometimes in writing during the thirteenth century, and could not be easily adjusted in line with subsequent inflation. Some payments, notably tallage, were often fixed by custom and levied at regular times—annually at Michaelmas or at some other festival, for example.[85] Entry fines, marriage fines, and recognition fines were sometimes pegged at

[84] P. Vinogradoff, *Villainage in England* (Oxford, 1892), 43–220; R. H. Hilton, 'Freedom and Villeinage in England', *P&P* 31 (1965), 3–19; P. R. Hyams, *Kings, Lords and Peasants in Medieval England: The Common Law of Villeinage in the Twelfth and Thirteenth Centuries* (Oxford, 1980); P. R. Schofield, *Peasant and Community in Medieval England 1200–1500* (Basingstoke, 2003), 12–17, 107–13.

[85] R. M. Smith, 'Some Thoughts on "Hereditary" and "Proprietary" Rights in Land Under Customary Law in Thirteenth and Fourteenth Century England', *Law and History Review*, 1 (1983), 95–128; E. King, *Peterborough Abbey 1086–1310: A Study in the Land Market* (Cambridge, 1973), 99–125; J. Hatcher, 'English Serfdom and Villeinage: Towards a Reassessment', in Aston (ed.), *Landlords, Peasants*, 247–84; Smith, 'English Peasantry, 1250–1650', 339–71.

customary levels, such as 2*s*. for a marriage fine, but they were changeable, and some payments, notably entry fines, posed real dangers for tenants. The many rules which seemed to restrict serfs were usually relaxed if a sum of money was paid, so that serfdom apparently became a financial problem. For example, in 1332 a tenant of John de Warenne, earl of Surrey, who lived at Sowerby in Yorkshire gave a fine of 6*s*. 8*d*., 'that he may not be molested for villeinage'.[86] The unfree were disadvantaged, but rather than being demoralized by their condition, then found ways of evading the rules. For example, the marriages of servile women were often concealed.[87] Peasants were able to manipulate the lords' courts through which many dues were collected because they provided the information for the court, declared the customs, made legal judgements, and administered the subsequent penalties.[88] In order to improve their conditions, for example, by removing or reducing a restriction or payment, they could negotiate with the lord, either informally or by presenting a petition. In extreme circumstances, and if their village could claim some former connection with the crown, villein tenants judged it worthwhile to collect money to pay a lawyer to bring a case in the royal court against their lord. The more direct confrontation between lords and tenants in the thirteenth or early fourteenth century almost always resulted in a victory for the lord, but disobedience, lawsuits, and occasional acts of violence played a part in the constant but often silent negotiations that went on between lords and peasants.[89]

The idea that peasant lives were controlled by lords can therefore be modified by showing that peasants resisted pressure by various covert or open methods. But if our attention is focused on the relationship between lords and tenants, there is a danger that we distort peasant lives which included many dimensions over which lords had no more than an indirect influence. Although tenants in villeinage are the section of the peasantry about whom we are best informed, near to half, perhaps even a majority, of the rural population was free. And we should not assume a great gulf in behaviour between free and unfree. The movement of people, many of them of servile origin but in no way inhibited by their condition, indicates clearly

[86] S. S. Walker (ed.), *The Court Rolls of the Manor of Wakefield from October 1331 to September 1333*, Wakefield Court Roll Series of the Yorkshire Archaeological Society, 3 (1982), 105.

[87] M. Müller, 'The Function and Evasion of Marriage Fines on a Fourteenth-Century English Manor', *Continuity and Change*, 14 (1999), 169–90.

[88] Z. Razi and R. M. Smith, 'The Origins of the English Manorial Court Rolls as a Written Record: A Puzzle' and P. R. Hyams, 'What Did Edwardian Villagers Understand by "Law"?', in Z. Razi and R. M. Smith (eds.), *Medieval Society and the Manor Court* (Oxford, 1996), 50–67, 69–102.

[89] C. Dyer, 'Memories of Freedom: Attitudes Towards Serfdom in England, 1200–1350', in M. L. Bush (ed.), *Serfdom and Slavery: Studies in Legal Bondage* (Harlow, 1996), 277–95; M. Müller, 'The Aims and Organisation of a Peasant Revolt in Early Fourteenth-Century Wiltshire', *Rural History: Economy, Society, Culture*, 14 (2003), 1–20.

an element of fluidity in late medieval society. Migration can be identified as a major feature of the period 1250–1350. The urban centres were drawing their populations from the countryside and other towns, and their movements are recorded in surnames deriving from the migrants' place of origin.[90] In early fourteenth-century Essex 4 per cent of the males aged over 12 left their village every year, and 5 per cent entered.[91] After the Black Death the rate of migration probably increased, in defiance of the new restrictions imposed under the labour laws. The turnover of surnames suggests that between a half and three-quarters of village families moved every half-century, and by 1500 only a few families in most villages and small towns were descended from residents of the late fourteenth century.[92]

Towns give the impression of being regulated and intensively governed. The majority of them were granted the status of a borough, and the lords who founded them thought that traders and artisans would be attracted by the privileges of burgage tenure, which included fixed cash rents, the ability to sell or bequeath or divide a holding, and the privilege of trading without payment of toll in the market. The borough would have its own administration, with a reeve or bailiff and a borough court. A number of towns, however, grew up without these advantages, and the inhabitants held their land by ordinary free tenure. Evidently in the more commercially active parts of the country, such as Norfolk, where only six of its twenty-four late medieval towns enjoyed burghal privileges, towns would grow without the stimulus of borough status.[93] Founders put more emphasis on formal privileges when they felt some uncertainty about the towns' prospects for urban growth. Once they were established, the larger self-governing towns produced a mass of regulations, which were supposed to prevent middlemen profiteering in the food trades, and to govern the activities of artisans through the ordinances of 'craft guilds'. In practice, much trade and manufacture was conducted in an informal and irregular fashion, with many deals being done outside the market-place, and much craft work being conducted by people without formal training.[94]

---

[90] P. McClure, 'Patterns of Migration in the Late Middle Ages: The Evidence of English Place-name Surnames', *Ec.HR*, 2nd ser., 32 (1979), 169–82.

[91] L. R. Poos, 'Population Turnover in Medieval Essex', in L. Bonfield, R. M. Smith, and K. Wrightson (eds.), *The World We Have Gained: Histories of Population and Social Structure* (Oxford, 1986), 1–22.

[92] e.g. R. J. Faith, 'Berkshire: Fourteenth and Fifteenth Centuries', in P. D. A. Harvey (ed.), *The Peasant Land Market in Medieval England* (Oxford, 1984), 154–5.

[93] *CUHB* i. 507, 510.

[94] C. Dyer, 'The Consumer and the Market in the Later Middle Ages', in C. Dyer, *Everyday Life in Medieval England* (London, 1994), 274–8; H. Swanson, *Medieval Artisans: An Urban Class in Late Medieval England* (Oxford, 1989), 35–9, 50–2, 115–18.

If regulations could not be enforced in the small space of a town, it comes as no shock to find that parliamentary legislation was generally ineffective. The labour laws which attempted to prevent an increase in wages after 1349 were vigorously enforced for thirty years after the Black Death, and may have slowed down the rise in pay, but in the long run wage rates were fixed by market forces. And the sumptuary law of 1363, which sought to control the quality of clothing, and to prevent the lower orders from dressing above their station, had no apparent effect, and was quickly repealed.

The systems invented by historians help to make sense of complex realities by providing points of reference, but they can give a false impression of order and uniformity. The midland field system, or the two- or three-field system, is well known to have been modified in a number of ways—in many cases crops were planted in rotation not on the basis of the fields, but on the subdivision of the fields, the furlongs. Often sections of the fields were taken into 'inhocs' and sown in the year when they should have been fallow. In some villages part of the land was sown continuously ('every years' land'), which made them resemble the arrangements in upland regions whereby an infield was cropped intensively and sections of the outfield were brought into cultivation in sequence. In the fifteenth century individuals took strips or groups of strips out of the fields, planted them in rotations of their own devising, or enclosed them or used them as pasture. Not only do these variations show that there were many departures from the ideal type, either by collective groups or individuals, but they also suggest that the village community, another possible source of control and regulation, was itself capable of changing rules, and did not always stifle individual initiatives.[95]

Inheritance customs fall into a similar category, as we find that the rules of primogeniture (inheritance by the eldest son), which in theory determined the transmission of property provided only one strand in the 'inheritance strategy' of each family. Through gifts in a father's lifetime, or by means of enfeoffment, or through bequests, provision was made for the daughters and younger sons who could not in theory have a share in the inheritance.[96] In the same way the apparent consequences of partible inheritance could be avoided, and on those not very frequent occasions when a holding was divided equally among a number of brothers, they might decide to grant or sell their acres to a single heir.[97] Again, the village community, which might be regarded as the enforcers of their local custom, would often, through a jury in the manor court summoned to declare custom, make some pragmatic

---

[95] *AHEW* iii. 175–7, 183–7, 210–14, 222–6, 254–9.
[96] Z. Razi, 'The Myth of the Immutable English Family', *P&P* 140 (1993), 8–10.
[97] Smith, 'Families and Their Land', 181–2.

judgement which solved a particular problem. An example of the jurors wrestling with a complex case and solving it with good sense is revealed by a dispute at Barnet in Hertfordshire in 1306. Walter Bartholomew had three sons, Walter (II), Robert, and John. Walter senior gave a smallholding to his youngest son John (with the lord's permission). When Walter senior died, Walter (II) inherited the main holding according to primogeniture. Sadly John also died, whereupon Robert, the second son, took John's land, but Walter, the eldest son claimed it by the rules of primogeniture. The jury decided that Robert should keep the land, by a local custom that land should revert to the next brother in order of birth. There may have been such a well-known rule, but it is possible, as these circumstances would have occurred so rarely, that they made the decision because that seemed the fairest solution.[98]

A final dimension of the supposed rigidities of medieval society relates to the classification of people into social categories. Some systems were devised by historians and others were used by contemporaries. The notion of a feudal hierarchy is to some extent an imposition by historians, though it is based on contemporary labels. In the feodaries, surveys, and extents people are defined by their tenure of land—knights hold by knight service, sergeants in sergeantry, villeins in villeinage, cottars hold cotlands, burgesses hold in burgage tenure, and so on. This did not provide an adequate basis for describing the numerous social ranks and varied functions, hence the adoption of terms in the thirteenth and fourteenth centuries such as franklin, esquire, vavasour, and yeoman.[99] Contemporaries, especially in the fourteenth century, reiterated the archaic tripartite division of mankind into warriors, prayers, and workers precisely because they sought some certainty in a shifting world, and found in the old verities a framework for criticizing the ills of society. But they knew that townspeople, professionals, and many other groups could not be fitted with ease into any of the three orders.[100]

A much more practical method of classifying people was devised after the Statute of Additions of 1413, and it became normal to divide the peasants into labourers, husbandmen, and yeomen, and the lesser aristocracy likewise were put into three categories: gentlemen, esquires, and knights. The townsmen, and rural artisans and traders, were identified by their occupation.

[98] L. R. Poos and L. Bonfield (eds.), *Select Cases in Manorial Courts 1250–1550: Property and Family Law*, Selden Society, 114 (1997), 2–3.

[99] N. Saul, 'The Social Status of Chaucer's Franklin: A Reconsideration', *Medium Aevum*, 52 (1983), 10–23; N. Saul, *Knights and Esquires: The Gloucestershire Gentry in the Fourteenth Century* (Oxford, 1981), 11–29; P. R. Coss, 'Literature and Social Terminology: The Vavasour in England', in T. H. Aston *et al.* (eds.), *Social Relations and Ideas: Essays in Honour of R. H. Hilton* (Cambridge, 1983), 109–50; R. Almond and A. J. Pollard, 'The Yeomanry of Robin Hood and Social Terminology in Fifteenth-Century England', *P&P* 170 (2001), 52–77.

[100] S. H. Rigby, *English Society in the Later Middle Ages: Class, Status and Gender* (Basingstoke, 1995), 182–3.

When these labels were used in the courts carefully, they reveal a complexity in the lives of individuals that is normally hidden from view. Individuals straddled the divide between landed and mercantile society, like Thomas Arnold of Cirencester, described as 'gentleman, alias clothman, alias wool-man, alias chapman' in 1459.[101] From other sources we know of 'gentlemen bureaucrats' like William Worcester, who occupied posts in the administration of the great lords, and in central government took over jobs previously done by clergy.[102] The parish clergy cannot always be easily separated from the laity: they would manage their own landed estates, and become entrepreneurs in the wool and grain trades, partly on the basis of their tithe revenues.[103] A glimpse can sometimes be caught of the activities of middlemen who are difficult to fit into the conventional occupational categories. They dealt in grain or in manufactured goods, like the peasant of Charingworth in Gloucestershire (recorded in 1424) who bought and sold ropes, or the livestock dealers (each called a *marchand de bestes*) who were scattered over the west of Yorkshire in 1379.[104] On the dividing line between peasants and aristocrats landholders are encountered who did not fit easily into either category. They were sometimes called franklins or farmers, but one suspects that no single convenient word could describe them. At the lower end of the social scale were the manual workers who appear in one place to perform a task for a few days and then disappear from the records. Many of them were local cottagers or subtenants finding employment to supplement their revenues from their few acres. Lists of numerous *garciones*, entered in the court records of the manors of Glastonbury Abbey before 1348, reveal a normally hidden substratum of landless workers.[105] Some wage-earners were itinerants, who might appear in groups organized among themselves, like the Welsh harvest workers, and Welsh dykers who dug ditches, moats, and fishponds. Individuals moved around to work, who were identified as labourers when they were employed or as vagabonds when they were travelling from job to job.[106]

[101] E. Power, 'The Wool Trade in the Fifteenth Century', in E. Power and M. M. Postan (eds.), *Studies in English Trade in the Fifteenth Century* (London, 1933), 53.

[102] K. B. McFarlane, 'William Worcester, a Preliminary Survey', in id., *England in the Fifteenth Century* (London, 1981), 199–224; R. L. Storey, 'Gentlemen-bureaucrats', in C. H. Clough (ed.), *Profession, Vocation and Culture in Later Medieval England* (Liverpool, 1982), 90–129.

[103] R. N. Swanson, *Church and Society in Late Medieval England* (Oxford, 1989), 238–42.

[104] Dyer, 'Market Towns', 31; Anon. (ed.), 'Rotuli collectorum subsidii regi a laiciis anno secundo concessi in Westrythyngo in comitatu Eboraci', *Yorkshire Archaeological and Topographical Journal*, 5 (1879), 3, 7, 9, 17, 19, 20, 21, 22, 23, 28, 35, etc.

[105] H. S. A. Fox, 'Exploitation of the Landless by Lords and Tenants in Early Medieval England', in Razi and Smith, *Medieval Society*, 518–68.

[106] C. Dyer, 'Work Ethics in the Fourteenth Century', in J. Bothwell, P. J. P. Goldberg, and W. M. Ormrod (eds.), *The Problem of Labour in Fourteenth-Century England* (Woodbridge, 2000), 39.

If the rules were not obeyed, and society was not ordered as those in authority wished, the 'new middle ages' contradicts the strongly held belief that decisions were made by the powerful elite, and that change was directed from above. A long historical tradition sets the aristocracy in the centre of the stage, and presumes the importance of their activities in promoting change, such as direct management of demesnes from *c.*1200 to 1400 (including an episode of high farming at the end of the thirteenth century), founding of markets, fairs, and boroughs between about 1070 and 1300, the imposition and exploitation of serfdom beginning around 1200, and the expropriation of the peasantry around 1500. Even in the thirteenth century, at the height of their wealth, the lords were managing directly a quarter or a fifth of the productive land, and had incomplete powers of social control. They were inhibited by the resistance of those below them, and by the limitations imposed by the state. In their foundations of commercial centres they were seeking to profit from points of exchange, but were not directing or initiating trade. Technical innovations tended to come from below, born out of the practical experience of peasants and artisans. The modern reputation for inventiveness enjoyed by monks, and particularly those of the Cistercian order, does not stand up to critical investigation. In the late fourteenth century the aristocracy were in danger of losing control, and struggled to keep powers over their tenants and to keep direct management of their demesnes. In the next century they learned to manage change, and minimize their loss of wealth and power, but they were nonetheless struggling against disadvantages.

The 'new middle ages' can be summed up as a period of flexibility and variety, which went through a process of commercialization in the thirteenth century, and emerged from the shocks of the fourteenth-century crisis with an enhanced capacity for change—a weakened aristocracy, a mobile and less restricted peasantry, and a lively industrial and urban sector. Many features of the period, from family structures to farming methods, bear a strong resemblance to those prevailing in the sixteenth and seventeenth centuries.

Transition from Feudalism to Capitalism

How should these new interpretations of the medieval economy and society affect our assessment of the debate on the 'transition from feudalism to capitalism'? One reaction has been to say that the old debate is totally outmoded. There was no transition, because the 'new middle ages' was clearly capitalist, with its developed market, and its lack of rigid domination by lordship, communities, or families.[107] Those who are arguing that capitalism had already arrived in the later middle ages are employing an imprecise definition of capitalism, often based on attitudes and mentalities. This assumption allows it to be said that a thirteenth-century peasant who bought a half-acre to add to his five acres was seeking profits and therefore had a capitalist outlook. In fact the extra land contributed to the consumption resources of the family, and would have meant that the tenant of this expanded holding needed to do agricultural work for others, or be employed in a craft, for eighty days in the year rather than a hundred days. If the word 'capitalism' is to have any useful historical meaning it should take note of cultures and ideas, but must also be based on concrete resources and organization. The three elements which have been generally regarded as essential to a capitalist economy are: first, the existence of entrepreneurs owning the means of production (that is, such assets as land, equipment, and capital); secondly, that production should be for the market, and the market provides the main means of articulating economic activity; and thirdly, that labour is provided by workers who depend mainly on wages for their livelihood.[108]

Much recent research has been affirming the vigour and effectiveness of economic activities within the traditional feudal structure. We have seen that the directly managed lord's demesne was capable of adaptability and efficiency, and represents a large unit of production aimed at the market. Similarly, the farming methods of the peasant holding changed in line with broader trends in demand. Industry expanded on the basis of the household workshop which was staffed mainly by family labour, and spread into the relatively unrestricted countryside. Yet at the same time the aristocracy maintained their position at the top of society. Rents for land were still often fixed in relation to the power of lords and the restraints of custom, rather than by market forces. A high proportion of agricultural production was destined for consumption in the households of the producers. And a great deal of labour was performed by peasants and artisans, or by members of their family, rather than by a hired work-force. Many of the workers had a small amount of land, or were working in their youth in the expectation of gaining a holding of land or a workshop of their own in later life.

In other words, commercialization could take place without creating a capitalist economy. As Adam Smith said, people have long had a tendency to 'truck, barter and exchange one thing for another', and if that activity grows it can lead to specialization in labour and a growth in productivity. But this falls

---

[107] A. Macfarlane, *The Origins of English Individualism* (Oxford, 1978).
[108] This traditional definition is restated in R. S. Duplessis, *Transition to Capitalism in Early Modern Europe* (Cambridge, 1997), 5.

short of structural changes in the ownership of workshops and equipment, and the nature of the labour force. Craft production at York in the tenth century can be shown from the surviving debris to have followed various trends as outlined by Smith, such as the division of labour under the influence of commerce, but as the work was carried out by artisans in their homes, that falls a long way short of capitalism.[109]

The problem that has always dogged the idea of a 'transition' has been the length of time separating the later middle ages and the most significant developments in production, marketing, and mentality: the agricultural and industrial revolutions did not have their full effect until the nineteenth century. Three or four centuries is too long for a continuous transition, and we might almost think of the period 1250–1750 as one when commercial farming, proto-industrialization, the 'consumer revolution', and the establishment of European hegemony over the rest of the world were at work. The growth of factory production and a waged labour force, together with rapid rises in agricultural productivity, belong to a distinct era of emergent capitalism after 1750.[110]

Recent research has made us question many of the assumptions made in the old 'feudalism to capitalism' debate. For example, the crucial opening period was always seen to be the fifteenth and sixteenth centuries, when enclosures and the early voyages of discovery occurred; in the older literature this was the time of 'the rise of the middle class'. Now we appreciate that the expansion of the market, or a growth in the proportion of those living on wages, is very much apparent in the thirteenth century.[111] And in England the fourteenth century was the great age of the merchant capitalists, who took over a larger share of overseas trade and replaced the Italians as lenders of money to the crown. The old picture of the enclosing lords in the fifteenth century evicting peasants in order to expropriate their land and create larger units of production does not accord with our general view of a weakening in lords' power, and our recognition of the self-confidence and rather assertive stance of the peasantry.

The thirteenth century was an age of economic growth seen in global terms. An estimate of gross domestic product for England would put the total in 1300 at £5 million, perhaps fifteen times the figure for 1086. As the numbers of producers and consumers fell in the fourteenth and fifteenth

[109] J. Richards, *Viking Age England* (London, 1991), 103–20.

[110] R. J. Holton, *The Transition from Feudalism to Capitalism* (London, 1985), 80–6; P. Sweezy, 'A Critique', in R. Hilton (ed.), *The Transition from Feudalism to Capitalism* (London, 1976), 46–52.

[111] R. H. Britnell, 'Commerce and Capitalism in Late Medieval England: Problems of Description and Theory', *Journal of Historical Sociology*, 6 (1993), 359–76.

centuries, naturally the GDP shrank, to perhaps £3.5 million in 1470. The share of the GDP per person increased, as the fifteenth century was an age of relative individual prosperity, so that the GDP per head can be calculated at £0.78 in 1300 and £1.52 in 1470. Historians have to judge the contribution of both global growth and the prosperity of individuals to changes in the economy as a whole.[112]

The towns cannot be depicted in the role of subverting the old feudal order, as we now see towns as developing at the same time as the emergence of the aristocracy, and indeed that aristocrats founded, encouraged, and patronized towns.[113] Towns were not alien growths in agrarian society, but provided the goods, services, and marketing centres for both lords and peasants. Lords in the thirteenth century were helped and strengthened by the urban economy. They took advantage of the peasants' ability to sell crops to increase rent demands, and used labour services in order to produce saleable surpluses from their demesnes. Nor can the towns in the fifteenth and early sixteenth centuries be seen as centres of special enterprise and innovation. A study of northern merchants, including those from York, suggests that their wealth and share of long-distance trade was diminishing at this time.[114] The protagonists of 'urban decline' may have lost the debate. Their opponents, however, are generally arguing that the towns held their own, sometimes showing signs of vitality, but not that the townspeople were taking on some new dominant role.[115]

If the 'transition from feudalism to capitalism' means the rise of the middle class, and the removal of peasants by commercial-minded gentry in the late fifteenth century, then it is a concept that has died. But the general idea will not go away, because we cannot escape from the profound changes that occurred between the thirteenth and the sixteenth centuries. These deserve some general recognition and assessment from historians. The period saw important shifts in the relationships between lords and tenant, state and subject, agriculture and industry, the public and private spheres. These changes were not merely cyclical. Unlike grain prices and wage rates, they did not swing back, and the English society and economy would never be the same again. Historians are very reluctant to employ the term 'feudalism', preferring 'seigneurial' or 'manorial'. These are more precise words, but

---

[112] N. Mayhew, 'Population, Money Supply, and the Velocity of Circulation in England, 1300–1700', *Ec.HR* 48 (1995), 238–57; S. R. Epstein, *Freedom and Growth: The Rise of States and Markets, 1300–1750* (London, 2000), 10.

[113] R. H. Hilton, *English and French Towns in Feudal Society: A Comparative Study* (Cambridge, 1992), 6–18.

[114] J. Kermode, *Medieval Merchants: York, Beverley and Hull in the Later Middle Ages* (Cambridge, 1998), 314–19.

[115] Dyer, *Decline and Growth*, 58–61.

'feudal' in the later middle ages, when vassalage and fiefs were diminishing in significance at a high social level, is a useful shorthand means of depicting a society in which lords wielded private jurisdiction, and where rents were fixed by power and custom rather than by supply and demand. This is closely linked to the political power wielded by the aristocracy at every level, which was based on allies and clients rewarded with patronage, gifts, and fees rather than the payment of salaries. The long-term dynamic element lay in the tendency for tenants to gain more autonomy. That escape from lords' control can be seen among aristocratic tenants in the twelfth century, and was spreading to the peasants by the fourteenth. In the reign of Richard II hundreds of thousands of serfs were still living on English manors, and lords' private justice was enforced in manorial courts which generated useful revenue. By the reign of Henry VIII serfdom was still present, but much diminished, and the manorial courts had lost some types of business and lacked the teeth previously used to enforce their authority.[116]

To see the impact of these overall changes on the lives of people at a local level, let us end with a glance at James Ford's parish of Navestock in Essex. In the thirteenth century the lord of the manor, St Paul's Cathedral, received rents and services from more than a hundred tenants (see Table 1.2), mostly with 4 acres of land or an even lower figure. By Ford's day it was dominated by twenty-five farms, half of them with more than 100 acres.[117] That development which transformed the agriculture and society of the village had begun decisively in the period on which this book is focused. By 1533 the number of tenants had halved. The court rolls of 1528–35 reflect the changes in landholding which can be paralleled throughout England. A number of tenants had collected two or three holdings previously held separately. Richard Ballard held both customary and free land. Lawyers like Robert Norwich, members of the local gentry, and a London merchant, William

Table 1.2. Landholding at Navestock, Essex, 1222–1840

1222	1533	1840
116 tenants (59% with 4 acres or below)	55 tenants	25 farms (48% with 100 acres or above)

Sources: see n. 117.

---

[116] D. MacCulloch, 'Bondmen Under the Tudors', in C. Cross, D. Loades, and J. Scarisbrick (eds.), *Law and Government Under the Tudors* (Cambridge, 1988), 91–109; M. Bailey, *The English Manor c.1200–c.1500* (Manchester, 2002), 178–88.

[117] Guildhall Library, Corporation of London, Ms. 25304; W. H. Hale (ed.), *The Domesday of St. Paul's*, Camden Society, 69 (1858), 74–85; *VCH Essex*, iv. 139–50.

Dyce, were buying up land formerly held by small producers, and no doubt subletting all or part of the land to cultivators. In 1524 tenants were defying the authority of the lord by refusing to pay their share of the 'common fine', an ancient tax acknowledging the lord's jurisdiction. Seven newcomers, according to a list compiled in 1532, were moving into the manor and neglecting to fulfil the legal formalities of residence by swearing a oath of legal responsibility. Here was a local society in which individuals were gathering more land, showed a great deal of mobility, and demonstrated by their actions that the lord's authority had diminished. Navestock had moved a long way since the thirteenth century; the combination of parallel movements throughout the country will be the subject of the rest of this book.

2

Community and Privacy

In all societies—and that of medieval England was no exception—a tension existed between public obligations and private rights. Collective activities, family interests, and communal values were of great importance, but at the same time individuals had possession of land, and private space was maintained, for example, in houses. At the end of the middle ages an episode that has attracted much attention was the appropriation of common pastures by the lords of manors, the enclosures of common fields, and the exclusion of the peasantry. This seems to represent a triumph of private interests over the common good.

My purpose in this chapter is first to demonstrate the long ancestry of the shifting boundaries between collective welfare and private property, and to show that the conflict between them was not confined to the period after 1350 or 1500; secondly, to argue that the conventional story of private interests overriding collective rights oversimplifies more complex and contradictory trends; and thirdly, to stress that the role of lords should not be overrated, as much of the pressure for 'privatization' came from below. This inquiry begins with the history of the family and domestic life, and then turns to common fields and communities.

Peasants' Families and Land

The peasant household normally consisted of parents and children, with a living-in servant or two in the case of the better off. But often during a phase in the family's life-cycle the resident group included a grandparent or grandparents. This phase when the family consisted of three generations was of limited duration, given the limited lifespan of the elderly. The old people seem often to have been accommodated in a separate building on the holding.[1] This could be the subject of an agreement, by which the old person on retirement gave up the holding to a younger tenant, often a son, daughter, or son-in-law but sometimes a non-relative, in exchange for a promise of receiving food and other benefits as an annuity or pension.[2] Estrilda Nenour of the manor of High Easter in Essex, a widow, in 1321 surrendered her holding of a messuage and half-yardland to her daughter Agnes, in return for a promise that she would be accommodated 'within the messuage', which could have meant a cottage among the outbuildings grouped around the main house. She was also to be provided with adequate food and clothing.[3] Agnes married Henry Poleyn, and six years after her retirement Estrilda brought a case in the lord's court against Agnes and Henry because she alleged that they had failed to provide maintenance. She won her case, recovered the tenancy of the land, and made a new agreement with another younger tenant, who was apparently not a relative.

The point to notice is that such an arrangement, even between parents and children, was subject to negotiations when land passed from one generation to the next, and if the bargain was not kept the old person could resort to law. The retired peasant had no automatic right to support, and land was in the possession of either the outgoing or incoming tenant—property did not belong collectively to the family. The younger generation was no doubt strongly influenced by social pressures which emphasized the duties of the young and able-bodied towards the elderly and infirm, and indeed they were reminded of their responsibilities in sermons.[4] Their resources were, however, stretched, especially when they had children, as a half-yardland (about 15 acres) was adequate to feed a family of four or five, but would be strained by the requirements of one or two extra adults. One can imagine the frictions that might grow between the family in the main house and demands coming from the old lady in the cottage across the yard, and these could become especially acute in a year of a deficient harvest.

A strong sense of family loyalty is apparent in the western parts of England, because most land was transmitted by inheritance. For example, on the intensively studied manor at Halesowen in Worcestershire, in 1270–1348 63 per cent of transfers took place between relatives, and a very high

---

[1] R. M. Smith, 'Rooms, Relatives and Residential Arrangements: Some Evidence in Manor Court Rolls 1250–1500', *Medieval Village Research Group Annual Report*, 30 (1982), 34–5.

[2] R. M. Smith, 'The Manorial Court and the Elderly Tenant in Late Medieval England', in M. Pelling and R. M. Smith (eds.), *Life, Death and the Elderly* (London, 1991), 39–61.

[3] L. R. Poos and L. Bonfield (eds.), *Select Cases in Manorial Courts 1250–1550: Property and Family Law*, Selden Society, 114 (1997), 55–6.

[4] G. C. Homans, *English Villagers of the Thirteenth Century* (Cambridge, Mass., 1941), 155.

proportion of land was inherited within the family.[5] In addition to the transmission of land, the kin, which includes relatives beyond the nuclear family, helped one another, both in practical ways and by supporting each other in their actions in the manor court.[6]

There was also a land market between people who were not related to one another, and in eastern England most transactions of land held on customary tenure consisted of surrenders of a holding by a tenant in the court for the use of an incoming tenant. Less than 20 per cent of the transfers recorded at Redgrave in Suffolk in 1260–1319 were between members of the same family.[7] This makes it appear that the more commercial pressures of eastern England seriously weakened family loyalties.

Other influences helped to create these regional differences, because in western England the land was held and transmitted in the standard units of virgates or yardlands, while in East Anglia these landholding units had been shattered into small parcels, and the very active land market in manors like Redgrave consisted of moving half- or quarter-acres constantly within the village from family to family. This reservoir of small parcels of land was simply not available at Halesowen or other manors in the midlands and the west, where most land was held in the official holdings. In this respect the lords were imposing some important controls, because in the manorialized regions it was they who insisted on maintaining these customary units of tenure. They also restrained and supervised any acquisition of free land by customary tenants.[8] Customary tenure went through a long evolution. In the thirteenth century servile land in theory belonged to the lord, though it passed by hereditary succession. During the fourteenth century tenants obtained a copy of the court roll entry which gave them some written evidence of their tenure, and in the fifteenth century tenants of copyhold land could seek protection in the royal courts.[9] By 1500, although inferior to free land because of the high rent and the continued rights of the lord (for example, to demand a variable entry fine), copyhold land had virtually become the property of the tenant.

After a lengthy period of adjustment to the fall in population and the epidemics of the fourteenth century, by the 1430s all over the country

---

[5] Z. Razi, 'Family, Land and the Village Community in Later Medieval England', in T. H. Aston (ed.), *Landlords, Peasants and Politics in Medieval England* (Cambridge, 1987), 361.

[6] Ibid. 365–6, 384–6.

[7] R. M. Smith, 'Families and Their Land in an Area of Partible Inheritance: Redgrave, Suffolk 1260–1320', in id. (ed.), *Land, Kinship and Life-Cycle* (Cambridge, 1984), 182–4.

[8] P. Schofield, *Peasant and Community in Medieval England 1200–1500* (Basingstoke, 2003), 65–9.

[9] R. M. Smith, 'The English Peasantry, 1250–1650', in T. Scott (ed.), *The Peasantries of Europe from the Fourteenth to the Eighteenth Centuries* (Harlow, 1998), 342–7, 366–70.

families lost some of their significance in the transfer of land.[10] Inheritance declined because many families lacked sons. This reflects both the high rate of mortality in epidemics of plague and other diseases, and the ease with which those who survived could find land away from their father's holding or their home village, and so did not have to wait to inherit. To take a characteristic case where no inheritance took place, Robert Scotors who held a small amount of customary land, a 'penyland' and an acre of meadow, on the Yorkshire manor of Sherburn in Elmet, died in 1438. For five years heirs were given the opportunity to claim it, but as none came forward, in 1443 the lord granted it to John Thomson, clerk, who was not related to Scotor.[11] There was probably a decline in the number of maintenance agreements for the elderly, because holdings encumbered with old people were not so desirable. Kin, who in earlier times can be observed co-operating with one another, ceased to do so with the same frequency.[12] Soon after the plagues, in the late fourteenth century, in the absence of a son holdings would be inherited by more remote relatives, such as nephews, but even these links within the extended family declined in the fifteenth century.[13]

All of this could be taken as evidence for an important change in the nature of the family, which began in the most commercially active region, East Anglia, and then spread to other parts of the country. Individuals, motivated by self interest, relied on the land market rather than family connections to build up their holdings. Sons did not help their fathers as was once the case, and in general kin connections were no longer valued. Families were weakened by the diminishing control over tenants by lords, who could only make feeble efforts to prevent migration, and who could no longer influence the succession to holdings.

This narrative of the rise of the selfish individual, or of the small, self-reliant nuclear family, is not the whole story. For example, the peasants of East Anglia did not lack family loyalties. If we look at the amount of land (as distinct from the number of parcels) passing between family members, we find figures in the early fourteenth century of 46 per cent at Redgrave in Suffolk.[14] So inheritance figured rather more prominently in the transmission of land than first appears, even in the parts of the country under strongest commercial influence. This reflected the tendency for the busy land market to consist mainly of small parcels, but for complete holdings containing 5, 10, or even more acres to be inherited. Also peasants in East Anglia and elsewhere were granting

---

[10] Z. Razi, 'The Myth of the Immutable English Family', *P&P* 140 (1993), 27–42.
[11] West Yorkshire Archive Service, Leeds, GC/M3/42.
[12] Razi, 'Myth', 22–33.
[13] Razi, 'Family, Land and the Village Community', 373–9.
[14] Razi, 'Myth', 17.

parcels (often ones which they had purchased) to their children, especially those who could not expect to inherit under the conventions of the local inheritance custom. So at Palgrave in Suffolk, where land was inherited by all sons by the rules of partible inheritance, in 1273 Edyth Dikeman was given 5 roods (1¼ acres) of land by her father, 'by the grant' of Hugh and William Dikeman, her brothers, who were also her father's heirs.[15] Lords allowed the device of 'deathbed surrender', by which fathers could pass land before death to those who had no formal right to inherit.[16] This desire to help all members of the family partly explains why the wealthier peasants, who built up large holdings both before and after the Black Death, failed to found dynasties, as their accumulations of land were often fragmented among their offspring towards the end of their lives or after death.

The transfer of land within the family was not permanently damaged by the easing of the pressure on land after 1348–9. Family bonds changed under the new circumstances. Parents in the west midlands (for example, on the Worcestershire manor of Kempsey) from the 1470s used the device of surrendering a holding only to receive it back as a joint tenancy for the lives of named individuals, as a method of manipulating inheritance in favour of a younger son. The eldest son, who had gone off to make his own fortune elsewhere, lost his claim, and his younger brother, who had stayed at home to help work the land, received his reward.[17] In the late fifteenth and sixteenth centuries, as the demand for land rose again transfers of land within the family picked up. Sons rediscovered, as holdings became harder to find and more expensive to acquire, that family solidarity had its merits. For example, at Hevingham Bishops in Norfolk less than 13 per cent of holdings went to relatives in the period 1425–43, but after 1498 the proportion of transmissions within the family rose above 30 per cent.[18]

This leads us to the conclusion that at any particular period peasants were probably not attached by any strong mystic bond to a specific holding. Peasants were motivated both by self interest and by loyalty and duty to others, and the balance was tipped one way or another depending on circumstances. The strength of their commitment to the family was bound to be influenced by the contribution to the work on the holding by family members, and the tendency for the holding to form the basis of social security for the old and inadequate. We should not assume that land and houses were

[15] Suffolk Record Office (Ipswich Branch), HA 411/40/1.

[16] L. Bonfield and L. R. Poos, 'The Development of the Deathbed Transfer in Medieval English Manor Courts', *Cambridge Law Journal*, 47 (1988), 403–27.

[17] C. Dyer, *Lords and Peasants in a Changing Society: The Estates of the Bishopric of Worcester, 680–1540* (Cambridge, 1980), 309–11.

[18] J. Whittle, *The Development of Agrarian Capitalism: Land and Labour in Norfolk 1440–1580* (Oxford, 2000), 120–77.

always acquired or inherited to be worked and occupied by the tenant. There were circumstances when land was held as an investment to be rented out to others, or to be sold to raise cash.[19]

Members of the community were concerned with the transfer of property. The leading figures acted as guardians of the inheritance customs in their position as jurors of the manor court. With their anxiety for the maintenance of good order, they wished to settle quarrels and attempted to prevent destitution. They sometimes came to the aid of old people who complained that their maintenance agreement was not being honoured, as in the case of Estrilda Nenour above, who was judged by a local jury to have been wrongly denied her maintenance. While they would be concerned to protect the elderly (they might all be old one day themselves), they would also favour the tenure of holdings by strong and active tenants, who would contribute to the village's obligations to lord and state and keep their land free of weeds. We can see that individuals needed to balance their own interests against those of their neighbours. They could behave ruthlessly in the time of bad harvests around 1300, buying up the holdings of their poorer neighbours who were encumbered in debt.[20] After the Black Death the more efficient or ambitious villagers engrossed holdings and acquired such a large share of resources as to endanger the neighbourly relations which kept the common fields running smoothly.[21] But even these selfish and wealthy individuals usually accepted that the community had a role, and participated in collective activities such as religious fraternities and the churchwardens' fund-raising.

To sum up this discussion, peasants transmitted holdings to their heirs, or bought and sold land, because their actions were for their own benefit, but they were also influenced by their lords, by their family commitments, and by neighbours. The degree of self interest varied with place and time, and it would be difficult to argue on the basis of the evolution of the land market that the period saw the continuous and linear growth of selfish individualism.

Space in Houses and Villages

An approach to analysing the relationship between the public and private spheres is to examine the allocation of space within and around the house.

[19] E. Clark, 'Charitable Bequests, Deathbed Land Sales, and the Manor Court in Later Medieval England', in Z. Razi and R. Smith (eds.), *Medieval Society and the Manor Court* (Oxford, 1996), 143–61.

[20] B. M. S. Campbell, 'Population Pressure, Inheritance and the Land Market in a Fourteenth-Century Peasant Community', in Smith (ed.), *Land, Kinship and Life-Cycle*, 113–20.

[21] R. H. Hilton, 'Rent and Capital Formation in Feudal Society', in id., *The English Peasantry in the Later Middle Ages* (Oxford, 1975), 203–4.

A shift towards greater privacy in houses has been identified in the late medieval and early modern periods. At the aristocratic level the lord and lady were supposed in the high middle ages to spend a good deal of time in the public space of the hall, where they dined and showed themselves before the assembled household of companions, servants, and guests, and only retired to the private chamber after meals. In the 1370s the poem *Piers Plowman* famously criticized lords for abandoning the hall and taking their meals in their private chambers.[22] This divisive trend has been identified by architectural historians in the design of late medieval houses, in which the hall diminished in size, and culminated in the allocations of space in the modern country house, by which the servants had their own hall below stairs and the family and household led strictly separate lives.[23]

The development of aristocratic houses does not entirely support this view. The separate apartments with ample space for the private lives of the aristocracy were already well established in twelfth-century domestic planning, when two-storey chamber blocks were being built as freestanding structures, or at the end of halls.[24] As early as the 1240s the countess of Lincoln was being advised to take a full part in the public life of the hall, as if there was an alternative of private meals, both for the lady herself and for the superior servants.[25]

The notion that halls diminished in importance in the fifteenth century cannot be regarded as a universal tendency, and there are some remarkable examples of new large halls being built, such as Gainsborough Old Hall (Lincolnshire) in the 1460s.[26] Much attention was being paid to the furnishing, heating, and lighting of the dais on which the lord and lady sat with their family, companions, and guests.[27] The ceremonies of public eating were being taught to the coming generation of young servants through the fifteenth-century courtesy books.[28] Much of the provision of private accommodation was not for the lord but for the superior servants, for whom lodgings—rows of small heated rooms, not unlike the accommodation for clergy in colleges—were being built in the fifteenth century.[29]

---

[22] G. Kane and E. Talbot (eds.), *Piers Plowman: The B Version* (London, 1975), 412 (ll. 98–103).

[23] M. Girouard, *Life in the English Country House: A Social and Architectural History* (New Haven, 1978), 30–59.

[24] J. Blair, 'Hall and Chamber: English Domestic Planning 1000–1250', in G. Meirion-Jones and M. Jones (eds.), *Manorial Domestic Building in England and Northern France*, Society of Antiquaries Occasional Papers, 15 (1993), 1–21.

[25] D. Oschinsky (ed.), *Walter of Henley and Other Treatises on Estate Management and Accounting* (Oxford, 1971), 402–7.

[26] J. Grenville, *Medieval Housing* (London, 1997), 89–120; C. R. J. Currie, 'Larger Medieval Houses in the Vale of White Horse', *Oxoniensia*, 57 (1992), 81–244.

[27] Grenville, *Housing*, 110–13.

[28] R. W. Chambers (ed.), *A Fifteenth-Century Courtesy Book*, Early English Text Society, os, 148 (1914).

[29] M. Barley, *Houses and History* (London, 1986), 95–100.

In peasant houses private accommodation increased with the addition of rooms in the sixteenth and seventeenth centuries. Domestic space is said to have been 'enclosed' in a move analogous to the enclosure of fields, suggesting parallel advances on the path to private property.[30] The processes often took place centuries apart, however, which makes the parallel seem less apposite. Peasant houses bore some resemblance to aristocratic houses, with a division by about 1200 between an accessible public room, the hall, and the chamber, a private inner room where the family slept and valuables were stored. House plans sometimes show two small rooms at ground-floor level in addition to the hall (Fig. 2.1).[31]

Upper rooms, or at least lofts, were being inserted in two- and three-room peasant houses in the midlands and the south-west even before 1350, and more regularly in the fifteenth century.[32] In the south-east the wealden houses, which were being built in some number from about 1380, combined an open hall with two-storey bays at one or both ends, giving the larger houses four or five rooms with the potential for separate sleeping accommodation for parents, children, and servants.[33] Private rooms clearly increased in number after *c*.1380, but they were not a complete novelty.

Fireplaces, as distinct from open hearths, in specially constructed smoke bays, or with smoke hoods built over the fire, were being inserted in the halls of superior peasant houses in the fifteenth century, in Wiltshire, for example.[34] The full modernization of houses, with a ceiling inserted over the hall, so that houses consisted entirely of two storeys, which was happening in the south and east in the sixteenth century, was delayed much longer in the north-west and south-west.[35] When the hall was ceiled, fireplaces and chimneys were inserted, not just in the hall but in other rooms, such as the parlour, which represented a new concept in domestic arrangements. The use of rooms was becoming more specialized. Peasants, even the wealthier yeomen, did not need to put on a show of ceremony and impress visitors with displays

[30] M. Johnson, *Housing Culture: Traditional Architecture in an English Landscape* (London, 1993), 164–77.

[31] M. Gardiner, 'Vernacular Buildings and the Development of the Late Medieval Domestic Plan in England', *MA* 44 (2000), 159–79.

[32] C. Dyer, 'English Peasant Buildings in the Later Middle Ages (1200–1500)', *MA* 30 (1986), 24, 41; Grenville, *Housing*, 147, 151–6.

[33] S. Pearson, *Medieval Houses of Kent: An Historical Analysis* (London, 1994); the complexity of the arrangements of rooms, in terms of access as well as construction and use, is revealed in D. Martin, 'The Configuration of Inner Rooms and Chambers in the Transitional Houses of Eastern Sussex', *Vernacular Architecture*, 34 (2003), 37–51.

[34] This is based on papers given at the winter meeting of the Vernacular Architecture Group in December 2001, and particularly on papers by R. Brunskill, J. Thorp, and P. Slocombe.

[35] The process of flooring the hall and inserting a chimney is discussed in E. Roberts, *Hampshire Houses 1250–1700: Their Dating and Development* (Winchester, 2003), 150–6.

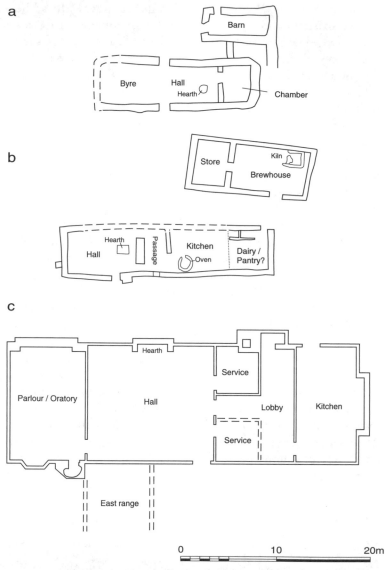

Fig. 2.1. Plans of peasant houses and manor houses. The four examples are (a) thirteenth-century 'long house' from a hamlet at Meldon Quarry near Okehampton (Devon), in which a hall, chamber, and byre lie under one roof, with a separate barn; (b) house of the fourteenth to early sixteenth centuries at Great Linford (Bucks.), with a hall, kitchen, and dairy (the chamber would have been on an upper storey), and separate brew-house (both of these peasant houses had stone foundations and a timber-framed superstructure); (c) manor house of the abbot of Walden Abbey at St Aylotts (Essex), built in 1500–1, of

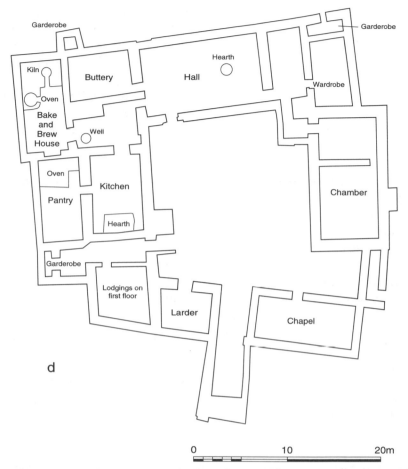

Garderobe

Garderobe

Hearth

Kiln

Buttery   Hall

Oven

Wardrobe

Bake
and
Brew   Well
House

Oven

Pantry   Kitchen   Chamber

Hearth

Garderobe

Lodgings on
first floor

Larder

Chapel

d

0   10   20m

brick with timber framing. This range in the plan originally had wings on either side, all contained within a moat; there were chambers and lodgings on the first floor. Novel features for its period include the parlour and the kitchen which was incorporated into the range; (d) manor house of the Cardinham family at Penhallam in Jacobstow (Corn.), which is a complex of stone buildings of mainly thirteenth-century date. The hall, chamber, chapel, and other rooms lie to the east of the courtyard, and kitchen and service rooms to the west.

Sources: D. Austin, 'Excavations at Okehampton Deer Park, Devon, 1976–1978', *Proceedings of the Devon Archaeological Society,* 36 (1978), 191–239; D. C. Mynard, R. J. Zeepvat, and R. J. Williams, *Excavations at Great Linford, 1974–80,* Buckinghamshire Archaeological Society Monograph Series, 3 (1991), 65–7, 126–7; A. Emery, *Greater Medieval Houses of England and Wales 1300–1500,* Vol II (Cambridge, 2000), 145–7; G. Beresford, 'The Medieval Manor of Penhallam, Jacobstow, Cornwall', *MA* 18 (1974), 90–145.

of opulence or ancestral weapons and coats of arms, as did the aristocracy, and their status did not depend so much on traditions of hospitality and patronage, so the large open hall diminished in significance in peasant houses earlier than in those of the gentry. In this respect, as in others, the peasants adopted new ways of living ahead of their social superiors (see pp. 28–9).

The plans of villages and hamlets were often devised and modified in the twelfth and thirteenth centuries. Public spaces, such as streets and greens, were clearly distinguished from the tofts and enclosures within which houses were built. In woodland and pastoral landscapes the houses and their tofts and crofts could appear as islands surrounded by extensive common pastures. In champion landscapes the houses would be grouped together in a nucleated village, with each house sandwiched between neighbours, facing on to a strip of roadside grass or a green of an acre or two, with common arable fields or common pasture sweeping up to the edge of the settlement (Fig. 2.2). The properties belonging to individual late medieval households were defined by ditches, hedges, fences, or walls, and peasant houses were provided with strong doors with iron hinges and locks.[36] Intruders intending to steal from a peasant would have had to enter the private space of the toft by negotiating a barrier or passing through a gate, and would then have had to cope with a locked outer door, followed by the inner door to the chamber, and finally would need to break into a padlocked wooden chest. Evidently late medieval villagers had a strong sense of private property, and distrusted outsiders. The records of felonies in the royal courts, and the accusations of petty housebreaking and theft which were heard in the lords' courts, suggest that precautions were justified.[37]

Protection of private goods is compatible with an element of co-operation and common purpose among peasants. We must not imagine that family life resembled that of our own times: one only has to visualize the family's sleeping arrangements, either confined in a chamber measuring 5 metres square, or with some members sleeping in the hall after its function as a room for food-preparation and eating had ceased. The household extended beyond the family to non-relatives, in view of the widespread employment of young living-in servants, and they had a share in the sleeping space. Medieval peasants' sense of community encouraged them to put much energy and time into the parish and fraternities. They devoted a high proportion of their resources to collective building projects, such as the fabric and fittings of the

[36] G. Astill, 'Rural Settlement: The Toft and the Croft', in id. and A. Grant (eds.), *The Countryside of Medieval England* (Oxford, 1988), 51–4.

[37] Individuals' awareness of legal rights and duties are discussed in A. Musson, *Medieval Law in Context: The Growth of Legal Consciousness from Magna Carta to the Peasants' Revolt* (Manchester, 2001), 84–134.

Fig. 2.2. Plan of the village of Broxholme (Lincs.), as it probably looked in the later middle ages. This is based on a map of *c.*1600, combined with recent fieldwork. It shows the boundaries around the houses, together with the public building of the church, and the common fields to the west and common pasture to the east.

Source: P. L. Everson, C. C. Taylor, and C. J. Dunn, *Change and Continuity: Rural Settlements in North-West Lincolnshire*, Royal Commission on the Historical Monuments of England (1991), 76–8.

parish church, church houses for parish functions, and guildhalls.[38] They also depended for their survival on the management of collective assets, above all the common fields, pastures, and woods. In many villages the main water supply was a well or stream shared between neighbours. They had to strike a balance between private interests and the common good, between households and communities, just as individuals had to define their relations with the family. The complex choices that had to be made cannot be forced into a single tendency towards greater privacy focused on a particular period.

Common Fields and Private Profit, Before 1350

The control of land was a central issue in agricultural production. Private property and collective interests coexisted, sometimes in harmony, but often also in competition. Here the focus will be on conflicts, because they arose in times of change and were also more likely to be recorded in writing.

Common land and land held in severalty or enclosure lay side by side throughout the middle ages. According to one calculation, about a half of all agricultural land had been enclosed by 1600, and one may estimate that about a half of that (a quarter of the total, and therefore *c.*2 million acres) lay in crofts and closes surrounded by fences and hedges before 1200.[39] Much enclosed land, intermixed with patches of common arable and some extensive common pastures, was concentrated in the woodland or wood-pasture land-scapes, which are found in western England from north Dorset and eastern Somerset through the west midlands to Cheshire and Lancashire, and in the south-east.[40] These areas of enclosure are recorded for the first time in the tenth and eleventh centuries, and they may at that time have been more extensive than later, as between about 850 and 1150 large villages were forming in the midland belt, and as part of that process former enclosed land in their territories was being turned into extensive common fields. We can glimpse the process by which common fields were growing at the expense of enclosures at Swannington in Leicestershire, when a hedged field created by assarting in a wooded landscape and held in severalty,

---

[38] e.g. B. Kümin, *The Shaping of a Community: The Rise and Reformation of the English Parish c.1400–1560* (Aldershot, 1996); V. Bainbridge, *Gilds in the Medieval Countryside: Social and Religious Change in Cambridgeshire c.1350–1558* (Woodbridge, 1996); K. L. French, *The People of the Parish: Community Life in a Late Medieval Diocese* (Philadelphia, 2001); C. Dyer, 'The English Medieval Village Community and its Decline', *Journal of British Studies*, 33 (1994), 407–29.

[39] J. R. Wordie, 'The Chronology of English Enclosure, 1500–1914', *Ec.HR*, 2nd ser., 36 (1983), 483–505.

[40] J. Thirsk (ed.), *The English Rural Landscape* (Oxford, 2000), 97–9, 105–15, 136–9.

in the thirteenth century was subdivided between a number of tenants to form a new open field.[41]

The opposite tendency, when individuals enclosed parcels of common pasture for cultivation or for the exclusive grazing of their own animals, was developing in the twelfth century and can be observed as a source of serious conflict in the early thirteenth. This was part of the assarting movement, which is usually regarded as a positive sign of economic growth, stimulated by the increase in population, agricultural profits, and land values. One man's improvement, however, meant a loss of assets for his neighbours.

The appropriation of common pasture, and the strong reactions that it caused, caused troubles in the large woodland parishes in north Worcestershire and Warwickshire, which are now absorbed into the southern suburbs of the city of Birmingham (Fig. 2.3). In the thirteenth century a rather small population was distributed in hamlets and isolated farms scattered on the edge of extensive heaths and woods. In 1221 the Justices in Eyre holding a session in Worcestershire heard that nineteen people from Yardley had pulled down the hedges of Thomas of Swanshurst.[42] He claimed that he had been deprived of his holding, and was supported by the lord of the manor, Ralph of Limesi. He stated that by the 'law of Arden' (Arden evidently stretched here across the boundary from Warwickshire) lords could build houses and raise banks and hedges on common pasture, provided that the encroachments did not damage those who used the commons. Here the local custom anticipated the Statute of Merton, which applied the same principle more generally in 1236.[43] The nineteen 'rioters', in fact respectable people protecting their grazing rights, defended their action by recalling an earlier dispute in the royal court from which a compromise was reached. A boundary had been defined around existing assarts to prevent further loss of common pasture, but Thomas had broken that agreement.

The lord of the manor, Ralph of Limesi, had been drawn into the dispute but he had not himself built a house or enclosed a section of the common pasture. The initiative had come from his tenant, and the lord was defending his interest in the rent that he would gain from the enclosed land. The root of the problem lay in conflicts between peasants. In three other complaints at

---

[41] J. Thirsk, 'The Common Fields', in R. H. Hilton (ed.), *Peasants, Knights and Heretics* (Cambridge, 1976), 21.

[42] D. M. Stenton (ed.), *Rolls of the Justices in Eyre, being the Rolls of Pleas and Assizes for Lincolnshire and Worcestershire 1221*, Selden Society, 53 (1934), pp. lxvi–lxvii, 448–51; the topography of the area is in V. Skipp, *Medieval Yardley* (London, 1970), 26–30.

[43] F. Pollock and F. Maitland, *The History of English Law Before the Time of Edward I*, new edn. (Cambridge, 1968), i. 622–30.

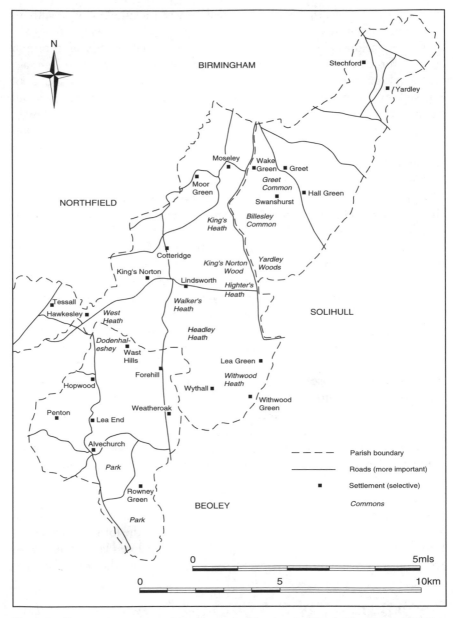

Fig. 2.3. Common pastures and landscapes in Alvechurch, King's Norton, and Yardley (Worcs.), 1221–1332. The map shows a woodland landscape to the south of the medieval town of Birmingham. Characteristic features include the large parishes, dispersed settlements, and extensive common pastures, heaths, and woods.

Sources: see n. 42, and information from Anne Baker and George Demidowicz.

the same eyre about the casting down of hedges at Yardley, those making the enclosures had ordinary names like Richard son of Edwin.[44] They were evidently peasants seeking to extend their holdings by taking in land from the common, which brought them into conflict with their (mainly peasant) neighbours.

The conflicts over the remaining open spaces of this district continued for another century. In 1273 a dispute broke out between the people of Alvechurch and King's Norton, a few miles to the west of the Yardley common pasture.[45] They shared common grazing on West Heath and *Dodenhaleshey*, but tenants of the Alvechurch manor were enclosing land on these two pastures, so the 'men of King's Norton' destroyed their banks and fences. As at Yardley, the lord of the manor of Alvechurch allied himself with his tenants, but as he was the bishop of Worcester he had an extra weapon against those who destroyed enclosures, and he excommunicated the offenders from King's Norton. The quarrel was patched up 'through the mediation of friends and neighbours', and it was agreed that the *Dodenhaleshey* enclosures would remain demolished, except those belonging to four named tenants, but the enclosures on West Heath could be kept in severalty. This was implemented by quitclaims granted by the Alvechurch tenants to the bishop, by which they gave up their enclosures. This compromise did not survive, as Alvechurch peasants were still seeking to extend their holdings by encroaching on pieces of common land. In the next settlement of the dispute in 1287 the King's Norton men gave up their claims to common pasture in *Dodenhaleshey* in exchange for keeping common rights on what remained of West Heath. They were also paid off with £6. 13s. 4d.

Later, in 1332, the battleground moved a short distance to the east, to King's Norton Wood, in which people from King's Norton, Yardley, and Solihull had claims to common grazing.[46] They all joined forces to attack a bank and ditch raised by Roger Mortimer, the aristocratic lessee of King's Norton, again not for his direct gain but for the benefit of tenants wishing to add to their holdings. The rioters were initially fined £300, perhaps to frighten them, but this was later reduced to £13. 6s. 8d. The large sums of money paid in compensation or in penalties reflect the large areas of land and the profits at stake in these campaigns of encroachment.

Riots in which communities defended their pastures make a good story, especially when they involve such incongruities to a modern reader as the

---

[44] Stenton (ed.), *Justices in Eyre*, 448–51.

[45] R. H. Hilton, *A Medieval Society: The West Midlands at the End of the Thirteenth Century*, 2nd edn. (Cambridge, 1983), 152; Dyer, *Lords and Peasants*, 57; Worcestershire Record Office, ref. 821, BA 3814 (*Liber Albus*), fos. 71, 79.

[46] *Calendar of Patent Rolls, 1330–4*, 268.

people of Solihull, a suburb now famed for its respectability and conservatism, defying the law in a destructive rampage, but they are greatly out-
numbered by the attempts of individuals to protect themselves through legal
process. In the Shropshire Eyre of 1256 twenty cases, under the assize of novel
disseisin, were brought, like the allegation of William Flemyng of Norbury
that Roger son of Celestine and Nicholas Tubbe had deprived him of pasture
for his cattle by cultivating 3 acres of heath.[47] These apparently isolated
complaints of deprivation of grazing, denial of access to wood, or obstruction
of passage along roads sought to preserve the common rights of a number of
local people, and the plaintiffs are likely to have been acting on behalf of a
group of tenants, or a whole community, who would have contributed to the
lawyers' fees.[48] While one man may have stood up for the common rights of
the many, the paradox needs to be remembered that the community's concern
to protect common grazing was based on a combination of the economic
interests of many individuals.

These disputes could be put before the king's court because they involved
free tenants or the lords of manors, and because conflicts between whole
villages attracted the attention of higher authority. Many lesser disputes
surfaced in the manorial courts. At Erdington, in the woodlands of north-
west Warwickshire, in 1336 the lord's court ordered an inquiry into a house
built on the waste by Thomas le Gardiner, and also distrained another tenant,
William Fox, to explain the construction of a bank (an enclosure) also on the
waste.[49] Those who were making private encroachments on the common
offended the manorial authorities by not seeking the lord's permission nor
paying rent for the new land. But neighbours would have been offended by
the threat to their common rights, and brought the offenders to the notice
of the court. The problem for the opponents of these assarts or enclosures lay
in the lord's perception that the new holdings gave him extra income once
they had been registered and a rent agreed.

The whole community could engage in direct negotiations with the lord
about common rights, as occurred at Brightwalton in Berkshire in 1294: the
communitas villanorum (community of villeins, rather than of villagers, but
most villagers here were villeins, or unfree tenants) agreed that common
rights previously enjoyed by the villagers and by the lord of the manor (the
abbot of Battle) in two woods should be reallocated so that the lord had
exclusive use of one, and he would withdraw from any claim to graze animals

---

[47] A. Harding (ed.), *The Roll of the Shropshire Eyre of 1256*, Selden Society, 96 (1980), 21.
[48] On collective action over common rights, see J. R. Birrell, 'Common Rights in the Medieval
Forest: Disputes and Conflicts in the Thirteenth Century', *P&P* 117 (1987), 22–49.
[49] Birmingham City Archives, 347851.

in the other.[50] The insistence in the official record on the spontaneity of the villagers' agreement, and the 'grace' shown by the lord, suggests that he had the best of the exchange.

Sometimes the lord seems to have had to make a concession, as when on the estate of Halesowen Abbey the peasant community of Oldbury (Worcestershire) in 1301 prevailed on the lord not to allow the common pasture of *Wellegrene* to be appropriated, though they had to pay 6s. 8d. as a a lump sum, and an annual rent of 4d., to save their grazing.[51] Many other small-scale negotiations were conducted without great commotion or even record, but the results of the give and take emerges in the arrangements revealed at a much later date. The understanding had evidently often been reached that land in a close would be exploited as the tenant wished, but that at the 'common time', after the harvest or in the year when a nearby section of the common fields of the village lay fallow, the gates should be opened and common grazing allowed.

In the woodland landscapes in which these disputes took place pasture was relatively plentiful. The problems of feeding livestock was felt much more acutely in the champion or feldon landscapes in the village belt of central England, where grazing depended on the stubbles and fallows of the arable fields, and only limited amounts of permanent pasture were available. In the thirteenth and early fourteenth centuries, when the pressures would have been at their height, complaints of encroachment are not so commonly found. On the Cotswolds, where villages shared upland pastures, one village would accuse another of exceeding its quota, and in retaliation would seize the offending animals. On Bredon Hill in Worcestershire in 1312 the men of Kemerton impounded 400 sheep and an ox belonging to villages on the other side of the hill. The injured peasants happened to be the tenants of the bishop of Worcester, who had no secular jurisdiction over the offenders, and so used his religious authority to excommunicate them.[52]

Frictions on a smaller scale were revealed when an individual tenant brought a plea of trespass against a neighbour whose cattle had strayed on to his land, often a garden or close in the vicinity of the village itself. Almost as a routine, peasants in considerable numbers would be accused of allowing their animals to consume the lord's crops and grass. On the Gloucester Abbey manor of Abbot's Barton in 1291 John Peris and Richard Moot were each

---

[50] F. W. Maitland (ed.), *Select Pleas in Manorial and other Seignorial Courts*, Selden Society, 2 (1888), 172.

[51] R. A. Wilson (ed.), *Court Rolls of the Manor of Hales*, part 3, Worcestershire Historical Society (1933), 158–9.

[52] R. A. Wilson (ed.), *The Register of Walter Reynolds, Bishop of Worcester 1308–1313*, Dugdale Society, 9 (1928), 40–1.

accused of putting 100 sheep to graze on the lord's meadow, and thirty-three other offenders were said to have consumed the lord's grass and corn with a total of sixty-eight other animals and six geese.[53] They would be amerced a few pence, and would often be found repeating the offence in the next year's court. Perhaps the peasants believed that the land on which their animals strayed had once been common and had been wrongly occupied by the lord. If such an issue of principle was involved, the lord would probably have reacted much more forcefully, so it seems that each amercement represents a substitute for a regular rent for pasture. The lord accepted some modest trespassing, as long as he received a flow of money to compensate for the crops and grass consumed. In the same way, those who dug marl or clay on the common were made to pay, not to prevent them from obtaining these materials, but to ensure that the lord received his share of their profits.

The relatively small number of records of violent conflicts over commons reaching the royal courts in the champion regions must reflect the maturity of the system. The delicate interlocking mechanisms of open-field farming by the thirteenth century were tried and tested, when the documents become abundant. Everyone knew the rules, and compromises between individuals and the community had long been agreed. The by-laws issued in the period 1270–1350 were mainly concerned with the harvest, a crucial time when tensions reached their height. Pasture was an issue then, as individuals were selfishly grazing animals in the stubble before the crops were carried. A more pressing concern seems to have been the danger of sheaf stealing, so harvest workers were not to be paid in sheaves, as it would be difficult to distinguish between corn honestly or dishonestly acquired as people left the harvest field, and sheaves were not to be carted away at night. The villagers showed some concern for the poor, but they were suspected of abusing the privilege of gleaning in the fields. In particular, potential harvest workers were either gleaning or seeking work in other villages.[54]

Most of the dozens of rules in each village governing the open fields and common resources were so well known that they were not rehearsed in the lords' courts, and were enforced by informal neighbourly pressure. To take one example, every village had an agreed quota of animals that could be kept on the common, the stint. It sometimes appears in writing when a free-holding was granted by charter, presumably because the change of ownership created a need for defining or even revising the rules. At Maisey Hampton in Gloucestershire, for example, in *c*.1300 new holders of 14 acres of arable were told that they could graze four beasts, a horse, and thirty sheep in

---

[53] Gloucestershire Record Office, D 936a, M1.
[54] W. O. Ault, *Open-Field Farming in Medieval England* (London, 1972), 27–38.

the common pasture.[55] Stints were not normally recorded in writing at this time.

The existence of so many well-known routines did not prevent the open-field village from making changes. The concern to limit gleaning at the end of the thirteenth century must relate to growing anxieties about the poor, and perhaps a shift in attitudes among the better-off peasants towards charity. In a more positive spirit, we have seen that villages were able to adjust the cropping of the fields in order to increase output, not so often through remodelling the whole cultivated area, as in the case of conversion from two to three fields, but in hitching or inhoking, that is, taking part of the fallow and planting crops on it.[56]

A potential source of stress in all parts of the countryside in the twelfth and thirteenth centuries lay in the need to accommodate an increased number of households. The division of existing holdings, which led the yardlands to be split into halves or quarters, need not have imposed any great strain on the common fields or pastures, as the rights and obligations would have been divided between the fractions. If the stint allowed sixty sheep per yardland, for example, the half-yardlands would be allocated grazing for thirty. The real threat to the welfare of the whole village came from a proliferation of cottagers and smallholders, who might be granted small parcels of the demesne, or settled on common land, often on the edge of roads. Some of the potential problems for the substantial villagers were avoided by allowing the cottagers very limited quantities of common grazing, such as pasture for a single cow, or even no guaranteed access to common grazing at all. This underlines the lack of an egalitarian spirit in villages. The full members of the community were the tenants of the more substantial holdings, the yard-landers and half-yardlanders. They were the main agricultural producers, who provided most of the rents and services to the lord, and contributed almost all of the village's tax payment. They served on the jury in the manor court, and acted as tithing men and chief pledges. They filled the offices of reeve and hayward for the running of the manor. This group—too large to be called an elite—insisted on fair shares of resources for themselves, and when they helped to frame the by-laws expressed their prejudices, for example, on the subject of harvest labour. At that time of year they wished to employ all the able-bodied villagers, and it galled them to see the cottagers and young men and women leaving for better wages.

To sum up the use of land before the Black Death, a dialogue between public and private interests was in progress. In the open-field villages the

[55] A. Clarke (ed.), *The English Register of Godstow Nunnery, near Oxford*, Early English Text Society, os, 129, 130, 142 (1905–11), 151.

[56] See above, p. 37.

tensions were contained within an intricate system of checks and balances. Outside the village belt the enclosure of common grazing land led to more readily visible clashes of interest. The lords were drawn into the conflict, and can be seen defending the enclosers, because they represented an increase in the number of tenants and the payment of rent. Many of the initiatives, however, both to enclose and to resist enclosure, and to regulate the use of common assets, came from the peasants themselves.

Common Fields and Private Profit, After 1350

Enclosure and Land Management

After the Black Death, the fall of population, the rise of rural industry, and the depression in grain prices, the whole emphasis of agriculture shifted from the cultivation of cereals to pastoral farming. Animal husbandry required less labour than tilling the fields, and consumers were demanding more meat and animal products.

The activities of lords have often been highlighted in this period, and especially between 1450 and 1520. In the terminology of historians such as Robert Brenner, they undermined peasant property, or in the more traditional vocabulary used by Maurice Beresford, were responsible for depopulating enclosure.[57] Contemporary commentators, most famously in the early sixteenth century but with antecedents going back to the 1450s, linked the greed of lords and their agents with the engrossing of holdings, the conversion of arable to pasture, the enclosure of common arable and pasture, the ruin of houses, the 'putting down of towns' ('town' meaning village at this time), and the expulsion of peasants from the land. These evils led to such social problems as vagabondage and unemployment. Private acquisitiveness was perceived not just as the enemy of the common people of the countryside. It threatened the whole commonwealth, by reducing the number of self-reliant and productive husbandmen and yeomen, who paid taxes, served as soldiers, relieved the poor, and generally provided the state and social order with its material and moral foundation.[58]

---

[57] R. Brenner, 'Agrarian Class Structure and Economic Development in Pre-industrial Europe', in T. H. Aston and C. H. E. Philpin (eds.), *The Brenner Debate: Agrarian Class Structure and Economic Development in Pre-Industrial Europe* (Cambridge, 1985), 10–63; M. W. Beresford, 'A Review of Historical Research (to 1968)', in M. W. Beresford and J. G. Hurst (eds.), *Deserted Medieval Villages: Studies* (London, 1971), 11–56.

[58] W. G. Hoskins, *The Age of Plunder: The England of Henry VIII, 1500–1547* (London, 1976), 66–72; A. McRae, *God Speed the Plough: The Representation of Agrarian England, 1500–1660* (Cambridge, 1996), 30–52; P. Slack, *From Reformation to Improvement: Public Welfare in Early Modern England* (Oxford, 1999), 5–28.

The complaints of the defenders of the commonwealth persuaded the government to set up a commission of inquiry, the so-called Domesday of Inclosures, which in 1517–18 investigated engrossment of holdings, enclosures, conversion of arable to pasture, and depopulation. The problems were felt most acutely in the champion counties, with the highest density of complaints from Berkshire, Buckinghamshire, Leicestershire, Northamptonshire, and Warwickshire.[59] The commissioners investigated many complaints, but they do not seem to have been on a sufficiently large scale to justify the outcry. In particular, in their investigation of the 'putting down of towns' they did not find many examples of deserted villages. In Buckinghamshire, for example, where the 1517–18 inquiry was conducted thoroughly, they found complaints of houses being ruined or abandoned, or people forced to leave, in seventy-nine places, but in most cases six houses or less were mentioned as being removed, and in only eight villages does the number of tenants expelled or the reference to the 'enclosure' or 'devastation' of the vill suggest that the commissions had uncovered a complete or near complete depopulation. As eighty-three deserted villages are recorded in the county, the full story of their abandonment cannot be told from this set of records.[60] The inquiry's terms of reference, which went back to 1488, allowed it to investigate a single short phase of a process which is apparent in the fourteenth century and continued until the age of parliamentary enclosure. In particular, the commissioners were able to report only the tail-end of an acute period of amalgamation of holdings, conversion of arable to pasture, and abandonment of houses in the fifteenth century.

The changes that were reported to the commission, and which are recorded in many other sources, are perhaps too well known to require detailed description here, but I will sketch a well-documented example to give a flavour of the events and the attitudes behind them. This dispute took place in the east Warwickshire villages of Upper and Lower Shuckburgh. Around 1400 the common grazing on the Inlondes, the lord's demesne, had

[59] I. S. Leadam (ed.), *The Domesday of Inclosures 1517–1518*, Royal Historical Society (1897).

[60] Leadam (ed.), *Domesday*, i. 158–214. The 8 places were Burston (7 houses decayed and 60 people evicted, so that the village is 'totally and wholly used for pasture'); Doddershall (24 messuages put down and 120 people withdrawn); Fleet Marston (1 messuage and 5 cottages for shepherds remain, 'and the rest is in decay'); Hogshaw and Fulbrook (11 messuages either put down or used to house shepherds, and 60 people left the village and hamlet); Lillingstone Dayrell (7 messuages and 4 cottages demolished and 40 people forced to leave; 'the whole vill was put down and remains totally devastated'); Littlecote ('whole hamlet . . . devastated'); Castle Thorpe (7 messuages devastated and 88 people withdrew). Beresford and Hurst (eds.), *Deserted Medieval Villages*, provide a list of 56 Buckinghamshire village sites. Subsequent research has raised the figure to 83: C. Lewis, P. Mitchell-Fox, and C. Dyer, *Village, Hamlet and Field: Changing Medieval Settlements in Central England*, 2nd edn. (Macclesfield, 2001), 125. The same source notes that 39 villages in the county are regarded as 'extensively shrunken' and 80 as 'shrunken'.

caused some dispute, and contention flared up again in 1490–1516.[61] The villagers claimed in the Court of Requests that they had been accustomed to graze land called Overchurchhull, Rugillhill, Nether Rugilhill, and the Playing Place. They had been excluded from access to these fields by the lord of the manor, Thomas Shuckburgh, who had 'dyked and enclosed' them. They claimed that if the parcels remained closed they would lose the means of feeding their cattle, and the enclosure had also deprived them of the use of a well. The complaint was investigated by three local gentry, Sir Edward Grevile, Sir Edward Ferrers, and John Spencer esquire. Grevile and Spencer were accepted by the parties to the dispute as arbitrators.

On 30 September 1516 the three heard the response of Thomas Shuckburgh. He stated that part of the land (which he insisted was called Combes, a field name denied by the villagers) was 'several pasture' of the demesne, which had been held by himself and his ancestors 'time out of mind'. The rest of the waste belonged to him as lord, which he 'improved himself' as he was legally entitled to do (by a thirteenth-century law, as we have seen) as long as he left the villagers with sufficient grazing. The lord was apparently claiming part of the demesne for his exclusive use, and extending his control over part of the common pasture. The same lord was reported to the enclosure commissions of 1517 to have allowed, in 1509, a holding consisting of a messuage and 14 acres of land in Lower Shuckburgh to fall into ruin, at which six people moved away. In the 1490s a similar decayed holding in Lower Shuckburgh was attributed to Thomas Catesby, and Wroxall Abbey was accused of enclosure at Upper Shuckburgh.[62]

The 1516 inquiry was biased in favour of Thomas Shuckburgh. It must have helped the lord that one of the commissioners was John Spencer. His family, once of Hodnell in Warwickshire and by 1516 of Althorp in Northamptonshire, had risen in wealth and status on the profits of grazing sheep and cattle on the former common fields of a dozen nearby villages, all of them decayed or totally deserted. Spencer kept his own copy of the 'certificate' recording the villagers' complaints and the lord's response, but he or his clerk mischievously changed the name of the leading complainant among the villagers, William Makernes, to William Makerude. Thomas Shuckburgh obviously shared this view of the villagers as troublemakers. He accused them of being vexatious, and mounted a separate suit against William Makernes, which was focused on Makernes's objection to paying a heriot (death duty) on his holding.

---

[61] C. Dyer, *Warwickshire Farming: Preparations for Agricultural Revolution*, Dugdale Society Occasional Papers, 27 (1981), 32; British Library, Add. MS. 75314 Althorp papers A14; TNA: PRO, REQ2 8/339.

[62] Leadam (ed.), *Domesday*, ii. 410–11.

The villagers' perspective can be glimpsed behind the conventional legal language. They complained in the usual fashion that Shuckburgh had 'threatened, troubled, and vexed' them, making them fearful of violence, and causing them expenses in defending themselves in lawsuits. In addition to these formal complaints, the communal culture of the village can be glimpsed. One notes from the details already given that the villagers used field names different from those favoured by the lord. We might speculate that the loss of the Playing Place, the football field, had special meaning for them. They told the king's court of a direct clash between the community and the lord. When they went on their annual rogation procession through the fields, the parishioners and inhabitants of Lower Shuckburgh would pause at a well called Ruggulhilwell, which 'servith all the said town of water for their cattle'. The procession kept alive memories of the parish boundaries, but also had the religious purpose of blessing the crops, and the custom of the parishioners was to 'say a gospel' at the well. However, after the ditches and banks of the enclosures had been 'digged', the way was blocked, and Shuckburgh himself with three armed servants prevented them from entering the field. The villagers were therefore able to represent themselves not just as cultivators deprived of customary grazing land and access to water, but as upholders of traditional values, the common good, and religion against the violence and selfishness of their lord.

The villagers' account of themselves was designed to attract sympathy, and it resonates with us, but we should not forget that there were limits to the communal values of Upper and Lower Shuckburgh. Soon after the inquiry, in 1524–5, when the new subsidy was levied, most of the twenty-seven taxpayers were assessed on goods worth between 20*s.* and 40*s.*, or on lands valued likewise at a pound or two. But William Makernes, who led the disputes, had goods valued at £12, and was by a long way the wealthiest man in the village.[63] When Thomas Shuckburgh and Makernes pursued a private lawsuit, hay was said to have been taken from Makernes's 'several ground' (an enclosed field), and he clearly had a considerable number of livestock, so he does not fall easily into the category of an indigent peasant ruined by his lord's oppressions, and only the conventions of legal language could include him among the 'poor subjects' who made the collective complaints.

Behind all of the arguments and different perspectives, on one point we can be certain. Not just by the allegations of the villagers, but also by his own admission, the lord had restricted the area available for common grazing, and there must be some substance to the complaints that he had thereby damaged

---

[63] TNA: PRO, E179/192/120, 122.

the peasant economy. Upper Shuckburgh eventually disappeared as a village, and Lower Shuckburgh still bears the scars of its shrinkage.

Many more anecdotes of such episodes can be told, and they represent a significant strand of rural conflict, but we have to be cautious about regarding them as the central tendency of the period. Removing peasants was not a straightforward task, as at least a few freeholders lived in many villages, and copyhold tenants could not always be dismissed without controversy.

The most effective strategy for a lord anxious to extend his pastures was not to evict tenants directly, but to overstock the common pasture, fence off the demesne to prevent common grazing, buy up the freeholders, and not to strive to attract tenants when a customary holding became vacant. If ambitious tenants who took over neighbours' land, or demesne farmers, were behaving badly towards the remaining villagers—for example, by ignoring the traditional husbandry routines which enabled the common fields to function properly—the lord might not discourage them.

These activities are not fully documented, but the various manoeuvres of the Verney family at Compton Murdak (later renamed Compton Verney) in Warwickshire suggest the strategy for taking over a village and its land, even if the precise tactics remain unclear.[64] Having purchased the main manor in 1435, the Verneys went on in 1437 to buy the second manor, which had belonged to the Durvassal family, and within a few years were leasing the land of the parish church, which was attached to the collegiate church of St Mary at Warwick. They were taking over every available acre in their territory, and removing any influential rival who could have challenged their actions. At this time the village was in serious decay, but it was being closed down in the 1450s and 1460s when Richard Verney was buying the few remaining freeholdings. The amount of land available for the villagers for common grazing was severely truncated when the Verneys converted most of the former arable fields into pasture closes, which gave much better returns in rent than the village had ever done.

When a lord embarked on this process he was usually removing the remnants of an already decayed village. The Compton Murdak peasants were living in a sickly community a generation before the Verneys moved into the manor. In around 1400 holdings were being amalgamated and buildings allowed to fall down. Absentee tenants from neighbouring villages were taking over holdings. Holdings, once in a regular structure of yardlands, were being dismembered and reassembled in new, unofficial combinations of

[64] C. Dyer, 'Compton Verney: Landscape and People in the Middle Ages', in R. Bearman (ed.), *Compton Verney: A History of the House and its Owners* (Stratford-upon-Avon, 2000), 49–94.

parcels. Field boundaries were not being maintained, groups of strips were held in groups, but not apparently enclosed, and animals from neighbouring villages were being driven to graze on the neglected and unguarded Compton fields. Rents were reduced to a low level, and the lord had difficulty in collecting them. This was not apparently to the advantage of tenants: the old families moved away, and newcomers took on land, stayed for a few years, and then left.

In other villages the painful decline cannot be examined in detail, but the village had evidently shrunk before the lord cleared away the remnants. At Burton Dassett, a few miles from Compton, in 1495 the villagers do not seem to have been so depleted or demoralized, and the lessee of the demesne, Roger Heritage, had run a mixed farm with moderate success in the previous twenty years. In 1497 Sir Edward Belknap, probably aided and abetted by John Heritage, Roger's son and successor as the farmer of the demesne, destroyed twelve houses and enclosed 360 acres. He was clearing away the rump of a community which before the Black Death had provided a living for more than eighty households and cultivated more than 2,000 acres.[65]

Outside the champion districts lords like Shuckburgh, Spencer, Verney, and Belknap had their counterparts, but they tended to enclose areas of common pasture in landscapes with a relative abundance of grazing. The gradual growth of enclosed pastures, alongside the conversion of arable to grass, can be traced through the descriptions of landholdings in conveyancing documents, the final concords, and in inquisitions post mortem. In Staffordshire, for example, the percentage of pasture recorded in the final concords between the mid-fourteenth century and the end of the fifteenth century rose from 3 per cent to 31 per cent, with an especially pronounced upward trend in the 1430s.[66] Alongside this slow accretion more dramatic appropriations of common grazing were being made, notably by the Wolseley family of Wolseley. Their manor lay on the northern edge of Cannock Chase, and they had common rights over pastures shared with many others in the bishop of Coventry and Lichfield's manor of Haywood. In 1465 Thomas Wolseley and his son Ralph were said to have enclosed a thousand acres of this land, causing a major dispute with the bishop and the people of the surrounding settlements. In the early 1480s Ralph Wolseley claimed exclusive rights in 200 acres in Wolseley itself, which brought him into conflict with those

[65] Leadam (ed.), *Domesday*, ii. 424–7; N. W. Alcock, 'Enclosure and Depopulation in Burton Dassett: A Sixteenth Century View', *Warwickshire History*, 3 (1977), 180–4; T. John (ed.), *The Warwickshire Hundred Rolls of 1279–80*, British Academy Records of Social and Economic History, NS, 19 (1992), 224–9.

[66] *AHEW* iii. 79.

claiming pasture rights, including other lords, John Aston esquire and the bishop.[67]

Extensive marshland grazing was also subject to the trend to privatization on Dengemarsh and Walland Marsh, parts of Romney Marsh in Kent. A grazier, Andrew Bate, in 1466 was keeping so many cattle that tenants were driven from one end of Dengemarsh. Landowners like the farmers Thomas Robyn and Thomas Holderness were systematically buying up smallholdings between 1480 and 1520, and the resident population was falling as the land came into the hands of gentry from the Kentish weald to the north, and by townspeople at Lydd, who kept mainly sheep. By 1525 it could be said, in an area formerly containing many smallholdings and which was once famous for its corn and cattle, that 'Many great farms and holdings are held by persons who neither reside on them, nor till or breed cattle, but use them for grazing'.[68]

Against these high-profile activities of the elite we need to place the significant and cumulatively larger-scale engrossing, enclosure, and conversion to pasture by the peasants themselves. Just as they were responsible for much of the enclosure before 1350, so they continued with these activities in subsequent centuries. The movement from arable to pasture could be accommodated in a number of ways within the traditional common fields. The land might be cropped less frequently, allowing more opportunities for fallow pasture, or part of the field could be grassed over as leys. Sometimes, in an apparent paradox, we find that land was being cultivated more intensively. In south Worcestershire and adjacent parts of Warwickshire and Gloucestershire, for example, villages which had been recorded with two-field systems in the thirteenth and fourteenth centuries had converted to three- and four-field arrangements by the fifteenth and sixteenth centuries.[69] But these changes related to the core of the fields which still survived in use as arable, while some of the outer furlongs were being used for grazing. The intensively cultivated arable may also have contributed to the feeding of livestock, as the acreage under fodder crops such as peas and vetch was probably also increasing. These developments should ideally have been carefully negotiated, as they

---

[67] G. Wrottesley (ed.), *Extracts from the Plea Rolls, temp. Edward IV, Edward V and Richard III*, Collections for a History of Staffordshire, NS, 6, part 1 (1903), 138–9, 150–2; G. P. Mander (ed.), *History of the Wolseley Charters*, Collections for a History of Staffordshire, 3rd ser. (1934), 53–94; C. Welch, 'Ralph Wolseley, a Fifteenth-Century Capitalist', *Staffordshire Archaeological and Historical Society Transactions*, 39 (2001), 22–7.

[68] M. Gardiner, 'Settlement Change on Denge and Walland Marshes, 1400–1550', in J. Eddison, M. Gardiner, and A. Long (eds.), *Romney Marsh: Environmental Change and Human Occupation in a Coastal Lowland*, Oxford University Committee for Archaeology Monographs, 46 (1998), 137–41; S. Dimmock, 'English Small Towns and the Emergence of Capitalist Relations, c.1450–1550', *Urban History*, 28 (2001), 5–24.

[69] *AHEW* iii. 224.

involved new rotations, new choices in the crops to be sown, and arrangements for physical access to land. The stream of offences reported in the manorial courts show that these adjustments could not always be made smoothly.

In woodland landscapes contention surrounded common rights in crofts and closes, when the tenant would allow the land to revert from arable to grass and then prevent neighbours having access in the 'open time', such as the period after the harvest when traditionally the stubbles were generally accessible. A typical case concerned Thomas Daukes and William Skinte of Brockencote in Chaddesley Corbett, Worcestershire, in 1442. They were amerced in their lord's court for unjust enclosure of a croft in the Middle Field, and making it several when it should have been common and 'open to the lord's tenants after the corn had been carried'.[70] Such conflicts sometimes reveal changes in rotations, because the offending tenant of the enclosed land was following some routine different from his neighbours. When they were planting crops for two years out of three, he kept his gates shut in the third year and cultivated land which should have been lying fallow.

Wherever there was common grazing, in districts of open field or of 'old enclosure' individuals caused offence by keeping more animals than were allowed by the customary stints, which damaged the pastures for their neighbours. A tenant with enough arable to justify keeping sixty sheep on the common would be reported to be grazing a flock of 300. Others with common rights would be restricting their neighbours' access to grazing by renting their share to outsiders, such as butchers and drovers.[71] Some villagers failed to contribute their customary share to the pay of the common herdsman. A dispute in 1453 at Willenhall near Coventry reveals the details of this potentially complicated procedure. Every tenant was to find food and drink for the 'servant called Hurdeman' (probably in rotation), and citizens of Coventry who held land in the village and were not on hand to provide the food should pay $1\frac{1}{2}d.$ for each animal for each quarter of a year (three months).[72] Villagers in many communities also failed to observe the disciplines designed to protect the crops during the harvest, by putting animals to graze the stubble too early or failing to tether horses properly. Not everyone repaired fences to protect the growing corn or the meadow from straying animals, and pigs were not kept ringed or yoked to prevent them rooting, which could leave a stretch of greensward looking like a badly ploughed field.[73]

---

[70] Shakespeare Birthplace Trust Records Office, DR5/2797; *AHEW* iii. 224–6.
[71] Dyer, *Warwickshire Farming*, 30–2.
[72] Northamptonshire Record Office, Spencer roll, 214.
[73] Ault, *Open-Field Farming*, 40–52.

The constant repetition of by-laws in the fifteenth century suggests that the system was being tested by changes in farming practice. The ever-present tension between the selfish behaviour of individuals and the defence of the common good was reaching a new fraught level. When offenders were identified and presented to the courts, they were often revealed as belonging to the upper ranks of village society. They were the people who had taken advantage of the cheapness of land to build up accumulations of two or three formerly separate holdings, and who were most anxious to increase their profitability by expanding their flocks and herds, which gave them the best prices at market and cost less in labour than cultivating grain.

These leading villagers could be accused of inconsistency, because they were the same people who, as jurors, helped to frame the by-laws. They should be seen as people who believed themselves to be representing the best interests of the community, who attempted to control and prevent destructive abuse of the common fields while allowing individuals, including themselves, to adjust to new economic circumstances. They could change their villages in radical ways, which resolved some of the conflicts but left no trace in the records. Sambourn, on the edge of the Warwickshire Arden, was a typical woodland community in which peasants lived in strung-out hamlets, and worked an open-field core surrounded by fields enclosed from the heaths and woods since they had been assarted in the twelfth and thirteenth centuries. After 1445 and before 1472 an agreement among sixteen tenants, each of whom held a half-yardland, led to the enclosure of about 240 acres of the arable, which must account for a high proportion of the common fields.[74] This bold move did not proceed entirely smoothly, as not all of the necessary exchanges were completed, and villagers who were not among the sixteen could claim common grazing rights within the new enclosures.

Similar changes in other villages would not be mentioned in documents, and so would not be observed by historians, if they had avoided these causes for dispute. At Stoke Fleming in south Devon for example, occasional references in the court records show that some consolidation and planting of hedges was in progress, and by 1500 virtually the whole open-field system had been converted into closes, which were used for growing corn. The same gradual enclosure movement, combined with the advance of pastoral farming, made north and east Devon into a mainly enclosed landscape by the sixteenth century, although there were many patches of open subdivided field two centuries earlier.[75] This hidden process in many regions must explain at

---

[74] Dyer, *Warwickshire Farming*, 26.
[75] H.S.A. Fox, 'The Chronology of Enclosure and Economic Development in Medieval Devon', *Ec.HR*, 2nd ser., 28 (1975), 181–202.

least part of the areas of 'old enclosure' which appear on maps and in surveys of the sixteenth and seventeenth centuries. In many cases the moves towards enclosure by agreement began with small closes formed out of the edge of the open fields adjacent to the tofts of the peasant houses, like the plots which tenants were allowed to enclose with hedges at Woodeaton in Oxfordshire in 1448, provided that fees were paid to the parish church and the lord.[76]

In most late medieval villages all of these development were being made among the peasants themselves. Individual peasants attempted to change their farming methods under economic pressure, and their neighbours, either individually or in some more concerted way, brought their objections to the notice of the manor court. The juries helped to make judgements about the complaints, and as the spokesmen for the 'homage', played an important part in making new by-laws or reiterating old ones. The lords' role was to make the courts available to settle quarrels, issue by-laws, and hear presentments. The lords had a general concern to maintain good order and protect their rent income, rather than to promote or prevent change.

The Village Community

The shift in the boundaries between private and public in the management of fields must be seen in the light of the land market and the developments in the character of the village community. A high rate of migration meant that few families remained in the same village for more than three generations. From the early fifteenth century in the midlands a higher proportion of land transfers took place between unrelated tenants, and inheritance declined. Tenants could acquire holdings from predecessors who were retiring, or departing, or simply wished to reduce the size of their holding, and from the land lying 'in the lord's hands'. A tenant who acquired two holdings needed only a single house, barn, carthouse, bakehouse, and accommodation for animals, so some buildings became redundant and were allowed to fall into decay. These tendencies undermined the former tenurial structure of the village.[77]

The village's communal discipline and agrarian economy was under threat. Occasional individuals appear in the courts as enemies of the rules which kept

---

[76] H. E. Salter (ed.), *Eynsham Cartulary*, Oxford Historical Society, 49, 51 (1907–8), vol. ii, p. lxxiii; *VCH Oxfordshire*, v. 314.

[77] On these tendencies in rural society, see such works as R. H. Hilton, *The English Peasantry in the Later Middle Ages* (Oxford, 1975); P. D. A. Harvey (ed.), *The Peasant Land Market in Medieval England* (Oxford, 1984); J. Hatcher, *Rural Economy and Society in the Duchy of Cornwall 1300–1500* (Cambridge, 1970); B. Harvey, *Westminster Abbey and Its Estates in the Middle Ages* (Oxford, 1977); J. A. Raftis, *The Estates of Ramsey Abbey* (Toronto, 1957); id., *Tenure and Mobility* (Toronto, 1964); Dyer, *Lords and Peasants*; Whittle, *Agrarian Capitalism*.

the community together, such as Henry Channdeler of Roel in Gloucestershire, who had engrossed five holdings in the village by 1400. He allowed
their buildings to decay, amalgamated a number of tofts, and built himself a
large house on the site. He was accused of overburdening the common
pasture with sheep, and must be seen as contributing to the eventual collapse
of his village (Fig. 2.4).[78] Even when those who engrossed holdings lived in
relatively healthy communities, they helped in the long term to change the
social character of the settlement. They acquired land when it was cheap, but
their successors in the late fifteenth or early sixteenth centuries, when demand
was reviving, would keep their accumulations of holdings intact. Whereas
during the population growth of the thirteenth century smallholdings pro-
liferated, in the similar circumstances in the sixteenth century the mean size
of holdings in many villages stayed the same or even increased. In Norfolk, a
county of smallholdings, the mean acreage of holdings on the manor of
Hevingham Bishops rose from 12 acres in 1509 to 15 acres in 1573, and
there were three tenants with 50 acres or more in 1573, compared with none
at the beginning of the century. In a period when numbers of would-be
tenants were increasing, this in effect deprived succeeding generations of the
opportunity to acquire land, and forced those without an inheritance to work
for wages or to leave their village. This is one dimension of the 'expropriation
of the peasantry', except that peasants did not need to wait for a lord to
undermine their tenancy: to quote Whittle, they expropriated one another.[79]

    The expected outcome of these changes would be the 'decline of the village
community', one of those historical processes claimed for every century from
the fourteenth to the twentieth. In particular after the Black Death, the
turnover of population, rise of engrossing yeomen, threats to the common
fields, and rampant individualism were all seen as destroying the cohesion of
the village. Yet religious and cultural historians have constructed an opposite
picture. They study the parish, which often coincided with the village, and
regard it not as merely surviving, but as entering into a flourishing golden age.
The churchwardens, whose origins go back to the thirteenth century, took on
ever-expanding roles in providing for the church fabric, furnishings, and
decoration. They became more adept during the fifteenth century at raising
 funds, and increased their income and expenditure. The surviving church
buildings bear testimony to these efforts. They were in many cases rebuilt
entirely at some time between 1380 and 1520, or at least received some major
alterations or additions. The wardens' accounts record how much they

    [78] C. Dyer, 'Peasants and Farmers: Rural Settlements in an Age of Transition', in D. Gaimster
and P. Stamper (eds.), *The Age of Transition: The Archaeology of English Culture, 1400–1600*
(Oxford, 1997).
    [79] Whittle, *Agrarian Capitalism*, 182–224, 307–9.

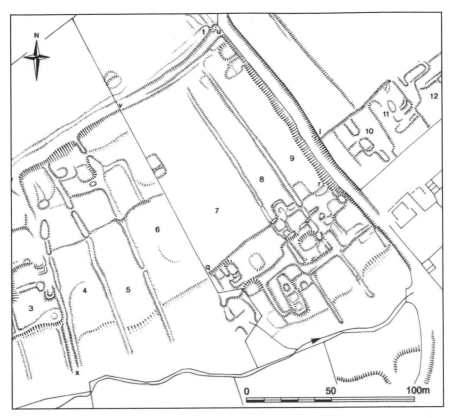

Fig. 2.4. Roel (Glos.), showing the house of Henry Channdeler, *c.*1400. The plan of the earthworks at the centre of the village of Roel (adjacent to Hawling) reveals the foundations of a large building *c.*25m long, which contrasts with the normal peasant houses, such as that in plot 12, *c.*15m long. The large house stands in plot 7, the large size of which is the result of the amalgamation of older, narrow plots of the type still visible in plots 4, 5, 6, 8, and 9.

Source: J. Bond and C. Lewis, 'The Earthworks of Hawling', *Transactions of the Bristol and Gloucestershire Archaeological Society.* 109 (1991), 150–1, 165–70.

provided in embellishments and artefacts which have subsequently been lost: images, screens, wall paintings, books, and vestments. While the churchwardens received some valuable donations and bequests, most of their money came from collective fund-raising, from the profits of church ales, plays, or entertainments organized by fraternities. As further physical proof of the growth of parish funds at this time, many parishes built a church house, where ales and other public events could be held. In parallel with the energy of the parish, and not in any rivalry with it, fraternities were being formed, especially in eastern England, where a single parish might have four or more. Again, these religious and social organizations required money and time from their members. They held feasts and processions, and attended the funerals of brothers and sisters. Their funds could provide the members with masses for their souls, which they could not have afforded as individuals. The fraternities and the churchwardens had charitable aims, and we hear of 'boxes' for alms, and poorhouses.[80]

The diverging accounts of the village community can be reconciled. Rural society before the Black Death cannot be described as egalitarian, as is all too apparent when the wealthy bought land from their poorer neighbours in hard times. In the thirteenth century most midland villages contained a good number of tenants with 15–30 acres, and a substantial minority with 5 acres or less. In East Anglia 80 per cent of the tenants often had less than 5 acres, and a prosperous minority cultivated 10–25 acres. The inhabitants of such places were bound together to some extent by a defensive mentality, and organized themselves to make the field systems work as efficiently as possible, and to protect themselves in their relations with the lord and the state.

Many villages by 1500 contained often a half-dozen substantial tenants holding at least 40 or 50 acres, who naturally had a strong voice in the decisions of the manor court and the parish. Smallholdings persisted, but in smaller numbers than before 1348–9. The villagers were more self-confident in running their own affairs, as the lord had retreated into the background. Surplus wealth could be used for the benefit of the whole community in church building and in relief of poverty. The state made demands and gave the leading villagers more responsibilities, and we can detect their civic sense as they passed numerous by-laws against idleness, gambling, gossiping, and theft of firewood from neighbours' hedges and fences.[81] They were the pillars of their manor courts, parishes, and fraternities, who imposed good order that reflected their interests as employers and property-holders.

Community, Privacy, and Oligarchy at Quinton in Warwickshire

These general tendencies can be seen at work in a single, exceptionally well documented example, that of the large manor of Quinton, now in Warwickshire, containing the villages of Lower and Upper Quinton. The lords were laymen until it was acquired in the late fifteenth century by Magdalen College in Oxford. The advantage of selecting this place for close investiga-

---

[80] See the works cited in n. 38.

[81] C. Dyer, 'The Political Life of the Fifteenth-Century English Village', *The Fifteenth Century*, 9 (2004), 135–57; M. K. McIntosh, *Controlling Misbehavior in England, 1370–1600* (Cambridge, 1998).

tion is that, as well as many manorial documents, the college archives also contain some petitions and letters in which motives and attitudes, as well as actions, are recorded.

Before the Black Death there were between forty and fifty households in the manor, divided between the two villages. Three-quarters of the tenants held their land by customary tenure, of whom about fifteen had standard units of yardlands, half-yardlands, and quarter-yardlands, a yardland amounting to about 40 acres of arable. Almost a half of the tenants (twenty-one) held cottages or a few acres.[82] As was normal in this champion landscape, most of the land was cultivated in common fields, two per village, but an unusually large area of meadow lay to the north, and the lord and the villagers had access to some hill pasture on Meon Hill, a promontory jutting out from the Cotswolds, to the south (Fig. 2.5).

By 1430 the place had gone through some familiar changes: population had dropped, some arable had been converted to pasture, and relations between lord and peasants had moved in favour of the tenants. At least ten dwellings had fallen into ruin, the number of tenants had almost halved, to twenty-four, and some had accumulated in excess of 60 acres. Part of the arable lay frisc, that is, was uncultivated. Most tenants held 'at will' for cash rents, and only one family was still identified as servile. The decline in prices of grain had not robbed arable cultivation of all of its profits. The tenants were paying rent of about 20s. per annum for a yardland, that is, 6d. per acre, and parcels of demesne were being rented at about 8d. per acre. The lord saw a future in intensive grazing, and in 1430–1 invested £9 in enclosing the Eastmeadow, with a hedge and ditch over a perimeter of 2,000 yards.[83] He was presumably expecting to use the hay crop to feed large numbers of livestock in the winter, and to pasture them on the meadow after the hay harvest.

Fifty years later the village almost collapsed, and its crisis, followed by recovery from the brink of disaster, tells us much about the English country-side around 1500. It would be easy to use the Quinton documents to construct a straightforward story of poor peasants victimized by ruthless gentry entrepreneurs, and saved by the intervention of kindly clergymen.[84] If we explore the internal history of Quinton, though, we find a more

---

[82] This is based on clues contained in fifteenth-century documents, and especially the manorial account of 1430–1 and a rental of 1472 (Magdalen College 35/9, 35/5). See also P. Franklin (ed.), *The Tax Payers of Medieval Gloucestershire* (Stroud, 1993), 64.

[83] Magdalen College, 35/9 (account of 1430–1).

[84] C. Richmond, 'The Transition from Feudalism to Capitalism in the Archives of Magdalen College', *History Workshop Journal*, 37 (1994), 165–9.

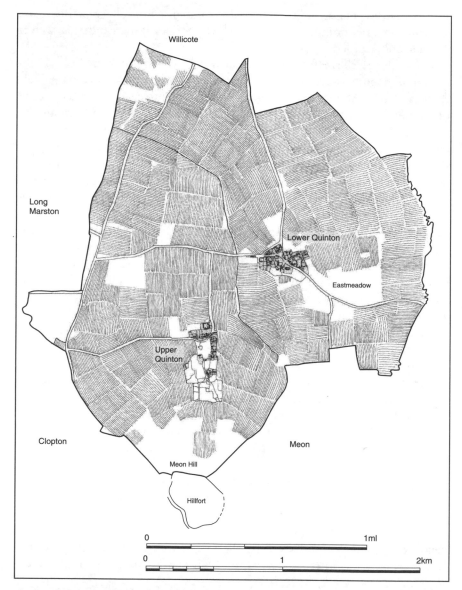

Fig. 2.5. Quinton (War., formerly Glos.) in the fifteenth century. The map shows ridge and furrow from the former arable fields, and the settlements, visible on aerial photographs of the 1940s.

Source: Warwickshire County Museum.

complex picture of wealthy yeomen manipulating change in their own favour.

The manor court at Quinton, acting in the lord's interest but also under strong influence from the leading villagers, made efforts to deal with difficulties in managing the fields and pastures. As tenant sheep-flocks increased, access to pasture had to be restricted. There were strains and conflicts arising from the use of two types of pasture, the permanent grazing on the common on Meon Hill and the separate enclosures, the leys, which had been taken out of the common arable by individual tenants. They could keep flocks on the slopes of the hill only from 24 June until 2 February according to a by-law of 1483. In 1477 grazing on the hill was explicitly forbidden from 2 February until Whitsun, in order to give the grass a chance to grow. Tenants were prohibited in 1483 from allowing their sheep on the hill to descend into the 'several lands of the tenants called the leys'. The leys were to be enclosed by their tenants according to a law of 1517. Animals could also be grazed on the stubbles and fallows of the open fields. The acreage of fallow pasture available had been reduced at some time before 1495, by which date the village had adopted a four-course rotation, so only a quarter of the land lay fallow rather than a half under the old two-field system. This tempted tenants to put sheep into the harvest field at the earliest possible time, leading to a rule in 1477 that sheep could not be grazed on the stubble until fifteen days after the peas had been carried. This time allowed the pods left behind to be gathered. Another problem was caused by driving sheep over the fields of Lower Quinton, perhaps after crops had been planted. Common rights were disputed, and cottagers had to be reminded that they had no right to common pasture at all.[85]

These conflicts between private profit and the common good were found in many villages. Quinton had in addition especially acute difficulties created by a succession of demesne farmers, who held on lease the 600 acres of arable, together with the meadow and pasture. The very large size of the demesne, and in particular the extensive enclosed meadow, must have attracted lessees with a special interest in grazing, and these were famous men in the 1470s and 1480s—the land was managed in turn by William Catesby, soon to be one of Richard III's advisers, William Spencer, a relative of John Spencer, the grazier, Thomas Rous, lord of the manor of Ragley, and Roger Heritage, farmer of Burton Dassett. Edward Empson bears a familiar surname, but nothing else is known about him.[86] It is hard to imagine a series of characters

[85] Magdalen College, 35/1 (court roll of Apr. 1477); 35/2 (court roll of Oct. 1477); 35/10 (court roll of Oct. 1483); 75/14 (court roll of 1495).

[86] The names are recorded in the petitions, Quinton 56 and 60, and in the accounts 35/13, 35/3, 35/12, 35/8, 35/25, 35/43, 35/26 (these are cited here in chronological order). For the farmers see

more unsympathetic to the welfare of the peasantry and the preservation of traditional husbandry than these, most of them having profited, or being about to profit, from the decay of villages and encroachment on common fields and common pastures. Most of the members of this rogues' gallery were too busy elsewhere to devote much of their own time and attention to Quinton, which figured as a small part of their portfolio of assets. For a time a local man, John Salbrygge, a husbandman of Willicote, acted as under-farmer. Willicote had by that time ceased to exist as a village, and its farmer from 1469 was William Catesby, so Salbrygge may have been an all-too-appropriate ally.

As under-farmer, no doubt encouraged by his superiors, Salbrygge discontinued the custom by which cottagers were allowed to grow crops on parcels of the demesne. He decided to deny them the use of these few acres after they had ploughed them in preparation for sowing, so they lost their labour as well as the land. He ploughed up some leys, whereby the villagers were deprived of some common pasture. These acts were the subject of a petition from the tenants in about 1480, which was probably written by the vicar, Humphrey Chapman, who in addition to the income from his benefice held a good deal of land from the manor.[87] The petitioners made the telling point that the old bond which once linked the demesne to the tenants had been broken: 'these men have occupied it as [if] the farm was of one lordship and the town of another.' The demesne was being run as a private enterprise, ignoring the impact on the community. They recommended that the next farmer should be a villager, Richard Davyes. He was a successful tenant who had acquired two yardlands (80 acres) and served as an official of the manor court as

---

J. S. Roskell, 'William Catesby, Counsellor to Richard III', *Bulletin of the John Rylands Library*, 42 (1959), 145–74; Dyer, *Warwickshire Farming*, 17, 19–21 (Catesby); William's father had connections with Magdalen College, conveying land to the college under the will of Alice Deincourt: History of Parliament Trust, London, unpublished article on William Catesby for the volume on 1422–61. (I am grateful to the History of Parliament Trust for allowing me to see this article in draft.) William Catesby's lease of Willicote is in Warwickshire County Record Office, CR 1911/16; H. Thorpe, 'The Lord and the Landscape, Illustrated Through the Changing Fortunes of a Warwickshire Parish, Wormleighton', *Transactions of the Birmingham Archaeological Society*, 80 (1962), 38–77 (Spencer); *VCH Warwickshire*, iii. 29; 5, 191 (Rous); C. Dyer, 'Were There Any Capitalists in Fifteenth-Century England?', in id., *Everyday Life in Medieval England* (London, 1994), 315–21 (Heritage); C. Carpenter, *Locality and Polity: A Study of Warwickshire Landed Society, 1401–1499* (Cambridge, 1992), 158–60, 163–4, 191–2 (Catesby); 186 (Spencer); 112, 202 (Rous); Empson is a mysterious figure, and there is no evidence that he was related to Richard Empson.

[87] Magdalen College, Quinton 56. There is information about Salbrygge, Chapman, and Davyes in Magdalen College, 35/5 (court roll of 1472) and 75/13 (court roll of a little earlier). In *c*.1477 Chapman owed rents of 45*s*. 4*d*. and Davyes 33*s*. (Magdalen College, 35/4), so they both held a good deal of land. In 1480 Chapman held more than a yardland; Davyes gave up a half-yardland, and Salbrygge and William Spencer jointly held 1½ yardlands and a cottage (35/13).

affeerer, who helped to fix penalties. He was not chosen to be farmer, and left his holding in 1480, we might suppose in disgust.

In the next ten years more houses were falling down—seven ruinous buildings were reported to a court in 1485, and five holdings lay vacant in 1486.[88] The next vicar, who succeeded in 1486, Thomas Elys, in a candid letter to the president of Magdalen College in 1490, painted a bleak picture of the village's prospects, as buildings worth 20 marks (£13. 6s. 8d.) had fallen down in the previous four years.[89] The village was 'near to the point of destruction'. He warned the college that if a single farmer was granted the lease of the demesne again, particularly if the farmer was a 'gentleman' or a 'gentleman's man', no more tenants would take up a holding in the village. This is supported by the turnover of people, which meant that of twenty-three tenant surnames in 1480, only three can still be found in the rental of 1517–18.[90] Holdings were being rented from year to year, presumably because tenants were reluctant to commit themselves to a manor with an uncertain future. Elys in his letter used the persuasive argument that there was a danger that the college might be seen as a greedy ('covetous') lord. For the sake of a high rent it ought not to set a bad example to laymen who 'cast down towns'.

Elys's letter of 1490 was written at a delicate stage of the negotiation with the farmer, Thomas Rous, who plotted over the future of the lease, offering to arrange for four tenants to take over from him. Elys advised the president of Magdalen that the lease should go to a larger group of local people: it was meritorious 'to support and succour a community', or as he interpreted that phrase, the college should lease the demesne to a consortium of farmers from the village.

Elys's advice was followed. Thomas Rous, the last of the gentleman farmers, left in a huff, still owing part of his rent, which was never paid.[91] When the college agreed 'to support...a community' it was apparently responding to the vicar's appeal to take the virtuous path which would help the parish church and the poor. It was, however, also accepting an attractive and profitable offer from Elys and five other substantial tenants. Elys helped the president to make the morally correct decision by offering the gift of a riding-horse. He promised that the farm of £30 per annum would be paid, and that the college would gain extra money from court profits if the peasantry survived.

---

[88] Magdalen College, Court Book no. 1.
[89] Magdalen College, Quinton 60. On Elys, Worcestershire Record Office, ref. b 716.093, BA 2648/7(i), p. 227.
[90] Magdalen College, 35/13, 35/7 (rentals).
[91] Magdalen College, 35/43, 35/28, 35/27, 35/41, 35/30 (manorial accounts showing Rous's unpaid debts).

Most of the new farmers had previously acquired two or three holdings, which gave each of them already between 45 and 66 acres. With their share of the demesne the farmers were tenanting well over 100 acres each. Elys, whose vicarage was already worth £18. 13*s*. 4*d*. per annum, was adding enough land to increase his income to £25 or more.[92] This apparently idealistic cleric resembles a shrewd businessman looking after his material interests and forming an alliance with his wealthiest parishioners. They certainly benefited from the leases as, when Quinton's contribution to the subsidy was assessed in 1524, the farmers were assessed at between £4 and £8, compared with £2 for those still holding the standard yardland and half-yardland holdings.[93] The lease had reinforced and promoted an elite. They could, like Catesby, Spencer, and Rous before them, have sublet all or part of their share of the demesne; if so, they still enjoyed the profit of the land, judging from their tax assessments. We do not know the details of their agricultural management of their new acquisitions, but when we have terriers of their holdings in the early seventeenth century they included both strips in the open fields, and areas of enclosed land both near to the village and on the hillside where former arable had been converted to pasture, so at some point there had been partial piecemeal enclosure.[94]

It may well be true that Elys saved the village, but it does not appear to have become a healthy and thriving community after the peasant farmers took over. Buildings continued to decay (ten messuages were reported as ruinous in 1495), and there was a constant turnover in tenants. The number of tenants (there had been twenty-four in 1430) fell to nineteen in 1517–18.[95] At least Quinton did not share the fate of neighbouring Meon, where the enclosure commissions found that five people, four of them with 30–40 acres each, had enclosed land in 1513, and the settlement was eventually abandoned. Again we can note the initiatives being taken by tenants.[96]

The general lessons that we learn from the example of Quinton, are that, first, acquisitive gentry could be a threat to villages, not just when they were lords of the manor, but also when they acted as farmers. Secondly, villages were especially vulnerable when they had decayed internally. Thirdly, predatory gentry did not always have their own way, and it appears that the villagers, helped and rallied by their vicar, offered an effective resistance which rid them, with the co-operation of the lord, of these dangerous

[92] *Valor Ecclesiasticus*, 6 vols., Record Commission (1810–34), ii. 502.

[93] TNA: PRO, E 179/113/20.

[94] Magdalen College, Adds. 75, 78. A by-law of 1517 refers to leys on Quinton Hill (Meon Hill) which were to be enclosed by Ascension Day (Magdalen College, ECB4).

[95] Magdalen College, 75/14, 68/6, 35/7.

[96] I. Gray, 'A Gloucestershire Postscript to the "Domesday of Inclosures" ', *Transactions of the Bristol and Gloucestershire Archaeological Society*, 94 (1976), 79–80.

outsiders. Fourthly, the initiative for developing a new type of farming, in larger units and with some enclosure of land, came from peasant cultivators. They may have been represented by Elys in their negotiations with the college, but they had clearly wanted to take over the demesne, and persisted in their arrangements for long after Elys's death. Fifthly, the word 'community' was not being used as an inclusive term by Elys, and it did not mean the whole body of villagers, but a minority of wealthy tenants. Sixthly, the village survived as the result of a working compromise between the common fields and private enclosures.

Quinton was a special case in its farming arrangements and in the documents that inform us about them, but in many ways it is characteristic of a section of rural England around 1500, where we find enterprising and acquisitive peasants as well as avaricious gentry. There were thousands of substantial tenants like the six farmers who took on their share of the Quinton demesne. They worked their many acres, often with new methods. Their type had scarcely existed before 1400, and their emergence is one of the most significant innovations of the period.

3

Authority and Freedom

The first part of this chapter is about those who exercised the strongest authority in medieval society, especially the landed aristocracy, both laymen and clergy. It attempts to make some assessment of their influence as producers in their own right, and their impact on the production of others. It makes a brief consideration also of the economic role of the state. The final section considers those below the ranks of the gentry.

The Role of Lords, 1200–1350

It is easy to gain the impression that the lords controlled the heights of the economy in the thirteenth century. We are told directly of their ability to command others, notably in the various treatises on estate management. In *c.*1240 the countess of Lincoln was advised: 'Tell high and low, and this do often, that they ought to execute all of your orders that are not against God, fully, quickly, and willingly.'[1] Another wise counsellor in the 1270s claimed: 'If he will keep the aforesaid rules, any lord will live...honourably of his own, and be wealthy and powerful as he may wish, without committing trespass or wrong against anyone.'[2]

The more mundane and factual surveys of lords' assets, and the financial accounts produced by bailiffs and reeves, show well-organized manors grouped in coherent estates, which at this time were active in agriculture, with cultivated demesnes, pastures for flocks and herds, sometimes on a very large scale, and managed woodlands producing fuel and timber. Lords brought land into productive use in their demesnes, but also, for motives

---

[1] D. Oschinsky (ed.), *Walter of Henley and Other Treatises on Estate Management and Accounting* (Oxford, 1971), 399.
[2] Ibid. 293.

partly economic and partly for display, altered the landscape to create parks, chases, ponds, and warrens.

The methods of administration on lords' estates tended to come from the same textbooks and training schools, leading to a standardization in documentation, whereby an estate survey or a manorial account looks much the same from one end of the country to another. But they employed a variety of agricultural techniques, so that when it came to choosing the crops to be sown or the animals to be kept, lords respected the judgement of local managers, realizing that production would be most successful if it followed the tried and tested methods of the locality. [3] Many estates were committed to programmes of improvement, to clear new land, to increase the fertility of the soil by marling and planting legumes, to adopt new rotations, combinations of crops, and fallowing regimes, and to build new barns and mills. On monastic estates monk wardens made decisions about farming matters, and such important officials as the cellarers would visit manors, while fellows of Oxford colleges were sufficiently engaged in agriculture to attend the harvest. Lords maintained a central control by calculating profits and making judgements about the effectiveness of their local officials and the different branches of production. Under the influence of the market, they specialized in the most profitable crops, and increased the intensity of production.[4]

Lords managed their demesnes in order to gain only part of their income; on most estates the tenants brought in more money. The bishop of Ely, for example, in 1298–9 obtained £2,100 from his tenants in rents and court profits, compared with £1,400 from the profits of agriculture.[5] The lords' influence on the peasants extended far beyond the collection of rents and dues in money and goods, and the levying of labour services.[6] They claimed to control the marriages and migration of their servile tenants, who were not allowed to make wills or sublet their land like their free neighbours. They manipulated the market. The sale of land held by customary tenure was conducted in the lords' courts, and was subject to charges levied by the court. They had a strong influence on the labour market by their position as the largest employers in many villages. Their preference for cash rents as distinct

---

[3] B. M. S. Campbell, *English Seigniorial Agriculture, 1250–1450* (Cambridge, 2000), 60–2.

[4] e.g. R. A. L. Smith, *Canterbury Cathedral Priory: A Study in Monastic Administration* (Cambridge, 1943), 100–12, 128–45; E. King, *Peterborough Abbey, 1086–1310: A Study in the Land Market* (Cambridge, 1973), 127–8; P. D. A. Harvey, *A Medieval Oxfordshire Village: Cuxham, 1240–1400* (Oxford, 1965), 87–90; E. L. G. Stone, 'Profit and Loss Accountancy at Norwich Cathedral Priory', *Transactions of the Royal Historical Society*, 5th ser., 12 (1962), 25–48; Campbell, *Seigniorial Agriculture*, 424–30.

[5] E. Miller, *The Abbey and Bishopric of Ely* (Cambridge, 1951), 94.

[6] R. H. Hilton, *A Medieval Society: The West Midlands at the End of the Thirteenth Century*, 2nd edn. (Cambridge, 1983), 127–48.

from labour services helped to push the peasants into selling a higher proportion of their produce, and adapting production to fit market conditions. By demanding that peasants pay a high proportion of their cash rents between September and December they distorted the grain market, by forcing the peasants to sell when supplies were abundant and prices were low, allowing the demesne grain to be sold later in the year when prices were rising. Some lords acted as middlemen in the wool trade, not just the large monasteries but also members of the gentry, collecting the fleeces of the local peasantry in order to make a bulk sale to a merchant.[7] They helped to determine when and where markets would be held by seeking market charters from the crown, and founding boroughs on their estates. The tolls from the transactions went to the lords, to add to the dues that they exacted on the sale of servile tenants' draught animals, and on the sale of ale on their manors.

Peasants' management of their holdings was subject to various controls, so they could not fell their trees without permission, and they could be ordered to keep buildings in good repair. They could be deprived of the manure of their animals, which were folded on the lord's demesne. Their access to grazing land and woods was controlled by lords, who might demand extra rents for pasturing animals and gathering wood. Peasants were forbidden to hunt even small animals and birds if their lord enjoyed the privilege of 'free warren'. Lords could exercise some choice over the transfer of holdings, forcing a widow who had succeeded to her husband's former holding to remarry. Tolls were levied for the use of the lord's mill, and the oven might also be a seigneurial monopoly. Through their powers of jurisdiction lords oversaw law and order; they could fine serfs for acts of immorality; as patrons of the local church they appointed the local clergyman. Of greatest economic importance, as landlords they could levy substantial rents, often in excess of 8*d.* per acre, and demand large extra payments in entry fines when a new tenant succeeded, sometimes at a rate of 24*d.* per acre. They could levy sums at other unpredictable times, notably as a recognition when a new lord or lady came into the estate. These extra dues, especially the entry fines, reflected more closely than any other rents the growing demand for land in the thirteenth century. They took away a sizable proportion of the peasants' surplus, and the larger sums would have forced the tenant into debt.[8]

The best indication of the success of lords in winning profits from demesnes and tenants comes from their increased incomes, which usually

[7] T. H. Lloyd, *The English Wool Trade in the Middle Ages* (Cambridge, 1977), 295–300; P. Nightingale, 'Knights and Merchants: Trade, Politics and the Gentry in Late Medieval England', *P&P* 169 (2000), 37–40.

[8] C. Dyer, *Standards of Living in the Later Middle Ages: Social Change in England c.1200–c.1520*, revised edn. (Cambridge, 1998), 110–17.

doubled between *c*.1200 and the early fourteenth century. The annual revenues of Canterbury Cathedral Priory, for example, rose from £1,406 in 1200 to £2,540 in 1331.[9]

This picture of an all-pervading and successful lordship is partly created by the distorting mirror of the lords' own archives. The treatises on estate management, however, which were prefaced with rather grand claims to wealth and power, sow doubts in the minds of modern readers by continuing with advice on countering the effects of dishonest officials, disloyal servants, and malicious workers. Lords were told that constant vigilance was needed to maintain revenues. Of course they were grand figures, with their own courts and huge incomes, and were major players in the economy, but we need to keep their role in perspective. Even in the thirteenth century lords could find themselves in serious financial difficulty, not just the gentry who ran up debts and had to sell land to a monastery, but also quite large monasteries which were bankrupted by an incompetent abbot or by a severe attack of sheep scab. We need to spend a short time appraising critically their importance in their period of maximum power, before moving to look at their contribution after 1400.

Even in the era of high farming in the late thirteenth century most lords' demesnes were not very large, with a mean of 200 acres of arable land. They accounted for a fraction of productive land, perhaps a quarter or a fifth.[10] Similarly, the bulk of the cattle, sheep, and pigs were kept by peasants, only in small numbers of three or four cattle on each holding, or thirty sheep at a time, but there were near to a million peasant holdings, and about 20,000 demesnes. Demesnes accounted for only a fraction of the produce that was put on the market, and three-quarters of the 10 million or so fleeces that were exported each year at the peak of the wool trade in the early years of the fourteenth century came from peasant flocks.[11] Demesnes produced very little of the industrial crops, such as flax, hemp, and dyestuffs, which came mainly from peasant gardens.[12] The busy trade in fruit and vegetables, honey and mustard, poultry and eggs, butter and cheese, which was focused on towns, was supplied by the peasantry, and particularly by peasant women.[13] Although demesnes kept many pigs, peasants were responsible for the bulk of the trade in bacon. A tendency in the fourteenth century took dairy cows out of the direct management of lords' officials, and long before the wholesale

[9] Smith, *Canterbury Cathedral Priory*, 12–13.
[10] Campbell, *Seigniorial Agriculture*, 57–8, 67.
[11] Ibid. 158–9.
[12] C. Dyer, 'Gardens and Orchards in Medieval England', in id., *Everyday Life in Medieval England* (London, 1994), 119–27.
[13] R. H. Hilton, 'Women Traders in Medieval England', in id., *Class Conflict and the Crisis of Feudalism* (London, 1985), 210–11.

leasing of demesnes each cow would be rented out for between 3*s.* and 6*s.* per annum, making the peasant lessee responsible for making and marketing the butter and cheese. Even in the case of grain, better-off peasants sold more of their crop than did the demesnes, because so much of the lords' production was used to pay servants, to feed animals, and to supply the household.[14]

There were limits to lords' control of people as well as their management of land. A gap is evident between the claims that lords made for their domination of villeins or serfs, and the reality of the serfs' lives. In spite of the undoubted disadvantages of their condition, tenants in villeinage were able to accumulate land, profit from the sale of produce, and indeed organize themselves to mount a spirited resistance (p. 35). The examples of restriction and interference mentioned were not imposed universally. A majority of peasants were free, and therefore not liable to the bulk of the exactions and controls. Other impositions were enforced inconsistently, or scarcely at all, such as the prohibition on migration. Labour services, which fell very unevenly even on the serfs, were commuted in growing quantities during the thirteenth century, leading to the estimate that only 8 per cent of work on demesnes in *c.*1300 was being done compulsorily by customary tenants.[15]

The tenants lived within a framework of rules devised by their lords, and were influenced in their activities by lordship, but there was a complex interaction between tenant and lord. Let us take the case of assarting. In woodland manors we find records of tenants taking on pieces of cleared land. Sometimes a lord would grant a parcel for a specified rent, or holdings of new land would be added to a rental or survey. This is often taken to mean that the lord had organized the clearance, and gained the expected benefit in the form of a rent. If so, the lord's actions would have been influenced by the demand for land among the peasantry, and may have been responding to pressure from them. In other cases the lord seems to have discovered an assart some time after the tenant had carried out the work, so his recording of a new rent represents the lord catching up with initiatives taken by tenants. Numerous cases of this kind are recorded at Wakefield in Yorkshire in 1316 in the extreme circumstances of the Great Famine, for example, when Thomas Bole of Dewsbury was found to have enclosed a rood (quarter-acre) of land in 1310, and was required to pay 15*d.*, which covered his accumulated rent of 2*d.* per annum for the previous six years, and 3*d.* penalty for the act of encroachment.[16]

---

[14] R. H. Britnell, *The Commercialisation of English Society, 1000–1500* (Cambridge, 1993), 119–23.

[15] Campbell, *Seigniorial Agriculture*, 3.

[16] J. Lister (ed.), *Court Rolls of the Manor of Wakefield*, Vol. IV, *1315–1317*, Yorkshire Archaeological Society Record Series, 78 (1930), 119. On the general phenomenon, M. Stinson, 'Assarting and Poverty in Early Fourteenth-Century West Yorkshire', *Landscape History*, 5 (1983), 53–67.

Similarly, lords are often given the credit for founding new towns. They certainly showed imagination and initiative, but their ambitions could be frustrated. In 1263, for example, Robert de Ferrers, earl of Derby, created a new borough on his manor of Agardsley in Staffordshire. Everything would seem to have favoured the success of the town (which came to be called Newborough). The lord provided the right institutional framework to attract settlers. They were given the privileges of the well-established county town of Stafford, with guaranteed freedom of tenure, and a modest fixed cash rent. The town was laid out by the lords' officials, each tenant being provided with a burgage plot of an acre on which to build a house, and two acres of arable land in addition.[17] The town was sited on a crossroads with good communications. The district in which it lay, Needwood Chase, was being developed through the assarting of land for cultivation and the exploitation of its pastures and woods. Colonists of cleared woodland needed a centre to sell and buy.[18] Nearby town foundations, like Tutbury and Uttoxeter, did well. And the town lacked for nothing in the support it received from its powerful founder. The earls of Derby dominated much of the surrounding countryside from their castle at Tutbury. If lordship was the crucial factor in the fortunes of a town, then Newborough would have been a triumphant success. It failed, because Ferrers could not compel people to take up the plots or stay in them. He provided the new town's constitution, but the migrants or potential migrants made the decisions, depending on the profits that they could expect from trade and crafts. The new town was near to two successful rivals, the rural surroundings did not expand quickly enough, and an urban economy could not be sustained. Lords like Ferrers were attempting to channel and profit from a surge of urbanization with its own sources of energy that they could not always grasp. Meanwhile other midland towns, such as Rugby (Warwickshire) or Rugeley (Staffordshire), were growing without being helped by their lords with a grant of borough status, because they were well sited for commercial growth.[19]

In the case of industry, which tended not to be rooted in one spot, and was sometimes an ephemeral or part-time activity, lords were often ineffective in profiting in any significant way. In the thirteenth century pottery manufacture, which had become a mainly rural industry, spread in woodlands where fuel and clay were plentiful, preferably near to transport routes which could

[17] D. Palliser, *The Staffordshire Landscape* (London, 1976), 149, 151; M. Bateson, 'The Laws of Breteuil', *English Historical Review*, 16 (1901), 334.

[18] J. R. Birrell, 'Medieval Agriculture', *VCH Staffordshire*, vi. 7, 11–12.

[19] C. Dyer, 'The Hidden Trade of the Middle Ages: Evidence From the West Midlands', in id., *Everyday Life*, 292, 300; id., 'The Urbanizing of Staffordshire: The First Phases', *Staffordshire Studies*, 14 (2002), 11, 20, 22.

carry the wares to markets and consumers. The potters were usually peasants, with a smallholding and some livestock, who pursued their craft as an extra source of income. Such a group of potters settled in the manor of Hanley Castle in Worcestershire, and flourished. We know about their activities because the remains of their kilns have been discovered and excavated, but mainly because their distinctive wares are found throughout the west midlands and the Welsh borders.[20] The pots were loaded into boats at a quay at Hanley, and taken up and down the river, but much was carried overland and distributed by middlemen. The lords of Hanley in the thirteenth and early fourteenth centuries were powerful magnates, first the Clares, earls of Gloucester, and then the Despensers. They ruled the manor with a light hand, by making only modest demands of the tenants who owed labour service, while many of their tenants were freeholders. It seems extremely unlikely that they intervened to found or encourage the industry. Instead, local officials noticed the potters, and took a profit from them by insisting that each pay 6*d.* for digging clay. Thirteen of them paid this small rent in 1296, and in 1315 the potters also paid an extra charge for fuel. The lord took a token share in the profits of the industry, which was conducted largely beyond any manorial supervision.[21]

Cloth-making, a much more profitable rural industry, provided employment for many hands in the various stages of manufacture, but lords had limited opportunities to profit from the scattered and mobile workers. Lords built fulling mills, in order to attract some revenue from one of the cloth-making processes, but again they are revealed as following the enterprise of others rather than leading or directing industrial development.[22]

Lords famously promoted watermills for grinding corn in the early middle ages. Here was an example of technology which was relatively expensive, but which was valuable for the users because it released them, especially women, from the drudgery of milling by hand. Continued investment in mills in the later middle ages rewarded many lords with substantial revenues, whether directly in the form of toll corn taken from the grain as it was being processed, or in rent paid by millers in exchange for the lease of the mill. Many manors and estates from the thirteenth century gained about 5 per cent of their total

[20] A. Vince, 'The Medieval and Post-Medieval Ceramic Industry of the Malvern Region: The Study of a Ware and its Distribution', in D. P. S. Peacock (ed.), *Pottery and Early Commerce* (London, 1977), 257–305; J. D. Hurst, 'A Medieval Ceramic Production Site and Other Medieval Sites in the Parish of Hanley Castle: Results of Fieldwork in 1987–92', *Transactions of the Worcestershire Archaeological Society,* 3rd ser., 14 (1994), 115–28.

[21] J. P. Toomey (ed.), *Records of Hanley Castle Worcestershire, c.1147–1547,* Worcestershire Historical Society, NS, 18 (2001), 143, 146, 147, 149.

[22] E. Miller, 'The Fortunes of the English Textile Industry During the Thirteenth Century', *Ec.HR,* 2nd ser., 18 (1965), 64–82.

income from mills, and in the north the proportion of estate revenues from mill tolls or rents could be a tenth or more.[23] The profits increased in the thirteenth century with the growth in the numbers of consumers and the price of corn. Some new watermills were built, and lords were enabled by the application of wind power to build mills in places which lacked the right streams and rivers. Lords who had rashly allowed mills to fall into the hands of tenants paying fixed rents took steps to recover them.[24]

Historians have tended to assume that the basis of the profits of milling lay in the lords' right to compel their tenants to grind their corn at the manorial mill (to do suit of mill), and there are celebrated cases, as at St Albans and Cirencester, when lords' officials confiscated tenants' hand-mills and smashed them. Suit of mill would be a point of contention between lords asserting their rights and rebellious tenants, as at Darnhall and Over in Cheshire on the estate of the Cistercian monastery of Vale Royal in the early fourteenth century.[25] The obligation to use the lord's mill was resented because of the high toll that might be charged, and the licence that the miller was being given to take more corn for himself and to do the work when and how he pleased. Those liable to do suit of mill might face the inconvenience of travelling to a mill sited at some distance, and the chance of having to waste time waiting in a queue. Tenants were tempted either to grind the corn at home, or to take it to another lord's mill which might offer lower tolls, less travel, and a more efficient service.

Lords could seek to enforce suit by punishing those who were absent from the appropriate manorial mill, but detection and enforcement were difficult and cumbersome. We can see small campaigns being mounted, as at Walsham-le-Willows, Suffolk, in 1332, when eight tenants were amerced in the manor court 3*d.* and 6*d.* each 'for not milling at the lord's mill'.[26] This was the first year of a new lord, Hugh de Saxham, and we might speculate that he wished to show that he was in charge of the manor. There were no new cases in the court for eight years, so either the confrontation succeeded, or more likely the lord gave up his attempt to impose discipline. In order to maintain mill revenues lords used some coercion by bringing tenants occasionally before the court, combined with providing an effective and convenient service.[27]

[23] R. Holt, *The Mills of Medieval England* (Oxford, 1988), 70–89.

[24] Ibid. 107–16; J. Langdon, 'Watermills and Windmills in the West Midlands, 1086–1500', *Ec.HR* 44 (1991), 424–44; R. Holt, 'Whose Were the Profits of Corn Milling? An Aspect of the Changing Relationship Between the Abbots of Glastonbury and Their Tenants, 1086–1350', *P&P* 116 (1987), 24–55.

[25] Holt, *Mills*, 40–4.

[26] R. Lock (ed.), *The Court Rolls of Walsham le Willows 1303–1350*, Suffolk Records Society, 41 (1998), 151.

[27] J. Langdon, 'Lordship and Peasant Consumerism in the Milling Industry of Early Fourteenth-Century England', *P&P* 145 (1994), 3–46.

The willingness of one lord to welcome to his mill the tenants of a neighbour reminds us of the competition between lords, which is found also when a lord founded a borough and hoped to attract other lords' tenants to take up burgage plots, and to attend the market and pay tolls. When new land was being assarted, the new tenants could again come from old settled land on other lords' estates. Strict control of subordinates was scarcely possible if the aristocracy showed such limited solidarity. Serfs who left a manor were not usually pursued by their lord in the period before 1348–9, as land was in such high demand that a vacant holding could be rented without difficulty. If serfs' sons and daughters departed, there was no point in restricting them rigorously as labour was so abundant. Those who fled would in any case be received on to the estate of another lord, if they brought cash and skill which would make them good tenants and workers. The state made little attempt to help lords pursue runaway serfs.[28] Indeed, the state could be regarded as another competitor, imposing limits on lords' rights of jurisdiction, offering to protect free tenants from ill-treatment, and taking part of the tenants' surplus wealth in taxes.[29]

The ability of lords to master their estates and subordinates was limited also by their dependence on their tenants for administration. The manor would not have worked without the peasants who served as reeves, haywards, and grangers, and the manor courts functioned with the information provided, among others, by the tithing men or chief pledges. Judgements were made by the jurors, the amercements were set by the affeerers, and the money collected by the beadle. Guarantees of future payments and good behaviour were obtained from peasants acting as pledges.[30] These office-holders served for the same mixture of reasons that led the gentry to accept positions in local government at county level. On the manor some were compelled to take on office, especially in the case of reeves, who were servile tenants. But most felt impelled by a sense of duty, combined with a calculation that the offices gave them opportunities to gain financial advantages (in the case of some reeves) or status, authority, and influence within the community. The lord gained from their local knowledge, and from their ability to persuade and cajole their neighbours into doing services and paying rents, which would have been resented much more strongly if the demands had come from an outsider. The disadvantage for the lord lay in the inefficiency of amateur, part-time officials who did their tasks reluctantly. With such an administration it was

---

[28] Royal writs helped lords to pursue fugitives in the twelfth century. See P. R. Hyams, *Kings, Lords and Peasants in Medieval England: The Common Law of Villeinage in the Twelfth and Thirteenth Centuries* (Oxford, 1980), 223–30.

[29] On the state as an independent actor, Britnell, *Commercialisation*, 134–40, 208–12.

[30] M. Bailey, *The English Manor c.1200–c.1500* (Manchester, 2002), 171–8.

easier to maintain the accepted routines than bring in novelties. At best the functionaries would drag their feet, and if pushed too far they could use their position of leadership in their community, their organizational skills, and their legal knowledge to agitate against the lord. A striking example was the reeve of Mickleover in Derbyshire, Nicholas son of Henry, who led a campaign against the abbot of Burton in 1280, and showed resourcefulness in his use of writs and the royal courts to counter the moves of his lord.[31]

Lords liked to claim that they were in command, as with their boast that they could demand tallages and fines at their own will. In practice, however, they found that the best results came from manipulating, persuading, and pressurizing their tenants. Medieval lords are said to have extracted their tenants' surplus, thereby transferring wealth from the productive section of society to those with political and social power. The lords were indeed attempting this, but were frustrated in achieving their goal effectively. We can point to customary tenants in Somerset, on the estates of church magnates such as Glastonbury Abbey and the bishops of Winchester, who as well as paying high rents and heavy services were required to pay in the late thirteenth century entry fines of £20 and more for their yardland (30 acre) holdings.[32] The money would have to have been borrowed, and the new tenants would have spent ten years and more repaying the loans. Here the surplus was indeed being effectively extracted, but we can find plenty of examples in the same period where the rents had been fixed at a few shillings, and fines were set at a modest sum of a shilling per acre, or only 30s. for a yardland.[33]

Lords' revenues from tenants tended to level off around 1300, partly reflecting the tenants' diminishing profits from agriculture, but also because lords were unwilling to push harder in the face of resistance. Incomes from some landed estates went through difficult times between the famine of 1315–18 and the Black Death of 1348–9.[34] Lords had kept abreast of inflation in the thirteenth century, but their real incomes were beginning to fall in the early fourteenth as the prices of manufactured goods, imported luxuries, and services such as building were rising.[35]

---

[31] D. Crook, 'Freedom, Villeinage and Legal Process: The Dispute Between the Abbot of Burton and his Tenants of Mickleover, 1280', *Nottingham Medieval Studies*, 44 (2000), 123–40.

[32] J. Z. Titow, *English Rural Society 1200–1349* (London, 1969), 73–8.

[33] C. Dyer, 'Seignorial Profits on the Landmarket in Late Medieval England', in L. Feller (ed.), *Le Marché de la terre au moyen âge* (Paris, 2004).

[34] M. Mate, 'The Agrarian Economy of South-East England Before the Black Death: Depressed or Buoyant?', in B. M. S. Campbell (ed.), *Before the Black Death: Studies in the 'Crisis' of the Early Fourteenth Century* (Manchester, 1991), 90–107.

[35] Dyer, *Standards of Living*, 101–3.

The Role of Lords After 1350

In the fourteenth century the lords faced threats to their whole way of life. The long-term decline in grain prices, which began after the Great Famine, reduced the profits of the arable cultivation, which led to piecemeal leases of parts of the demesnes before 1348.[36] The Black Death did not immediately put an end to the demesne economy, because wages did not rise as rapidly as might be expected, and grain prices remained high, partly because of a series of poor harvests, until 1375.[37] Between 1380 and 1420, under pressure from low prices and high wages, complete demesnes were leased out in large numbers, and most of the magnates' estates gave up production of corn for the market.[38] At the same time the scarcity of tenants reduced the overall rent income. Even before the Black Death variable rents were often tending to level off or decline. After 1349 not only were tenants in a stronger bargaining position because of their scarcity, but also their relations with lords were soured by the political actions taken by lords to protect their private interests, in such measures as the Statute of Labourers and the poll tax.[39] This new role of the state helped to provoke the rising of 1381, and that event encouraged tenants and put lords on the defensive in negotiations over the next half-century. Rents fell, and many dues, such as tallage, were forgotten during the first half of the fifteenth century. In 1381 there had been tens of thousands of servile families. By 1450 handfuls of serfs survived in pockets on some estates, but they were severely depleted in numbers, and the various restrictions and penalties associated with serfdom survived only sporadically. Land might still be described as *native* (servile), and it would take some time for the stigma to be forgotten.[40]

The great estates had pulled back from a prominent economic role—they were no longer involved in production, but had handed their demesnes over to lessees or farmers. They did not intervene in the market or intrude into the economy of the peasant household as they had once done. The magnates should not be regarded as ineffective, as they still took huge sums of money out of the hands of others and then spent it in distinctive ways. They still held their private courts (though with diminishing authority), but were active in local government and the law, and exercised influence through their retainers

[36] E. Miller and J. Hatcher, *Medieval England: Rural Society and Economic Change, 1086–1348* (London, 1978), 238–9, 246.

[37] A. R. Bridbury, 'The Black Death', *Ec.HR*, 2nd ser., 26 (1973), 577–92.

[38] *AHEW* iii. 22–3, 573–6.

[39] Ibid. 753–60, 768–72.

[40] R. H. Hilton, *The Decline of Serfdom in Medieval England*, Economic History Society (1969), 32–55.

and followers. The laity were active in the land market, with the result that large numbers of manors changed hands, but they were perceived not as units of production but as generators of a steady flow of rent.

The Gentry

These generalizations apply to the magnates, but what of the gentry? This is a term taken here to mean the whole of the lesser aristocracy, from knights through esquires to the lesser lords, and which therefore includes those with landed incomes as high as £200–£300, and at the lower end even dipping below £10.[41] They have always been regarded as careful and adaptable managers, responsive to change, and indeed more likely to be personally committed to production.

To begin in the period before 1400, the most distinctive characteristics of the gentry derived from their need to live on limited resources. The wealthiest knights rarely held more than ten manors, and the lesser gentry often had only one, or a collection of lands which did not even constitute a conventional manor. Given these limited resources, they had to give estate management the highest priority. They often lived on their lands, and supervised them directly. The great lords respected their expertise by employing them as estate officials, and one could argue that because the magnates tended to lease out their manors before 1200, while the knights kept their lands under their direct control, the large estates were adopting the methods of the small landowners when they went over to direct management.

Gentry estates lacked servile tenants, or even large numbers of tenants of any kind, and one type of manor was provided with a high proportion of land held in demesne, so they were perforce involved in the marketing of produce, and without labour services they used wage labour. An example was James Grim of Sibthorp and Brampton in Huntingdonshire, whose landholding was recorded in 1279–80, with a demesne of 542 acres (worth at least £20 per annum), and rents producing annually less than £4.[42] This has led to the belief that by the thirteenth century—perhaps earlier—the gentry manors resembled modern capitalist farms more closely than the larger units of production on the magnate estates. They might have supplied their households directly with their own produce, but they needed a substantial cash income, as their status could only be maintained if they lived in defended

[41] N. Saul, *Knights and Esquires: The Gloucestershire Gentry in the Fourteenth Century* (Oxford, 1981), 30–5.

[42] E. A. Kosminsky, *Studies in the Agrarian History of England in the Thirteenth Century* (Oxford, 1956), 265–7.

houses, rode on good horses, wore superior clothes, and drank wine at least occasionally.[43]

A sample of gentry manors for which accounts have survived has been examined by Britnell. He concluded that many of them accorded with the model suggested above, with demesnes accounting for a high proportion of their resources.[44] They sold a great deal of produce, and invested a relatively high proportion of their income. For example, Lionel of Bradenham, from his Essex manor of Langenhoe in the first half of the fourteenth century, was regularly selling grain worth £15–£20 per annum, and wool and livestock brought in more money. He sometimes spent 10–15 per cent of his income on capital investment. But Britnell argued that these special characteristics derived from the small size of the manors, rather than from a more progressive or 'modern' approach. The lords showed no distinctive mentality in their management of their lands, and made no great innovations.

Looking at another sample of gentry manors in the thirteenth and fourteenth centuries, likewise I have not found much evidence for special enterprise or distinctive systems of production. The gentry were heavily influenced, like the magnates, by local economic environments. So we find gentry manors in the intensely manorialized part of west Gloucestershire with high rent incomes, resembling in that respect nearby magnate manors. An example would be the manor of Sir Nicholas Poyntz at Tockington in 1345, with less than 200 acres in demesne and rents worth £59.[45] We should remember also that relying on manorial accounts introduces a bias, because they tended to be kept by knights or the higher ranks of esquires, whose manors were scattered, and who therefore needed to employ estate officials who created the written evidence. Nonetheless, they demonstrate that some lords were running estates in the same fashion as Grim and Bradenham. Sir John Jernegan's manor of Somerleyton in Suffolk, for example, in 1359–60 received only £3. 11s. 6½ d. in rents and commuted labour services, while sales of grain and profits of the dairy alone came to £33.[46]

Alongside these conventional bureaucratic documents, more irregular jottings occasionally survive, like the accounts of the de Filleigh family in Devon in the early fourteenth century.[47] The categories in which the information

[43] F. Lachaud, 'Dress and Social Status in England Before the Sumptuary Laws', in P. Coss and M. Keen (eds.), *Heraldry, Pageantry and Social Display in Medieval England* (Woodbridge, 2002), 105–23.

[44] R. H. Britnell, 'Minor Landlords in England and Medieval Agrarian Capitalism', in T. H. Aston (ed.), *Landlords, Peasants and Politics in Medieval England* (Cambridge, 1987), 227–46, esp. 236–41.

[45] Saul, *Knights and Esquires*, 222–3.

[46] Bodleian Library, Oxford, Suffolk Rolls, no. 29.

[47] Devon Record Office, 1262 M/M82, M84, M90.

was gathered was somewhat jumbled—building costs were entered in a paragraph headed 'Cost of ploughs'. The accounting period did not run in the conventional way from Michaelmas to Michaelmas. In these and many other gentry accounts household expenditure was mingled with estate matters, reflecting the close relationship between consumption and production where the agricultural land and buildings lay adjacent to the manor house. This emphasis on direct supply is found everywhere on gentry estates together with a practice of paying for household purchases from the revenues of the manors: for example at East Carleton in Norfolk in 1274–5, from which the household of William Curzon received wheat, malt, cattle, and pigs, and the sergeant paid for herring and candles. At Holcombe Rogus in Devon in 1371–2 the reeve bought grain, cheese, and butter for the lord's household, in addition to supplying produce from the demesne.[48]

Unconventional accounting documents could be seen as evidence of administrative slackness. They lack many traces of professional auditing, but that should not lead us to regard the gentry manor as inefficient. Rather, we should see the accounts as evidence of a useful informality, reflecting the supervision of a resident lord, who oversaw the manor in person, and carried out audits verbally. A large section of the gentry below the de Filleighs kept no accounts at all, or at least none that have survived. This could be the result of a personal attention to management, which in the hands of an able lord could have been responsive to opportunities. After all, some of the most successful businessmen of the early fourteenth century, the wool merchants, appear to have kept no systematic written accounts for their trading activities. Some of the accounts for gentry manors contain hints of the lord's managerial presence, as he is recorded authorizing payments in person, like Thomas de Filleigh at Buckland, who attested to the sale of grain and authorized the purchase of iron and steel. Such a lord knew about the prices in local markets. The direct supervision of labour gave the lord the advantage of being able to hire farm servants flexibly, rather than taking them on for a full year as normally happened on magnate estates. At Buckland in Devon in 1315–16, a difficult year, one servant was taken on for five weeks and another for fourteen.[49]

The gentry lords investigated here employed no special production methods, other than those characteristic of the region in which the manors were located, such as beat burning (paring turf, burning it, and spreading it on the land as a fertilizer) in Devon, and rabbit rearing in East Anglia. The tendency for the gentry to supply their households directly from their estates

---

[48] John Rylands Library, Manchester, Phillipps ch. 17; Devon Record Office, DD 54890.
[49] Devon Record Office, 1262 M/84.

discouraged them from specialization; so, for example, the demesnes of Nettlecombe and Rowdon in Somerset in 1379–80 provided the household of John de Bourwash with a high proportion of its supplies, including grain, cheese, butter, cattle, pigs, sheep, and poultry.[50]

At the end of the fourteenth century the gentry faced the same problems as the great magnates in the simultaneous decline in agricultural profits and rents. John Catesby, a wealthy esquire based at Ashby St Ledgers in Northamptonshire, in 1385 and 1386 carried out a remarkable exercise in reviewing the 'state' of his manors, of which he held five, together with four smaller properties (Fig. 3.1).[51] The bulk of his revenues came from rent. His farming was entirely conventional, with a mixture of corn and livestock. He cultivated about 100 acres on four of his manors, and in 1386 kept twenty-nine horses, 132 cattle, 426 sheep, and eighty pigs. The novelty of the document does not lie in the agriculture that it depicts, but in its calculations of profit. These revealed that cultivating the demesne of one manor, Ladbroke, was not worth anything: 'husbandry there, beyond the costs, of no value.' The tenant holdings also caused concern, as some lay in the lord's hands, rents were 'decayed', and £18 was estimated as the cost of rebuilding eight houses that had fallen down. The whole estate was valued at £123 per annum, but a sum of £7. 11s. 5d. was in arrears.

John Catesby's realistic assessment of his estates was pointing towards the leasing of demesnes, and soon after 1400 many of Catesby's contemporaries went through the same change in management as on the great estates. Robert Darcy esquire of Maldon in Essex in 1447–8 gained an income of £99 from rents of twenty-two properties, four of them manors worth between £14 and £21 each, and Sir John Bishopsden of Bishopton in Warwickshire had apparently leased out all of his demesnes by 1422.[52] A common arrangement, which is also found on monastic estates, involved leasing out most of the manors, but keeping one as a home farm to supply the household. In the 1430s this was happening on the Govytz family estate in Dorset, with much of the demesne rented out, but enough was cultivated to keep the household in bread and ale, and to give a surplus of grain that could be sold.[53] At the Waterton's manor of Methley in Yorkshire in 1435–6 the 'husbandry' of the manor provided the household with wheat and malt and thirty-four cattle, eighteen pigs, 134 wethers, and calves and piglets.[54] The administration of

[50] Somerset Archive and Record Service, DD/WO/Box 42/Bundle 3.
[51] J. R. Birrell (ed.), 'The *Status Maneriorum* of John Catesby, 1385 and 1386', in R. Bearman (ed.), *Miscellany I*, Dugdale Society, 31 (1977), 15–28.
[52] TNA: PRO, SC6/848/14; SC6/1043/28.
[53] Ibid., SC6/833/24–28.
[54] West Yorkshire Archive Service, Leeds, MX/M6/3/10.

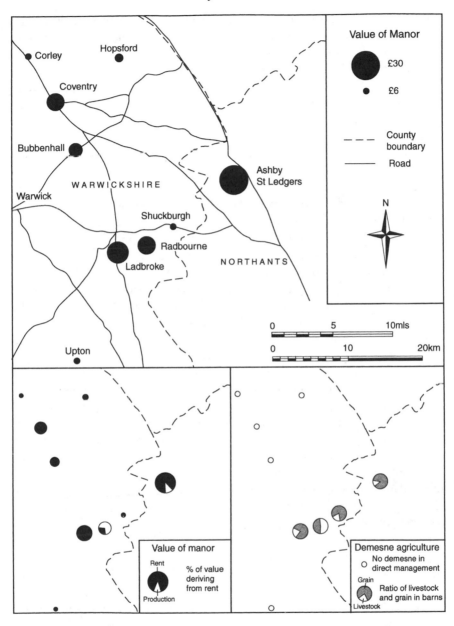

Fig. 3.1. The estate of the Catesby family, 1386. The maps show the values assigned to each manor, income deriving from rent and agriculture, and the relative importance of livestock and grain in the demesne economy.

Source: see n. 51.

rent income at Methley was kept separate from the records of agriculture, and on some small estates the 'husbandry' was not formally written into an account at all. On some gentry manors, such as Holcombe Rogus in Devon after 1434, and Whalesborough in Cornwall after 1440, incidental references in accounts mainly concerned with rents reveal that some agriculture was being practised by the lord, but there are no details to indicate its scale.[55]

The desire for a degree of self-sufficiency even extended to the urban gentry, like Thomas Creyke of Beverley in Yorkshire, who was growing grain on land outside the town, and keeping cattle, sheep, and pigs, which are recorded in 1488.[56] Direct supply of the household, which gentry evidently regarded as convenient, could also be achieved by taking on a lease of tithe corn from the local rectory. This was done by Thomas Malory of Newbold Revel in Warwickshire, the author of the impractically chivalric *Morte D'Arthur*, who was practical enough to lease the tithe corn of nearby Stretton-under-Fosse in the 1440s.[57] Alternatively a demesne could be rented out for a share of the crop (the third sheaf), which enabled John Heydon of Hackford in Norfolk to obtain direct supplies of oats and barley without the trouble and expense of cultivating the land himself.[58]

In a sense an estate based mainly on rents, on which many gentry lived in the fifteenth century, represented a retreat from active economic management, and might be regarded by historians as a safe option by which the lord could focus his or her attention on important matters of government or the practice of the legal profession, and receive the regular agreed payments from the tenants. In reality such an estate needed constant attention, as tenants were reluctant to pay rents or attend courts, and would have taken advantage of any sign of slackness. Records that survive from a gentry estate, like the court rolls kept carefully by the Bishopsden family already mentioned, show the vigilance that was needed to keep tenant buildings in repair, and to make sure that land transfers were made through the court, and to enforce the payment of heriots, entry fines, and other occasional dues. Gentry lords would also 'renew' rentals in order to keep track of tenants, rents, and holdings.[59] The choice of lessees for demesne lands and mills emerges from the letter collections, especially those of the Paston family, as a constant

---

[55] Devon Record Office, DD 54925; Somerset Archive and Record Service, DD/WO/Box 46/Bundle 1.

[56] J. Raine (ed.), *Testamenta Eboracensia*, 4, Surtees Society, 53 (1868), 34–9.

[57] P. J. C. Field, 'Thomas Malory and the Warwick Retinue Roll', *Midland History*, 5 (1979–80), 20–30.

[58] Norfolk Record Office, Aylsham 733 T 189B.

[59] Warwickshire County Record Office, CR 1911/2–7. On rentals, see C. Carpenter, *Locality and Polity: A Study of Warwickshire Landed Society, 1401–1499* (Cambridge, 1992), 163–4 ff.

concern. In 1460 Robert Calle the bailiff wrote to John Paston about the difficulty of finding a tenant for land at Mautby, and having identified someone suitable, John Daye, proposed to send him to see Paston for a personal interview. Such lessees had to be watched to ensure that they paid their rents, repaired buildings, and observed the conditions of their contracts. Farmers would break their bargain and reduce their payments in order to negotiate for lower rents in the middle of their term, like the farmer of Saxthorpe in Norfolk who ran up arrears of £45, who was said to have 'had great favour in his payments'.[60]

To some extent the gentry who lived on rents were maintaining as best they could the structure of the manors that they had inherited from their predecessors, and their main task was to hang on to as much as possible of the rents and dues that had been paid in the past. Sometimes, however, we see novel estate structures being created, like the new manor at Cheshunt in Hertfordshire, built out of forty-four pieces of land acquired mainly by purchase, and then rented out for an annual total of £31. 10s. 10d.[61] On more traditional gentry estates which had opted for a rent income, which was bound to decline, the only sure way to expand landed wealth was to acquire more property by marriage and purchase.[62]

Some gentry during the fifteenth century adopted a new style of directly managed demesne production, and their activities have rightly received a good deal of attention from historians. Mixed enterprises, which combined cultivation of grain with animal husbandry, can be found on gentry estates, not just at the beginning of the fifteenth century, when in 1408–9 a Hampshire esquire, John Champflour, sowed large areas of arable and kept cattle and 3,254 sheep, but also in 1494 when Martin de la Mare in Yorkshire used four teams of oxen for cultivation and owned sixty cows and 1,200 sheep.[63] In the case of the Catesbys of Ashby St Ledgers in Northamptonshire, they concentrated their endeavours on a single manor, Radbourne in Warwickshire which had been used for pasture in 1386 (Fig. 3.1).[64] Here they acquired exclusive use of a large pasture—the peasants had left the village in unknown circumstances, and the Catesbys took leases of adjoining lands

[60] N. Davis (ed.), *Paston Letters and Papers of the Fifteenth Century* (Oxford, 1971 and 1976), ii. 191–2, 217–18; R. Britnell, 'The Pastons and Their Norfolk', *Ag.HR* 36 (1988), 141–2.

[61] P. Glennie, 'In Search of Agrarian Capitalism: Manorial Land Markets and the Acquisition of Land in the Lea Valley, *c*.1450–*c*.1560', *Continuity and Change*, 3 (1988), 11–40.

[62] E. Acheson, *A Gentry Community: Leicestershire in the Fifteenth Century, c.1422–c.1485* (Cambridge, 1992), 68–71.

[63] British Library, Add. Roll 26869; *VCH Hampshire*, ii. 367, 382; Raine (ed.), *Testamenta Eboracensia*, 4, pp. 100–1.

[64] C. Dyer, *Warwickshire Farming 1349–c.1520: Preparations for Agricultural Revolution*, Dugdale Society Occasional Papers, 27 (1981), 18–21.

belonging to other lords, such as the monks of Combe Abbey. On this consolidated block of a thousand acres of grassland, carved into closes with ditches and hedges, they kept a large flock of sheep, rising in number from 1,600 in 1447 to 2,700 in 1476, together with between twelve and fifty-four cows, a herd of beef cattle (forty-five in one year), and a dozen horses. Part of the land was occupied by rabbits, on such a scale as to yield 300 couples in one year. Some of the livestock were consumed in the household at Ashby, but the main purpose of Radbourne was to generate cash from the sale of wool and fattened beef cattle. The cattle were sold at markets such as Warwick and Banbury, and one of the purchasers of bulk quantities of wool was a merchant of Stratford-upon-Avon, John Hannes.[65]

A more extensive federation of properties was built up by 1500 by Thomas Kebell, the Leicestershire lawyer, whose 3,684 sheep and 188 cattle were distributed over ten pastures.[66] The largest gentry sheep-masters known to us were the Townshends, based on pastures within a 6 mile radius of their manor house at East Raynham in west central Norfolk.[67] By arrangements peculiar to East Anglia, the sheep were pastured not on the lord's demesne lands (many of which were leased out) but on fold courses. These derived from lords' possession of the rights to pasture sheep on the fallows of the common fields. The flock rose from almost 12,000 in 1490 to a total of 18,000 by 1516. The Townshends cultivated some arable land and sold quantities of barley, but their main enterprise was geared for the sale of wool and surplus animals to merchants at King's Lynn and in the small towns and villages of the locality, including butchers from such villages as Appleton and Wells-next-the-Sea.

Gentry participated in the industrial and commercial economy as well as the more profitable branches of agriculture. In Derbyshire a number of families invested in lead-mining and smelting, and in millstone quarries.[68] The Willoughbys of Wollaton in Nottinghamshire exploited coal-mining on a relatively large scale, gaining annual profits in 1498–1503 of £200 from pits which could have yielded annually about 500 tons. By the 1520s production had almost doubled.[69] Some gentry lords built tile kilns, or owned ships, or at

---

[65] C. Dyer, 'Medieval Stratford: A Successful Small Town', in R. Bearman (ed.), *The History of an English Borough: Stratford-upon-Avon 1196–1996* (Stratford-upon-Avon, 1997), 57, 58–9.

[66] E. W. Ives, *The Common Lawyers of Pre-Reformation England: Thomas Kebell: A Case Study* (Cambridge, 1983), 330–53, 440–2.

[67] C. E. Moreton, *The Townshends and their World: Gentry, Law and Land in Norfolk c.1450–1551* (Oxford, 1992), 162–90; Norfolk Record Office, Bradfer Lawrence V X45; MS 1475 IDF.

[68] S. M. Wright, *The Derbyshire Gentry in the Fifteenth Century*, Derbyshire Record Society, 8 (1983), 21–2.

[69] J. Hatcher, *History of the British Coal Industry*, Vol. I, *Before 1700: Towards the Age of Coal* (Oxford, 1993), 165–6.

least a share in a ship (like Sir William Ryther of Yorkshire in 1475), and were involved in partnerships with merchants.[70] Well placed to take advantage of local raw materials and markets, John Brome of Baddesley Clinton in Warwickshire ran a profitable pastoral business by buying beef cattle from Wales for fattening and then sale mainly for consumption in towns, and also invested in a tile works, a stone quarry, and fishponds.[71]

Can we identify these gentry enterprises as a new form of capitalism? It has been argued that magnate estates in the thirteenth century were capitalistic, in the sense that the demesnes were large units of production, which sent much produce to market, with investment in drainage and buildings.[72] The fifteenth-century gentry estates had a number of special qualities which mark them off as different from their magnate forerunners.

The first of these lay in the willingness of the gentry lords to rearrange property and consolidate their lands for administrative and economic efficiency.[73] Earlier estates tended to work within old units of landholding and existing patterns of fields. Exceptions in the thirteenth century were the new centres of agrarian production on the hillsides and moorlands of the north and west, or sometimes in drained marshes and assarted woodlands—the vaccaries, bercaries, granges, and new demesnes.[74] The late fifteenth- and early sixteenth-century gentry were much more ready to change the landscape to create their pastures, putting together demesnes, common fields, glebes, and pieces of land acquired by purchase or lease in order to build an efficient expanse of enclosed fields. For example, the Giffards of Weston Subedge in Gloucestershire in the 1440s leased out to tenants their arable demesnes at Weston and adjacent Norton Subedge, but took on the lease of the nearby grange of Combe, most of which was occupied with a sheep pasture on the Cotswold upland, and which had a common boundary with the pastures at Weston.[75] This combination of land enabled them to keep at least 2,000 sheep and fifty cattle. In champion country gentry, more than other types of lord, replaced villages and open fields and common pastures, which had functioned in many cases for five centuries, with a single expanse of pasture, as at Radbourne (pp. 103–4). They also turned former arable landscapes into

[70] J. Raine (ed.), *Testamenta Eboracensia*, 3, Surtees Society, 45 (1864), 217–18; K. B. McFarlane, 'The Investment of Sir John Fastolf's Profits of War', in id., *England in the Fifteenth Century* (London, 1981), 179–84, 195–6.

[71] C. Dyer, 'A Small Landowner in the Fifteenth Century', *Midland History*, 1 (1972), 1–14.

[72] e.g. in Smith, *Canterbury Cathedral Priory*.

[73] Carpenter, *Locality and Polity*, 128–30.

[74] R. A. Donkin, *The Cistercians: Studies in the Geography of Medieval England and Wales* (Toronto, 1978), 68–79, 98–100, 103–34.

[75] Dorset Record Office, D10/M231, 233; M229/1–5.

parks, which had practical value as pastures as well as prestigious pleasure grounds.

The second quality of gentry lords lay in their degree of specialization and market orientation. We have seen that gentry lords often escaped entirely from corn growing, or kept it going for household consumption and as a minor source of saleable surpluses. The focus of their activities lay in keeping livestock, not just the infamous sheep but also cattle for beef, and to a lesser extent horses and rabbits. They can be observed using convenient markets, which included those in the smaller towns, where their informants no doubt told them of local demand, or of good prices which could be obtained without high transport costs.

This can be connected with the third characteristic of the gentry lords, which is their degree of personal supervision and direct decision-making. The 'improving' magnates of the era of high farming took a close interest in estate management, but they worked through a council and a staff of administrators. We cannot imagine Henry of Eastry of Canterbury Cathedral or a bishop of Winchester showing the degree of personal concern evident from some of the most active gentry. Sir Roger Townshend had a large array of properties, as big as many monastic estates, and spent much time away from Norfolk, so, as on a magnate estate, he employed a 'sheep reeve', John Stalworthy, with responsibility for co-ordinating the work of dozens of shepherds and other staff. But Townshend still took a direct interest: a note in an account book of 1479–82 remarked on the lightness of fleeces from one pasture, which should be discussed with the lord. The shepherd was probably suspected of failing to look after the animals with sufficient care.[76] Townshend personally compiled memoranda about husbandry matters, including small details. Old hurdles should be sold, or taken to the household for firewood. Shepherds should look out for dogs; the building in which the sheepskins were stored needed repair; hedges were to be better maintained. The tone was not very encouraging, as he complained about slackness and inefficiency—horses and harness were not being properly prepared for work, dung could be used to better advantage, and harrowing was not being done thoroughly enough at the right time, 'for if my land was well tilled, it would bear as good corn as other men's, and for default of tilling I lose all'. One imagines Townshend riding round his estate, casting a critical eye over the work that he sees, and talking to his employees who, judging from his writings, had their errors explained to them with some force: 'we must see these things amended' was his final comment.

[76] Norfolk Record Office, MS 1475 1DF; C. E. Moreton and C. Richmond, ' "Beware of grazing on foul mornings": A Gentleman's Husbandry Notes', *Norfolk Archaeology*, 43 (2000), 500–3.

John Pennington, a Lancashire knight, kept records between 1486 and 1512 in books which reveal his continuous personal involvement in the estate.[77] Part of it was leased, and the tenants were supervised by the lord in person, even to the point of collecting small instalments of rent: 'The same day and year [17 July 1507] William Halylon for the farm of Martinmas past [11 November 1506], 20*d*.' On the production side, he sold cattle, sheep, sheepskins, cattle hides, and wool, and he made arrangements with shepherds: 'I reckoned with Robin Gyffard for the sheep of Byrkis, 12 July 1491, the which day was put forth to the pasture 585 of old sheep and 124 lambs...' Some of the sales involved major contracts for large sums with traders from Kendal and Manchester, but often small-scale sales were made by him to local people; nonetheless he recorded the date, name of buyer, and price. Other gentry lords who kept less detailed and personal records nevertheless were clearly paying close attention to estate business—Robert Waterton of Methley (Yorkshire) himself bought sheep in 1436, and the lord of Bere Regis in Dorset attended the sheep-shearing on his manor of Waterston.[78] If circumstances prevented the lord from exercising personal supervision, he might delegate the task to a member of his family. The Paston women are prime examples of this, as is Thomasin Hopton, who looked after the affairs of her husband, John Hopton, on his Suffolk manors in the 1470s.[79]

The fourth and final characteristic of gentry lords might be their attention to investment and profit. The incompleteness of the financial accounts, and their sometimes informal nature, means that we are rarely able to calculate the percentage of their revenues used on capital assets such as buildings and improvements to land. At Radbourne, for example, in each of two years about £10 was spent on hedging and ditching, but in other years much smaller sums were involved. The early years of running a specialized large pasture would have required heavy expenditure on sheepcotes, fencing, and the purchase of stock, but the cost of subsequent maintenance would not have been so high. John Spencer at Wormleighton in Warwickshire in 1500–1, at the point when the shift to pasture was being made, spent £30 on improvements, including a new barn, and in the next year £7 on fencing, but outlay on this scale may not have been needed in subsequent years. Perhaps capital formation was no higher than on the large estates in the thirteenth century, as the 4 per cent of income spent on investment at the gentry manor of Waterston in Dorset in 1434–9 suggests.[80]

[77] Cumbria Record Office, Carlisle, D/Pen/200; TNA: PRO, E101/691/41.

[78] West Yorkshire Archive Service, Leeds, MX/M6/3/10; TNA: PRO, SC6/833/24.

[79] C. Richmond, *John Hopton: A Fifteenth Century Suffolk Gentleman* (Cambridge, 1981), 115–21.

[80] British Library, Add. MS. 75314, Althorp Papers A14; TNA: PRO, SC6/833/24–28.

Pastoral farming was especially attractive because of its low labour costs, and we note the handful of shepherds who were employed at Radbourne and the other pastures. The herdsmen could be rewarded partly in cash and partly with a share of the pasture for a small flock of their own animals, which probably increased their incentive to look after the whole flock with care. They were expected to be more productive than their predecessors who worked as demesne shepherds on magnate estates, as they were responsible for about 400 animals each, while under the old system before 1400 each shepherd was assigned between 250 and 300.[81] One obvious contrast between conventional manors on magnates' estates *c.*1300 and gentry pastures under direct management around 1500 lay in the complete absence of labour service at the later date. In the earlier period lords of manors were investing money received in traditional feudal rents, deriving from such sources as commuted labour services and entry fines. Gentry estates also had rent income, both from assize rents of free and customary tenants, and from leaseholds, which could provide funds for investment. A number of the lords whose affairs have been analysed here were also lawyers, and they had often bought land, and invested in improvements, putting the surplus from their professional earnings to profitable use. The attraction of the purchase of land for gentry who had acquired cash from the law, office, or war lay in the safety and stability of their assets, and the steady return that they received. They were probably content that land gave then 5 per cent of the purchase price in annual income. For much of the fifteenth century income from land was won with difficulty, as tenants expected rent reductions and might leave altogether, and even the produce from livestock was not very lucrative, as wool prices slid to a low level after about 1441.[82] Nonetheless, transformations of manors which previously consisted of a demesne with mixed land use and a decaying village could yield in some cases a threefold increase in profits for the lord— Compton Verney in Warwickshire was valued as a conventional manor with demesne and tenant land at £24 towards the end of the fourteenth century; in 1461, as an enclosed pasture of about 1,500 acres, it was said to be worth £60. A similar growth must have occurred at Wormleighton, where William Cope in 1500–1 was receiving £66. 13*s.* 4*d.* from 'three fields of pasture'.[83]

The lesser gentry remain something of a mystery, and most of the examples that have been quoted here were well-heeled knights and esquires worth a

---

[81] D. Farmer, 'The *famuli* in the Later Middle Ages', in R. Britnell and J. Hatcher (eds.), *Progress and Problems in Medieval England: Essays in Honour of Edward Miller* (Cambridge, 1996), 221–3.

[82] *AHEW* iii. 512–16.

[83] C. Dyer, 'Compton Verney: Landscape and People in the Middle Ages', in R. Bearman (ed.), *Compton Verney: A History of the House and Its Owners* (Stratford-upon-Avon, 2000), 89–90; British Library, Add. MS. 75314, Althorp papers A14.

minimum of £100 per annum. A remarkable commonplace book belonging to a Cheshire gentleman, Humphrey Newton, contains jottings of accounts and memoranda on economic matters for 1498–1506.[84] It also included poetry, prayers, legal notes, and medical recipes. As has already been remarked, the unsystematic nature of such records should not be taken as evidence of inefficiency, but in Newton's case show his close personal interest which could have contributed to profitability. He acted as his own bailiff, paying wages, collecting rents, and managing small-scale arable cultivation, animal husbandry, and a fishpond. Rents from land at Newton rose in his time from £11 to £14. The unspecialized nature of the farming reflects the need to supply the household, but he saw the profits that could be made by cattle-rearing, and he went to Chapel en le Frith (Derbyshire) to sell cattle, expecting to obtain a better price than in the more local markets. In 1503 he kept eighty sheep, and in one year he sold a dozen cattle. He was an innovator on a modest scale, working on the fishpond and a corn mill and fulling mill, and devoting a great deal of money to the marling of his arable land. One is reminded by his willingness to try almost any source of income of the 'economy of makeshifts' practised by cottagers—in comparison with the Townshends or Catesbys, he was struggling to keep up an income on modest assets.

Did most gentry live on rents, or become involved in direct management? A clumsy way of judging their commitment to agriculture is to see how many of them bequeathed in their wills grain, animals, or equipment which might indicate farming activity. From a sample of sixty-three gentry wills proved in the archdiocese of York in 1485–1500 only eleven mention these signs of direct agricultural production. Some of these gentry confirm their knowledge of farming matters by mentioning details of husbandry, like Nicholas Conyers of Stokesley (Yorkshire), who left 12*d.* to 'my herd who keeps my cows'.[85] A number of them would have been running home farms rather than a large-scale pastoral enterprise of the type discussed above. On the other hand, a knight or esquire active in commercial agriculture was capable of writing a will without bequeathing animals or dung carts to his relatives, supporters, and servants! With these important qualifications, the model provided by Catesby, Kebell, or Townshend appears to have applied only to a minority. In any case, specialized pastoral farms and investment in industry were by no means confined to the gentry, as a few larger monasteries, such as Fountains and Winchcombe abbeys, were keeping sizeable numbers of

---

[84] D. Youngs, 'Estate Management, Investment and the Gentleman Landlord in Later Medieval England', *Historical Research*, 73 (2000), 124–41.
[85] Raine (ed.), *Testamenta Eboracensia*, 4.

cattle and sheep in the late fifteenth and early sixteenth centuries.[86] Many
magnates drew revenues from coal-mining and tile houses, and the bishopric
of Durham profited from lead extraction. In 1455–6 the duke of Norfolk
invested 66s. 8d. at Stottesdon in Shropshire in a new pond to power a mill
for ironmaking, a 'bloom smithy', and hired a skilled operator to run the new
machinery, searching for the right man first in the Forest of Dean, and then in
Sheffield 'for the lord's greater profit'.[87] It can be said, however, that none of
these larger owners committed as much of their resources or time to these
enterprises as did gentry of all kinds, from the Townshends to Newton, nor
did they gain more than a small fraction of their income from them.

The gentry's profit-seeking was of course entirely compatible with the
culture and tastes that prevailed in their age, as Newton's commonplace
book suggests. The lords who calculated the profit that could be made
from their pastures read Arthurian romances, and expressed strong religious
convictions in their wills. They were active in common law, politics, and
administration. The different aspects of their lives did not always work in
harmony. William Catesby, who calculated with skill the profits from wool
sales and his rabbit warren, was capable of a fatal political miscalculation
when he gave enthusiastic support to Richard III.[88]

To sum up the whole of this discussion of the economic role of the
medieval aristocracy, lords, even at the height of their power in the thirteenth
century, were influential but were not as significant as producers, nor as all-
encompassing in their power over their subordinates, as they would have
wished. The large estates slipped in their domination after 1350 and especially after 1400. Some members of the gentry, who had always differed from
the magnates in the management of their affairs, developed new types
of agrarian enterprise in the fifteenth and early sixteenth centuries. These
activists were too few and scattered to change the whole economy. The
aristocracy, though divided between clergy and laity, and between its higher
and lesser ranks, had fundamentally similar ways of exercising authority and
gaining an income, and the whole class's economic importance shrank in the
later middle ages. If we estimate that about a quarter or a fifth of the
productive land in England was under the direct management of lords in

[86] *AHEW* iii. 4, 573–5; West Yorkshire Archive Service, Yorkshire Archaeological Society, MD
335; D. J. H. Michelmore (ed.), *The Fountains Abbey Lease Book*, (Yorkshire Archaeological Society
Record Series, 140 (1981); *Valor Ecclesiasticus*, 6 vols., Record Commission (1810–34), ii. 456–9.

[87] J. M. W. Bean, *The Estates of the Percy Family 1416–1537* (Oxford, 1958), 49–51; R. I. Jack
(ed.), *The Grey of Ruthin Valor*, Bedfordshire Historical Record Society, 46 (1965), 129–31; I. S. W.
Blanchard, 'Seigneurial Entrepreneurship: The Bishops of Durham and the Weardale Lead Industry
1406–1529', *Business History*, 15 (1973), 97–111; Hereford Record Office, A 63/I/399.

[88] J. S. Roskell, 'William Catesby, Counsellor to Richard III', *Bulletin of the John Rylands Library*,
42 (1959), 145–74.

c.1300, the figure in *c*.1500 would be much less than tenth, even as little as a twentieth.

The State

Any consideration of the economic and social significance of those in authority must include, in addition to the role of lordship, some assessment of the contribution of the state. Some theories relate economic growth to the development of political freedom, in particular in the seventeenth and eighteenth centuries.[89] 'Liberal' concepts of freedom are not found in the middle ages, when freedom tended to mean 'privilege', in the sense of jurisdictional liberties, or in the use of the term 'freeman' in towns to describe full members of the civic body by right of birth, apprenticeship, or wealth.[90] The state of the later middle ages, although its resources were small and its agents few, influenced the lives of its subjects in many different ways.

The English state was famously unified, and its centralized character stands out when compared with its continental contemporaries. With the exception of the palatinates of Durham and Chester, and the marcher lordships, English lords were not able to wield the judicial, military, and fiscal independence available to the lords of immunities on the continent. England had no city states which ruled over the smaller towns, lords, and peasants of the surrounding countryside. Its towns had little power beyond their immediate boundaries, and could not enforce monopolies on trade and manufacture.[91]

Throughout the land the English lived under the same system of law, used the same currency, and generally paid the same taxes. The country was by no means free of institutional obstacles to trade. We do not know enough about tolls levied on the road system, for example, but toll stations are known which charged a halfpenny on passing carts.[92] The state failed in its objective of imposing uniformity of weights and measures, and local bushels for measuring grain persisted into modern times. Londoners used their influence and trading privileges to make life difficult for their provincial rivals, as in the

---

[89] S. R. Epstein, *Freedom and Growth: The Rise of States and Markets in Europe, 1300–1750* (London, 2000), 12–37.

[90] A. Harding, 'Political Liberty in the Middle Ages', *Speculum*, 55 (1980), 423–43; S. H. Rigby, *English Society in the Later Middle Ages: Class, Status and Gender* (Basingstoke, 1995), 162–3.

[91] Cf. the situation in Germany: T. Scott, *Freiburg and the Breisgau: Town–Country Relations in the Age of Reformation and Peasants' War* (Oxford, 1986).

[92] e.g. on the roads through Droitwich (Worcestershire) and Melton Mowbray (Leicestershire): C. Dyer, *Bromsgrove: A Small Town in Worcestershire in the Middle Ages*, Worcestershire Historical Society, Occasional Publications, 9 (2000), 36–7; J. Laughton and C. Dyer, 'Seasonal Patterns of Trade in the Later Middle Ages: Buying and Selling at Melton Mowbray, Leicestershire, 1400–1520', *Nottingham Medieval Studies*, 46 (2002), 168.

domination of cloth exports by the Merchant Adventurers. Still, these cannot be compared to the hindrances to carrying and trading goods across the European continent.[93] The relative stability of the currency until the reign of Henry VIII must be judged to have been to the advantage of English traders, though they suffered, like their continental counterparts, from a shortage of coin. Unlike their contemporaries on the continent and in Scotland, the English had only gold and silver coins, and so lacked a base-metal small change for everyday transactions, but they seem to have coped, one suspects by delaying payment until the debt was cancelled by some reciprocal transaction, or until a sum had accumulated that could be settled with a coin.

One of the most important contributions that the state could make to economic well-being was to create a secure environment, so that people did not live in constant fear of robbery or destructive armies, and enjoyed stable property rights. Late medieval England has a reputation for criminal and political violence, but we must doubt whether these had major economic effects. Horrific stories can be told of bands of ruffians, often led by members of the gentry, riding across the country to attack a manor house or threaten a rival, yet the loss of life from these disturbances was not very great, and crime was channelled and controlled in a way which limited its general impact.[94] As many commentators have remarked, we can search but cannot find in the numerous local records much evidence for destruction of property or serious economic disruption resulting from the Wars of the Roses.[95] Whatever psychological scars were caused by the risings of 1381 and 1450, we can only be impressed by the rapid return to apparent normality, even in the epicentres of the revolts. Anyone working on the records of manors and estates notices that large sums of money were in constant motion around England, being carried from the manorial reeves, bailiffs, and rent collectors to the lords and their officials. Theft en route was quite rare, and estate records make no reference to guards or security precautions by the officials responsible for sending or collecting the cash. There was much complaint about the cumbersome legal process and the wealth of lawyers, and one cause of aristocratic violence, such as forcible entry, was the perceived need for the parties to help their case with some extra-legal pressure.[96] Disputes often went to arbitration rather than being settled by the judgements of the court. But there was a general acceptance of the authority of the law, one indication

---

[93] P. Spufford, *Power and Profit: The Merchant in Medieval Europe* (London, 2002), 215–27.
[94] P. C. Maddern, *Violence and Social Order: East Anglia 1422–1442* (Oxford, 1992), 226–35.
[95] A. E. Goodman, *The Wars of the Roses: Military Activity and English Society, 1452–97* (London, 1981), 213–24; C. Carpenter, *The Wars of the Roses: Politics and the Constitution in England, c.1437–1509* (Cambridge, 1997), 259.
[96] J. G. Bellamy, *Bastard Feudalism and the Law* (London, 1989), 34–56.

being the high levels of litigation. The lawyers would not have been so rich if people with money had not been prepared to pay for their services. Recovery of debts could be slow and difficult, but the procedures were used and the fear of non-payment did not prevent bargains being struck and sales agreed. Some debts would be described as 'desperate' and would never be recovered, but this also happens in advanced modern economies.

The English state had been an efficient collector of taxes in the fourteenth century, and on occasion demanded so much that subjects complained of their damaging effects, especially around 1340 and in the period 1371–81. With the winding down and then the end of the French war in the mid-fifteenth century the tax burden cannot be regarded as high or oppressive. The calculation has been made that the load of taxes in the late fifteenth and early sixteenth centuries amounted to 1 shilling per head per annum, that is, less than three days' wages for a labourer, and under the graduated system by which direct taxes were assessed few actual labourers would pay more than a few pence. The tax revolts of 1489, 1497, and 1525 were provoked by experiments in the method of assessment rather than an unsupportable weight of financial demands.[97] The routine subsidy, though based on an archaic assessment, was administered by the local communities in ways that seem to have been accepted by the taxpayers. They were perceived to be fair, in the sense that the aristocracy paid a share. A reflection of the stability of English politics and society could be seen in the prevailing low rate of interest, which has been calculated at 10 per cent in the thirteenth century but at only 5 per cent in the fifteenth.[98]

The development of 'political society' from the late fourteenth century undoubtedly saw a coming together of the state and the landed interest, in which the crown shared law-enforcement and government with the local aristocracy acting as JPs.[99] But this was not the creation of an *ancien régime*, in which the nobles became dependent on the monarchy for pensions and patronage. It was more of a partnership, which undoubtedly helped the aristocracy to cope with their economic problems as their incomes from land declined. The state cannot, however, be regarded simply as a collective expression of the narrow interests of the upper class, as it established a new and direct relationship with those below the aristocracy. The servile peasantry wrongly believed in the thirteenth and fourteenth centuries that the royal

---

[97] M. Ormrod, 'England in the Middle Ages', and P. K. O'Brien and P. A. Hunt, 'England, 1485–1815', in R. Bonney (ed.), *The Rise of the Fiscal State in Europe, c. 1200–1815* (Oxford, 1999), 19–52, 53–100.

[98] Epstein, *Freedom and Growth*, 61–2.

[99] G. L. Harriss, 'Political Society and the Growth of Government in Late Medieval England', *P&P* 138 (1993), 28–57.

courts would protect them from the demands of their lords, but they were right to recognize that the state had an interest in establishing sovereignty over them. As the serfs gained their freedom after 1350, mainly by migrating to places where their status was unknown or overlooked, the king gained many thousands of new subjects, as the ex-serfs were now able to exercise their rights in the common-law courts. They still held their land by copyhold and tenancy at will, which had their origin in the servile tenures of the thirteenth century. In the late fifteenth and early sixteenth centuries the law provided some protection, hesitantly and ambiguously, towards copyhold tenants, who took cases to Chancery, and were said by lawyers to be able to bring trespass actions against their lords under common law.[100] The crown had for a long time engaged the village elite as jurors in the courts, and as tax assessors, and eventually they extended their public role in the administration of the poor law. The leading peasants and artisans believed themselves to be part of the political community as early as 1450. In moves very different from the rebels of 1381, Cade's followers put forward programmes written for them by lawyers, demanding reforms in government which showed that they sympathized with ideas expressed in parliament.[101] Those in government behaved inconsistently over such issues as enclosure, when they paid lip service to the interests of the peasantry, especially when they embraced 'commonwealth' rhetoric, but still tolerated the 'improvements' made by landlords.

Below the Gentry

The 'freedom' in the title of this chapter refers not just to the 'liberation' of the serfs, though that was an important change, but to the whole process by which lords suffered a reduction in their control of their subordinates, and withdrew from the forefront of economic activity. The space that they left was not filled by the state. People below the aristocracy gained more resources, such as the demesnes which they took on lease, and were able to retain more of their income as rents and taxes stood at a relatively low level. They had more say in the conduct of their own lives, and here we will begin to ask what they did with that freedom.

The material circumstances and outlook of those below the ranks of the gentry can be investigated through their probate records, which are most plentiful in eastern England from the 1430s. There are various types of

---

[100] C. M. Gray, *Copyhold, Equity, and the Common Law* (Cambridge, Mass., 1963); J. H. Baker, *The Oxford History of the Laws of England*, Vol. VI, *1483–1558* (Oxford, 2003), 631–52.
[101] I. M. W. Harvey, *Jack Cade's Rebellion of 1450* (Oxford, 1991), 186–91.

probate document, but in this and subsequent chapter for the sake of brevity I will call them wills. It is not necessary to go into all of the qualifications and reservations about their use, but it is worth mentioning that they belonged to a genre of writing, with standard formulae and conventional phrases, so the words used do not express the personal thoughts of the testator—the phrases would often have been suggested or added by the clerk. Wills give a very incomplete account of the disposal of property, because many gifts and sales had been made, and trusts and groups of feoffees had been set up, during life, or even on the deathbed. The instructions given in the will were often not carried out, through the failings of the executors, or their impractical nature, as many testators overestimated their wealth and underrated their debts. The majority of wills are disappointingly brief and uninformative, telling us little more than the name, place of residence, and burial-place. A minority are packed with details about the testator's status or occupation, lands, houses, goods, family, and associates. A small number of inventories have survived from the archives of the prerogative court of Canterbury and of the probate jurisdictions in York. The great advantage of wills for our theme is that, in contrast with the records of manorial administration, they were not serving the administrative priorities of the lords and their courts. Wills were also the product of an administrative machine, that is, the bureaucracy of the church courts, but at least they give an alternative approach, a non-seigneurial perspective.[102]

The sample of wills which is analysed here is heavily biased towards the better-off, so we find in them very little information about cottagers or labourers. Women made wills, but they are under-represented. Because many of them come from the courts of the archdeacons and ecclesiastical peculiars, that is, local church courts, the wills that survive were often made by people below the ranks of the gentry. This allows us to focus on the non-aristocrats who took the initiative when the lords adopted a lower economic profile. They include, in the countryside, the tenants who accumulated a number of holdings, or who occupied a lord's demesnes on lease, or who were involved in rural trade and manufacture. In the towns the sample includes traders and craftsmen. Most testators are not assigned a specific status in the will, and most would in other records (in the royal courts, for example) be called husbandmen or yeomen, or have an occupational description such as draper, chapman, carpenter, fuller, and so on.

---

[102] M. Zell, 'Fifteenth- and Sixteenth-Century Wills as Historical Sources', *Archives*, 14 (1979), 61–74; M. Spufford, 'The Limitations of the Probate Inventory', in J. Chartres and D. Hey (eds.), *English Rural Society, 1500–1800: Essays in Honour of Joan Thirsk* (Cambridge, 1990), 139–74; T. Arkell, N. Evans, and N. Goose (eds.), *When Death Us Do Part: Understanding and Interpreting the Probate Records of Early Modern England* (Oxford, 2000).

John Hall of Holgate near York, identified as a husbandman, who died in 1468 was among the poorest people to have left an inventory before such documents became commonplace after 1540. He represents the middling peasantry. When the inventory was compiled on 9 August, before the harvest, he had 11 acres under crop, suggesting that his holding (allowing for fallow land) contained not much more than 20 acres of arable, and he owned four horses, five cattle, and a pig. The total inventory was worth £8. 15s. 10d., of which the rather basic household goods were valued at £2. 8s. 10d. Cash was often in short supply: Hall's purse contained 6d., and he owed £2. 3s. 1d. His unfortunate widow and children therefore received a very modest inheritance.[103] Most of those for whom we have inventories, or detailed wills, had more goods and assets than Hall.

Future chapters will deal with specific occupational groups, such as farmers and clothiers, but at this stage I wish to indicate some of the common characteristics of the will-makers, and I will deal with three aspects of their lives: as producers, participants in the market, and members of society.

Production

Many testators had more than one source of income. They usually held some land, and here the striking feature is its varied nature. When we rely on manorial records for evidence of landholding, the investigation has to be confined to a single manor, though we are sometimes able to observe contiguous manors, and tenants can be found to have acquired holdings from more than one lord. The wills confirm that by the late fifteenth century ambitious tenants would hold land from two or more lords, and in more than a single village. To take a Norfolk example, John Seyve of Rollesby in 1482 held land in Rollesby, Burgh, Ormesby, and Winterton, all villages in the same district to the north of Great Yarmouth, together with a plot of land in Yarmouth itself.[104] The wills often identify the land as being held by different tenures: freehold, leasehold, and customary. In the mid-fifteenth century people were still conscious of the disadvantages of servile tenure, but as so many of the burdens of serfdom had faded away freemen were more willing to take naif or bond land. To return to John Seyve, he held a free messuage, a free tenement, and parcels of naif land totalling 6½ acres in Rollesby, and a similar combination of bond and free holdings in other villages. Manorial sources tell us that he also held a piece of land in Rollesby on lease for a rent of £8.[105]

---

[103] Borthwick Institute of Historical Research, York, D. and C. wills, 1468, Hall.
[104] Norfolk Record Office, NCC wills, 200, A. Caston.
[105] Norfolk Record Office, EST 15 (receiver's account of bishopric of Norwich).

The largest accumulations of land tended to belong to those, like John Seyve, who held a lease of demesne land among their portfolio of holdings. But some large multiple holdings appear to have been made by those who engrossed land which had previously belonged to a number of tenants, like Thomas Ridhale of Wisbech, Cambridgeshire, who held 232 acres of mainly freehold land, or Edward Artour of the same, with 178¾ acres, both recorded in 1493.[106] Commonly in East Anglia landholdings were combined with a trade or craft, like those of Thomas Amys, a grain merchant of Barton Turf in Norfolk, who held more than 60 acres of both free and bond land in 1495. John Overy of Kentford in Suffolk held 28 free and customary acres in 1477, and was also a skinner.[107]

The will-makers were all tenants, paying rents and dues for their holdings, though their obligations to their lords was rarely mentioned in their wills. They regarded the land, not just those parts of their holding held freely, as their property: they use phrases such as 'my own land'.[108] Their references to ploughs, carts, and livestock show that they worked the land themselves, though some had rented at least part of it to subtenants. John Leven of Great Bricett in Suffolk in 1472 pastured at least twenty-seven cattle and fifteen sheep, so he was using part of his land for production, while subletting a holding to a tenant who was to be allowed to occupy it for six months after his death.[109] Subletting would be the only practical use for land located some miles from the tenant's home village, like the holding in Winterton, 5 miles from John Seyve's village of Rollesby. When arrangements were being specified for the use of land after the testator's death, subletting provided the ideal way of generating a stable rent to maintain a relative with an income, or as a source of revenue for a future series of religious services. A contribution towards the maintenance of Margery Overy of Kentford in Suffolk in her widowhood, by the provisions of her husband's will proved in 1477, would come from the rent of 14 acres paid by a subtenant. The problem that the land was held by the Overys on customary tenure, which in theory could not be sublet except with the lord's permission, was not mentioned in the will.[110]

The great majority of testators can be judged, from their place of residence and their occupation, to have belonged either to the country or to the town, but a few held both rural and urban property. This may have originated in an

---

[106] TNA: PRO, PROB 11/10, fos. 12, 79. They both appear as brewers, landholders, and litigants in the court rolls of Wisbech in the 1470s: Cambridge University Library, EDR C9/2/88.

[107] TNA: PRO, PROB 2/102; PROB 11/10, fo. 224; Suffolk Record Office, Bury St Edmunds Branch, IC500/2/11, fo. 104.

[108] e.g. William Clerk of Stratford St Mary, Suffolk, left 'my own land': Suffolk Record Office, Ipswich Branch, J421/2, fo. 3.

[109] Ibid., fo. 233.

[110] Suffolk Record Office, Bury St Edmunds Branch, IC500/2/11, fo. 104.

accident of inheritance, as the result of a marriage or migration. One suspects that in the case of some of those based in a village, their tenement in a town gave them a convenient base for sales of produce, as in the case of John Seyve's Yarmouth property. A rural tradesman, Thomas Bronnewyn of Wetheringsett in Suffolk, does not reveal his specialism in his will of 1457, but he does refer to his stall in the market at Eye, presumably as an outlet for his goods, and another stall in his own village at the churchyard gate, as well as land in two villages.[111] Townspeople would hold property in more than one centre, like John Frethorne, whose 1494 will shows that he occupied a house in Broad Street, Worcester, and also held three burgages and other land in the small Gloucestershire town of Moreton-in-Marsh.[112] Urban property could be combined with rural assets. When Geoffrey Samwyse from Dorset, before his death in 1486, travelled from his house inland in Dorchester to visit his houses in the small adjacent ports of Weymouth and Melcombe Regis, he could have inspected his flock of sheep at rural Upwey, midway between the towns.[113] Sometimes the land in the countryside was held simply as an investment and rented out, but often it contributed to a townsman's business activities. Edward and William Atwell, Northampton butchers, who both died in 1485, recorded in their wills their land in nearby villages of Denton, Grafton Regis, and Eastcote, where cattle and sheep could be kept before slaughter.[114] Many wool merchants and clothiers acquired pastures on which they grazed sheep, like Thomas Mayhew, a clothier of Chew in Somerset, who left 100 sheep in 1495 as well as broadcloths, cloth-shears, and dyeing equipment.[115]

For those who divided their time between a craft or trade and agriculture, the two sources of income need not have been directly connected, but supplemented one another. William Pethode of Ringland in Norfolk wove hair cloth, used in the malting process. The contents of his shop in 1493 were valued at £8, which does not suggest manufacture on a large scale, but his three landholdings enabled him to keep two cows and 130 sheep, and had yielded 7 quarters of grain. The grain and dairy produce would have made his household almost self-sufficient in those foodstuffs, and the sheeps' wool would have been sold to provide a decent cash income.[116]

The wills and inventories confirm the message of other sources that few individuals or households pursued a single occupation. Those who had no

---

[111] Suffolk Record Office, Bury St Edmunds Branch, IC500/2/9, fo. 206.

[112] TNA: PRO, PROB 11/10, fo. 67.

[113] Ibid., PROB 11/8, fo. 28.

[114] Northamptonshire Record Office, Early Will Register, fos. 39–40.

[115] TNA: PRO, PROB 2/97; F. W. Weaver (ed.), *Somerset Medieval Wills*, Somerset Record Society, 16 (1901), 326.

[116] TNA: PRO, PROB 2/63; PROB 11/10, fo. 3.

agricultural land would involve themselves in a number of trades. Hugh Grantham, a York mason who died in 1410, bought and sold grain on a large scale, and Thomas Hunt of South Molton in Devon was, at the time of his death in 1496, a dealer in salt and iron as well as a clothier.[117]

Investment and capital assets figure in a number of wills. Townspeople refer to the buildings and structures connected to their trade, such as fulling mills, tenteryards, warehouses, and tanyards. They make clear the great contrast between most artisans' relatively cheap equipment and materials, like the tailor's tools which were valued at 11*s.* in 1485, and the £100 or £200 commonly tied up in a merchants' wares and ships that could be worth £30 and more.[118] The most valuable assets in the hands of the better-off rural testators were their flocks and herds, which could be appraised at £20 or more, and make credible the complaints in manorial court rolls that common pastures were being overburdened with 100, 200, or 300 sheep or a dozen cattle at a time.

Rural will-makers mention new buildings, like Robert Colas of Melbourn in Cambridgeshire, who when he died in 1497 had acquired timber cut for constructing a barn on a copyhold tenement.[119] Some stated that their houses and buildings were new, like William Clerk of Stratford St Mary in Suffolk, who in 1458 referred to his new house and weaving shop.[120] Both in town and country testators expressed the wish that the buildings would be kept in good repair by their successors. At this time manorial court rolls were full of complaints that customary tenants were letting their buildings fall into ruin, and lords made efforts, often fruitlessly, to push tenants to carry out repairs.[121] The wills give another picture, of new construction and tenants anxious to maintain the buildings that *they* needed, as distinct from those that their lords wished to be kept in good condition.

Those rural producers whose wills are available to us expressed their expectation that their heirs and successors would use good agricultural practices. John Petre of Melton in Suffolk, in bequeathing land to his wife in 1461, enjoined her to make sure that the land should be 'well and faithfully ploughed and sown', and others referred to the need for hedging and ditching, and the preservation of trees.[122] Again, this contrasts with the

---

[117] Raine (ed.), *Testamenta Eboracensia*, 3, pp. 47–53; TNA: PRO, PROB 11/11, fo. 99; PROB 2/106.

[118] H. Swanson, *Medieval Artisans: An Urban Class in Late Medieval England* (Oxford, 1989), 129; E. Roberts and K. Parker (eds.), *Southampton Probate Inventories 1447–1575*, Southampton Records Series, 34 (1992), 1, 2–9, shows Richard Thomas, merchant, in 1447 with an inventory worth £301, including iron worth £9. 13*s.* 0*d.*, and 'an old ship' valued at £35.

[119] TNA: PRO, PROB 11/11, fo. 121.

[120] Suffolk Record Office, Ipswich Branch, J421/2, fo. 3.

[121] *AHEW* iii. 84, 171, 606–7, 627–9.

[122] Suffolk Record Office, Ipswich Branch, J421/2, fo. 48.

complaints in court rolls of failure to plough, the neglect of ditches and hedges which blocked roads with floods and overhanging branches, and the illicit felling of trees. The wills give us a much more positive image of conscientious, or at least well intentioned, peasants and farmers. Of course the two types of evidence are not incompatible: court-roll presentments of delinquents imply a body of opinion in favour of good husbandry, and the will-makers were aware of the danger of neglect which they no doubt saw among their less responsible neighbours.

The wills make regular references to employees. For the clothiers, out-workers, such as spinners, were remembered. Living-in servants were mentioned more frequently, and were left cash, clothing, and even pieces of land. Thomas Schorthose, a weaver of Sudbury, in 1459 bequeathed household goods to a *famula* (female servant) and a loom and other equipment to an apprentice.[123] Servants formed an important part of the late medieval work-force, but their significance may be exaggerated in the wills because of the loyalty and intimacy that naturally developed between masters and employees living and working in the same household. Thomas Schorthose, for example, had no living children at the time when he made his will, and he regarded his young servant and apprentice almost as his heirs. Many of the testators, especially those who made their living in agriculture, would have commonly employed through the year labourers by the day, especially at harvest time, but they would be less likely to make bequests to such workers.

Marketing

The will-makers took the market for granted. Its constant presence was assumed, and its operations understood. Those who lived in the country showed their familiarity with towns, for example, by leaving money to friaries, which were often located in urban centres 10 or 20 miles from their homes. The clothiers of the west country knew the places where cloth could be sold or to which it would be carried, not just their local ports of Bristol or Poole, but also London. A grazier from Geddington in Northamptonshire, Henry German, left money in 1486 to all of the parish churches on the road to Royston in Hertfordshire, which was presumably the route he took in driving animals towards the capital.[124] Townspeople were anxious to maintain the roads essential for their trades, like the Sudbury man who left £10 in 1496 to repair the roads from Sudbury to another Suffolk cloth town, Nayland.[125]

---

[123] Suffolk Record Office, Bury St Edmunds Branch, IC 500/2/9, fo. 236.
[124] Northamptonshire Record Office, Early Will Register, fos. 45–6.
[125] TNA: PRO, PROB 11/11, fo. 42.

The market for land is known to historians primarily from entries in manorial court rolls and from deeds. The wills give us another perspective, as they show that the sale and purchase of land were relatively commonplace actions. Thomas Malcher of Waldingfield in Suffolk remembered in 1457 that he had bought a holding, a cottage, and various parcels in his home village, and had acquired the reversion of two holdings in Monk Illeigh. All were to be sold by his executors in order to pay for charitable bequests.[126] Other testators mentioned that some of their own properties had been purchased, partly because they adhered to the old custom that the eldest son should come into the inherited land, while the younger son would be granted the land acquired during the lifetime of his father. Joan Reynham of Nayland in Suffolk, a clothier, in 1495 was still paying the instalments of the sale price of land that she had previously purchased, and required her executors to pay a further £25. 6s. 8d. to complete the transaction.[127] Many testators needed to turn their properties into money in order to make cash bequests, often to relatives, but also for charitable purposes. Accordingly they instructed their executors to sell land, and more remarkably, they made arrangements for their sons in effect to buy their inheritance, instructing them to pay a sum of money over a number of years. So John Stodde, son and heir of William Stodde of Stonham Aspall in Suffolk, was required in 1491 to pay for his inherited land 10 marks, in instalments of 1 mark (13s. 4d.) per annum, to his mother. His elder brother, Thomas, was to pay £26. 13s. 4d. for his holding, at £1. 6s. 8d. per annum.[128]

The more detailed instructions for the sale of land tell us something about the mechanics of the process, and the profit-seeking attitudes that prevailed. Executors would be instructed, like those of Robert Rider of Peterborough in 1497, to sell land 'to the most advantage', and a Fakenham (Norfolk) woman in 1464 expected 'the best price in cash'.[129] When relatives were to be given the chance to buy, they were sometimes to be offered advantageous terms, such as 40s. below the market price, but often they were expected to meet the full price: 'Paying therefore as much money as every other man will pay.' A few Suffolk wills mention the price that was expected to be paid, between £1 and £3. 4s. 0d. per acre, which are comparable with prices occasionally recorded in manorial court rolls.[130] Prices would vary with the quality of the land and its situation, but a certain stability was expected, as one testator (at Helmingham, Suffolk, in 1495) thought that the executors would obtain

---

[126] Suffolk Record Office, Bury St Edmunds Branch, IC 500/2/9, fo. 262.

[127] TNA: PRO, PROB 11/10, fo. 217.

[128] Suffolk Record Office, Ipswich Branch, J421/3, fo. 126.

[129] TNA: PRO, PROB 11/11, fo. 168; Norfolk Record Office, NCC wills, 111 Grey.

[130] Suffolk Record Office, Ipswich Branch, J421/3, fo. 117; John Sprouce, in J421/3, fo. 104, required payment of £10. 10s. 0d. for 4 acres.

for a piece of recently acquired land the same price that he had paid for it. In renting out land the same spirit of obtaining a just market price prevailed. A Suffolk widow in 1477 was to receive 'the profit and true value' of a plot of land, and some makers of wills might specify the rent that they thought was appropriate, such as 10*d*. per acre in Cambridgeshire in 1496.[131]

Wills and inventories contain ample evidence for the goods which were bought and sold: both the surpluses of grain, animals, wool, and cheese, and the stocks of manufactured and traded goods which the will-makers sold, and the goods that they bought, notably clothing and household items, such as metal cooking vessels. The inventories give no impression of extravagant expenditure on consumer goods, but rather of modest plain living, with farm stock greatly exceeding in value the household goods and furnishings. A typical ratio is revealed by the contents of the household and farm of Henry Sperk of Bishop Burton in Yorkshire, whose domestic possessions in 1522 were worth a little less than £10, and his corn and animals just over £80.[132] Widows and other beneficiaries of bequests were expected to live on modest sums, in some cases as little as 1*d*. per day. As in the case of land, testators showed that they expected any sales of goods to operate according to the rules of the market, though at Eriswell in Suffolk a friend of the deceased was to be allowed to buy sheep 'within the just price by the judgement and discretion of the Rector and the churchwardens'.[133]

The credit system which underpinned market transactions is fully displayed in wills in the lists of debts owed by and to the testator appended to inventories, and by the anxiety of testators that debts should be settled in both directions. Some mention large sums owed to them by named individuals; others, more troubled, feared that when their obligations had been discharged there would be little left for their relatives or the pious works on which the salvation of their souls depended.[134] The more sophisticated traders, especially in towns, owned a counter in their office for keeping written records, and some mention their 'book of debts'. Many relied on memory of oral contracts. In 1489 the executors of Henry Punt of Dalbury and Littleover in Derbyshire were expected to wind up his affairs on the basis of 'debts confessed from his own mouth by the aforesaid Henry on his sick bed before his confessor and a certain notary'.[135]

---

[131] TNA: PRO, PROB 11/10, fo. 191; Suffolk Record Office, Bury St Edmunds Branch, IC 500/2/11, fo. 104; TNA: PRO, PROB 11/11, fo. 11.

[132] Borthwick Institute of Historical Research, York, D. and C. wills, 1522, Sperk.

[133] Suffolk Record Office, Bury St Edmunds Branch, IC 500/2/11, fo. 37.

[134] e.g. John Yorke of Etwall in Derbyshire in 1497 was concerned that if his executors spent too much on charity, they would 'defraud [his children] of their portions': TNA: PRO, PROB 11/11, fo. 118.

[135] Ibid., PROB 2/29.

Society

Wills tell us a great deal about social ties and obligations, in which the nuclear family of husbands, wives, and children occupied a central position. Inheritance customs allowed widows a free bench, as long as they remained single, and favoured the transmission of land eventually either to the eldest son or all of the sons in the areas of partible inheritance. Fathers and mothers were anxious to share their assets among the children, by leaving land to younger sons, or by imposing on the executors and the heir the obligation to make cash grants to their brothers and sisters. The wills support the statistics derived from the manorial court rolls in showing that families were not attached to their ancestral land by some fixed bond. They were prepared to sell the family holding, and sons were not always available to inherit, having acquired their own land elsewhere. Will-makers in towns were more likely to make reference to more remote relatives, such as nephews, and to leave money or goods to non-relatives, such as godchildren and servants.[136]

Lords do not make a prominent appearance in wills. The prosperous peasants, farmers, artisans, and traders whose wills have come down to us seem to present themselves in a position of independence. They knew that if they held customary or copyhold land certain procedures would be necessary in manor courts to accomplish their wishes, and a few refer to the need for executors to pay entry fines and to secure the court's consent for the transfer of a holding.[137] The heriot, the death duty of best beast or chattel, would have been taken before an inventory had been compiled, so there was no need to mention it. The influence of lords over the rest of society was not confined to questions of tenancy, and the will-makers reveal relationships of clientage when they appointed members of the gentry to be their overseers. This can be seen in the case of artisans and traders in the Suffolk cloth towns, such as John Barker of Long Melford, a fuller, who in 1457 named John Clopton esquire to give counsel on the sale of property.[138] Presumably the support of an influential aristocrat, who probably had legal expertise, was of great help in ensuring that the transfer was properly conducted according to the testator's wishes. This was one of the services that a 'good lord' could provide to townsmen who joined his affinity and wore his livery, as recorded in other parts of the country in the records of the royal courts and the military surveys of 1522.[139]

---

[136] D. Cressy, 'Kinship and Kin Interaction in Early Modern England', *P&P* 113 (1986), 54.

[137] Norfolk Record Office, NCC wills, 138 Typpes; in this will Thomas Wodeward of Battisford in Suffolk requires that the lord's consent is needed for a transfer.

[138] Suffolk Record Office, Bury St Edmunds Branch, IC 500/2/9, fo. 215.

[139] G. Wrottesley (ed.), *Extracts from the Plea Rolls of the Reigns of Henry V and Henry VI*, Staffordshire Historical Collections, NS, 17 (1896), 6–7, 29–32, shows Lichfield men being granted

Wills contain many expressions of support for local communities, above all by making bequests to the parish church, but also very often to fraternities. If they left money to the poor, or the upkeep of roads and bridges, or other charitable works, these were usually focused on the home parish or those in the immediate vicinity. They used the appropriate language of community— a bequest in 1489 by John Myller of Thornham Episcopi in Norfolk would be for the 'use and profit of the whole community of the vill for ever'.[140] Many bequests made to people with no stated kinship relationship suggest networks of associates, partners, and friends, many of them located within the same village or town.

At the same time testators often refer to places at some distance from their homes, with which they were acquainted through commercial contacts, or perhaps because they or relatives had moved there but kept in touch, or their wives came from a distance. John Staloun of Mildenhall in Suffolk made bequests to churches at Moulton, Newmarket, Brandon, and four other places, between 4 and 10 miles from his home. He also left money to the friars at Babwell on the fringes of Bury St Edmunds, and to a relative who was a tanner at Haverhill.[141] Movement was normal, not because poverty drove people to seek their fortune at a distance, but because migration allowed ambitious traders and farmers to hope to take advantage of opportunities.

The will-makers sometimes showed a concern for sobriety, self-discipline, and decent behaviour. John Caldewell, an Ipswich merchant, in 1460 wished that his son be 'well ruled and governed'. A servant should be 'well behaved and of good conversation, and honest to my wife and executors'. Concern was expressed that a daughter might choose a husband without seeking wise advice.[142] Many shared the widespread belief that charity would be used most effectively if it went to almshouses and churchwardens who would select recipients who were most deserving, though a good number also left money for indiscriminate distribution. Thomas Amys of Barton Turf was not un-usual in his stipulation that his charitable gift should go to those in 'most need', but he went further than most in ensuring that his gift would not be wasted, because instead of a sum of money the poor would receive at Christmas 'blankets, sheets, shirts, and smocks'.[143]

liveries by Hugh Erdeswick and other local gentry; M. A. Faraday (ed.), *Worcestershire Taxes in the 1520s*, Worcestershire Historical Society, NS, 19 (2003), 61–2, shows the numerous retainers of the marquis of Dorset in north Worcestershire.

[140] Norfolk Record Office, NCC wills, 43 Wolman.

[141] P. Northeast (ed.), *Wills of the Archdeaconry of Sudbury 1439–1474, Part 1*, Suffolk Records Society, 44 (2001), 257.

[142] Suffolk Record Office, Ipswich Branch, J421/2, fos. 87–8; Suffolk Record Office, Bury St Edmunds Branch, IC500/2/11, fos. 2, 104.

[143] TNA: PRO, PROB 11/10, fo. 224.

The testators' beliefs and attitudes were not just formed by oral tradition, sermons, performances of religious drama, images on church walls, and word of mouth. A few, like a farmer of Chipping Campden in Gloucestershire, in 1488 owned a book, the *Golden Legend* in English, and presumably quite fresh from the printing press. Stephen Smyth of West Mersea in Essex in 1492 more conventionally owned a number of service books. Thomas Aysheley of Wickham Market in Suffolk in 1492 believed that literacy was a useful preparation for life as a small-town tradesman, and advised his wife to keep their three sons at school until they could read and write, and be 'able to set at crafts'.[144]

Conclusion

The indestructible aristocracy were not ruined by the economic trends of the later middle ages, but their wealth was eroded and their coercive power diminished. Elements within the gentry adapted to market conditions and developed new styles of production, but this was an influential movement rather than a decisive change. The state was shaken but not seriously damaged by political upheavals, including the English defeat in the Hundred Years War and the internal upheaval of the Wars of the Roses. Unified institutions made England a single market, with a relatively stable economic environment.

When we first glimpse the activities and sentiments of the section of English society below the gentry from their probate records, we are observing a well-established section of society who had played an important economic role well before the mid-fifteenth century. A brief overview cannot do justice to the complexity of this previously hidden group of people. The plurality of their existence must be emphasized, in their landholding, occupations, and connections to town and country. They cannot be easily pigeon-holed, but they had in common their reliance on the market, their attachment to families and communities, and their social attitudes which, if expressed in the seventeenth century, would be labelled 'puritan'. The sources from which the fifteenth-century economy is usually depicted tell us of physical decay, recession, and social fragmentation. In the will-makers' world new buildings were being constructed, land was being carefully cultivated, money was being made, families looked after their members, villages came together in parish churches and guildhalls, but at the same time had horizons well beyond their place of residence. Lords were shadowy figures, of no great significance to these workers and traders who pursued their own lives.

---

[144] TNA: PRO, PROB 11/8, fo. 120; PROB 2/21; PROB11/10, fos. 261, 137.

4

Consumption and Investment

The study of consumption in the middle ages is a relatively new field of enquiry; it repays investigation because it tells us about material conditions, levels of individual wealth, the dynamic forces behind production, and mentalities. In this chapter I have linked consumption and investment, partly so that I can consider the relative importance of these rival claims on resources, but also because investment was closely linked to the demand for consumer goods.

Consumption in Modern Times—A Standard of Comparison

Consumption has been studied by anthropologists and sociologists who specialize in field of material culture, as well as historians.[1] Much of the enquiry into material culture in the later middle ages has been advanced by archaeological research into structures and artefacts.

A well-known and thoroughly researched episode in the history of modern consumption has been the identification in the eighteenth century of a 'consumer revolution'.[2] There are four principal elements in the interpretation of economic behaviour in the period leading up to the industrial revolution.

---

[1] G. McCracken, *Culture and Consumption: New Approaches to the Symbolic Character of Consumer Goods and Activities* (Bloomington and Indianapolis, 1990); D. Miller (ed.), *Acknowledging Consumption* (London, 1990); M. Douglas and B. Isherwood, *The World of Goods: Towards an Anthropology of Consumption* (London, 1996).

[2] N. McKendrick, J. Brewer, and J. H. Plumb, *The Birth of a Consumer Society: The Consumer in Eighteenth-Century England* (London, 1982); L. Weatherill, *Consumer Behaviour and Material Culture in Britain, 1660–1760* (London, 1988); C. Shammas, *The Preindustrial Consumer in England and America* (Oxford, 1990); J. Brewer and R. Porter (eds.), *Consumption and the World of Goods* (London, 1993).

First, it is argued that in the early eighteenth century or in the decades before 1700 incomes rose, for example, among London merchants and artisans. Household earnings (that is, the income of the whole family including women and children) were enhanced by the 'industrious revolution' and the high levels of employment which have been identified in this period.[3] The changes in agricultural methods and consequently lower prices of farm produce reduced the proportion of household budgets which was spent on food, leaving money to spare for manufactured goods. Secondly, the old hierarchies were eroded by a new phase of social mobility. Former subordinate groups became wealthier, and in an atmosphere of social competition sought to emulate the style of life of their superiors. They bought fine clothes, furniture, utensils, and ornaments. Ordinary houses were provided with clocks and mirrors. The urban upper middle class looked to the aristocracy for models. Farmers sought to live like gentlemen, and artisans imitated merchants. The old elites, anxious to differentiate themselves, adopted different styles, and acquired even more luxurious goods which were beyond the reach of the aspiring lower ranks.[4] Thirdly, the merchants and manufacturers stimulated demand by making available more luxury goods, such as textiles and furnishings, and they imported greater quantities of the commodities associated with the new styles of life, such as tea, coffee, and chocolate. Fourthly, the new consumerism, linked with a stronger sense of individualism and privacy, was fuelled by innovation and rapid change. Fashion, advertising, and new-style shops developed, which helped to mould and develop demand and consumer choice.

The advocates of this interpretation of the eighteenth century are not just seeking to explain an upswing in the trade cycle, but rather to identify a structural change in demand which made a permanent difference to the future development of society and economy. The concepts of a 'consumer society' and a 'consumer revolution' in the eighteenth century have encountered some criticisms and revisions, such as doubts about whether wealth and incomes were rising in the manner that is assumed, and the notion of an 'industrious revolution' has attracted some scepticism.[5] But these debates do not concern us directly, as our main interest is the relevance of the consumer-revolution model for the later middle ages. The historians of the eighteenth century who believe that they are dealing with an entirely new phenomenon

---

[3] J. de Vries, 'Between Purchasing Power and the World of Goods: Understanding the Household Economy in Early Modern Europe', in Brewer and Porter (eds.), *Consumption and the World of Goods*, 85–133.

[4] D. Miller, *Material Culture and Mass Consumption* (Oxford, 1987), 134–42; McCracken, *Culture and Consumption*, 13–15.

[5] B. Fine and E. Leopold, *The World of Consumption* (London, 1993), 74–84, 128–37.

naturally tend to play down its antecedents, even within the modern period, and some of them are typically scathing about the puny level of consumer demand before 1500, one of them referring to the 'medieval void' in the history of consumption, and another commenting on the 'remarkably few personal possessions' owned by medieval people.[6] One researcher has noted the much wider range of items listed in probate inventories after *c*.1540, when compared with the 'principal goods' compiled in *c*.1350–1440 by manorial lords seeking to maintain the assets on customary peasant holdings. This suggests a great expansion in material wealth between the fifteenth and sixteenth centuries.[7] The manorial lists, however, had their own specialized purpose, which led to a concentration on such items as ploughs, carts, and metal cooking pots, and excluded the smaller and cheaper implements and furnishings which fell within the scope of those writing inventories.

Consumption in the Later Middle Ages

There is no value in announcing yet another revolution, but we can recognize consumerism in the middle ages, and identify episodes and characteristics in the material culture of our period which have some similarity with those of the eighteenth century. The argument will be advanced here that consumption changed significantly in the later middle ages, and this led to new patterns in the acquisition and use of material goods, which had a wider impact on the whole economy.

Incomes and Expenditure

The first characteristic of the period 1375–1520 which bears a resemblance to the tendencies of the consumer revolution is the increase in spending power. Beginning with the late medieval wage-earners, rising wage rates reflected the scarcity of labour in a period of continued demand, especially after legal restraints faded into insignificance in the thirty years after the Statute of Labourers in 1351. An unskilled labourer obtained 4*d*. per day in the late fifteenth century, compared with a penny 200 years earlier. Between 1300 and 1480 a craftsman's wage in the south of England rose from just below 3*d*.

---

[6] Brewer and Porter (eds.), *Consumption and the World of Goods*, 1; Miller, *Material Culture*, 136.
[7] C. Muldrew, *The Economy of Obligation: The Culture of Credit and Social Relations in Early Modern England* (London, 1998), 24–8; R. K. Field, 'Worcestershire Peasant Buildings, Household Goods and Farming Equipment in the Later Middle Ages', *MA* 9 (1965), 121–5, 137–45; P. Hargreaves, 'Seignorial Reaction and Peasant Responses: Worcester Priory and Its Peasants After the Black Death', *Midland History*, 24 (1999), 60–2.

per day to 6*d*. or more. The reduced and steady grain prices meant that real wages were at least three times higher in the late fifteenth century compared with the period around 1300.[8] High daily wages would not necessarily lead directly to a comparable increase in earnings, because of the tendency for people who had been paid well for a few days' work to be satisfied with the money that they had obtained and take a rest.[9] This is a large issue to which I will return, but let it be sufficient here to say that evidence for the involvement of women in the labour force is one reason for suggesting that households were apparently maximizing their incomes at this time.[10] We should envisage the possibility that in about 1500 a labourer's family with two able-bodied parents and a teenage child could have received an income for part of the year of 8*d*. per day.

Peasants' incomes were adversely affected by the reduced price of grain, so that although they could provide their households with ample supplies of basic foodstuffs, their cash surplus in the market was being eroded. They could also be disadvantaged by the higher cost of hired labour, which tenants even of modest holdings of 15 acres would need for peak seasonal tasks, and which would be used on a more continuous and permanent basis for peasants with larger accumulations of land. On the other hand, many peasants increased the quantity of land under their management, so that in much of the midlands, south, and the north-east those with 15 acres formed a relatively poor minority, whereas in the late thirteenth century they lay near the centre of the social spectrum. They could also offset the impact of low prices and high wages by using a higher proportion of their land as pasture, thereby increasing their production of wool, cheese, butter, and animals, the prices of which tended to hold up better than grain. They could, by keeping more animals and growing less corn, economize on hired labour.[11] In addition, they had more opportunities to supplement their incomes from industrial employment, especially through the earnings of women, so peasant households with two female members might be gaining as much from spinning as from wool or bacon production. John Rede of Soham in Cambridgeshire in 1417 owned as his principal agricultural asset a flock of at least 140 sheep, but in his parlour, presumably for use by his wife, was a

---

[8] *AHEW* ii. 760–79; iii. 467–94.

[9] e.g. G. Persson, 'Consumption, Labour and Leisure in the Late Middle Ages', in D. Menjot (ed.), *Manger et boire au moyen âge* (Nice, 1984), 211–23.

[10] P. J. P. Goldberg, *Women, Work, and Life Cycle in a Medieval Economy: Women in York and Yorkshire c.1300–1520* (Oxford, 1992), 82–157.

[11] C. Dyer, *Standards of Living in the Later Middle Ages: Social Change in England c.1200–1520*, revised edn. (Cambridge, 1998), 140–50, though this made some dubious assumptions about trends in grain yields. The consensus now is that yields probably fell after 1400 because of the reduction in labour inputs.

spinning-wheel and 4 lbs of flax ready for spinning into thread.[12] At a higher level of rural wealth were the farmers and graziers, who appear as new large-scale producers from around 1400. While a moderately prosperous peasant like Rede had an inventory of goods, money, and debts owed to him worth £11. 10s., a farmer of a demesne could have possessions valued at £150.[13]

Urban incomes present us with a wide range of experiences. Merchants had gained a larger share of overseas trade in the fourteenth century, and continued thereafter to obtain high profits from exporting wool and cloth and the distribution of imports. They went through many short-term ups and downs in the trade, notably the depression of the mid-fifteenth century.[14] The only direct attempt to calculate merchants' wealth has indicated that in the fifteenth century northern merchants, from York, Beverley, and Hull, had their incomes reduced, which can mainly be attributed to the concentration of trade in the hands of the London exporters, and to the rise of the West Riding cloth-makers.[15] In other words, mercantile wealth was being redistributed from one group to another, and the class as a whole was not necessarily losing income. Urban artisans sometimes suffered from rural competition in cloth-making, but in terms of the incomes of artisans over the whole country, by the early sixteenth century increased numbers of quite prosperous rural weavers, fullers, and shearmen represented a net gain. Half of the urban population lived in small towns, those with fewer than 2,000 inhabitants, and though individual towns often housed fewer people in 1500 than they had done in 1300, most market towns continued to function as centres for rural hinterlands, and their traders and craftsmen derived some benefit from the larger holdings and higher wages of their customers.[16] Sometimes they found a niche that gave them a wide hinterland for a specialist product, like the scythe-blades made in Birmingham, the horse-bits from Walsall, or the knives of Thaxted.[17]

---

[12] TNA: PRO, PROB 2/1.

[13] Ibid., PROB 2/457 (Roger Heritage, farmer of Burton Dassett, Warwickshire: the sum of £150 includes debts owed to him).

[14] The precariousness of merchant fortunes is vividly presented by P. Nightingale, *A Medieval Mercantile Community: The Grocers' Company and the Politics and Trade of London, 1000–1485* (New Haven and London, 1995), 371–2, 395–8, 441–6, 469–88, 545–6.

[15] J. Kermode, *Medieval Merchants: York, Beverley and Hull in the Later Middle Ages* (Cambridge, 1998), 305–22.

[16] C. Dyer, *Bromsgrove: A Small Town in Worcestershire in the Middle Ages*, Worcestershire Historical Society, Occasional Publications, 9 (2000), 55–6.

[17] R. Holt, *The Early History of the Town of Birmingham 1166 to 1600*, Dugdale Society Occasional Papers, 30 (1985), 18–21; *VCH Cheshire*, v. pt. 1, 66; C. Dyer, 'The Urbanizing of Staffordshire: The First Phases', *Staffordshire Studies*, 14 (2002), 20; D. Keene, 'Small Towns and the Metropolis: The Experience of Medieval England', in J.-M. Duvosquel and E. Thoen (eds.), *Peasants and Townsmen in Medieval Europe: Studies in Honorem Adriaan Verhulst* (Ghent, 1995), 234–6.

The aristocracy's incomes were reduced as rents declined. The land was constantly redistributed as families died out, contracted marriages, and bought and sold land. Some of them were able to supplement their landed income from service, war, and the law, but these employments were not entirely new. So while fresh names appear with increased spending power, the aristocracy as a whole lost income until the first half of the sixteenth century, when they could take advantage of an upturn in land values.[18]

Clearly we are dealing with a mixed picture, but we can in general say that while a section of the elite, especially those dependent on land, experienced a decline in income at this time, the lower ranks of society, and not just the wage-earners, enjoyed an increase in their spending power.

The pattern of consumption of foodstuffs and manufactured goods changed decisively after the Black Death. Expenditure on food per head of the mass of the population increased. Calculations from the late fourteenth and fifteenth centuries show that contemporaries reckoned that an adult could be fed on a penny per day, which is probably more than double the cost of feeding labourers in about 1300.[19] A higher proportion of cereals was consumed as bread rather than in some form of boiled pottage. Bread was baked more often from wheat instead of rye or barley. More meat was eaten and ale drunk. More of the meat and fish was fresh, not salted. The ale was more frequently brewed from barley malt, rather than malt made from oats.[20] These changes can partly be traced from direct evidence for food consumption, and partly from the shifts in production that reflected demand, such as the increase in barley acreage in the late fourteenth century to provide for the increased sales of brewing corn.[21] The superior diet of artisans can be appreciated from the example of building workers recorded between 1377 and 1440 (Table 4.1). The meals provided by their employers can be analysed through expenditure on different types of foodstuff, and this reveals a diet containing a very high proportion (between a third and a half by value) of fish and meat and also a prodigious quantity of ale. This combination of food and drink resembles the diet of early fifteenth-century harvest workers in Norfolk,

---

[18] *AHEW* iii. 580–6.

[19] S. Thrupp, *Merchant Class of Medieval London (1300–1500)* (Ann Arbor, 1948), 142 n.; in his will of 1462 Roger Smethis of South Elmham, Suffolk, left Isabella his wife 26s. 8d. per annum, if she did not wish to live with John, Roger's son: Norfolk Record Office, NCC wills, 2, 3 Cobald. Elena Godesday of Brenchley, Kent, was also to be paid 26s. 8d. per annum, with accommodation in a house: Centre for Kentish Studies, Maidstone, DR6/P Wr 2, fo. 4.

[20] C. Dyer, 'Did the Peasants Really Starve in Medieval England?', in M. Carlin and J. T. Rosenthal (eds.), *Food and Eating in Medieval Europe* (London, 1998), 67–9.

[21] J. A. Galloway, 'Driven By Drink? Ale Consumption and the Agrarian Economy of the London Region, c.1300–1400', in Carlin and Rosenthal (eds.), *Food and Eating*, 87–100; B. M. S. Campbell, 'Matching Supply to Demand: Crop Production and Disposal by English Demesnes in the Century of the Black Death', *Journal of Economic History*, 57 (1997), 835–9.

except that in the harvest field more cheese was provided, and an even higher share of expenditure went on ale. Harvest workers a century earlier were issued with a much smaller proportion of ale, meat, and fish, and we must assume that the same was true of skilled building artisans at that time.

People could afford this more varied, nutritious, and pleasurable diet partly because the prices of basic cereals after 1375 remained quite low, and instability in prices was reduced. The threat of bad harvests and food shortages receded. A serious famine threatened only once between 1375 and 1520, in the late 1430s, and the occasional seriously deficient harvests, which had been frequent in the fourteenth century, became quite rare between 1440 and 1520.[22]

A labourer's family in the fifteenth century could have fed itself according to the new standard for 3*d.* per day, and family earnings, as we have seen, could have exceeded 6*d.* per day, so they had some spare cash for housing, clothing, and manufactured goods.[23] The opportunity to spend on goods other than food must have been shared by a wide section of the lower ranks of society.

The total number of consumers had halved during the fourteenth century, from 5–6 million to 2.5 million, but as each household could afford to buy more goods, global consumption fell by much less than a half, and in cases such as meat or cloth the total may well have increased. A reduced number of traders and artisans were kept busy supplying the demand, and their increased workload brought them higher incomes. The proportion of the population living in towns probably remained stable, or may even have increased a little. The numbers working in industry, especially in rural cloth-making, rose to satisfy the known growth in the export market, and an assumed expansion in domestic demand.[24]

Social Mobility and Emulation

The advocates of the eighteenth-century consumer revolution suggest that a more competitive society helped to create demand, as the lower orders advanced themselves by emulating their superiors. Now historians of late medieval society are only too familiar with this tendency, as so many contemporaries complained that wage-earners in particular were subverting the social hierarchy by eating and dressing above the accustomed standard of their status group. The issue was raised in the poem *Winner and Waster*, conventionally dated to the 1350s, and was addressed two or three decades later in *Piers Plowman*; it provoked typical moral indignation from

[22] Dyer, *Standards of Living*, 261–8.

[23] Shakespeare Birthplace Trust Records Office, Stratford-upon-Avon, BRT/1/3/40.

[24] C. Dyer, 'How Urbanized Was Medieval England?', in Duvosquel and Thoen (eds.), *Peasants and Townsmen*, 169–83.

Table 4.1. Expenditure on meals given to building workers, 1377–1440 (with some comparisons)

	Bread	Ale	Fish and meat	Vegetables, oatmeal, salt, mustard, oil, butter, cheese	Total
Stratford-upon-Avon (Warwicks.), 1431					
Money	10s. 4d.	14s. 7d.	17s. 5½d.	2s. 3½d.	44s. 8d.
%	23	33	39	5	100
Wyre Piddle (Worcs.), 1377–8					
Money	2s. 0d.	2s. 0d.	2s. 4d.	0s. 8d.	7s. 0d.
%	29	29	33	9	100
Sherborne (Dorset), 1439–40					
Money	4s. 0d.	6s. 4½d.	10s. 7½d.	0s. 10d.	21s. 10d.
%	18	29	49	4	100
Harvest workers, 1424					
%	15	41	34	10	100
Harvest workers, 1326					
%	39	17	21	23	100
Bridport priests, 1456–7					
%	26	27	41	6	100
Luttrells, 1425–6 (with wine)				(wine)	
%	16	23	35	3	23	100
Luttrells, 1425–6 (without wine)					
%	21	29	46	4		100

Note: All percentages are based on expenditure, or the valuation of food.
Sources: T. H. Lloyd, 'The Medieval Gilds of Stratford-upon-Avon and the Timber-Framed Building Industry', University of Birmingham, MA thesis (1961), 228–31; TNA: PRO, SC6/1071/5; Dorset Record Office, D204/A14; Dyer, 'Changes in Diet', 82; id., *Standards of Living*, 56.

John Gower. Chaucer, with characteristic irony, described urban artisans, a carpenter, weaver, and dyer whose knife scabbards were trimmed with chapes made from silver, not brass, and who wore high-quality girdles and pouches; their wives lived in the hope of being addressed as 'madam', if the husband should become an alderman.[25] The wearing of inappropriately expensive

[25] S. Trigg (ed.), *Wynnere and Wastoure*, Early English Text Society, 297 (1990), 13 (ll. 37–80); G. Kane (ed.), *Piers Plowman: The A Version. Will's Visions of Piers Plowman and Do-Well* (London, 1960), 344–5 (ll. 287–95); E. W. Stockton (ed.), *The Major Latin Works of John Gower* (Seattle, 1962), 210; L. D. Benson (ed.), *The Riverside Chaucer* (Oxford, 1988), 29 (ll.361–78).

clothes was the subject of failed legislation in 1363, and in 1406 it was said that country people were taking jobs in towns 'for pride of clothing'.[26]

The elite responded by making moves to differentiate themselves from the aspiring lower orders. For example, before 1400 the fur most commonly worn was that of squirrels from northern Europe. By the fifteenth century, however, artisans' wives were acquiring garments lined with squirrel skins. As that type of fur, therefore, lost its exclusive status, it was worn less often by the royal court and the upper classes in general. The wealthiest consumers opted for extremely luxurious sable and marten fur, which no artisan could possibly afford.[27]

While wage-earners, peasants, and artisans were buying more food and clothing than their predecessors had done, were they motivated by emulation? In making their choices in consumption, did they imitate models provided by their superiors? This is not easily answered. It would be true to say that their new diet, with its high proportion of meat and fish, increased quantity of ale, and greater opportunity to eat white wheat bread and ale brewed from barley malt brought the lower classes nearer to the daily fare served in aristocratic households. Members of such households had consistently, throughout the whole period 1200–1500, been allowed each day a pound or two of white bread, a gallon of ale, and between one and two pounds of meat or fish.[28] A precise comparison can be made between the food and drink of building workers and the diet of clerical and gentry households (Table 4.1). The artisans enjoyed a diet which was statistically very similar to that consumed by chantry priests at Bridport, Dorset, in 1456–7. A knightly household, that of the Luttrells of Dunster in Somerset, was distinguished by its high proportion of spending on wine, and if that factor is taken out of the calculation, the balance of expenditure on the diet of the knight and his servants was not markedly different from that of the artisans, though no doubt the portions were larger and the cooking more elaborate.

But perhaps the preferences for a high-protein diet with wheat bread and ample alcoholic drink cannot be attached to a particular social class—white wheat bread for example was palatable, with an attractive appearance, texture, and flavour, and was also easily digestible, which has made it preferred by almost all consumers until recent times. A more precise imitation of aristocratic styles of eating can be seen in the occasional grand meals which better-off peasants organized for weddings and funerals, when venison, wine, or

---

[26] *Statutes of the Realm*, 11 vols., Record Commission (1810–28), i. 380–3; ii. 157.

[27] E. Veale, *The English Fur Trade in the Later Middle Ages* (Oxford, 1966), 134–41.

[28] C. M. Woolgar, *The Great Household in Late Medieval England* (New Haven and London, 1999), 124–7; B. Harvey, *Living and Dying in England 1100–1540* (Oxford, 1993), 51, 55–6, 58–9.

spices were served.[29] Urban artisans who belonged to fraternities would similarly attend an annual feast at which the ingredients of aristocratic meals, including spices such as ginger and pepper, were used for the sauces to accompany such high-status meats as veal and goose, and wine was drunk. The fraternity at Stratford-upon-Avon in the early fifteenth century ensured the authenticity of the meals by hiring cooks who had worked in gentry households. Not just the food but the whole occasion followed aristocratic models. The diners sat in hierarchical order, with the elite on a dais at the end of the hall, and they were entertained by minstrels.[30] A clue to the influence of aristocratic food preparation on peasant households comes from their possession of stone mortars, which were appropriate for a specific style of cooking, such as the grinding of meat for dishes such as mortrews and tartlets.[31]

The most remarkable example of the downward diffusion of aristocratic style, driven by the aspirations of the lower ranks of society, is provided by the adoption in the 1340s by the courtly elite of short, close-fitting clothes, which then spread to the rest of society in the next few decades.[32] The transmission probably did not work by direct imitation of the dress of the local lord by peasants and labourers, but rather by the new fashion's being adopted first by townspeople, and encountered by the rural population on their regular visits to markets. The key figures in spreading new forms of dress must have been the tailors, who were numerous in large cities such as York, and were present throughout the country in small towns and occasionally in rural settings.[33]

The naming of the main rooms of peasant houses as 'hall' and 'chamber', with 'speres' at the end of the hall marking the passage through the house between opposed doorways, may seem to us a little incongruous and pretentious. How could a small room, measuring perhaps 15 feet by 15 feet, or at

[29] A. Watkins, 'The Woodland Economy of the Forest of Arden in the Later Middle Ages', *Midland History*, 18 (1993), 23; Borthwick Institute of Historical Research, York, D. and C. wills 1468, Hall (wine worth 12*d.* was bought for the funeral of John Hall of Holgate, husbandman); occasional peasant purchases of spices can be deduced from the presence of spicers in small market towns which catered mainly for the consumption needs of those below the gentry, e.g. Dyer, *Bromsgrove*, 33.
[30] G. Rosser, 'Going To the Fraternity Feast: Commensality and Social Relations in Late Medieval England', *Journal of British Studies*, 33 (1994), 430–46; [W. J. Hardy] (ed.), *Stratford-on-Avon Corporation Records: The Guild Accounts* (Stratford-upon-Avon, 1880), 8–10, 12–19.
[31] D. D. Andrews and G. Milne (eds.), *Wharram: A Study of Settlement on the Yorkshire Wolds*, Society for Medieval Archaeology Monograph, 8 (1979), 127–8; C. B. Hieatt and S. Butler (eds.), *Curye on Inglysch: English Culinary Manuscripts of the Fourteenth Century*, Early English Text Society, special ser., 8 (1985), 84, 89, 137.
[32] F. Piponnier and P. Mane, *Dress in the Middle Ages* (New Haven and London, 1997), 65–70, 86–9; S. M. Newton, *Fashion in the Age of the Black Prince* (Woodbridge, 1980), 6–13.
[33] Piponnier and Mane, *Dress*, 28–31; H. Swanson, *Medieval Artisans: An Urban Class in Late Medieval England* (Oxford, 1989), 45–50.

Fig. 4.1. House at Tyddyn Llwydion, Pennant Melangell (Montgomeryshire). This house, which was built from timbers felled in 1554, resembles many built in the western part of England and eastern Wales in the fifteenth and early sixteenth centuries. It has low stone foundations, and a timber frame based on five pairs of crucks. The hall was heated by an open hearth, and there were three other rooms. That to the right of the hall was a chamber or parlour.

Source: W. J. Britnell and R. Suggett, 'A Sixteenth-Century Hallhouse in Powys: Survey and Excavation of Tyddyn Llwydion, Pennant Melangell, Montgomeryshire', *Archaeological Journal*, 159 (2002), 142–69.

most 30 feet by 15 feet, though called a hall, possibly resemble the great public spaces of a castle or manor house? There can be no doubt that hall and chamber were the words current among the peasants themselves, as they were consistently employed in manorial courts and wills, and must reflect the prevailing vocabulary in the villages (Fig. 4.1). The use of the word hall allowed Chaucer to comment ironically in his description of a poor widow's house on the contrast between the grandeur of the concept and the 'narrow cottage' to which it belonged.[34] Peasants appear to have expressed through their possession of a hall their aspiration to a style of life resembling that of the aristocracy. The ground-plans of houses at both ends of the social scale had developed simultaneously before 1300 (see pp. 52–3). In occupying his or her hall the peasant was echoing, however faintly, the hierarchy and formality of the manor house. Peasant houses before the sixteenth century

[34] Benson (ed.), *Chaucer*, 253 (l. 2832).

were commonly furnished with a single chair, on which the male head of household sat at meals at the head of the table, while his wife, children, and any servant whom he employed occupied benches beside the table.[35] Even households based on a few acres of land owned a tablecloth, and we should imagine, therefore, that the table was set out in preparation for the meal in a dignified fashion. Better-off peasants possessed metal basins and ewers, like John atte Wall, who died at Leigh in Worcestershire in 1394, holding about 75 acres of land. His basin and ewer were valued at 12*d.*, and he also owned a towel, which suggests that meals were preceded with hand-washing, bringing a little refinement and ceremony into the household routine.[36]

Towns exercised a powerful influence on the architecture of rural houses, as the routine construction of two-storey dwellings began in towns from the twelfth century and spread into the countryside in the fourteenth and fifteenth.[37] The impact of urban styles was felt earliest and most strongly in the south-east with its 'wealden' house, consisting of an unceiled open hall, flanked on one or both ends by two storey structures, with chambers on the first floor (Fig. 4.2). Eventually, ahead of the aristocracy, peasants developed houses without an open hall, with two storeys throughout, again in line with urban trends.[38] The rural adoption of the jetty demonstrates conclusively that peasant houses were imitating urban designs. The jetty, by which the upper floor juts out by two or three feet beyond the wall of the ground floor, most commonly at the front of the house, had a practical function in a crowded urban street, providing extra floor area for the upper storeys without encroaching into public space at street level. In the country, where there were no constraints from narrow burgage plots, the jetty was adopted primarily for reasons of style. Jettied houses showed to their neighbours and visitors that their owners were sophisticated and in touch with urban fashion.

Not every change in material culture resulted from downward transmission through social ranks, or lateral influence from town to country. Peasants showed a degree of self-confidence, adopted their own way of life, and developed their own culture. A peasant settlement consisted commonly of tofts, a grouping of enclosures to contain buildings. The toft, with its arrangement of house and buildings for food-preparation and agriculture, often placed around a yard, and associated with a garden, animal pens, ricks, and dunghills, provided a practical combination of living and working

[35] Field, 'Worcestershire Peasant Buildings', 138; Borthwick Institute of Historical Research, York, D. and C. wills, 1468, Hall; 1481, Akclum; 1494, Gaythird.

[36] Field, 'Worcestershire Peasant Buildings', 142–3.

[37] S. Pearson, 'Rural and Urban Houses 1100–1500: "Urban Adaptation" Reconsidered', in K. Giles and C. Dyer (eds.), *Town and Country in the Middle Ages: Contrasts, Contacts and Interconnections, 1100–1500*, Society for Medieval Archaeology Monograph, 22 (2005), 40–60.

[38] J. Grenville, *Medieval Housing* (London, 1997), 151–6.

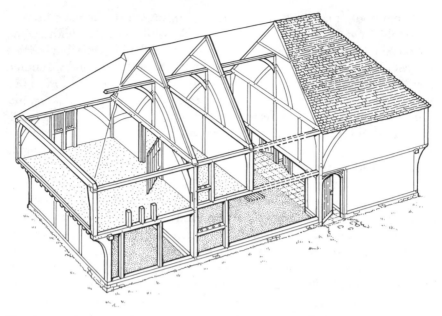

Fig. 4.2. Little Bursted farmhouse at Upper Hardres (Kent), a wealden house, which probably dates from 1500–30. Like many wealden houses it has two storeys at each end, with a hall in the middle open to the rafters with an open hearth. A less typical feature is the extra room on the first floor jutting into the hall, providing the inhabitants with six rooms rather then the customary five. Both ends of the house were jettied, so that the upper storey overhangs the lower.

Source: S. Pearson, *The Medieval Houses of Kent: An Historical Analysis*, Royal Commission on the Historical Monuments of England (1994), 110, 151; P. S. Barnwell and A. T. Adams, *The House Within: Interpreting Medieval Houses in Kent*, Royal Commission on the Historical Monuments of England (1994), 130.

space.[39] Public buildings in the village, such as the guildhall and the church house, expressed in material form the commitment of the peasantry to a collective life.[40] Competitiveness within the village encouraged some display of status. The jetty has already been mentioned as an indicator of 'modernity', to which could be added the plentiful display of timber in the 'close studding' of the front of a house as a signal of the wealth of the builder. Once inside the

---

[39] G. G. Astill, 'Rural Settlement: The Toft and the Croft', in G. Astill and A. Grant (eds.), *The Countryside of Medieval England* (Oxford, 1988), 51–60.

[40] K. Farnhill, *Guilds and the Parish Community in Late Medieval East Anglia, c.1470–1550* (York, 2001), 94; E. H. D. Williams, 'Church Houses in Somerset', *Vernacular Architecture*, 23 (1992), 15–23.

hall, visitors would be impressed by decorative carved timbers, features which are found as far apart as north Wales and the weald of Kent.[41]

Consumer-oriented Production

In the eighteenth-century consumer revolution, in addition to social competition among the consumers, the producers stimulated demand by developing and making available new commodities.

The overall demand for aristocratic building did not increase in the late fourteenth and fifteenth centuries. Surveys of manor houses in Northamptonshire and Oxfordshire show that new building projects were more numerous in the thirteenth and fourteenth centuries, with a distinct drop in 'starts' in the fifteenth century. A larger sample covering the whole country, and based on precise scientific tree-ring dates from structural timbers, suggests a peak of new construction in the first third of the fourteenth century, and then a decline from which numbers recovered during the mid- to late fifteenth century.[42] New buildings followed distinct trends in accommodation and in style. The design of castles emphasized convenient space for a household and an impressive exterior. Standards of comfort increased with the number of smaller rooms, provision of heated lodgings, and the fitting of larger glazed windows. The builders (the key figures here being the master masons) could offer their clients houses with a more ornamental appearance, such as the new styles in brick with patterns picked out in different colours. The castle would be conceived as part of a designed landscape, surrounded by pools, and gardens with walkways and 'herbers' which offered pleasure and beauty.[43]

Craftsmen aimed to profit from the rising spending power among lower-class consumers. Metalworkers developed techniques of increasing output, which cannot be described precisely as mass production, but used multiple moulds to cast dozens of identical belt-buckles and dress accessories in a single operation (Fig. 4.3).[44] They aimed to produce showy, though still quite cheap, fittings and ornaments from lead, tin, and pewter rather than copper

[41] R. Suggett, 'The Chronology of Late-Medieval Timber Houses in Wales', *Vernacular Architecture*, 27 (1996), 28–35, esp. 33–4; S. Pearson, *The Medieval Houses of Kent: An Historical Analysis*, Royal Commission on the Historical Monuments of England (1994), 90–101.

[42] C. R. J. Currie, 'Larger Medieval Houses in the Vale of White Horse', *Oxoniensia*, 57 (1992), 81–244; S. Pearson, 'The Chronological Distribution of Tree-ring Dates, 1980–2001: An Update', *Vernacular Architecture*, 32 (2001), 68–9.

[43] M. W. Thompson, *The Decline of the Castle* (Cambridge, 1987), 71–102; C. Taylor *et al.*, 'Bodiam Castle, Sussex', *MA* 34 (1990), 155–7; M. Johnson, *Behind the Castle Gate: From Medieval to Renaissance* (London, 2002), 19–54.

[44] G. Egan and F. Pritchard, *Dress Accessories, c.1150–c.1450*, Medieval Finds From Excavations in London, 3 (1991), 18–20, 122–3.

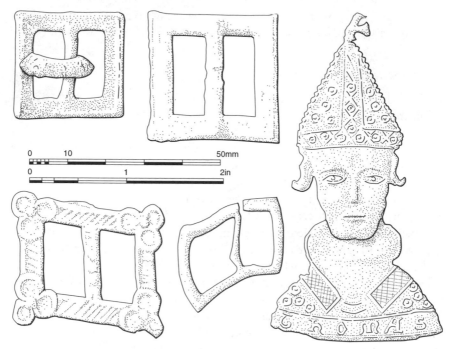

Fig. 4.3. Cast metal buckles from excavations in London, and a pilgrim badge of the head of St Thomas of Canterbury from Salisbury (Wilts.). These lead/tin alloy objects were probably made in the fifteenth century.

Source: see nn. 44 and 45.

alloys. The lower melting point of the metals allowed more rapid and cheap manufacture, and the objects when new had an attractive silvery appearance. The products were not always finished with great care (for example, the pieces of waste metal from the casting process might not be filed away), and the buckles and other functional objects were not very durable, suggesting that the customers were not discerning. One specialist product of the cheap metal-casting industry, pilgrim badges, were sold in large numbers, allowing the wearers not just to decorate their hat or clothing, but also to proclaim their piety and ability to travel to far-off places.[45]

These inexpensive dress fittings were aimed at a wide market, including wage-earners. More costly products were the pewter tablewares which are sometimes recorded as being produced and sold in market towns with

[45] B. Spencer, *Pilgrim Souvenirs and Secular Badges*, Salisbury Museum Medieval Catalogue, 2 (1990), 6–94.

hinterlands in which the main demand came from peasants and artisans, such as Eynsham in Oxfordshire.[46] The gentry equipped their households with dozens of pewter vessels and at least a few silver plates, saucers, and cups. Artisans and peasants by *c*.1500 not uncommonly owned a dozen or half-dozen pewter plates.[47] One of the attractions of pewter lay in its aristocratic associations, and its superficial resemblance to silver, hence the custom of calling it 'counterfeit'. Those below the gentry could not usually afford silver plate, but they could hope to buy a few silver spoons which, judging from references in wills, they regarded with great pride as symbols of their success.[48]

The ceramic pottery industry catered for a very wide market, and its wares were bought in varying quantities by every household. The potters worked mainly in the countryside, where fuel, clay, and labour were easily obtainable. Under a variety of pressures in the fourteenth and fifteenth centuries, including the need for economies of scale and efficient marketing networks, the industry became concentrated in a limited number of manufacturing centres.[49] Ceramic pots faced competition from industries using more durable materials, notably brass cooking pots and pans, which led to the production of forms imitating cast-metal vessels. On the other hand, especially in the fifteenth century, ceramics could enter into direct competition with the cheap products of the wood-turners, especially with cups and mugs which could replace wooden cups and bowls. The pottery vessels were more expensive than 'treen ware', but they lasted for a longer time, and had a much more attractive appearance, as they were often given coloured glazes. Some were decorated with comical face designs, to amuse the drinkers. The expansion of ale drinking, and the tendency for more ale to be consumed in specialist ale-houses rather than being sold for home consumption by part-time ale-wives, may be connected with the production of a range of vessels, from large cisterns with bungs to a variety of drinking vessels (Fig. 4.4). It has been suggested that the potters were catering for a 'drinking culture'.[50]

[46] British Library, Harleian Roll F21 (borough court roll for Eynsham, 1453).

[47] J. Hatcher and T. C. Barker, *A History of British Pewter* (London, 1974), 55–6, 80; York Minster Library, L2/4, fo. 274 (a husbandman of Helperby, Yorkshire, with 7 pewter vessels); TNA: PRO, PROB 11/10, fo. 199 (farmer of Church Lawford, Warwickshire, with half garnish of pewter); a number of the rebels hanged in Kent for rebellion in 1451 each owned 8–16 pieces of pewter, TNA: PRO, E357/42.

[48] Suffolk Record Office, Ipswich Branch, J 421/1, fos. 42, 126; J 421/3, fos. 20, 21; TNA: PRO, PROB 11/10, fo. 30.

[49] G. Astill, 'Economic Change in Later Medieval England: An Archaeological Review', in T. H. Aston *et al.* (eds.), *Social Relations and Ideas: Essays in Honour of R. H. Hilton* (Cambridge, 1983), 226–30; M. Mellor, 'A Synthesis of Middle and Late Saxon, Medieval and Early Post-Medieval Pottery in the Oxford Region', *Oxoniensia*, 59 (1994), 93–150.

[50] Mellor, 'A Synthesis', 118–32.

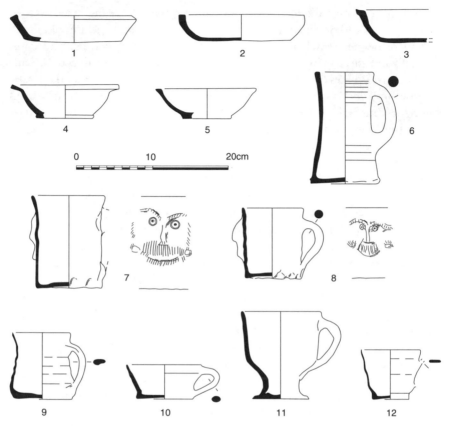

Fig. 4.4. Pottery drinking vessels made at the Brill/Boarstall kilns on the Buckingham-shire/Oxfordshire border. They include dishes and bowls (1–5) influenced by wooden originals; cups and mugs (6–11), two of which are decorated with human faces; and a three-handled tyg (12) made in thin, glazed Cistercian ware.

Source: see n. 50.

English potters, especially those serving the south-eastern market, com-peted with accomplished continental products by providing more attractive glazed wares, such as so-called 'Tudor Green' and 'Cistercian ware'. The manufacture of the first began well before 1485, and the second was not made or owned exclusively by monks, but both became more abundant toward the end of the fifteenth century and were used by a great variety of consumers. At this time kilns in different regions produced wares of standard type, such as Cistercian ware, helping to spread designs with a nationwide appeal.[51]

[51] Astill, 'Economic Change', 223–6; D. Gaimster and B. Nenk, 'English Households in Transition *c.*1450–1550: The Ceramic Evidence', in D. Gaimster and P. Stamper (eds.), *The Age*

Ever since the commercial growth of the thirteenth century, the ceramics industry had presented the consumers with pots of many different fabrics, textures, forms, size, colours, decorations, qualities, and prices. A single village would at any one time be obtaining its pottery from three or more centres of manufacture.[52] Either on visits to market stalls in nearby towns, or in response to the displays of travelling pedlars, the purchasers (almost certainly women) exercised choice. The distribution of pottery was in the hands of middlemen, who would act as a channel of communication between purchasers and suppliers. The surviving fragments of pottery show the manufacturers and traders seeking to attract the consumer with glazes, shapes, and decorations, sometimes imitating the techniques of competitors, or in the case of some drab and ill-made pot, seeking to undercut rivals in price. We can observe the interaction between producers and consumers, and demonstrate that the purchase of goods in the middle ages was not just a matter of satisfying utilitarian needs.

Fashion and Shopping

Finally, in this review of late medieval consumption, is there any equivalent in our period to the fashion-consciousness, advertising, and shopping practices of modern times? Printed advertisements aimed at a mass readership could not be found in our period, though traders brought their goods to the attention of potential customers by displays outside their premises, by hanging signs above their shop, by decorating the outside of the shop with carvings and paintings, by shouting their wares, and by sending huxters to sell in the street or from door to door. Goods may not have been branded as in recent times, but makers' marks, on knives for example, as well as on more expensive metalwork made customers aware of the object's origin.[53] Some products were associated with particular places, and thereby consumers were informed about the type of goods and their quality. In woollen textiles there were Bristol reds and Stroudwaters; in linen Aylshams had a good reputation; Thaxted knives were distinct presumably from those produced in dozens of other places; Banbury and Essex cheeses were well known.

Fashion, with its sometimes radical changes in the form and style of goods, was fully established in parts of the medieval world of consumption. A series

of Transition: The Archaeology of English Culture 1400–1600, Society for Medieval Archaeology Monographs, 15 (1997), 173–9.

[52] e.g. C. Bell and B. Durham, 'Archaeological Excavations at Lawn Farm, Bulkington, 1994', *Wiltshire Archaeological and Natural History Magazine*, 90 (1997), 77–90.

[53] J. Cowgill, M. de Neergaard, and N. Griffiths, *Knives and Scabbards*, Medieval Finds From Excavations in London, 1 (1987), 17–24.

of changes in the shape and construction of shoes can be followed in surviving examples, contemporary depictions, especially on tombs, and from comments (of a disparaging character) made at the time.[54] Extremism and extravagance in shoes led to moral condemnations, and the moralists did not always exaggerate. The notorious *poulaine* shoe, with toes up to 4 inches long, which was kept rigid by packing the tip with moss or animal hair, was indeed worn in London in the late fourteenth century.[55] It may have been a mainly London fashion, but others almost as distinctive, such as the square toe favoured around 1500, were adopted throughout the country.

In clothing fashion, reference has already been made to the close-fitting short garments which spread from the royal court in the second half of the fourteenth century. Women's veils and head-coverings are known mainly from upper-class examples to have changed from the veiled, to the *crespine*, to horns and 'butterflies', though Chaucer's mockery of the enormous head-dress worn by the wife of Bath (an artisan in the textile industry) suggests a downward diffusion of these styles.[56]

The variety of textiles and garments which the clothing industry produced to stimulate and satisfy consumer demand is revealed by the descriptions of cloths in merchants' warehouses. A London draper, Thomas Gylbert, when he died in 1484 had more than a hundred pieces of cloth 'in the shop' and 'in another shop on the other side of the street', much of which was described as russet and tawny, but his stock also included green medley, tawny medley, light tawny, violet, mustardvylers, white, red, crimson, murrey, scarlet, northern green, frieze, kersey, white kersey, and popinjay.[57]

Fragments of textile recovered by excavation from waterlogged deposits in which organic material is preserved provide more direct insights into the weave of textiles and the cut of garments. This evidence is especially abundant on the Thames waterfront in London.[58] The fragments show changes in manufacture, such as the spinning of thread by wheel rather than by hand with a distaff, and different weaving techniques and finishing methods. All of these influenced the appearance and texture of the cloth, and the ways that it could be used in making up garments. Cloth tends to lose its colour after five centuries in wet earth, but scientific analysis allows its original appearance to be reconstructed. As well as the variety of colours from one cloth to another,

[54] F. Grew and M. de Neergaard, *Shoes and Pattens*, Medieval Finds From Excavations in London, 2 (1988), esp. 112–22.

[55] Ibid. 28–36.

[56] M. Clayton, *Catalogue of Rubbings of Brasses and Incised Slabs* (London, 1968), 22–4; Benson (ed.), *Chaucer*, 30 (ll. 453–4).

[57] TNA: PRO, PROB 2/12.

[58] E. Crowfoot, F. Pritchard, and K. Staniland, *Textiles and Clothing c.1150–c.1450*, Medieval Finds From Excavations in London, 4 (1992).

many of them were rays (striped) or medleys in which the warp and weft had been dyed different colours before weaving. Among the London finds was a cloth of black-and-pink check. Purely decorative features of late medieval clothes included *dagges*, strips of cloth cut into jagged shapes and sewn on to the edges of garments. Slashing, in which the garment was cut in order to reveal a lining of a contrasting colour, is found in the preserved clothing, and was another feature which attracted moral disapproval. Buttons were used in quantity, partly as decorative features.

Only rarely can a preserved garment be linked to a specific rank or occupation. Excavations in a fifteenth-century coal-mine at Coleorton in Leicestershire produced a remarkable piece of clothing, a tunic of woollen cloth, the lower part of which had been ornately cut into strips.[59] The place of its recovery must suggest that it had been worn by a coal-miner, though whether it had been acquired second-hand from a gentry household, as the excavator suggested, or represented the clothes that a worker on 6*d.* per day could afford, remains a mystery.

A feature of modern fashion has been the growth of groups with their own tastes and preferences, based not just on the distinction between rich and poor, but also on differences of age. Again, medieval consumers were by no means homogeneous, and we know of youth groups who conducted their own social life, like the guilds of young men and women who met in parishes in the south-west, though they signalled their integration into adult society by making contributions from their festivities to church funds.[60] Material goods can be linked with children, who were provided with playthings such as spinning-tops, and dolls and models that would be used in make-believe and imaginative play.[61]

In modern studies of material culture the concept of 'patina' is used, referring to the attachment to old objects and buildings, even while fashion and consumerism insists on a constant stream of novelties.[62] The association with traditional material things might even confer some degree of status. The gentry clung to their draughty open halls, because of their association with traditions of aristocratic hospitality and hierarchical displays at public meals. Monasteries which were proud of their traditions may have cherished the older part of their buildings, even when they were constructed in such outmoded styles as Romanesque. William Cosyn from East Bergholt in Suffolk, who was not aristocratic but held a substantial quantity of land,

[59] R. Hartley, 'Coleorton', *Current Archaeology*, 134 (1993), 77.
[60] E. Hobhouse (ed.), *Church-Wardens Accounts*, Somerset Record Society, 4 (1890), 3–43.
[61] G. Egan, *Playthings from the Past* (London, 1996); N. Orme, *Medieval Children* (New Haven and London, 2001), 167–76.
[62] McCracken, *Culture and Consumption*, 31–43.

expressed in his will of 1444 the desire that the timber screen 'standing in the hall should not be removed out of the house but should remain there for ever'.[63]

Shops and shopping have a long ancestry, and had reached an advanced stage of development in the later middle ages. Stalls in market-places at a very early stage of their construction had often become permanent structures; in London in particular, but to a lesser degree in the provinces, selds, the precursors of modern shopping malls, tempted the customers with closely packed rows of stalls, boards, and chests offering goods, often with groups of traders, such as tanners or ironmongers, selling side by side.[64] The front rooms of houses accessible from the main streets contained retail outlets, which might be connected with the living accommodation at the rear, or separated and rented to traders who lived elsewhere. Timber booths would be built facing on to streets along walls and boundaries, against church walls, for example, or on the edge of churchyards. The shops that have survived from the fifteenth century in towns such as Saffron Walden have distinctive wide window openings, often two together, for display purposes, with provision for boards which could be extended into the street.[65] At Chester, and on a smaller scale in other towns, first-floor galleries provided access to a second tier of shops.[66] In Southampton and elsewhere shoppers would enter undercrofts opening from the street into the space below the house where goods could be displayed and sold.[67] Initially trading may have been confined to a market day, but larger towns had more than one market day, and shops were open six days a week—indeed, judging from regulations on Sunday trading, some opened on the seventh as well.

Fifteenth-century letters, and dialogues written for language instruction show that shopping included bargaining over price, and discussion of the quality of goods between buyers and sellers.[68] Sometimes the results were frustrating, if the customers were as demanding and discriminating as the women of the Paston family, who complained in their letters of the poor choice available in the shops of Norwich as compared with London.[69] Making purchases could be regarded as pleasurable, hence in fairs the

[63] Suffolk Record Office, Ipswich Branch, J 421/1, fo. 25.

[64] D. Keene, 'Shops and Shopping in Medieval London', in L. Grant (ed.), *Medieval Art, Architecture and Archaeology in London*, British Archaeological Association (1990), 29–46.

[65] Grenville, *Medieval Housing*, 171–4.

[66] A. Brown (ed.), *The Rows of Chester*, English Heritage Archaeological Reports, 16 (1999).

[67] P. A. Faulkner, 'Medieval Undercrofts and Town Houses', *Archaeological Journal*, 123 (1966), 120–35.

[68] H. Bradley (ed.), *Dialogues in French and English by William Caxton*, Early English Text Society, extra ser., 79 (1900), 14–19.

[69] N. Davis (ed.), *Paston Letters and Papers of the Fifteenth Century*, 2 vols. (Oxford, 1971 and 1976), i. 227, 236, 247, 252, 263.

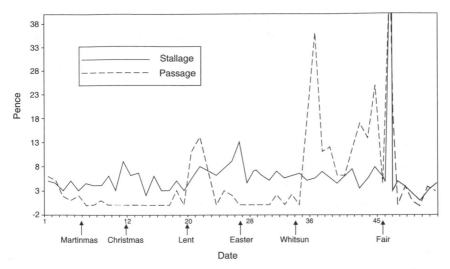

Fig. 4.5. Fluctuations in market tolls at Melton Mowbray (Leics.). The accounting year began on 29 September 1498. Stallage came from rents paid for market stalls, and passage from payments made by goods, animals, etc. being taken through the town. The most dramatic peak came from the tolls of the August fair. Others coincide with Christmas, Lent, Easter, and immediately after Whitsun.

Source: see n. 70.

entertainments alongside the booths where hard bargains were struck. At fifteenth-century Melton Mowbray in Leicestershire, where we know the rhythms in the volume of trade through the year, peaks in the trading cycle were at Easter and Whitsun, when religious holidays were combined with more secular pleasure-seeking (Fig. 4.5). A pre-Christmas rush can be detected, with slackening demand in the following weeks.[70]

Changing Medieval Consumption Patterns

The conclusion can be reached, therefore, that consumerism is a useful concept to apply to a period before the eighteenth century, and there are parallels—in a lower key perhaps—between the development of consumption around 1700 and in the period 1375–1520. Was there indeed a growth in our period in demand in goods and services, especially at the lower end of the market?

[70] J. Laughton and C. Dyer, 'Seasonal Patterns of Trade in the Later Middle Ages: Buying and Selling at Melton Mowbray, Leicestershire, 1400–1520', *Nottingham Medieval Studies*, 46 (2002), 162–84.

This subject can be readily tackled in anecdotal fashion. A great volume of miscellaneous goods imported from the continent were clearly designed to satisfy a widespread consumer interest in luxurious and even frivolous purchases. For example, a ship which arrived in Southampton in December 1509 carried among its very miscellaneous cargo seven gross of playing-cards, eight dozen large and small mirrors, a gross of spectacles, two dozen painted heads of St John, nine dozen pairs of small knives, and thirty gross (that is, 4,320) rings of counterfeit.[71] The stock in trade of John Skyrwyth of London was listed in 1486. He was known as a leather seller, though he also traded as a haberdasher and mercer. His wares give an impression of the large demand for small consumer goods, which must have been distributed far beyond the capital and purchased by a wide section of society. He had for sale in the 'shope with haberdascher ware' thimbles, buckles, bells for horses, dogs, and 'players', bridle bits, spurs, needles, pins, combs, hat-bands, girdles of various textiles, pouches, beads of glass and bone, penknives, ink-horns, thread, kerchiefs, and spectacles. The quantities are impressive, such as more than 150,000 beads, at least 500 bells, and almost 500 spectacles.[72]

The purchasers of such goods cannot be identified precisely, and we do not know if trade in these items was rising and falling. Small luxuries may be symptomatic of the existence of spare cash, but most individuals did not buy them in great quantity. We need to focus on textiles and housing, which after food were for most consumers the main items of expenditure. We can sometimes attempt a profile of the likely consumers, and we can follow some trends in demand. To begin with cloth, exports of woollens had been quite high in the thirteenth century, and after a decline in the early fourteenth century they rose from very modest totals in the 1340s to between 80,000 and 90,000 cloths in most years in 1500–30.[73] The background to this overseas trade was the industry's ability to satisfy domestic demand. The English cloth-makers were catering for a wide range of consumers. Much of the output in about 1500 consisted of high-quality cloth which retailed for about 3s. per yard, but included kerseys and other textiles which were worth about 1s. per yard. Much of this cheaper material was intended for the home market. The total quantity, or the amount bought by individuals, is a matter of guesswork, but some figures can be suggested. One way of estimating is to look at the number of cloth-workers. For example, in Babergh Hundred in Suffolk, a clothing district which included Lavenham and Boxford, 120

[71] T. B. James, *The Port Book of Southampton 1509–10*, Southampton Records Series, 32 (1990), pt. 1, p. 55.

[72] TNA: PRO, PROB 2/15.

[73] E. M. Carus-Wilson and O. Coleman, *England's Export Trade 1275–1547* (Oxford, 1963), esp. 138–9.

weavers were listed in 1522.[74] A weaver is said to have produced ten cloths per annum, so the annual output of this group of small towns and villages could have been 1,200 cloths or 28,800 yards. At least thirty districts with similar concentrations of weavers could be found in Devon, Essex, Gloucestershire, Kent, Lancashire, Norfolk, Somerset, Suffolk, Wiltshire, and West Yorkshire. There were also hundreds of villages and towns with half-a-dozen weavers in these and other counties. The number of cloths woven each year cannot have been less than 200,000.[75]

Individual ownership of clothes can be investigated from inventories, though many exclude garments, or confine themselves to the more valuable items. Hats, caps, shoes, or shirts are rarely mentioned, and many houses must have contained old and shabby gowns and tunics of negligible value. John Jakson of Grimston in Yorkshire in 1468, a peasant with a modest landholding, was credited with three garments, a tunic, and two gowns, worth in total 7s. 4d. He also owned sheets and a coverlet.[76] Robert Bell of Helperby in 1450 had an Irish gown, a black tunic, and a red hood.[77] Most peasant households were equipped with linen tablecloths and towels as well as bed-linen and woollen coverlets. With 3 yards of cloth to a gown, adults seem therefore to have owned garments containing about 9 yards of cloth, and another few yards in their bedding. The relatively small number of garments that they owned at any one time must have forced them to replace at least one of them every year or two, and this is confirmed by maintenance contracts for retired peasants which mention allowances of new clothing to be provided annually or every other year.[78] Bedding would have been renewed much more infrequently. This picture of clothing among the peasantry may not have been radically different from that prevailing around 1300, judging from the maintenance agreements. New demand in the fifteenth century came from the farmers, yeomen, traders, and others of the relatively wealthy minority, who from their inventories would also sometimes be credited with only three garments, but could aspire to as many as nine, and from the valuations of individual gowns or tunics, which varied from 4s. to 10s., were able to buy the higher-quality cloth at 3s. per yard.[79] The other growth area was likely to have been among the labourers and other wage-earners, who, with their new earning capacity, could have bought cloth at some stages

[74] J. Pound (ed.), *The Military Survey of 1522 For Babergh Hundred*, Suffolk Records Society, 28 (1986).

[75] For the amount of cloth produced by a weaver, J. H. Munro, 'Textile Technology in the Middle Ages', in J. H. Munro, *Textiles, Towns and Trade* (Aldershot, 1994), 17.

[76] Borthwick Institute of Historical Research, York, D. and C. wills, 1464, Jakson.

[77] York Minster Library, L2/4, fo. 265.

[78] Dyer, *Standards of Living*, 175–7.

[79] e.g. TNA: PRO, PROB 2/57, 69, 86, 106, 151, 696.

of their lives on a scale comparable with the middling peasantry. Those without regular incomes, and indeed many with more substantial means, would have obtained second-hand clothing by purchase or gift. Such a regular trade is implied by the values put on garments, not just in inventories but in the course of legal proceedings when prices were put on stolen goods and on the confiscated chattels of felons.

If in 1500 a million-and-a-quarter adults were buying annually an average of 3 yards of cloth each, assuming that peasants and some wage-earners could afford to replace a garment every year, and the elite's more plentiful purchases offset the inability of the poor to buy new clothes regularly, that means that home demand accounted for almost 4 million yards of cloth, or 160,000 whole cloths, double the total of exports. Woollens were not imported in any quantity, but other materials were, especially linen. Part of the linen needed each year to renew sheets, shirts, underwear, and some outer garments such as coverchiefs came from the English linen-weavers, but much was imported. In 1384 200,000 ells of linen (almost 240,000 yards) came through London. By 1480–1 the scale of imports had increased, amounting to 420,000 ells (a half-million yards) into London, together with raw flax. Total annual consumption must have attained a million or 2 million yards.[80]

Once the cloth had been woven, the garments had to be designed, cut, and stitched by tailors, a craft which had been numerous before 1350 but became even more prominent at the end of the middle ages. For example, in Babergh Hundred, with a population of about 10,000, forty-six tailors were listed scattered among the towns and villages. In Northampton, Leicester, and Norwich in the early sixteenth century tailors were the second or third most numerous craft. At Northampton twenty tailors worked in a town of 3,000–4,000 inhabitants. At the small town of Bromsgrove in Worcestershire in 1358 six tailors were employed. Perhaps 400 people lived in the town, though we should allow here and in the other towns for the population of the surrounding countryside who would also use their services.[81] The tailors named in our documents would be the masters in charge of a shop in which assistants (servant and apprentices) were working. If there was a tailor for every 200 adults, this suggests that a high proportion of the population were making use of their specialist services. We can gain some insights into

---

[80] H. S. Cobb, 'Textile Imports in the Fifteenth Century: The Evidence of Customs' Accounts', *Costume*, 29 (1995), 1–11; A. F. Sutton, 'Mercery Through Four Centuries, 1130–*c*.1500', *Nottingham Medieval Studies*, 41 (1997), 100–25; id., 'Some Aspects of the Linen Trade, *c*.1130 to 1500, and the Part Played by the Mercers of London', *Textile History*, 30 (1999), 155–75.

[81] Pound (ed.), *Military Survey*; W. G. Hoskins, 'English Provincial Towns in the Early Sixteenth Century', in id., *Provincial England* (London, 1963), 79; Swanson, *Medieval Artisans*, 45–6; J. F. Pound, 'The Social and Trade Structure of Norwich, 1525–1575', *P&P* 34 (1966), 55; Dyer, *Bromsgrove*, 31–2.

the techniques of cutting and stitching garments from the fragments of clothing preserved in the wet soil of the London waterfront.[82] The tailoring revolution of the later middle ages required complicated construction of garments from a number of carefully cut pieces of cloth designed to fit the body closely. Tailors needed to do a great deal of fine stitching, with 5–6 stitches to the centimetre in some cases. They used techniques often thought to have been developed in modern times, such as 'bias' cutting to improve the hang and look of the garment.

New evidence is emerging for a surge of new house-building in this period. If research was based entirely on documents this would come as a great surprise, because the principal written sources for rural houses, manorial court rolls between about 1380 and 1480, are full of references to buildings falling into ruin. Tenants were ordered to carry out repairs, and new tenants were required to carry out specified repairs or even to put up a completely new house or barn.[83] Finding that coercion had only a limited effect, as tenants ignored orders to repair and failed to carry out promised new building, lords would offer inducements, such as letting tenants off their rents or arrears for a period, so that they could use the money for construction work. Occasionally lords, despairing of their attempts to force or cajole their tenants to carry out renovations, hired masons and carpenters, and paid for the work themselves.[84] This 'great housing crisis' was entirely to be expected in view of the halving in the population, the abandonment of houses and even whole settlements, and the amalgamation of holdings consequent on engrossing. As the number of households in England had fallen from a million to a half-million, a half-million houses became redundant. One reason for neglect was that tenants had acquired two or three houses along with their holdings of land, and unless they wished to have subtenants they needed only one dwelling. The archaeological findings fit exactly with this state of affairs, as dozens of houses have been excavated that were left to fall down between about 1380 and 1520.[85] But the evidence—both from the documents and the material remains—is biased. We know most about the decayed houses from the documents, because lords were concerned to maintain the housing stock which, if kept in good repair, they hoped would be rented separately again to tenants. Archaeologists usually excavate deserted settlements, so they will only find abandoned houses.

---

[82] Crawford *et al.*, *Textiles and Clothing*, 150–98.

[83] C. Dyer, 'English Peasant Buildings in the Later Middle Ages (1200–1500)', *MA* 30 (1986), 22–4, 28–9; Hargreaves, 'Seignorial Reaction', 62–71.

[84] e.g. N. W. Alcock, 'The Medieval Cottages of Bishop's Clyst, Devon', *MA* 9 (1965), 146–53.

[85] A systematic bibliography of these sites up to 1968 is to be found in M. W. Beresford and J. G. Hurst (eds.), *Deserted Medieval Villages* (London, 1971), 149–68; for more recent work see M. Beresford, *The Lost Villages of England*, revised edn. (Stroud, 1998), pp. xii–xxviii.

We have seen that wills mention new houses and barns, but these documents only refer infrequently to the state of buildings, so they are not sufficiently numerous to counteract the testimony of the court rolls. The vital quantifiable evidence comes from the surviving timber-framed houses, of which thousands built in the middle ages are still standing and still occupied (though by advertising executives and management consultants rather than peasants and artisans). For a long time the dates of these houses remained uncertain, though on architectural typology it was clear that some wealden houses of the south-east went back to 1400 or earlier. The other candidates for early dating were the cruck houses of the western part of the country, that is, houses based on a timber frame of which the main load-bearing timbers were pairs of curved timbers, the crucks. (see Fig. 4.1) It was believed that many of these houses were medieval, but when exactly within the period were they built? And surely a high proportion of them belonged to the sixteenth and seventeenth centuries? The view that most surviving buildings belonged to the 'Tudor' period was helped by the archaeological interpretation that medieval peasant houses were built by the peasants themselves, using flimsy and perishable materials, and that permanent houses were not constructed until a late date, even after 1500.[86]

Now we have the results of dendrochronology, by which dates of the felling of timber can be calculated from scientific analysis of the growth rings of trees from structural timbers. This technique has given us dates for dozens of wealden and cruck houses. The date of the felling of the timbers can occasionally be precisely determined to a particular year, and often the dates are accurate to within ten years, depending on how much of the tree near to the bark, the sapwood, which includes the outer and latest rings, was trimmed away in preparing the timber. A few of these dated peasant houses were built before the Black Death, as early as 1262 in the case of a building now used as a public house at Cottingham in Northamptonshire.[87] The majority were built after 1380, and the dates continue into the early sixteenth century, with a peak for Kentish houses between 1440 and 1509, and in the case of midland cruck houses between 1400 and 1510. (Fig. 4.6).[88]

The sample of dated houses is now large enough for us to assert that many people made the decision to build new houses precisely during the 'great housing crisis', when so many were falling into ruin. There is no real

[86] The debate on 'impermanent' houses and the 'vernacular threshold' is summed up in Grenville, *Medieval Housing*, 123–33.

[87] N. Hill and D. Miles, 'The Royal George, Cottingham, Northamptonshire: An Early Cruck Building', *Vernacular Architecture*, 32 (2001), 62–7.

[88] Pearson, *Medieval Houses of Kent*, 67–70; the midland dates have been published in *Vernacular Architecture*, 18 (1987), 56–8; 24 (1993), 61–5; 29 (1998), 136–42 and subsequent issues; M. Moran, *Vernacular Buildings of Shropshire* (Almeley, Hereford., 2003), 351–70.

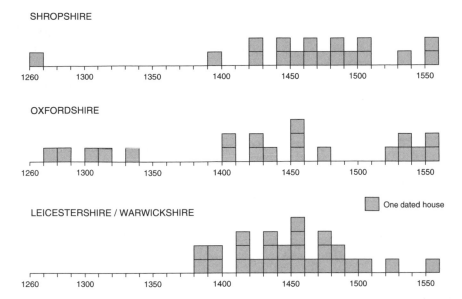

Fig. 4.6. Dated rural cruck houses from the midlands, 1260–1560. These were mainly peasant houses, as urban buildings and those of high status have not been included. The dates depend on dendrochronology (analysis of tree rings). Many houses must have been built in the period 1260–1350, but were less likely to survive to allow their timbers to be dated.

Source: see n. 88, and information from Dr Nat Alcock.

contradiction in these dates. The new houses were generally not new developments, but were on old sites, replacing decayed predecessors. Their builders were probably not grudgingly accepting orders from their lords, and very few of the surviving houses are likely to have been built directly by lords, as this was a relatively rare occurrence. Rather, tenants were putting up new houses to a higher standard, perhaps in some cases helped by the extra resources gained from amalgamating holdings. Peasants were employing skilled labour, of which the carpenters were the key to the quality of construction; their average daily wage topped 5*d*. from the 1430s. Some of the materials, including timber, would have been purchased. A house would have cost a minimum of £2, and some records suggest expenditure rising up to £6–£7.[89] The quality of their materials and carpentry can still be judged, as so many have survived. In Kent alone 2,500 late medieval houses still stand, which suggests that more than a tenth of those once built have endured

[89] Dyer, 'England Peasant Buildings', 28–32; B. Harrison and B. Hutton, *Vernacular Houses in North Yorkshire and Cleveland* (Edinburgh, 1984), 4–5; *AHEW* iii. 171, 863–5; Northamptonshire Record Office, Spencer MS, roll 109; Lincolnshire Archives, LMR 16/2.

through the accidents, stresses, and changes of five centuries.[90] One factor in their permanence was the increasing use towards the end of the middle ages of durable roofing materials such as stone slates and ceramic tiles, rather than the traditional thatch. Also the houses were constructed in a way which allowed their conversion to modern requirements, such as the insertion of upper storeys, without the need for demolition. Some peasants built well, in order to enjoy the comfort and convenience of a new house, to enhance the value of the holding, to provide dry storage for crops and implements and shelter for livestock, and no doubt (as has been suggested above) to impress their neighbours.

Finally, the expansion of consumer demand per head is reflected in the development of the local distribution network. The many markets held in village streets founded in the thirteenth and early fourteenth centuries tended to disappear, but these were rather fragile institutions, which in some cases had never flourished.[91] Their main function was to allow peasants to sell produce in order to obtain money for rents and taxes, rather than serving their consumption needs. By contrast, the essential elements of the network of small towns which had been established by *c*.1300 survived the changes of the fourteenth and fifteenth centuries, and though their populations had fallen, so had those of the surrounding villages, and a scatter of towns, such as Birmingham (Warwickshire), Chelmsford (Essex), and Buntingford (Hertfordshire), remained the same size or even grew. Buildings in small towns, like those in the villages, were being renewed in the fifteenth century, and particularly in the period 1430–90.[92]

The common characteristic of all of these towns lay in the wide range of their artisans and traders, often with one or two representatives of each specialism, so that the local rural population could obtain all of their basic needs in terms of clothing, leather goods, iron implements and utensils, and foodstuffs. Luxuries were also supplied, but not in every town, and usually on a small scale, by spicers, goldsmiths, and haberdashers. The wares available from a small-town mercer are revealed by the inventory of Harry Bodiham, who died at Goudhurst in Kent in 1490. His shop contained buckram, and linen from Holland, Flanders, and Brabant, many of these in small pieces of between 1 and 6 ells. He also kept pieces of fustian, canvas, and 7½ yards of crimson say.[93] His 'haberdash ware' and 'grocery ware' were not itemized,

[90]   Pearson, *Medieval Houses of Kent*, 146.
[91]   J. Masschaele, 'The Multiplicity of Medieval Markets Reconsidered', *Journal of Historical Geography*, 20 (1994), 255–71.
[92]   *CUHB* i. 636–7, 315; C. Dyer, 'The Archaeology of Medieval Small Towns', *MA* 47 (2003), 111–13.
[93]   TNA: PRO, PROB 2/35.

except for a reference to caps, though the omission can be partly filled if we turn to the goods in the shop of Thomas Pikring, who traded in another small town, Farnham in Surrey. In 1500, as well as a similar range of brabant, holland, and buckram, together with a small quantity of silk, he kept in his shop a gross of points (lace-ends for fastening clothing), six men's caps, and a dozen straw hats.[94] The contents of Bodiham's shop were worth less than £20, and Pikring's £28, so these were small traders, but nonetheless their businesses reveal the level of modest luxury that was available to the ordinary consumers who lived within a few miles of these two towns.

Conclusion on Consumption

To sum up this discussion of consumption, there were important changes in the period 1375–1520. The mass of the population enjoyed a more ample and varied diet, and consumption per head of clothing, housing, and goods and services in general increased. Demand was influenced by fashion, and was encouraged by tailors, carpenters, mercers, and others who gained their living from the increase in spending.

The study of consumption helps us to make a reassessment of the whole medieval economy. Concentration on the production side encourages rather pessimistic views of the standard of living and the extent of deprivation and poverty, whereas the study of consumption leads us to glimpse a more affluent dimension. In the decades around 1300 all calculations of peasant budgets and real wages bring us to the same gloomy conclusion, that only a small minority of peasants enjoyed any expendable surplus, and the majority of middling peasants, smallholders, and wage-earners struggled to keep alive. An examination of consumption, however, reveals a busy trade in ale in most villages. Selling ale helps to explain how some poor households, especially those of widows, kept going, yet to whom did they sell if most of their neighbours were all living on bread and water? Not many peasant houses survive from that period, largely because of the passage of time rather than their flimsiness, as many were solidly constructed, judging from excavated examples. The few still standing were apparently built by craftsmen using quite sophisticated methods. The iron industry was busy at this time, presumably supplying the million peasant households with the materials for ploughshares, knives, horseshoes, and nails. The many towns and towns-people were selling goods to country people as well as buying and processing

---

[94] Ibid., PROB 2/175B.

their products. Widespread poverty undoubtedly existed, but to see the whole picture we must take account of the complexity of a varied society.

The expansion of demand in the 150 years following the Black Death should not be underestimated. A well-rooted prejudice among economic historians links population growth with economic expansion, as in the period of the industrial revolution. Yet it is not only in our own time that a stable population can be reconciled with increased individual prosperity and economic achievement. To go back to an earlier medieval period, there is no reason to believe that the number of people was growing rapidly in the tenth and eleventh centuries, and indeed population levels were much the same as in 1375–1520, around 2.5 million, yet this early medieval period saw remarkable creativity and innovation in fundamental economic structures such as villages, manors, and towns.[95]

The increase in consumption per head stimulated the whole economy. We have seen that cloth-making expanded to meet the demand at home as well as overseas. Tin production in Cornwall, in spite of the fall in numbers of potential consumers and in workers in the mining of ore and its processing, actually achieved output around 1400 comparable with the peak in the 1330s (excluding the peak year of 1332), and after the mid-fifteenth-century slump climbed back to that level again in 1515–21.[96] Changing consumption contributed to innovation in industry, such as the larger scale of beer and ale brewing that developed in the fifteenth century.[97]

One measure of changes in the complexity of the economy is provided by the proportion of the working population who were not employed in primary production, especially in agriculture. In the century before the industrial revolution in England the proportion of those with occupations other than agriculture reached high levels, of 50 per cent (in *c.*1760), and 40 per cent in 1688.[98] This is a higher proportion than that found on much of the continent, notably in France, and has promoted the idea that the English and French economies diverged, perhaps in the late sixteenth century. The military survey of 1522, however, suggests high figures for non-agricultural occupations in industrialized districts, such as 34 per cent in Babergh Hundred in Suffolk. In counties with large towns as well as rural industry, such as Norfolk, and counties with numerous small towns and again many

[95] R. Hodges, *The Anglo-Saxon Achievement: Archaeology and the Beginnings of English Society* (London, 1989), 150–85.

[96] J. Hatcher, *English Tin Production and Trade Before 1550* (Oxford, 1973), 156–60.

[97] J. M. Bennett, *Ale, Beer, and Brewsters in England: Women's Work in a Changing World, 1300–1600* (New York, 1996), 79–92.

[98] E. A. Wrigley, 'Country and Town: The Primary, Secondary and Tertiary Peopling of England in the Early Modern Period', in P. Slack and R. Ward (eds.), *The Peopling of Britain: The Shaping of a Human Landscape. The Linacre Lectures 1999* (Oxford, 2002), 226.

rural artisans, such as Devon and Staffordshire, the proportion could have been near to the 1688 figure. The divergence between the England and the continent could be located in the late fifteenth century, as population growth after the Black Death and subsequent epidemics resumed in France and Italy while the English population remained at the same level until the mid-sixteenth century.[99] The long-term history of urbanization, industrialization, and development of the distribution system needs to take into account both the commercial growth in the whole late medieval period and the shifts in consumption after 1375.

Investment

Lords and Tenants

Consumption can be the enemy of investment, and it is commonly said of the middle ages that savings were non-existent. A few rich people hoarded wealth unproductively, like Richard Fitz Alan, earl of Arundel, who at his death in 1376 had £60,000 in cash.[100] Most aristocrats spent every penny they received, and often before it was received, on food, drink, servants, and display, rather than investing in buildings, equipment, and other capital assets. This is said in particular of the greater lords, and even in the era of high farming around 1300 they put a very small proportion of their estate income back into agriculture. On some estates less than 5 per cent of total money received was invested in that way.[101] Rather higher figures have been calculated for estates such as those of Isabella de Fortibus, Bolton Priory, and the bishops of Winchester, on which investment could have been around 10 per cent.[102] The argument has been made that the most appropriate assessment would be the proportion of agricultural income which was expended on buildings, drainage work, and other capital projects. If this is done the figure is usually much higher than 5 per cent, and would have been adequate to

[99] C. Dyer, 'Rural Europe', in C. Allmand (ed.), *The New Cambridge Medieval History*, Vol. VII, *1415–1500* (Cambridge, 1998), 110–13.

[100] C. Given-Wilson, 'Wealth and Credit, Public and Private: The Earls of Arundel, 1306–1397', *English Historical Review*, 106 (1991), 1–26.

[101] R. H. Hilton, 'Rent and Capital Formation in Feudal Society', in id., *The English Peasantry in the Later Middle Ages* (Oxford, 1975), 174–214; M. M. Postan, 'Investment in Medieval Agriculture', *Journal of Economic History*, 27 (1967), 576–87.

[102] M. Mate, 'Profit and Productivity on the Estates of Isabella de Forz (1260–92)', *Ec.HR*, 2nd ser., 33 (1980), 326–34; I. Kershaw, *Bolton Priory: The Economy of a Northern Monastery 1286–1325* (Oxford, 1973), 117–31; J. Z. Titow, *English Rural Society 1200–1350* (London, 1969), 49–50. I have benefited from information supplied by Dr Christopher Thornton on his researches on the Winchester estate.

maintain production. After the Black Death lords' capital expenditure increased, partly because of rising wages for building-workers. On the Canterbury Cathedral Priory estate in the 1450s and 1460s capital expenditure has been found to vary between 7 and 16 per cent per annum.[103] Lords also put more money into building at the time when the demesne was being leased, as they would find a tenant more easily, and gain a higher rent, if manors were in good condition. After demesnes were all in the hands of lessees, lords might still invest in demesne buildings such as mills, and in tenants' houses, though this rarely accounted for more than 10 per cent of their income.[104] Smaller estates devoted resources on capital assets, as buildings and equipment had to be maintained for a relatively small acreage of productive land. Also, as we have seen, some smaller estates continued with at least some direct management after 1400 (pp. 100–4).

The levels of investment, even after revisions have been made to the figures, can still be contrasted with the very high expenditure on daily living and domestic buildings. The first duke of Buckingham, who died in 1460, seems to epitomize an extravagant aristocratic lifestyle. His estate income suffered from falling rents and high levels of arrears, but his household lacked nothing in wine and spices.[105] This high living had wider implications, because of the damage inflicted on his tenants. Not only did the duke, like all lords, extract rents, thereby reducing the tenants' capacity to invest, but he also bought grain, hay, and livestock from those living near his principal residences of Maxstoke and Writtle, and delayed paying for these goods for many years. The tenants were in a weak position to insist on payment of the money owed—they were probably persuaded that it was in their interests to extend credit in exchange for 'good lordship'.

Recent research suggests that we should modify somewhat this judgemental view of aristocratic investment. Investigation of household accounts shows that lords, if they found that they were falling into debt, checked their expenditure and cut back if there was a danger of overindulgence.[106] Lords audited the accounts personally, and required budgets to be calculated in order to control spending. At the lower end of the scale extravagance was

[103] M. N. Carlin, 'Christ Church, Canterbury and Its Lands, from the Beginning of the Priorate of Thomas Chillenden to the Dissolution (1391–1540)', University of Oxford, B.Litt. thesis (1970), 112–19.

[104] C. Dyer, *Lords and Peasants in a Changing Society: The Estates of the Bishopric of Worcester, 680–1540* (Cambridge, 1980), 172–4.

[105] M. Harris (ed.), 'The Account of the Great Household of Humphrey, First Duke of Buckingham, For the Year 1452–3', in *Camden Miscellany XXVIII*, Camden Society, 4th ser., 29 (1984), 1–57; C. Rawcliffe, *The Staffords, Earls of Stafford and Dukes of Buckingham 1394–1521* (Cambridge, 1978), 115–21.

[106] Dyer, *Standards of Living*, 86–108.

simply not possible, and gentry households could not afford much in the way of wine or spices. Cutbacks in hard times can be seen in the case of institutions with incomes similar in scale to those of the gentry. The fellows of Exeter College, for example, in the mid-fifteenth century when their rents from urban properties and tithes were in decline, had to forgo the bonuses which they had previously paid themselves to celebrate Christmas, Easter, and Whitsun.[107]

The minor gentry are not well documented, but were capable of high levels of investment, relative to their income. The accounts of Humphrey Newton of Newton, Cheshire, as we have seen, give evidence of his direct management of farming. In the years 1498–1506 Newton lived off a small manor with 250 acres of arable and rent income of £14 per annum. His unsystematic jottings reveal expenditure of £3. 13s. 4d. on the mill, which he rented out for 22s. 4d. per annum. Typically he valued this asset not just for the cash that he received, which repaid his investment in just over three years, but also for the 'commodity and pleasure and ease' that he derived from having the corn for his household ground as it was needed and without toll payment. In 1502 he paid the very high sum of £5. 18s. 2d. to have his land marled, and took a close personal interest in the work, recommending that only 'able marl' should be spread on his fields.[108]

Landlords also invested in their urban property. Large estates are found to be putting money into building houses and shops, as in the case of the canons of St Paul's Cathedral in London, who embarked on major projects in the capital such as the construction of a row of eighteen shops in 1370.[109] Such a rich institution could well afford this outlay, and more impressive was the building activity of a small institution entirely dependent on urban rents, which absorbed a high proportion of income. The Holy Cross Guild of Stratford-upon-Avon was accumulating an impressive estate within the town during the fifteenth century, and increased its annual total of rents from £15 to £50. The guild attempted to make its tenants responsible for some repairs and rebuilding, but it was prepared to spend regularly £5 per annum in repairs to tenants' buildings. Over the whole century the master and aldermen decided to invest about a fifth of their income in rebuilding and repairs, and in the two years 1468–70, when they were very concerned about

---

[107] A. F. Butcher, 'The Economy of Exeter College, 1400–1500', *Oxoniensia*, 44 (1979), 38–54.

[108] D. Youngs, 'Estate Management, Investment and the Gentleman Landlord in Later Medieval England, *Historical Research*, 73 (2000), 124–41.

[109] L. F. Salzman, *Building in England: Down to 1540*, 2nd edn. (Oxford, 1967), 443–4; Royal Commission on Historical Manuscripts, *Ninth Report*, part 1 (1883), 24; D. Keene, 'Landlords, the Property Market and Urban Development in Medieval England', in F.-E. Eliassen and G. A. Ersland (eds.), *Power, Profit and Urban Land: Landownership in Medieval and Early Modern Northern European Towns* (Aldershot, 1996), 93–119.

a growing total of decayed rents and empty properties, they spent all of their rent income on building-work.[110]

The contribution of landlords to investment, especially on the smaller estates, should clearly not be dismissed. The lesser landlords who spent a higher proportion of their limited incomes on repairs and improvements were managing more land and assets cumulatively than the magnates. The bulk of investment, however, came from non-aristocratic sources, and from individuals rather than institutions. Most urban property was held by the townspeople themselves, some as owner-occupiers, or as small-scale landlords who sublet a few houses in order to gain a rent income which was commonly below £5 per annum. Cumulatively these minor property-owners were responsible for the bulk of the building and repair work in towns, though this activity is scarcely ever to be found in documents.[111] Tenants in both town and country, freehold, copyhold, and leasehold, were often expected to pay for their own buildings, hedging, and fixed assets. Just as we are aware of 'hidden trade' in the middle ages, being conducted in unofficial places without documentation, so we need to explore the 'hidden investment' which was paid for by people who have left no accounts and few other records.

The idea of 'improvement', both moral or material, developed in the sixteenth century, but had earlier origins. Bishop Veysey of Exeter, who patronized his home village of Sutton Coldfield in Warwickshire, provided it in 1528 with a new borough constitution, a paved market-place, access to land on the wastes, and enjoined the new 'warden and society' who were put in charge of the place to help the poor with their tax payments, building costs, and the expense of marrying their daughters.[112] This improver is thought to be typical of the new spirit of the commonwealth men, and indeed, before becoming a bishop he served on the commissions to investigate depopulation and enclosures in 1517–18. Those whose activities were reported to those inquiries themselves believed in improvement. The Northamptonshire and Warwickshire grazier John Spencer responded to the accusations made against him over the enclosures at Wormleighton by claiming that he was not responsible for the enclosures but bought the land at a high price after William Cope 'improved it', and he went on to argue that the

---

[110] T. H. Lloyd, *Some Aspects of the Building Industry in Medieval Stratford-upon-Avon*, Dugdale Society Occasional Papers, 14 (1961); C. Dyer, 'Medieval Stratford: A Successful Small Town', in R. Bearman (ed.), *The History of an English Borough: Stratford-upon-Avon 1196–1996* (Stroud and Stratford, 1997), 50–2.

[111] Keene, 'Landlords', 103–10.

[112] *VCH Warwickshire*, iv. 233–4; P. Slack, *From Reformation to Improvement: Public Welfare in Early Modern England* (Oxford, 1999), 23.

hedges contributed to the 'commodity and common wealth for the country there'.[113]

A notion of forward planning, and a pride in development, can be found well before Veysey and Spencer expressed their divergent visions of improvement. William Worcester, surveyor to Sir John Fastolf, believed that Castle Combe, the Wiltshire clothing village, had benefited from the encouragement of its lord and his employer from about 1411.[114] Fastolf had promoted charters for a market and a fair. He regularly bought cloth from the Castle Combe clothiers, and these sums 'were the principal cause of the growth in the common good, riches, and new building in the said vill'. Worcester reported with approval in 1454 that forty-eight of the tenants had built their houses and other structures, some of them in stone. We should note that the landlord's contribution lay in establishing an environment in which clothiers and artisans could prosper and pay for their own buildings.

The idea that good management could bring profit was one shared by peasants, though they can rarely be found expressing their views directly. They must have seen their drainage of fenland and the clearance of woodland in this light, and also modifications to field systems and the introduction of new rotations. In 1341 the tenants of a yardland of 40 acres at Admington (Warwickshire), Nicholas and Petronilla Shad, faced a claim from Gilbert Ricardes that he was the rightful heir to the holding.[115] The decision as to who had best claim was made by 'all of the customary tenants', and as we are told that one of them disagreed, this was evidently not just a legal formula but was a real expression of a collective judgement. They based their opinion on pragmatism rather than the letter of the law. Ricardes was known to them as an awkward character, and though he had the best claim, they decided that he should be content with a cottage built in a corner of the holding. The Shads had been tenants for twenty-four years, and had won the respect of their neighbours: 'the aforesaid holding has improved in the time that the same Nicholas held it, to the value of 20*s.* and more.' The sum of money probably referred to the increase in the annual income that came from the land under Shad's care, and their statement makes it plain that this group of peasants had a conception of profit, and believed that good husbandry could lead to an increase in returns. Our main evidence, though, that tenants planned for the future must come from the barns, enclosures, and other structures which they built and which are sometimes still in use.

[113] I. S. Leadam (ed.), *The Domesday of Inclosures 1517–1518*, Royal Historical Society (1897), ii. 488–9.

[114] E. M. Carus-Wilson, 'Evidences of Industrial Growth on Some Fifteenth-Century Manors', *Ec.HR*, 2nd ser., 12 (1959), 198–205; British Library, Add. MS. 28,208, fos. 2–28.

[115] Gloucestershire Record Office, D 676/96.

The level of expenditure by leaseholders, for example, those who took over the lords' demesnes in the fifteenth century, is normally concealed from us because of the lack of accounts. Some hints of the possible sums can be gained from the occasional interventions made by lords to pay for buildings, perhaps to help a farmer in difficulty, or in an effort to raise the value of the demesne before a new letting. Between 1496 and 1507 at Overton in Hampshire the bishops of Winchester paid a total of £34 for a new farmhouse and £47 for a large barn, the high quality of which can be judged from the buildings which are now still used for their original purposes.[116] The bishop of Worcester, when he bought a piece of hilly land at Dowdeswell in the Gloucestershire Cotswolds in order to endow his college at Westbury-on-Trym, spent £41 on a building to house sheep and to rid the pasture of bushes. It brought its new lord a rent income of about £8 per annum.[117] Also in Gloucestershire, 2,000 yards of fencing around a single sizeable meadow at Lower Quinton in 1431–2 cost £9, leading to the conclusion that a more extensive programme of enclosure to create a large new pasture farm would have cost five times that amount.[118] After that initial expenditure any further improvements would have been passed on to the lessee. Farmers would have been called on to build entirely new dwellings, barns, and animal houses when a demesne was split into separate units for the first time (see pp. 203–4). Occasionally a renewed lease will reveal that the previous tenant had improved the farm, like the two sheepcotes on a pasture at Upper Ditchford in Blockley (Gloucestershire) in 1507, which had probably cost £20 each.[119]

Mills

Lessees and tenants were usually expected to pay for the maintenance and rebuilding of mills. Lords had arranged for the construction of most mills initially, up to 15,000 by 1300. Most were corn mills driven by water or wind power, but some watermills were used for industrial processes, especially the fulling of cloth. Lords in the thirteenth and fourteenth century would employ a miller, and take the toll-corn for sale or consumption within the manor; or they would let the mill on a short lease. By the late fifteenth and early sixteenth centuries they were usually leased, often on quite long terms of twenty or thirty years. The leases were acquired by a wide range of people, including gentry and merchants, but mostly by specialists who called them-

---

[116] E. Roberts, 'Overton Court Farm and the Late-Medieval Farmhouses of Demesne Lessees in Hampshire', *Proceedings of the Hampshire Field Club*, 51 (1996), 89–106.

[117] Dyer, *Lords and Peasants*, 174.

[118] Magdalen College, Oxford, 35/9.

[119] Dyer, *Lords and Peasants*, 250.

selves millers, or in the case of the fulling mills, fullers, walkers, or tuckers. Some were acquired by craftsmen, especially carpenters, who had the skills to keep them in good repair.[120] In the great majority of cases the tenants were expected to pay for repairs or reconstruction, though the leases often contained assurances that the lord would provide the larger timbers. In effect the lessees were entrepreneurs, making a profit by attracting customers by offering a convenient milling service. The millers sometimes changed the use of a mill, particularly when a mill housed more than one set of machinery. One mechanism would power a corn mill, while another might be converted to operate fulling stocks. The arrangements would be changed, depending on local demand. Suit of mill, which had always been difficult to enforce, had faded into disuse, though with at least a fifth of mills in decay after the mid-fourteenth century many communities had easy access to only one mill. Some mills seem to have escaped from the control of lords, in particular those originally built by a lord but which had been ill-advisedly rented out (typically in the twelfth century) and had become freeholds, paying a nominal rent to a lord.[121] New mills were built in the later middle ages by entrepreneurs. At Gaydon in Warwickshire, for example, in 1539 a millwright was contracted to a free tenant, without apparent reference to the lord of the manor, to build a new windmill for £8. Independent mills of this type would not pay a rent to the lord, but would be subject to regulation by the court leet, where the miller would be fined for taking excessive tolls, which often provides the only means of discovering their existence.[122]

The increased number of mills founded and built by tenants rather than by lords is especially apparent when we examine the growing application of water power to industrial processes. In the tin mining and smelting industry of Devon and Cornwall the technology of the mid-thirteenth century depended on manual labour unaided by machinery. Ore was extracted from the stones and pebbles washed down by streams by workers equipped with picks, shovels, and wheelbarrows. Streams would be diverted and channelled to wash and separate the ore. The ore would then be broken up with hammers and smelted in bowl furnaces using hand-operated bellows. The processes were relatively simple, but the industry was highly organized, with capital provided by merchants for the costs of the often arduous

[120] J. Langdon, 'Water Mills and Windmills in the West Midlands, 1086–1500', *Ec.HR* 44 (1991), 424–44; R. Holt, *The Mills of Medieval England* (Oxford, 1988), 159–70.

[121] R. Holt, 'Whose Were the Profits of Corn Milling? An Aspect of the Changing Relationship Between the Abbots of Glastonbury and Their Tenants 1086–1350', *P&P* 116 (1987), 3–23; Holt, *Mills*, 165–7.

[122] Shakespeare Birthplace Trust Records Office, Stratford-upon-Avon, DR37/35, no. 2140. The contract requires the structure to be 'as substantial windmill as any is within Warwickshire' (I owe this reference to Dr P. Upton); Holt, *Mills*, 166–7.

prospecting for deposits and the long process of collecting the metal together for coining and sale.[123] New techniques for extracting the ore developed during the later middle ages, by which shallow lode-back pits, or openwork with wide trenches, were dug into the rock. Ultimately shafts were dug with underground galleries, provided with drainage adits and ventilation shafts. These methods of mining were laborious, but allowed the veins of ore to be worked productively. The ore was crushed in stamping mills, in which water power was used to operate trip hammers, and the pieces of ore were ground to a powder by a crazing mill. The ore, having been prepared in this way, was mixed with charcoal and smelted in a blowing house, in which the required temperature was reached with the help of water-powered bellows.[124]

The various elements of this technology were fully in place by the sixteenth and seventeenth centuries, but had begun to emerge even before 1348. The first reference to a blowing house is found in 1332, and the recruitment of Cornish miners to dig an adit at the Combe Martin (Devon) silver mine in 1296 suggests that at that time some miners were already sinking shafts into the rock. Crazing mills and stamping mills appear for the first time in the fifteenth and early sixteenth centuries. For example, a stamping mill was built on a new site to serve an openwork mine at West Colliford on Bodmin Moor in the mid- to late fifteenth century (Fig. 4.7).[125] The mills were expensive, not just for their stone foundations and carpentered superstructures and machinery, but also for the associated structures like the stone-lined buddles where the ore was separated from stone, and wooden water channels. Above all, the mills, if they were to be located near the works, might not be near the best source of water, and consequently long leats had to be built across country to bring water to the mill. Leats dug in the late fifteenth and early sixteenth centuries could be 5 miles or even 12 miles in length.[126] The money came from rich outsiders who relied on the labour of the tinners, or working tinners who formed groups and held shares in the mines and mills. The industry was dominated by the merchant tinners before the Black Death, but by the fifteenth century a lower proportion of the tin that was brought to be coined (stamped and taxed) was presented by London merchants or other large-scale traders. There was more opportunity, therefore, for local entrepreneurs, people like Simon Aysshe of Chagford in Devon, a yeoman who

[123] J. Hatcher, *English Tin Production and Trade Before 1550* (Oxford, 1973), 43–88; S. Gerrard, *The Early British Tin Industry* (Stroud, 2000), 25–80.

[124] Gerrard, *Tin Industry*, 81–139.

[125] Ibid. 93, 104, 120, 129; D. Austin, G. A. M. Gerrard, and T. A. P. Greaves, 'Tin and Agriculture in the Middle Ages and Beyond: Landscape Archaeology in St. Neot Parish, Cornwall', *Cornish Archaeology*, 28 (1989), 62–123.

[126] Gerrard, *Tin Industry*, 47.

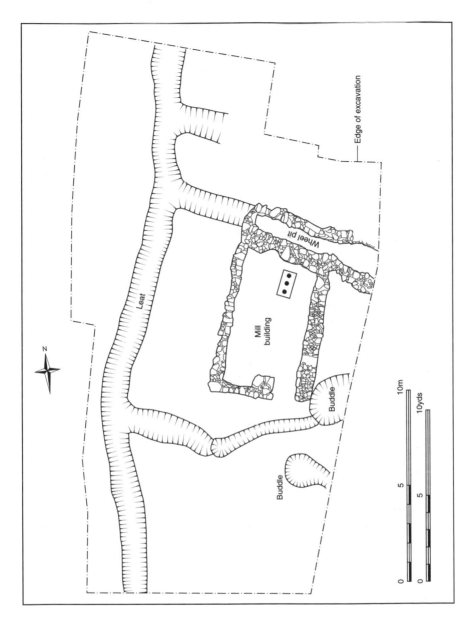

Fig. 4.7. West Colliford stamping mill, St Neot parish (Corn.). The plan of the excavated structures shows part of the leat (a channel), by which water was brought to power the mill-wheel, of which the pit is visible. The stone foundations of the mill building housed the machinery which converted the rotary movement of the wheel into the upward and downward movement of the hammers. Ore was placed on the mortar stone (which is shown with three hollows) and crushed by the hammers. The material was then transferred to the buddles, where it was 'dressed' and the ore separated.

Source: see n. 125.

in 1501 owned fractional shares (a tenth, a sixth, and a half) in five
stanneries.[127]

In iron-making water power was applied to hammers and to bellows in the
thirteenth century, and the references to this type of mechanization seem to
increase towards the end of our period with the building of more mills for
iron-working in the weald of Sussex, culminating in the introduction of the
first English blast furnaces in the 1490s. Some of the capital for the iron-
works came from lords of the manor, like the bishop of Durham, who ran an
iron-works under direct management at *Byrkenott* in the early fifteenth
century, but usually the ironmasters were putting up the money.[128] They
were apparently successful in the case of the Weardale producers, as they were
able to undercut their Spanish competitors in price, and won the custom of a
major local consumer, Durham Priory.[129]

These early phases of mechanization were part of a movement on the
continent, which was especially decisive in its influence in central Europe, in
the mid- to late fifteenth century, with the use of such devices as hydraulic
wheels for pumping mines, and the introduction of the Saiger process for
extracting silver from copper ore.[130] Metal industries were reacting to an
increased demand from consumers for such finished household goods as
pewter plates, and for greater quantities of iron for implements on farms,
for fittings in buildings, and for tools in a wide range of manufactures. The
machinery was essential if output was to be maintained or increased when
labour was in such short supply, and the capital came from those most
directly involved in the industry. Fulling mills spread in clothing districts
through the initiatives of clothiers and wealthier artisans. At Shaw in Berkshire, near to the clothing town of Newbury, a Newbury entrepreneur built a
fulling mill in 1436, and paid 12*d.* per annum to the lord for the use of the
water. In the same way mills were working in the fifteenth century along the
Stroud valley in Gloucestershire, but their presence is known from lawsuits
and other occasional references, not from any rents paid to the lord.[131]

---

[127] TNA: PRO, C131/85, no. 36.

[128] G. G. Astill, *A Medieval Industrial Complex and Its Landscape: The Metal-Working Watermill
and Workshops at Bordesley Abbey*, Council for British Archaeology Research Reports, 92 (1993);
H. R. Schubert, *History of the British Iron and Steel Industry from c. 450 B.C. to A.D. 1775* (London,
1957), 133–65; H. Cleere and D. Crossley, *The Iron Industry of the Weald* (Leicester, 1985);
G. T. Lapsley, 'The Account Roll of a Fifteenth-Century Iron Master', *English Historical Review*,
14 (1899), 509–29. I am grateful to Stephen Moorhouse who has shown me medieval water-
powered ironworking sites in Wensleydale.

[129] M. Threlfall-Holmes, 'Late Medieval Iron Production and Trade in the North-East', *Archaeologia Aeliana*, 5th ser., 27 (1999), 109–22.

[130] P. Braunstein, 'Innovation in Mining and Metal Production in Europe in the Late Middle
Ages', *Journal of European Economic History*, 12 (1983), 573–91.

[131] M. Yates, 'Watermills in the Local Economy of a Late Medieval Manor in Berkshire', in
T. Thornton (ed.), *Social Attitudes and Political Structures in the Fifteenth Century* (Stroud, 2000),
184–201; Carus-Wilson, 'Industrial Growth'.

The expansion of milling is a characteristic example of the failure of the conventional written sources to provide a full record of economic activity. Manorial mills are faithfully documented in rentals, surveys, and accounts. They show an overall decline in mill numbers from an estimated 10,000 in 1300 to 8,000 in 1500, which reflects the reluctance of lords to fund unprofitable mills in places with falling populations.[132] Even so, the number of manorial mills did not decline as much as the human population, and if we were able to count the mills outside manorial control, both those inherited from the past and those built to cater for new demands, and in particular the needs of industry, we would find that mill numbers may not have declined at all. Water power may well have become a more important source of energy in the economy as a whole by the early sixteenth century than it had ever been.

Clothmaking

A final assessment of the role of investment in manufacturing must take account of the largest and most expansive of late medieval industries, woollen cloth production, again an industry that was responding to a rise in consumer demand, in England and on the continent. The bulk of the capital of the clothiers was tied up in trading costs, as these were entrepreneurs handling raw materials and finished products rather than making cloth themselves. So a clothier like Robert Rychard of Dursley in Gloucestershire in 1490 had wool, yarn, and dyestuffs to be issued to spinners, weavers, and dyers, and cloth ready for sale, worth a total of £173.[133] He also had much money owing to him, some of it arising from the sale of cloth. Buildings would not be valued in an inventory, but his will mentions a house in the market town of Berkeley, as well as properties in Dursley. The inventory names the structures in which goods were kept and processed: a warehouse, wool loft, dye-house, and shop. Commonly clothiers were putting money into the other dimensions and stages of cloth-making—economists would call it 'vertical integration'—for example, by buying sheep pastures and sheep flocks. The possession and operation by clothiers of working premises and equipment associated with some of the processes of manufacture—we find them owning fulling mills, tenter yards, dye-houses, and weaving shops, together with looms, vats, and spinning wheels—suggests that at least on a small scale they carried out processes on their own premises, and employed workers directly on some of the stages of manufacture.[134] Legends of the sixteenth

[132] J. Langdon, *Mills in the Medieval Economy. England 1300–1540* (Oxford, 2004), 9–15, 21–64.
[133] TNA: PRO, PROB 11/9, fo. 142 (will); PROB 2/57 (inventory).
[134] e.g. William Bradwey of Chipping Campden, Gloucestershire; John Barker of Long Melford, Suffolk; John Benett of Cirencester, Gloucestershire; John Mayhew of Chew, Somerset; Walter and

century claim that John Winchcombe or Jack of Newbury (of that Berkshire town) employed in large shops 200 weavers and 200 spinners, together with carders, wool sorters, dyers, shearmen, and fullers. A more sober source, John Leland, reports seeing the buildings of Malmesbury Abbey in 1542 full of looms belonging to the clothier William Stumpe. These operations resembled factories, that is, workplaces in which wage-earners in some number were employed by the owner.[135] We can sometimes see in surviving clothiers' houses—of which there is a fine example at Southfields near Dedham in Essex—rooms built around a courtyard capable of accommodating workshops as well as warehousing, but the majority of clothiers were organizing spinners, weavers, and other specialists who worked in their own houses.[136]

The principal innovations among clothiers would have been in co-ordination and financial management, rather than in the techniques of manufacture. The only signs of mechanization (apart from the proliferation of fulling mills, which was a twelfth-century invention) was, first, the advance of the spinning-wheel in supplementing, though never entirely replacing, the distaff. This seems to have been a feature of the fourteenth century. The second mechanical device came in the form of the gig mill, which raised the nap on cloth for shearing, an important part of the finishing process. They are recorded in the fifteenth century, but were resisted.[137]

Peasant Investment

A considerable cumulative investment in production is found among the peasantry. Again the conventional sources suggest the opposite, with the complaints in court proceedings that buildings, fences, and ditches were neglected. Inventories do not suggest either that peasant equipment required much expense: John Hall, a husbandman of Holgate near York, in 1468 had agricultural implements valued at 25s. 10d. out of a total of all of his goods of

Joan Mayhew of Croscombe, Somerset; TNA: PRO, PROB 2/10, 21, 97, 133; PROB 11/8, fo. 120; PROB 11/11, fos. 42, 90; F. W. Weaver, (ed.), *Somerset Medieval Wills (1383–1500)*, Somerset Record Society, 16 (1901), 346–8.

[135] E. Lipson, *The History of the Woollen and Worsted Industries* (London, 1921), 46–8; L. Toulmin Smith (ed.), *Leland's Itinerary in England and Wales* (London, 1906), i. 132. I am indebted for the advice of Margaret Yates.

[136] *VCH Essex*, x. 163–4.

[137] Crowfoot *et al.*, *Textiles and Clothing*, 16–17, 26–7; P. Chorley, 'The Evolution of the Woollen, 1300–1700', in N. B. Harte (ed.), *The New Draperies in the Low Countries and England, 1300–1800* (Oxford, 1997), 7–33; J. H. Munro, 'Industrial Energy From Water-Mills in the European Economy, 5th to 18th Centuries: The Limitations of Power', in S. Cavaciocchi (ed.), *Economia e Energia, Secc. XIII–XVIII*, Istituto Internazionale di Storia Economica 'F. Datini', Prato. 34 (2002), 262–3; all of this discussion on clothiers has been informed by an important study of their activities in the sixteenth century: M. Zell, *Industry in the Countryside: Wealden Society in the Sixteenth Century* (Cambridge, 1994).

£8. 15*s*. 10*d*. His most expensive acquisition, as was commonly the case, was his cart with iron-bound wheels, valued at 23*s*. 4*d*.[138]

Most peasant investment went into livestock, buildings, and the management of the holding. Complaints of overburdening the common pasture provide an indication of the numbers of animals kept by the more substantial tenants, and flocks of 300 sheep or twenty cattle were not unusual from the end of the fourteenth century onwards. They grazed on the commons, leading to complaints. Peasants grew fodder crops for their own livestock. Everywhere they tended to expand the area of land under grass, and more rarely turned over their former arable entirely to pasture. We find them specializing also in the most profitable animals, like the cattle of the Forest of Arden.[139] The change from oxen to horses for pulling carts and ploughs, though difficult to investigate in detail, seems to have gathered pace at this time. John Hall, for example, owned four horses, and they were apparently his main source of traction. Animals were increasing in size at this time, perhaps because they were better fed, and also may have benefited from selective breeding. These changes in husbandry would have been mainly carried out on peasant holdings, as they were keeping the great majority of animals.[140]

Peasant buildings, especially barns, seem to have been constructed from the same materials and using the same craftsmen as their houses, so their effectiveness may have increased. Peasant holdings were also provided with accommodation for animals, especially sheepcotes, byres, and stables, as well as specialist buildings such as shelters for carts and wains. The remains of houses can tell us something of the scale of peasants' farming in the fifteenth century, like the two barns at Caldecote in Hertfordshire each more than 60 feet long, which provided sufficient storage space for the crops of 160 acres of corn, though these buildings may also have been used for hay. The owner had, like many of his contemporaries, engrossed smaller holdings.[141]

[138] York Minster Library, L2/4, fo. 317; Borthwick Institute of Historical Research, York, D. and C. wills, 1468, Hall.

[139] A. Watkins, 'Cattle Grazing in the Forest of Arden in the Later Middle Ages', *Ag.HR* 37 (1989), 12–25.

[140] U. Albarella and S. J. M. Davis, 'Mammals and Birds from Launceston Castle, Cornwall: Decline in Status and the Rise of Agriculture', *Circaea: The Journal of the Association of Environmental Archaeology*, 12 (1996 for 1994), 42–57, date the increase in size to the sixteenth and seventeenth centuries, but in Staffordshire earlier dates are proposed: R. Thomas, 'Animals, Economy and Status: The Integration of Historical and Zooarchaeological Evidence in the Study of a Medieval Castle', University of Birmingham, Ph.D. thesis (2003).

[141] *Medieval Village Research Group Annual Report* (1974), 22–3; the calculation on the capacity of the barns is based on D. Oschinsky (ed.), *Walter of Henley and Other Treatises on Estate Management and Accounting* (Oxford, 1971), 475.

In addition to construction costs, the organization of the land in the holding required investment. The acquisition of extra land could be seen as a contribution not just to the scale of farming, but also to its increased efficiency. The land could be exploited most effectively if it lay in compact blocks, thus cutting down travelling time between parcels. Again we can glimpse that process of consolidation through purchase, leasing, and exchange, and in its most advanced form piecemeal enclosure. Even at the nadir of land prices, buying land could cost the purchaser £1–£2 per acre in central Norfolk (see below, pp. 182–3).

Investment in the Infrastructure

We tend to focus our attention on individual investment by the owners or managers of productive enterprises, but in the later middle ages, as now, the expenditure of public bodies could make a significant contribution to the economy. The infrastructure of roads, bridges, wharfs, and harbours was essential for the flow of trade.

The late medieval transport system did not always deserve the bad press it has received from historians (pp. 21–3). On the more important roads most of the river crossings had been provided with a bridge by the early fourteenth century.[142] A good number of these had been rebuilt, or wooden bridges replaced with stone, or the approach to the bridge improved with a causeway to take traffic over potentially marshy ground by the early sixteenth century, when that observant traveller John Leland reported seeing many new or recently repaired bridges. Famous new structures include the bridge over the Thames built by the local fraternity at Abingdon in 1415, and the Clopton bridge replacing a timber predecessor at Stratford-upon-Avon, which was funded in about 1490 by a London merchant with local roots. Less celebrated examples show that roads which were not of the first importance were being equipped with bridges away from towns, suggesting that the whole transport system, and not just the main arteries, was being funded. At Barford in Bedfordshire an expensive stone bridge was being built in the 1420s which took traffic over the Ouse between northern Northamptonshire and the Great North Road, which avoided the road through Bedford and St Neots. Thousands of small bridges allowed local traffic to cross minor streams.[143] But these are mere anecdotes. If we calculate the total of larger

---

[142] D. Harrison, 'Bridges and Economic Development, 1300–1800', *Ec.HR* 45 (1992), 240–61.

[143] *CUHB* i. 346–7, 376, 446, 532; *VCH Warwickshire*, iii. 224–5; A. Simco and P. McKeague, *Bridges of Bedfordshire*, Bedfordshire Archaeology Occasional Monograph Series, 2 (1997), 26–9; the fifteenth-century bridge-building phenomenon, including minor bridges, was noticed in W. G. Hoskins, *The Making of the English Landscape*, revised edn. (London, 1988), 110–13.

bridges which can be dated by documents or the standing structure, taking as an example the northern counties of England, at least thirty-six had been constructed by 1350. Few river crossings were provided with an entirely new bridges in the following two centuries, though at Kexby in East Yorkshire a ferry is recorded in 1396 and a bridge in 1539. The stone fabric of at least twenty-two bridges in the region were either rebuilt or were extensively repaired between 1400 and 1540.[144]

A decision to build a new bridge was not necessarily an expression of prosperity. The Abingdon bridge was evidently part of a bid to divert trade from rival centres such as Wallingford, and the bridge at Stratford was built at a time when the town's fortunes had dipped. The building and maintenance of bridges were often a collective effort, organized by a fraternity, and rebuilding is some indication of a community's self-confidence and an ability to co-ordinate efforts and marshal resources. Roadworks may be interpreted in the same light, and some prospering towns, such as Lavenham in Suffolk in the fifteenth and early sixteenth centuries, were improving the network in the surrounding district, apparently in a co-ordinated effort as so many wills included bequests for road improvements. Eighteen wills between 1485 and 1540 each left an average of £25 for this purpose.[145] These were private acts of charity, of course, comparable with spending money on the fabric of churches, but that does not mean that the gifts and bequests to the local bridge or road had no economic motive—the charitable intent would only be achieved if the works were of public utility.

A considerable achievement in works to improve the flow of trade, not fully recognized until recent archaeological research, was the building of the London waterfront in stone.[146] After numerous successive replacements of the timber waterfront throughout the middle ages, which had resulted in a considerable extension of the city's built-up area into the Thames, stone revetments were built by individual wharf owners in the late fourteenth and early fifteenth centuries. Finally, a contribution by private capital was made to transport facilities by the building of inns, in towns, in villages on main roads, and in isolated spots, where travellers could obtain shelter, storage space, stabling, and both cart-drivers and their horses could be fed.[147] Some were

---

[144] E. Jervoise, *The Ancient Bridges of the North of England* (London, 1931).

[145] A. Betterton and D. Dymond, *Lavenham: Industrial Town* (Lavenham, 1989), 16, 113–15.

[146] G. Egan, 'Industry and Economics on the Medieval and Later London Waterfront', in G. L. Good, R. H. Jones, and M. W. Ponsford (eds.), *Waterfront Archaeology: Proceedings of the Third International Conference*, Council for British Archaeology Research Reports, 74 (1991), 9–12; G. Milne, *The Port of Medieval London* (Stroud, 2003), 135–42.

[147] e.g. E. Roberts, *Hampshire Houses 1250–1700: Their Dating and Development* (Winchester, 2003), 193–5; W. A. Pantin, 'Medieval Inns', in E. M. Jope (ed.), *Studies in Building History: Essays in Recognition of the Work of B. H. St. J. O'Neil* (London, 1961), 166–91; P. Spufford, *Power and Profit: The Merchant in Medieval Europe* (London, 2002), 203–8.

built by institutions as an investment, but as always many more were constructed by individual laymen without leaving documentation, apart from
references in rentals, deeds, or court records to their distinctive signs (the
Hart, the Griffon, the Talbot, and so on) and to the ostlers' breach of
regulations in the sale of ale or horse bread (coarse bread baked specifically
for horses).

Conclusion

The period between the Black Death and the early sixteenth century saw
some important changes in the quantity and quality of consumption. The
increased expenditure on consumer goods did not prevent investment. Lords
probably invested less in the long run, but the newly active groups, such as the
farmers, and the entrepreneurs and artisans who financed the industrial mills,
spent much more. New trends in demand for cloth and meat encouraged the
building of fulling mills, dyeworks, and sheepcotes. Urban industry seems
less subject to change, but the brewing industry provides an excellent example
of a response to consumer preferences. Growth in ale drinking promoted a
move away from part-time small-scale production by ale-wives, towards the
concentration of brewing in fewer, more specialized ale-houses. The introduction of hopped beer converted customers to a new taste, mostly in eastern
England. Because beer did not deteriorate as quickly as ale, the drink could be
stored for longer and distributed over long distances. This encouraged an
increased scale of production. Specialist brewers were routinely investing £20
in equipment which rarely cost the ale-wife more than a pound or two. In this
and other parts of the economy, consumption and investment went hand in
hand.[148]

---

[148] R. W. Unger, 'Technical Change in the Brewing Industry in Germany, the Low Countries
and England in the Late Middle Ages', *Journal of European Economic History*, 21 (1992), 281–313;
Bennett, *Ale, Beer*, 49, 79–92.

5

Subsistence and Markets

We must accustom ourselves to the paradox that in a period of recession, and particularly in the fifteenth century, the structures of society and economy were changing in ways that make them appear more 'modern', which flies in the face of our customary assumptions about the link between growth and 'progress'.

The argument presented in this chapter is that while the volume of economic activity contracted, the ingrained habits of marketing and the employment of credit and money continued. This was an age of opportunity and prosperity for many individuals, and various groups carved out a new place for themselves in the social hierarchy. These arguments will be demonstrated with an example of a particularly significant group of entrepreneurs, the farmers.

The Retreat From the Market

There is some evidence for a declining quantity of market activity, and also a movement away from the use of money. As we would expect after the pronounced fall in population of the fourteenth century, towns shrank in size, giving rise to complaints of decay and desolation among contemporaries, and the 'urban decline' of historians in the last century.[1] The volume of trade apparently shrank, judging by the fall in tolls collected at weekly markets. At Melton Mowbray in Leicestershire, for example, the lord of the town received in a year in the late thirteenth century market and fair tolls of £20, but in most years in the period 1427–96 these had fallen to between £3 and £6 for the market and £1–£4 for the fair. When we know that in other markets a toll of 1*d*. was paid on each sale of a horse, a cow, eight sheep or pigs, or a cartload

---

[1] The controversy is summed up in A. Dyer, *Decline and Growth in English Towns 1400–1640* (Cambridge, 1995).

of grain, this could mean that the number of transactions in the market liable to toll had fallen from perhaps 10,000 to less than 2,000 in the worst years.[2]

Primary products, such as grain and wool, which formed a high proportion of the commodities which passed through markets such as Melton, fell in price as the number of consumers shrank more rapidly than the area of land devoted to corn growing and sheep grazing. Those who grew and sold these crops complained about the low rewards for their efforts, such as members of the Paston family, faced with the problem of making a profit from Norfolk barley in a glutted market in the mid-fifteenth century. A book of school exercises produced at the end of the fifteenth century, which gave common-place sentiments in English to be translated into Latin, commented that peasants felt the same disappointment, as the scholar expresses his sympathy for 'the poor husbands' who wished to 'make money of their stuff for the king's silver', but 'the price of corn and sheep and of all beasts is abated in so much that they sell much things for little silver'.[3]

Household economies were organized to take account of this situation. A survey of 1411 made for Coventry Priory shows that instead of requiring the farmers of their manors (mainly in Warwickshire) to pay the usual cash rent, the monks arranged for specified quantities of grain and other basic foodstuffs to be delivered directly to the monastery.[4] This was the method by which monasteries arranged supply from their estates in the eleventh and twelfth centuries, before the commercial revolution. The monks in the early fifteenth century may have judged that potential farmers would have been daunted by the difficulties of raising large sums in cash in a sluggish market. Later in the century we occasionally find tenants on other estates who were contracted to pay their rents in cash persuading their lords to accept cartloads of grain or hay instead of money.[5] A symptom of the difficulties that tenants experienced in finding cash was their inability to pay on time, which was one of the causes of the accumulation of arrears which are a notorious feature of lords' accounts in the fifteenth century. On some manors the total of payments in arrears, most of them resulting from rents that had not been paid in full, exceeded the annual revenues.[6]

---

[2] J. Laughton and C. Dyer, 'Seasonal Patterns of Trade in the Later Middle Ages: Buying and Selling at Melton Mowbray, Leicestershire, 1400–1520', *Nottingham Medieval Studies*, 46 (2002), 166–70.

[3] R. H. Britnell, 'The Pastons and Their Norfolk', *Ag.HR* 36 (1988), 137–9; W. Nelson (ed.), *A Fifteenth Century School Book* (Oxford, 1956), 91–2.

[4] TNA: PRO, E164/21.

[5] C. Dyer, *Lords and Peasants in a Changing Society: The Estates of the Bishopric of Worcester 680–1540* (Cambridge, 1980), 183.

[6] Ibid. 179–80; T. B. Pugh (ed.), *The Marcher Lordships of South Wales, 1415–1536: Select Documents* (Cardiff, 1963), 161–2, 182.

As peasants accumulated more land, a higher proportion of them became self-sufficient in basic foodstuffs. If we regard 12–15 acres as the amount of land that could provide a family with all of the grain that it needed, then in 1280 in the east midlands at least 42 per cent of rural households were inadequately provided, and therefore had to buy at least part of their food.[7] In 1480 about two-thirds of rural households in the midlands had enough land to produce all of the grain for their food needs.[8] This was all to the benefit of the peasants, we might think, and indeed, a poem of about 1500 celebrates the material well-being of the husbandman, with his house well stocked with bacon, salt beef, malt, and onions.[9] But if they wished to take advantage of the opportunities to build up larger holdings, the market was not very encouraging, as they sold produce cheaply while labour was expensive. As labour contributed a major element to the prices of manufactured goods, or to the cost of building work, these items of expenditure were not easily affordable.

Although peasants (and producers on a more substantial scale) were required to pay rents and taxes in cash, and they expected to be able to spend money in the local markets, they avoided using coins. They engaged in transactions of all kinds—buying and selling goods, hiring labour, and paying rents for subletting land—without handing over any money, or perhaps with no more than a few pence in 'earnest money' to seal a bargain. After the passage of time debtors and creditors would meet and draw up a 'reckoning' or a 'counter', in which various transactions would be put together, and might even cancel each other out, leaving the parties on a level footing or able to settle with a modest payment. For example, when the Cotswold grazier and wool merchant Thomas Heritage was owed 40s. by his cousin, Thomas Palmer of Lemington (Gloucestershire), in 1510, Heritage took nineteen loads of firewood from Palmer worth 19s. in part payment.[10]

An obstacle to the use of money lay in the shortage of the coins themselves, especially in the middle years of the fifteenth century.[11] The old sources of silver on the continent were yielding less precious metal, and the amount in circulation was reduced by wear, hoarding, and the flow of silver from Europe to the east to pay for imported luxuries. This inconvenience of cash payment encouraged the use of reckonings and barter. In 1446, after the death of Joan Giffard of Weston Subedge in Gloucestershire, her executors settled her debts

---

[7] E. A. Kosminsky, *Studies in the Agrarian History of England in the Thirteenth Century* (Oxford, 1956), 216–23.

[8] *AHEW* iii. 636–7; Dyer, *Lords and Peasants*, 300; id., *Warwickshire Farming: Preparations for Agricultural Revolution*, Dugdale Soc. Occasional Papers, 27 (1981), 8.

[9] W. Hazlitt, *Early Popular Poetry of England*, 4 vols. (London, 1866), i. 210–11.

[10] Westminster Abbey Muniments, 12258, fo. 84.

[11] P. Spufford, *Money and Its Use in Medieval Europe* (Cambridge, 1988), 339–62.

and made her bequests in sheep, of which she owned large numbers, rather than cash.[12] They sent thirteen of the animals to a tradesman who had sold her cloth, and four to pay for the mending of a roof, and so on. All over the country those making wills bequeathed goods such as animals or bushels of corn, which was a traditional practice, but reinforced by the testators' knowledge that they owned little ready money, and that it might not be easily obtained. When tenants rented land to subtenants—which is not recorded as often as it occurred because it could be in breach of manorial rules—they would sometimes use the device of champart, that is, the tenant paid a fraction, often a third, of the crop in rent. Similarly, it was common to pay workers partly with meals, pasturage of animals, and other benefits in kind, though these were not necessarily new practices but are just recorded for the first time.[13]

In the countryside in the thirteenth and fourteenth centuries, if the parties failed to agree because they fell into dispute over defective goods, or because work had not been done properly, or because a cash loan was not repaid, or most commonly when payment had not been made for goods or services, the injured party brought a plea of debt before the manor court. In many manor courts by about 1430 or 1450 these pleas were reduced in number or had even virtually disappeared, giving the impression of a fall in the number of financial transactions. That was partly because of changes in the status and authority of the court. At the mercantile level the legal framework for the registration and recovery of debt did not decline, yet the number of debts recorded, and the amount of money in dispute, did diminish in the early fifteenth century, showing that as the supply of money was reduced, so was the availability of credit.[14]

The Market Continues

These symptoms of a retreat from the market after the Black Death give a misleading impression of the period. It is true that the really decisive commercial growth occurred at an earlier period, especially in the thirteenth century. That expansion involved much more than a quantitative increase in the volume of traded goods, or in the numbers of people buying and

[12] Dorset Record Office, D10/M231.

[13] A subletting contract is recorded in a plea of trespass in the court roll of Blackwell (Warwickshire) in 1412: Alice Lette, who held a half-yardland, let 2 selions to Robert Bocher 'for the third sheaf', but she claimed that he took too large a share of the produce: Worcester Cathedral Library, E46; J. Hatcher, 'England in the Aftermath of the Black Death', *P&P* 144 (1994), 23, 29–31.

[14] P. Nightingale, 'Monetary Contraction and Mercantile Credit in Later Medieval England', *Ec.HR*, 2nd ser., 43 (1990), 560–75.

selling, or in the number of trading places and occasions. The exchange economy seeped into every corner of society, involving smallholders as well as the better off, and extended into every region. It changed the way of life of everyone, as not just those who migrated into towns but also those who were left behind in the country learned new methods of production and acquired new tastes in consumption.[15] The commercial growth reinforced rather than threatened the social order, as lords managed the changes and hoped to profit from them, for example, by founding towns and markets. Peasants were made bolder by their contact with the market, but the towns were not offering any challenge to lords. The towns enjoyed the patronage of the aristocracy, and the leading townsmen, while sometimes joining political movements such as the baronial reform campaign of 1258–65, tended to focus on defending their particular liberties within the existing political and social framework.[16]

The intellectuals came to accept the commercial way of life. Such influential figures as the Merton Calculators (at Oxford) of the late thirteenth century had experience of practical affairs of estate and domestic management through occupying administrative positions in their academic institution.[17] Philosophers throughout Christendom accepted the idea that trade was based on a mutual and just exchange, and that money provided the best means of measuring value and therefore ensuring equality of gain between the parties. The level of prices was established by the market, so the just price was in effect fixed by supply and demand, and the mechanism for setting prices should not be distorted by monopolies. The view was developed that extra payments could be levied by lenders in order to obtain compensation for losses incurred by the absence of the money loaned. The cash, had it not been lent, might have been profitably invested. It was argued that merchants were entitled to some profit in recompense for their risk and skill. Local and royal courts devised their own rules and practices in the thirteenth and fourteenth centuries on moneylending, the setting of prices (especially for food and drink), and the cornering of the market by unscrupulous traders, known as regrating and forstalling. Sometimes the central courts borrowed from local practice, and sometimes ideas diffused down from the centre. The debates on the morality of moneylending continued into the fifteenth century, when the legitimacy of the lender's profit was defended, providing that the amount charged was not excessive—usury was defined as interest above 10 per cent.

[15] P. R. Schofield, *Peasant and Community in Medieval England, 1200–1500* (Basingstoke, 2003), 131–56.

[16] S. H. Rigby, *English Society in the Later Middle Ages: Class, Status and Gender* (Basingstoke, 1995), 160–77.

[17] J. Kaye, *Economy and Nature in the Fourteenth Century* (Cambridge, 1998), 32–6.

In spite of these compromises, usury in particular, and moneygrubbing in general, continued to be regarded with suspicion and even with contempt.[18]

While an important sea-change both in the use and perception of market exchange occurred in the thirteenth century, we should not in consequence regard the period after the crisis of the fourteenth century as a backwater or a period when people withdrew from the market. Once a whole population had been immersed in habitual buying and selling, it could not readily unlearn the lessons or dismantle the mechanisms based on money. The shortage of money was not as desperate as at first appears, as the number of coins shrank but so did the population, meaning that the volume of coinage in circulation actually increased from a figure variously estimated at 3*s.*–7*s.* per head in 1300 to 8*s.* per head in 1480. The number of convenient silver coins (pennies, half-groats worth 2*d.*, and groats worth 4*d.*) declined, which meant that the quantity of silver per person fell to as little as 1*s.*–2*s.* in 1422. In the late fifteenth century traders were handling significant numbers of gold coins worth 6*s.* 8*d.* and 3*s.* 4*d.*, which created difficulties when the majority of everyday transactions required payments of sums lower than a shilling.[19]

Though faced with practical problems, the market maintained a high level of activity in the fifteenth century. For example, tenant obligations in the countryside were converted by about 1400 almost entirely from labour to cash. This was not part of 'the rise of the money economy', but reflected the new relationship between lords and tenants. Lords were abandoning the direct cultivation of their demesnes, and had no need themselves of the labour services of tenants. They could have granted the labour services of the tenants to the leaseholders who took on the demesnes, as they had done in the twelfth century, but it would have been difficult to persuade the tenants to accept such a transfer. The tenants had always preferred to pay in cash, partly because it removed the practical inconvenience of turning out to do labour on the demesne when they would have been more gainfully employed on their own holdings, and partly because free tenants paid money rents, and customary tenants aspired to all of the benefits of free tenure. In a world with relative plenty of land and a shortage of tenants, their views carried considerable weight.

---

[18] J. T. Noonan, *The Scholastic Analysis of Usury* (Cambridge, Mass., 1957); N. Jones, *God and the Moneylenders: Usury and Law in Early Modern England* (Oxford, 1989), 8–14; O. Langholm, *Economics in the Medieval Schools: Wealth, Exchange, Value, Money and Usury According to the Paris Theological Tradition, 1200–1350* (Leiden, 1992), 586–93; D. Wood, *Medieval Economic Thought* (Cambridge, 2002); G. Seabourne, *Royal Regulation of Loans and Sales in Medieval England: 'Monkish Superstition and Civil Tyranny'* (Woodbridge, 2003).

[19] N. J. Mayhew, 'Population, Money Supply, and the Velocity of Circulation in England, 1300–1700', *Ec.HR* 48 (1995), 243–50; M. Allen, 'The Volume of English Currency, 1158–1470', *Ec.HR* 54 (2001), 606.

The lords, especially the greater lords, took a step away from self-sufficiency and direct supply of food to their households when they leased out their demesnes. This was quite convenient, because as basic foodstuffs were cheap they could be bought as they were needed in markets or by direct negotiation with producers. Wealthier lords, from the late thirteenth century, were ceasing to travel constantly from manor to manor. They occupied a few houses for a longer time each year, like the dukes and duchesses of Buckingham, who spent most of each year in the fifteenth century at Kimbolton (Huntingdonshire), Maxstoke (Warwickshire), and Writtle (Essex).[20] From these more permanent residences supplies of basic foodstuffs were bought locally, and the cost was saved of keeping large numbers of habitable manor houses across the scattered estate. Direct production was also going out of use within some of the larger households, as many of them stopped brewing their own ale but instead bought it by the barrel from local brewers.[21]

Among peasants money was still much used. They had to sell produce not just to pay their money rent—which was not so new, because a high proportion of their obligations were being paid in cash before 1300—but they also spent money on their own account. We have seen that they went in for a good deal of moneyless exchange through delaying payments for their daily dealings with neighbours, which were periodically settled through 'reckonings'. But these calculations show that even when no money was being paid immediately, each sale or service was given a monetary value. As the intellectuals said, the fairness of an exchange measured in money made its use a practical necessity and gave it a moral standing as well, in villages as well as in the counting houses of merchants. The market pushed peasant production towards specialization in the fifteenth century just as it did in the thirteenth; indeed, to a greater degree, in that some of them became entirely committed to pastoral agriculture, as in the north Warwickshire township of Bordesley by *c*.1500.[22] They expanded production of marketable crops such as saffron in the south-east.[23]

Wills demonstrate the assumptions of peasants and artisans that everything had a monetary value, and that cash could be raised through moveable assets and landed property. John Broun of Hopton in Suffolk, for example, who died in 1453, in typical peasant style left malt to repair the church fabric of Burgate.[24] It was probably intended that the churchwardens would brew the

---

[20] C. Rawcliffe, *The Staffords, Earls of Stafford and Dukes of Buckingham 1394–1521* (Cambridge, 1978), 66–7, 86–7.

[21] C. Dyer, *Standards of Living in the Later Middle Ages: Social Change in England c.1200–1520*, revised edn. (Cambridge, 1998), 57–8.

[22] *AHEW* iii. 227.

[23] J. Thirsk, *Alternative Agriculture: A History* (Oxford, 1997), 16, 17.

[24] Suffolk Record Office, Bury St Edmunds Branch, IC500/2/9, fo. 151.

malt and hold a church ale at which money would be raised. He also left a bushel of malt to each of his godchildren. But he bequeathed more than a pound in cash in small parcels to various pious causes, and to friends and relatives. He specified that his wife should have a holding for life, after which it should be sold, and left another holding (together with household equipment and agricultural implements such as a cart and a plough) to his son John, providing that he paid £10 over a period of four years in equal instalments. This money was presumably to pay debts, maintain John's mother, and to fund other bequests, notably to pay for a chaplain's prayers for a year. The cash was intended to finance annual expenditure, so it was convenient that it be paid over a number of years, but it also helped John Broun junior that he was not expected to raise the whole sum at once.

Broun was by no means alone among peasant testators in his insistence that sons should pay for their land. It could be said that they were being given an option to buy their inheritance. A more accurate description would be that they were being committed to fulfil their obligations to other relatives. Sometimes the executors were told to sell land to family members at advantageous prices, but often they were expected to obtain the full market value. This was linked with the payment of debts, but the money was also needed to maintain a widow or other dependants, who often at this period received a regular cash income rather than the liveries of grain which were commonly granted in the thirteenth and fourteenth centuries.

We now know from numerous local studies of manorial court rolls in East Anglia before 1350 that only a minority of transfers of customary land involved inheritance or even grants of holdings between members of the same family during their lifetime. On many manors only a fifth of transactions were between family members. By the fifteenth century in every region inheritance was in decline. Even in Halesowen in Worcestershire, where careful reconstitution of families allows us to observe land passing in the decades around 1400 between uncles and nephews, and to cousins and in-laws, land was no longer being transferred between relatives on a large scale by the 1430s.[25] Therefore, the market in land was being extended in the sense that a high proportion of land, often 80 per cent or more, was being acquired by people unrelated to the outgoing tenant. It could be said that this state of affairs was only temporary, because in the sixteenth century, as the value of land and its produce increased, a rising proportion of land was again transmitted and inherited within the family. But this does not mean that peasants had begun to behave as peasants should, according to modern expectations, and rediscovered the bond that linked a family and its land. On the contrary,

---

[25] Z. Razi, 'The Myth of the Immutable English Family', *P&P* 140 (1993), 27–33.

the peasants were behaving rationally, because as land became more valuable sons realized that as heirs they were on to a good thing, and stayed to inherit a valuable asset.[26] Previously, before 1500 or 1520, they had been able to go out in their early twenties and pick up pieces of land which were relatively plentiful, and did not have to wait for their inheritance. During the early sixteenth century these 'starter' plots were not so readily, or cheaply, available. We can conclude that in their land dealings peasants, in all parts of the country, had adopted the view that land could be bought and sold, and that the ups and downs of the market, rather than sentiment, played an important role in their decision-making.

The evidence for a land market consists normally of entries in manorial court rolls where a tenant surrenders a holding to the lord, for the use (*ad opus*) of another tenant, who then comes to the court and carries out the ceremonies necessary to be admitted as a tenant. The payment of money to the lord is always recorded—the entry fine or *gersuma*—and this often changed with fluctuations in the market, and so gives the impression that the main payment made was to the lord. In that case land would appear to have become very cheap indeed in the fifteenth century, because on most manors entry fines declined, either to very low levels of a few shillings for a holding of 15 or 30 acres, or just to some token payment of hens or geese, as if to keep alive the memory that a fine was payable. The manorial record usually tells us nothing about the bargaining between the incoming and outgoing tenants that accompanied these legal formalities, but wills leave us in no doubt that executors were regularly told to sell a holding (including customary land) at the most advantageous price.

Money changed hands between the tenants of customary holdings, and we should expect these not to have been negligible sums, because free land was often sold, even in the depressed years of the middle of the fifteenth century, for fifteen or twenty years purchase, that is, for at fifteen or twenty times the rental value of the land. Customary holdings were inferior to free land because they were subject to restrictions and extra payments such as the variable entry fine, but the differences were less acute after about 1400, as the labour services and some of the more resented obligations such as tallage were commuted or abolished, and entry fines ceased to be burdensome. We could even say that the markets for free and customary land moved closer together, as gentry and urban purchasers bought customary holdings, and landholders of all kinds held portfolios of property which included free, customary, and leasehold land in various combinations.[27]

[26] J. Whittle, *The Development of Agrarian Capitalism: Land and Labour in Norfolk 1440–1580* (Oxford, 2000), 120–77.

[27] P. R. Schofield, '*Extranei* and the Market for Customary Land on a Westminster Abbey Manor in the Fifteenth Century', *Ag.HR* 49 (2001), 1–16.

Rarely, payments between tenants were recorded in manorial court records, and particularly in Norfolk. The sums were normally of no direct interest to the lord, but when it was agreed that the money should be paid in instalments, the contract would specify that failure to pay would result in the land reverting to the seller, which would mean that the lord would find a former tenant returning to the holding. Also a contract registered in the court roll on a public occasion would make the payment enforceable. A typical agreement was made at Blickling in May 1439, when William Bryston and Margaret his wife surrendered into the lord's hands a messuage and 3⅞ acres of land for Nicholas Clerk, shoemaker, and Katherine his wife (and John Porter, an heir), on condition that Nicholas and Katherine pay £5. 3s. 4d. in eight annual instalments, every Easter, first 10s. and then 13s. 4d. in each subsequent year.[28] The sum would therefore be fully paid, and the grant would become 'firm and stable', at Easter 1447. The lord's entry fine amounted to 13s., which was unusually high for the period by comparison with the fines normally encountered outside East Anglia. This was a typical case because of the discrepancy between the purchase price of land and the entry fine, as the seller received 26s. 8d. per acre, while the lord's fine was set at 3s. 4d. per acre. The buyer was an artisan, and Blickling lay in an industrialized district, near Aylsham, where linen and worsted cloth were woven, which helps to explain the high land values (Table 5.1). At Costessey and Hevingham Bishops the prices, like those at Blickling, varied alarmingly from one holding to another, but averaged 25s.–36s. per acre in the mid-fifteenth century, rising on the latter manor to 49s. per acre in 1513–28.[29] Interpreting these figures involves many complexities, not least the inconsistency and variability in the prices which are concealed in the means and medians given in Table 5.1. Arable land commanded a lower price than orchard; very small holdings carried a higher price per acre than larger acreages; some of the transfers included an obligation to maintain an old person, or were part of the settlement of affairs under the terms of a will.

This commercialized part of a rich county presumably gives us an indication of how high prices could rise, but we know from occasional revelations of price that land carried a value in other, less intensively farmed and less industrialized parts of England. Prices per acre in Essex in the late fourteenth century vary from 12s. to 47s.; Suffolk wills of 1454 and 1486 record sales for 20s., 26s. 8d., and 52s. 6d. per acre, and in fifteenth-century East Sussex purchasers paid 12s. 6d. and 13s. 4d.[30]

[28] Norfolk Record Office, 11262 26A4.

[29] Whittle, *Agrarian Capitalism*, 110–13.

[30] C. Dyer, 'The Social and Economic Background to the Rural Revolt of 1381', in R. H. Hilton and T. H. Aston (eds.), *The English Rising of 1381* (Cambridge, 1984), 22; Suffolk Record Office, Bury St Edmunds Branch, IC500/2/9, fo. 175; Ipswich Branch, J421/3, fo. 104; M. Mate, 'The

Table 5.1. Some prices of customary land in Norfolk, 1390–1543 *(per acre).*

(a)

Manor	1390–9	1400–9	1410–19	1420–9	1430–9	1440–9	1450–9
Blickling*	44s. 0d.	19s. 10d.	22s. 7d.	—	36s. 0d.	42s. 0d.	20s. 0d.
Costessey*					25s. 6d.	24s. 8d.	19s. 9d.

(b)

Manor	1444–60	1483–97	1448–1512	1513–28	1529–43
Hevingham	36s. 4d.	30s. 0d.	25s. 4d.	27s. 8d.	48s. 8d.
Bishops†					

Note: *median price; †mean price.
Sources: Norfolk Record Office, NRS 11253; 91101; 11262 26A 4; 10192; Staffordshire Record Office, D641/3/D/1/29; Whittle, *Agrarian Capitalism*, 112.

Land may have been the most expensive purchase a peasant made, but it was one of many. The number of monetary transactions would clearly not match the 250 in a year recorded in the accounts of an eighteenth-century Lancashire farmer, Richard Latham. Dozens of separate sales of grain, wool, cheese, and livestock would be routinely contracted each year in the late fifteenth century on a larger holding practising mixed husbandry in lowland England, together with sales of smaller surpluses from garden and yard, such as fruit, honey, eggs, and poultry. If we add purchases the purchases for the farm of replacement livestock, horseshoes, and spare parts for implements, tar for treating sheep disease, wages for part-time help at harvest and for a full-time servant, as well as the consumption expenditure, including the purchase of ale, fish, and other foodstuffs, it would be difficult to believe that the total of payments in a year would have fallen far below a hundred.[31] Often the sums paid in each sale or purchase would have been less than a shilling, but a holding of 50 acres would have had a cumulative turnover of at least £5 each year.

All of these transactions, but especially the larger ones, would have depended on credit, yet the mechanics of lending and borrowing for the lower ranks of society remain something of a mystery. The litigation in the manor court, by which those who claimed debts would bring proceedings, provide us with the most abundant source of information. These have been

East Sussex Land Market and Agrarian Class Structure in the Late Middle Ages', *P&P* 139 (1993), 51–2.

[31] C. Muldrew, *The Economy of Obligation: The Culture of Credit and Social Relations in Early Modern England* (Basingstoke, 1998), 84.

investigated for the late thirteenth and fourteenth centuries, with important results for understanding social stratification in villages, the relationship between credit and the land market, and the economic consequences of harvests fluctuations on rural society. One conclusion has been that a wealthier stratum of peasants were able to exploit the indebtedness of their poorer neighbours to accumulate larger holdings in periods of food shortage. A sample of debts that came before the Blickling court in the 1430s, at the time of the purchase of land by Nicholas Clerk, arose from the sale of barley, malt, geese, barley straw, bread, and ale, and from unpaid wages for thatching work. The money owed commonly varied from 7*d.* to 3*s.* 4*d.*, which was similar to the sums which predominated in litigation before 1350. In the Blickling court a few unusually large debts appear, between £2 and £10, for sums of money supposed to have been paid for a holding of land, five cattle and twenty-four sheep, and substantial quantities of cloth.[32] Such large debts are normally absent from manorial courts, as they involved sums beyond their legal competence.

Church courts dealt with debts, some of them arising from probate disputes, for example, when an executor failed to make a payment required in the will. Ecclesiastical law was also concerned with the offence of breaking of oaths, and many loans involved the borrower swearing to repay. For example, in the Wisbech (Cambridgeshire) court held by the official of the bishop of Ely, among the cases of adultery, sabbath-breaking, absence from church, and failure to pay tithe, Margaret Roray was said in 1468 to have broken her oath by failing to repay 2*s.* 10*d.* owed to John Jackson. This amount of money involved lay near to the upper end of the range of sums claimed by litigants in the Wisbech court between 1467 and 1480, half of which fell between 4*d.* and 18*d.*, with no more than 12 per cent reaching 10*s.* or above.[33]

Occasionally we are told that the sum disputed in a court case was the result of a loan, presumably in cash, and it is possible to envisage that someone buying land, like Nicholas Clerk, or paying for a new house, would have borrowed small sums from a succession of neighbours. If this happened we do not hear much about it, because debt cases tend to disappear from manor courts in the fifteenth century. This does not mean that loans ceased, but rather that a credit network which had always existed was now

---

[32] P. R. Schofield, 'Access to Credit in the Early Fourteenth-Century English Countryside', in id. and N. J. Mayhew (eds.), *Credit and Debt in Medieval England c.1180–c.1350* (Oxford, 2002), 106–26; C. Briggs, 'Creditors and Debtors and Their Relationships at Oakington, Cottenham and Dry Drayton (Cambridgeshire), 1291–1350', in Schofield and Mayhew (eds.), *Credit and Debt*, 127–48; Norfolk Record Office, 11262 26A4.

[33] L. R. Poos (ed.), *Lower Ecclesiastical Jurisdiction in Late-Medieval England*, British Academy Records of Social and Economic History, NS, 32 (2001), 270–313.

being regulated and enforced mainly by neighbourly pressure and unofficial actions. Studies of credit within early modern communities show that people were very anxious to maintain their good reputation by keeping up with payments.[34] If individuals failed to honour their obligations, all of their business operations would be hampered by gossip and the resulting lack of trust. Community institutions would have offered opportunities for disputes over loans to be resolved, like the love days held by small-town fraternities, at which the master and aldermen would act as arbiters and persuaders.[35] More forceful action might include the seizure of cattle or other goods in distraint by the creditor, which helps to explain some of the incidents that came before the courts under the guise of thefts or trespasses.

A glimpse of the scale of borrowing in a single village comes from the Suffolk community of Dennington. Here Lady Katherine Wingfield had bequeathed £20 as a loan fund, to be kept in a chest in the parish church and distributed to applicants by local worthies who guarded the keys and kept rather inconsistent accounts.[36] In one year, in 1488, they recorded fourteen residents, each of whom borrowed between 6s. 8d. and 40s., which made a total of £18. 10s. 8d. The borrowers included some of the more credit-worthy members of the village, some of whom were required to deposit in the chest for security 'evidences' or title deeds of pieces of land.

This village loan chest was an unusual institution, but facilities existed for borrowing money on a similar scale from fraternities, which were especially numerous in eastern England. The fraternities accumulated cash reserves from the entry fees paid by new brothers and sisters, bequests from members, and rents from land that they acquired by gift or purchase. They could put this money to make substantial profits by lending it to members on short terms and at an interest rate often of 10 per cent. These 'stocks' contributed to the reserves of borrowable cash in a community, and could make a very useful source of finance for the 'stockholders' who were buying land or making some other major outlay. In the small town of Wymondham in Norfolk, for example, the fraternity in 1500 lent a total of £11. 18s. 9d. to thirty-one people, in sums varying between 2s. and 20s.[37] The fraternity could hope to recover its money because of the closeness of the bonds among its members, and the shame and humiliation which would felt by a bad debtor.

[34] Muldrew, *Economy of Obligation*, 148–72.

[35] G. Rosser, 'Going to the Fraternity Feast: Commensality and Social Relations in Late Medieval England', *Journal of British Studies*, 33 (1994), 440–1.

[36] Suffolk Record Office, Ipswich Branch, FC 112/A/1; J. J. Raven, 'Extracts from the Parish Book of Dennington, Co. Suffolk', *The East Anglian or Notes and Queries etc.*, NS, 3 (1889–90), 273–4.

[37] K. Farnhill, *Guilds and the Parish Community in Late Medieval East Anglia, c.1470–1550* (York, 2001), 68–9.

Neighbourly pressure alone would not always be effective, as is demonstrated in the Wisbech church court when the fraternity of St Katherine of Newton in 1469 brought cases against people who owed 13s. 4d., 23s. 4d., 40s., and 73s. 4d.[38] The widespread availability of credit through fraternities is suggested by the 'stocks' recorded in 1524 in Suffolk belonging to sixty-one fraternities and five other 'stocks' attributed to villages when the collectors of the subsidy in the county decided to bring them within the net of taxation.[39]

Other sources of credit included parish clergy, local monasteries and other religious institutions, and also traders, especially those from the nearby towns. But this does not rest on any great quantity of hard evidence. The parish clergy, for example, were quite often involved in debt litigation, and there are inventories, such as that of the vicar of Wharram le Street in Yorkshire, Thomas Grissaker, who died in 1511, who refers explicitly to three loans of cash, using the Latin word *mutuum*, of sums of 40s., and two of 6s. 8d., and his executors despaired of recovering loans in the same range from 5s. to 6s. 8d. (see Table 5.2).[40] The vicar, like many parish clergy, ran a small agricultural holding as a source of income. His sales of sheep had brought in more than £7, suggesting that he kept a flock of at least a hundred. The accounts of a merchant operating in the countryside, those of Thomas Heritage of Upper Ditchford, show that he was slow to pay his suppliers, so in his normal wool-trading activities the growers were advancing credit to him. But neighbours approached him for loans in quite separate negotiations. In 1520 he recorded that he had lent sums such as 6s. 8d., 10s., 13s. 4d., and 20s. to ten people, like William Bumpas of Longborough (Gloucestershire), who was one of his suppliers of wool.[41]

No English peasant accounts survive, but better-off peasants have left inventories of their possessions, including lists of their debts. In a few cases probate accounts give details of the affairs of the deceased as known to the executors. John Rede of Soham in Cambridgeshire, described as a shepherd and owning a flock of 140 sheep, in 1417 had assets worth £11. 10s. 3d., of which 31s. 11d. consisted of debts owed to him. However, his appraisers could also list 'desperate debts' that would in their view never be paid, of £4. 3s. 6d.[42] Most of those testators for whom we have inventories owed money and were owed money, like John Jakson of Grimston in Yorkshire, whose goods in 1464 were valued at £10. 13s. 1d., including in cash the princely

---

[38] Poos, *Ecclesiastical Jurisdiction*, 299–300.

[39] S. H. A. H[ervey] (ed.), *Suffolk in 1524: Being the Return for a Subsidy Granted in 1523*, Suffolk Green Books, 10 (Woodbridge, 1910), *passim*.

[40] Borthwick Institute of Historical Research, York, D. and C. wills, 1511, Grissaker.

[41] Westminster Abbey Muniments, 12258, fo. 76.

[42] TNA: PRO, PROB 2/1.

Table 5.2. Evidence of credit from inventories and accounts, 1464–1520

(a) Some debts listed in Yorkshire inventories.

Owed to Thomas Grissaker, vicar of Wharram le Street, 1511
Clear debts
Robert Halbern and Richard Croppton for sheep, 18s.
Robert Wankar of Wetwang, for lambs, 53s. 4d.
Richard Skelton of Marton, for 39 wethers, £3. 13s. 8d.
Thomas Houtbye, *ex mutuo*, 40s.
Robert Houtbye, *ex mutuo*, 6s. 8d.
Thomas Bol3ar, *ex mutuo*, 6s. 8d.
Robert Haubbern and Richard Cropp', £3. 10s. 0d.

Total £13. 8s. 4d.

Desperate debts
Peter Irnkynson, 7s.
William Kexbye, 10s.
Henry Raythe, 12s.
Robert Dice, *ex mutuo*, 6s. 8d.
Herre Gre', *ex mutuo*, 5s. 0d.
Robert Marton, *ex mutuo*, 6s. 8d.
Edward Bigott, £3. 6s. 8d.
Peter Bigott, 45s.
Sir Thomas Faunke, £3
The said Sir Thomas, 30s.
The said Sir Thomas, 26s. 8d.
Bryan Tayl3our, 26s. 8d.

Total £15. 2s. 4d.

Owed by John Jakson of Grimston, 1464
John Cotes of York, 5s.
Thomas Cotyngham, chaplain, 4s.
Richard Sporete, for farm, 4s.
Alex' Froste, 2s. 3d.
John Bysshop, 10d.
Robert Strensall, herring monger, 21d.
Richard Parke, fishmonger, 12d.
William Patan, 15d.
Robert Smyth of York, smith, 14d.
Thomas Brandesby, chaplain, 14d.
John Tylson of Holtby, 2s. 8d.
Thomas Cowper of York, 6s. 8d.
Agnes Scharp, 5s.
Brothers and sisters of St Elen's guild near York, 2s. 2d.
William Swan of Fulford, 12d.
John Johnson of Lund, 12d.
John Scalon of Heslington, 8d.
Thomas Sigrave of Grimston, 4½d.

(*continued*)

Table 5.2. (*Continued*)

Thomas Bullok, 2s. 5d.
Ralph Michell, 12d.
William Thomson of Elvington, 21d.
James Diconson of Grimston, 4d.
Clerk of the parish church of St Nicholas in the suburb of York, 3d.
Richard Sprote, for farm, 16s.
John Gurnard, chaplain, 2s. 3d.
James Bronne, 5d.
John Sigrave, for a bridle, 12d.

Total 67s. 4½d.

Owed by John Gaythird, husbandman, of Acomb, 1494
Lord, for farm at Whitsun and Martinmas, 15s.
Mr Lasse, for farm, 52s.
Mr John Deyce, for sheep, 10s.
James Lonsdale, 20s.
Joan Watson, 9s. 5½d.
John Blenco, 4s.
John Stanehous, 5s.
Guy Frankland, 7s.
Brother Robert Massam, 2s.
Gybson's wife, 3s. 2d.
John Herryson, 20d.
Thomas Pereson, 10d.
Common herdsman, 8d.
For threshing barley, 13d.
Mr John Deyce, for sheep, 13s. 4d.
For the fine of the tenement of his sister, 21s. 8d.
William Meylbe for wage (9s. 8d.) and livery (3s.), 12s. 8d.
Joan Sala for salary (7s. 8d.) and livery (7s. 8d.)
John Salo, 20d.
To Crow of Acomb, for free rent, 5s.
To Robert Schipton, 4d.

Total £9. 13s. 11½d.

Sources: Borthwick Institute of Historical Research, York, D. and C. wills, 1511, Grissaker; 1464, Jakson; 1494, Gaythird.

(b) Debts owed to Thomas Heritage of Upper Ditchford, Gloucestershire, 1520

First, Thomas Lee of Burton [Dassett], 13s. 4d.
William Bumpas of Longborough, 20s.
Thomas Mansell of Northwick, 13s. 4d.
John a Woode of the Furde (?), 20s.
William Mannsell of Bourton-on-the-Hill, 6s. 8d.
William Palmer of Bourton, tailor, for a horse, 13s. 4d.
Item, in money lent to the said Palmer, 6s. 8d.

Table 5.2. (*Continued*)

Item to Stevyns of Paxford, 10*s.*
To young John Whete of Aston [Magna, in Blockley], 10*s.* (paid, 7*s.* 3*d.*)
William Powle of the Furde, 6*s.* 8*d.*

Total £6

Source: Westminster Abbey Muniments 12258, fo. 76ʳ.

sum of 2*d.* He was owed 15*s.* 2*d.*, and owed more than £3. In some cases a high proportion of a peasant's assets consisted of debts. In 1494 John Gaythird, who probably came from Acomb near York, had assets worth £33, of which a half consisted of money owed to him, mainly for a building which he had sold, while he in turn owed nearly £10. (Table 5.2) William Akelum of Wharram le Street, when he died in 1481, owed £12. 14*s.* 0½ *d.*, but his goods were valued at only 57*s.*[43] The debts included small items of consumption expenditure. Some of Jakson's debts arose from purchases from tradesmen in York, such as 21*d.* owed to a herring-monger, 12*d.* to a fishmonger, and 14*d.* to a smith. One sum of 12*d.* was said to have been paid for a bridle. Jakson also owed sums to people from villages within 4 miles of Grimston, probably for animals or work on the holding, which varied between 4*d.* and 2*s.* 8*d.* These debts resemble in size and type those that were pursued through the manorial courts. Small sums were often owed to clergy, presumably for offerings or tithes. Rent payments are mentioned. Jakson owed 4*s.* and 16*s.* as farms (leasehold rents). Gaythird's list included 15*s.* and 52*s.* for two separate farms, 5*s.* for a freehold rent, and 21*s.* 8*d.* for an entry fine that he was paying on behalf of his sister. This is the counterpart from the peasant's perspective of the arrears of rent which lords' bailiffs recorded in their accounts. Jakson also owed money for sheep purchased, and wages, both to two regular employees, probably servants, to a hired worker who threshed barley, and a share of the pay of a common herdsman.

We might ask how the local worthies who drew up the inventories, usually the neighbours and social equals of the deceased, were able to itemize twenty or thirty individual debts. While one of their sources would undoubtedly have been the creditors, who would have been anxious to volunteer information, such oral evidence would not have been given by those who owed money, and especially the 'desperate' debtors. The likely conclusion must be that written evidence of some kind was kept by peasants, and this was used by the appraisers. Sometimes the testator had been able in his last illness to

[43] Borthwick Institute of Historical Research, York, D. and C. wills, 1464, Jakson; 1494, Gaythird; 1481, Akclum.

remember his debts, dictating the information to a clerk and therefore creating written records (see p. 122). Another source of information would have been the widow, who was often the joint tenant of land and in some sense a partner in her husband's dealings.

Credit was a normal, and indeed very important, part of peasant lives. The imbalance between William Akelum's assets and debts may reflect the run-down state of his holding in his old age or after a period of illness, and the disadvantage of using probate inventories is that they tend to reflect the economy of a household in its declining phase. In general we would expect that the more active the peasant, both in terms of his life-cycle and the scale of his assets, the larger would be his debts on both sides. A late fifteenth-century peasant who has left us with an account book, or rather a collection of jottings and memoranda, was Benedetto del Massarizia from a village on the outskirts of Sienna, who acquired much land and led a stormy life—his second wife walked out in 1481, giving him extra financial problems.[44] He lived well, with a silver buckle on his belt, and he bought an expensive bed. He held much land on various tenures, as did our better-off English tenants, and like them went in for a number of moneymaking ventures, such as lime burning. The more money he made, or was in prospect of making, the more he fell into debt, and throughout his life he owed money to his landlords and many others. He acquired his largest holding in 1466, and in order to pay the rent also went in for sharecropping. His lime burning was designed to supply an income which would pay off his debts in annual instalments. The experiences of our Yorkshire husbandmen would not have been so very different.

The Role of Towns

If the economy after the fourteenth-century crisis had been reverting back to subsistence and self-sufficiency, then the towns would have been in great difficulties. There are many symptoms of decline, such as decayed buildings and falling rents, and some historians have even detected signs of de-urban-ization. Populations fell, the built-up area shrank, basic industries migrated, the volume of trade slumped, and civic finances gave the administrators cause for complaint. These would be the consequences that we would expect if the producers of foodstuffs were concentrating on providing for their own needs rather than selling into urban markets, and were cutting back on their consumption of goods produced in towns or traded through them. This is not the place to rehearse the debate for and against urban decline, except to

[44] D. Balestracci, *The Renaissance in the Fields* (Philadelphia, 1999).

say that some of the evidence produced for a catastrophic reduction in urban fortunes may exaggerate the problem. The dramatic fall in market tolls at Melton Mowbray (see p. 173 above), which is found in many other towns, cannot represent an accurate index of the volume of the town's trade, and must reflect wholesale exemption and evasion of tolls. Many towns appear to have lost population in proportion to the general fall in numbers—that is, the number of their inhabitants was halved—but the urban centres remained in relative terms as large, and occupied a similar position in the commercial system as they had before the plagues and famine. In the last two centuries before the Reformation, in the context of the shrinkage in the population and size of towns, a mature urban system was developing in sophistication and adjusting to new economic influences.

Mercantile capitalism had gone through an important period of growth in the thirteenth and fourteenth centuries. Before 1300 international and more local trade had grown to a very high level, with the exports of wool and imports of wine reaching their peaks in the first decade of the fourteenth century. The English merchants had been prevented by continental competitors from profiting fully from the flow of goods, but during the fourteenth century they came to control a higher proportion of trade. Although when they raised capital and formed business partnerships they lagged behind the techniques of their Italian contemporaries, their methods seem to have served their purpose in moving goods and yielding profits. Merchants were pushed into organizations such as the staplers to carry wool to Calais and the Merchant Adventurers to export cloth to the Low Countries, eventually focusing on Antwerp. They used credit instruments to transfer money from the continent to London which functioned as bills of exchange.[45]

The advanced accounting systems which had been developed in Italy had no impact in England, and merchants' accounts consisted of memoranda of expenditure and income, rather than systematic calculations of profit. These must have been very difficult to use for any other purpose than checking that debts had been paid. This has been taken as marking the inadequacy of medieval merchants in England and indeed in much of northern Europe, but

---

[45] A. Hanham, *The Celys and their World: An English Merchant Family of the Fifteenth Century* (Cambridge, 1985), 186–202, 398–414; J. I. Kermode, 'Money and Credit in the Fifteenth Century: Some Lessons From Yorkshire', *Business History Review*, 65 (1991), 475–501; P. Nightingale, *A Medieval Mercantile Community: The Grocers' Company and the Politics and Trade of London, 1000–1485* (New Haven and London, 1995), 524–9; J. I. Kermode, *Medieval Merchants: York, Beverley and Hull in the Later Middle Ages* (Cambridge, 1998), 223–47; A. Sutton, 'The Merchant Adventurers of England: Their Origins and the Mercers' Company of London', *Historical Research*, 75 (2002), 25–46.

the deficiency was not confined to the middle ages, and some firms had not adopted double-entry bookkeeping in the early nineteenth century.[46]

The most important changes concerned the functioning of the network of towns and trading places. This amounts to a development in 'market integration', in the economists' phrase. London, always the largest town and the hub of communications, rose to a pre-eminent position in the fifteenth century. Already by the early fourteenth century the strength of London's coastal trade can be judged by the close correlation in wheat prices between London and Exeter. The prices moved in roughly the same fashion, but then diverged temporarily in the 1350s and 1360s; from 1370 they coincided once more, and continued to track one another through the fifteenth century, a period when prices were not given to striking volatility.[47]

Debt disputes brought before the court of common pleas show that by 1424 London's commercial links had extended far beyond the south-east and over the whole of the midlands. York was still a regional capital in the sense that lesser traders in Yorkshire would obtain their goods from York suppliers, but in Devon, for example, the petty traders would deal directly with Londoners, and not through intermediaries in Exeter. In the next 150 years York came under stronger influence from London, while the commerce of Devon developed greater independence.[48] London grocers were prominent in supplying the provinces with spices and dyestuffs, and London mercers dominated the linen trade. London had a long-term leading role in the luxury trades, so it is not surprising that the bishop of Carlisle bought his spices in London, and London marblers and bell-founders were selling memorial brasses and church bells in Leicestershire and Northamptonshire.[49] London, the administrative capital since the twelfth century, was developing its role as an economic metropolis. This was achieved to some extent through the political power and influence of the Londoners, who, for example, manipulated the Merchant Adventurer's company to the disadvantage of merchants

[46] B. S. Yamey, 'The Functional Development of Double Entry Bookkeeping', in C. Nobes (ed.), *The Development of Double Entry: Selected Essays* (New York, 1984), 136.

[47] J. A. Galloway, 'One Market or Many? London and the Grain Trade of England', in id. (ed.), *Trade, Urban Hinterlands and Market Integration c.1300–1600*, Centre for Metropolitan History Working Paper Series, 3 (2000), 23–42.

[48] D. Keene, 'Changes in London's Economic Hinterland as Indicated by Debt Cases in the Court of Common Pleas', in Galloway (ed.), *Trade, Urban Hinterlands*, 59–81.

[49] Nightingale, *Mercantile Community*; A. Sutton, 'Some Aspects of the Linen Trade, c.1130 to 1500, and the Part Played by the Mercers of London', *Textile History*, 30 (1999), 155–75; Cumbria Record Office, Carlisle, DRC 2/15; M. Norris, *Monumental Brasses: The Memorials* (London, 1977), 73–92, 132–53; C. M. Barron, 'Johanna Hill (d. 1441) and Johanna Sturdy (d. *c.*1460), Bell-Founders', in C. M. Barron and A. F. Sutton (eds.), *Medieval London Widows, 1300–1500* (London, 1994), 99–111.

outside the capital. In general the advance of the Londoners depended not on the exploitation of monopolies but on the economic advantages for provincial dealers and customers dealing directly with the importing and distributing merchants. The Londoners had been able to reduce transaction costs, one method being the deployment of their intelligence and news-gathering systems, evident from such sources as the letters written by members of the Cely family in the 1470s and 1480s. Political news and gossip carried at considerable speed across the country, but information concerning prices and local gluts and shortages, or the activities of competitors, enabled traders to respond profitably.[50]

The provincial urban network was established before 1300, in the sense that towns had been founded by then, and they already formed a hierarchy which enabled the trade of each region to flow up from the smaller market towns to the larger provincial towns, and the goods from the larger towns could be distributed through the smaller centres. In the midlands, Coventry had emerged by the early fourteenth century as the capital of the whole region, served by the ports of Boston to the east and Bristol in the west. The larger towns, such as Leicester and Worcester, lay below Coventry in the hierarchy, and dependent on them were the hundred or more smaller towns of the region. Each town developed its own rural hinterland, which varied in shape depending on the road system and the location of competitors, but consistently included the villages and hamlets within a radius of 6 miles.[51] This pattern shifted between 1350 and 1550, but was not transformed. Boston and other east-coast ports lost a good deal of trade, and the region came under stronger influence from London. A few of the weaker small towns ceased to be urban, and perhaps Betley in Staffordshire provides an example of that demotion. Village markets which had been founded during the market mania of the thirteenth century mostly disappeared, which concentrated trade in the market towns. Changes in the countryside, notably the rise of rural industries in such areas as south Gloucestershire and north Worcestershire, encouraged the growth of new trading centres, some of which, like Redditch in Worcestershire, remained small and informal, while others developed into flourishing small towns, notably Stourbridge in the same county and Stroud in Gloucestershire. A parallel shift in the urban pattern is found in the cloth country of Suffolk, with the rise of places like Nayland and Lavenham.[52]

Trade was apparently flowing along the channels influenced primarily by the availability of transport and the interaction between producers and

[50] Henham, *Celys and their World*, 62–6.
[51] *CUHB* i. 622–38.
[52] Ibid. 765–6.

consumers, but it was not controlled or monopolized by institutions, such as chartered markets and fairs or privileged boroughs. If it suited buyers and sellers to set up a market at a crossroads, it could become a centre of trade which was unregulated by the local lord, and where no tolls were charged. Many transactions were conducted by private treaty, on the farm, in a warehouse, or in an inn.[53] The households of institutions or aristocratic families would commonly obtain their grain, hay, or livestock by such negotiations.

Informal commerce responded readily to the new demands of industrial development, so we find new or growing towns of the fifteenth century in rural clothing or metalworking districts. They needed outlets for their manufactures, and a local market where food, drink, and everyday purchases could be made by the industrial workers. If historians are too preoccupied with the old institutions, they will gain an impression of decline and miss the unofficial new growth.

Farmers: Introduction

Farmers, those who held demesne land on lease, offer us an opportunity to look at a new group who were responding to the market and occupying the role in production previously occupied by lords. Contemporaries realized that they represented a distinctive category, appearing for the first time officially in the schedule of assessment for collecting the second poll tax in 1379. The graduated scale of payments required most peasants, artisans, and wage-earners to contribute 4*d.*, but the 'farmers of manors and rectories' were equated financially with lesser merchants, franklins, and innkeepers, and were expected to find, 'according to their estate', between 1*s.* and 6*s.* 8*d.*[54] If they paid the highest sum, this put them on a level with the lower ranks of the landed gentry, the 'esquires of less estate'. In the actual levying of the tax, in Warwickshire and Yorkshire for example, farmers paid no more than 3*s.* 4*d.*[55] At that time they were rather thinly and unevenly scattered across the villages, and many lords were still, in 1379, managing their own demesnes. By 1509,

[53] C. Dyer, 'The Hidden Trade of the Middle Ages: Evidence From the West Midlands', *Journal of Historical Geography*, 18 (1992), 149–53.

[54] V. H. Galbraith (ed.), *The Anonimalle Chronicle 1333–1381* (Manchester, 1970), 127. They were included in the same category as 'merchants of beasts'. The list is conveniently translated in R. B. Dobson, *The Peasants' Revolt of 1381* (London, 1970), 105–11.

[55] C. C. Fenwick (ed.), *The Poll Taxes of 1377, 1379 and 1381*, part 2, British Academy Records of Social and Economic History, NS, 29 (2001), 647–73; Anon (ed.), 'Rotuli collectorum subsidii regi a laiciis anno secundo concessi in Westrythyngo in comitatu Eboraci', *Yorkshire Archaeological and Topographical Journal*, 5 (1879), 1–51, 241–66, 417–32.

when Edmund Dudley wrote, farmers were well-established and prominent members of the commonwealth. He regarded them as rich, equating 'wealthy graziers and farmers' with 'substantial merchants', and thought of them as tending to avarice and ruthlessness, so that he urged them not to 'covet great lucre', and instead to be charitable.[56]

The farming out of manors and other sources of revenue, such as rectorial tithes and mills, had a long ancestry, and many of these assets had been put in the hands of tenants in the twelfth century.[57] Although lords' demesnes and mills were often brought into a system of direct management around 1200, and continued under the control of officials until about 1400, the leasing of demesnes persisted throughout the thirteenth and fourteenth centuries in some regions, such as the far north, or perhaps went through a relatively brief phase of direct management before being farmed out in the early fourteenth century.[58] Many lords of manors had been moving away from direct management of all their assets during the fourteenth century, when parcels of land, mills, and herds of cows were leased out, while the central operations of grain and wool production continued. Leasehold was also used as a form of tenure for peasant holdings, and many customary tenements were converted to leasehold in the late thirteenth and fourteenth centuries.[59] So farming and farmers were not entirely new around 1400. There was novelty, however, in the leasing of some thousands of demesnes, varying in size between 100 and 500 acres, and amounting to a quarter or a fifth of the land in lowland England. Assets which had been run by lords and their officials for two centuries were being put under the management of new tenants, mostly within a span of forty years between 1370 and 1410. Decision-making about crops, livestock, buildings, equipment, marketing, and labour were being transferred from the aristocracy to entrepreneurs who came mostly from lower-class origins.

Contemporaries were conscious that this was a momentous change. The auditors of the Duchy of Lancaster justified the decision to their superiors when they stated persuasively and bluntly in 1388 with reference to two Northamptonshire manors, Raunds and Higham Ferrers, that 'husbandry... is of no value beyond the costs there which are so great each year that the said

[56] D. M. Brodie (ed.), *The Tree of Commonwealth: A Treatise Written by Edmund Dudley* (Cambridge, 1948), 45–6, 89.

[57] R. Lennard, *Rural England, 1086–1135: A Study of Social and Agrarian Conditions* (Oxford, 1959), 142–212.

[58] R. A. Lomas, 'The Priory of Durham and Its Demesnes in the Fourteenth and Fifteenth Centuries', *Ec.HR*, 2nd ser., 31 (1978), 341, 345; E. Miller and J. Hatcher, *Medieval England: Rural Society and Economic Change, 1086–1348* (London, 1978), 236.

[59] R. H. Hilton, 'Gloucester Abbey Leases of the Late Thirteenth Century', in id., *The English Peasantry in the Later Middle Ages* (Oxford, 1975), 161–73.

husbandry is a great loss to my lord, wherefore the demesne lands ought to and can be leased at farm as in other places'.[60] We can sense the reluctance of many lords, who leased out part of the demesne, or who tentatively began with a short-term letting for perhaps six years, or who experimented with a period of leasing and then took the land back temporarily into their own hands again. The larger estates tended to let their arable demesnes go to farmers, but to hang on to their profitable sheep pastures. With reluctance, a few decades later in the mid-fifteenth century, in view of falling wool prices they had to give them up. Most of them must have known that leasing was a permanent move. They commonly commuted the last labour services at the time of the leasing of the arable, and were thus severing for ever the close link between the demesne and the tenant land which had formed the basis of the manorial economy.

The leasehold tenants were recruited from a wide range of social types, including the middling and wealthy peasants, artisans such as carpenters and fullers, merchants, including wool-dealers and clothiers, clergy, and gentry. The latter would include those who were making their main living from legal practice, and various estate officials such as stewards, receivers, and auditors. Studies of particular estates and regions have shown that the peasant element was most prominent in the first phase of leasing, and that gentry became involved in the late fifteenth and early sixteenth centuries.[61] In some counties, such as Warwickshire and Wiltshire, most farmers came from peasant backgrounds throughout the period.[62] Demesnes were sublet, both with and without the lord's permission, and as the gentry were most likely to need under-farmers, this would tend to increase the proportion of peasants who were actually managing the land.

Often the initial grant was made to a familiar figure, and the reeve or bailiff who had been responsible to the lord for the demesne became the first farmer. We detect the nervousness of estate officials who felt more comfortable in making their first move into unknown territory if they were putting the assets

---

[60] G. A. Holmes, *The Estates of the Higher Nobility in Fourteenth-Century England* (Cambridge, 1957), 126–7.

[61] F. R. H. Du Boulay, 'Who Were Farming the English Demesnes at the End of the Middle Ages?', *Ec.HR*, 2nd ser., 17 (1965), 443–55; B. Harvey, 'The Leasing of the Abbot of Westminster's Demesnes in the Later Middle Ages', *Ec.HR*, 2nd ser., 22 (1969), 17–27; B. F. Harvey, *Westminster Abbey and Its Estates in the Middle Ages* (Oxford, 1997), 148–63; Dyer, *Lords and Peasants*, 209–17; Lomas, 'Priory of Durham', 339–53; G. Draper, 'The Farmers of Canterbury Cathedral Priory and All Souls College on Romney Marsh *c*.1443–1545', in J. Eddison, M. Gardiner, and A. Long (eds.), *Romney Marsh: Environmental Change and Human Occupation in a Coastal Lowland*, Oxford University Committee For Archaeology Monographs 46 (1998), 109–28.

[62] C. Dyer, *Warwickshire Farming 1349–c.1520: Preparations for Agricultural Revolution*, Dugdale Society Occasional Papers, 27 (1981), 4–5; J. N. Hare, 'The Demesne Lessees of Fifteenth-Century Wiltshire', *Ag.HR* 29 (1981), 1–15.

into the hands of a trustworthy local man. Later the demesnes were leased to outsiders, who were strangers to the manor. Such 'new men' would pose a risk because they might prove to be unreliable or dishonest, and they lacked the former reeve's familiarity with the fields and the tenants, but on the other hand they had the advantage that they were unencumbered with the baggage of alliances and rivalries which a local man inevitably brought to the task. The great boon of engaging the services of a carefully selected outsider lay in the talents for management and marketing which would enable him to pay his rent in full and on time, and perhaps even to improve the demesne as an asset which would attract future lessees.

All farmers were 'new men' in the sense that, whether they came from the locality or from outside, taking on a lord's demesne transformed their whole way of life and economic behaviour. The peasants who made up the majority of the new generation of farmers had previous experience of managing a holding of perhaps 30 acres. Overnight they found themselves having to run an enterprise of 300 acres. Those who had recently acted as reeves would adapt more readily, but they were still taking on new challenges and responsibilities. The collective experiences of thousands of farmers at the beginning of the fifteenth century amounts to one of those episodes in history when a combination of circumstances compelled people to take a step upwards in skills, talents, and achievements.

Farmers and the Market

The most important adjustment required of the farmers came from their exposure to the full forces of the market, as they moved from a holding in which most of the crops were absorbed in the subsistence of the tenant's household, to one so large that at least three-quarters of its produce was sold.

The connection between the leased demesne and the market was built into the contract between the lord and the farmer. The contract evolved in the first stages of leasing, and some of the early leases retained some of the traditional and even archaic ties of lordship. The conservative Benedictine estate of Winchcombe Abbey in Gloucestershire in 1390 experimented with letting the demesne at Roel and the grange at Cutsdean to a customary tenant of the manor of Roel, Thomas Jannes, for a term of twenty years.[63] They made the unusual decision to grant the lease in the manor court, so that it was written into the court roll, and Jannes was to hold by customary tenure, in servility (*native*). As tenant of a new customary holding, Jannes was saddled with arduous conditions, to rebuild a barn and plant 400 saplings. He was

---

[63] Gloucestershire Record Office, D678/98C (Winchcombe Abbey court roll).

provided with stock and equipment (two ploughs with harness and two teams, each of eight oxen, together with a cow, a sow, and poultry), and the lord contributed to some of the maintenance of buildings. The lessee was expected to pay part of his rent in kind: wheat, drage, and oats for the monastery, peas to feed the abbey's sheep flock, and litter for the abbot's horses. He was to return the land at the end of the term with a specified number of strips in named furlongs planted with particular crops. In other words, the terms of the lease prevented the tenant from making any changes in the types of grain grown or the rotation of crops in the fields. The 59 quarters of grain that he paid in rent represented a high proportion of the saleable surplus, and the most profitable part of the demesne, the sheep flock, was retained in the lord's hands. To underline the continuity in the demesne under its old and new management, the lessee was granted the labour services of the tenants, and two servants who had been recruited by compulsion from the serfs of the manor. Jannes was being assigned the role of a caretaker, with little more opportunity to make profits for himself than a servant, and he would have enjoyed few advantages as a tenant farmer. The lease can scarcely have been negotiated freely, but was presumably dictated to him.

The arrangements at Roel and Cutsdean are an extreme example of a general tendency in the early days of leasing for lords to seek to maintain control over farmers. Many servile and customary tenants, among them former reeves, were persuaded or pressured to take on leases, and the lords hoped that by appointing such men, and sometimes by inscribing the lease into the manorial court rolls, that they could supervise them through the court. Farmers might be required to do suit of court, even suit of mill, and their heirs would be expected to deliver a heriot when they died.[64] As the social climate changed in the late fifteenth and early sixteenth centuries another method of binding the farmer to the lord could be achieved by appointing him to a manorial office such as woodward, and issuing him with a livery of clothes.[65] The farmers of Fountains Abbey in Yorkshire, right up to the Reformation, were expected to attend the abbot when he visited the locality, as if they were part of his retinue.[66]

In spite of these survivals of traditional lordship, most fifteenth-century demesne leases were based on negotiated contracts, reflecting the forces of the market. The document recording the terms of the bargain was in the form of an indenture, so that each party had a copy. We know from contemporary

[64] e.g. Gloucester Cathedral Library, Register C, 4–5. (Lease book of Gloucester Abbey, lease of Pitchcombe, Glos., in 1501).

[65] Ibid. 27–9; the lease of Frocester, Glos., in 1501 includes the office of Woodward of Bokeholt Wood, and a gown each year worth 6s. 8d.

[66] D. J. H. Michelmore (ed.), *The Fountains Abbey Lease Book*, Yorkshire Archaeological Society Record Series, 140 (1981), pp. 1xx–1xxi.

letters that the terms were negotiated, often over a considerable period, and the farmers were able to insist on conditions favourable to them. In most cases the rent was paid in cash, which presumed that the farmer was selling a considerable part of the produce from the land. Rents in kind, and champart rents for a proportion of the crops, often for the 'third sheaf', occur only sporadically. On the Fountains Abbey estate granges were leased to 'keepers', who received a herd of cattle and delivered a fixed quantity of butter and cheese to the monastery.[67] The farmer in most cases was taking over fixed assets only, that is, land and buildings, without livestock or equipment, which meant that to acquire these he had to pay out a considerable capital sum but was under no compulsion to continue with a particular type of agriculture. The farmer was usually expected to pay for the upkeep of buildings, though lords often agreed to provide materials such as stone or timber. A lord sometimes accepted responsibility for a specific building. Husbandry clauses, which insisted that a quantity of land be cultivated or manured, were few and not very restrictive. Lords were attempting to prevent the running down of their estates, as in clauses which enjoined farmers to use the manure on the demesne and not to sell it, but such a provision still left lessees with much freedom to choose their own economic strategy.[68] The demesnes were separated from the manors, without links of labour service or rents. Labour services had usually been converted into cash payments by about 1400, but rents were still collected for the lord by local officials, so the lord's income from each manor consisted of the tenants' rent, profits of justice and other manorial revenues, and the substantial leasehold rent from the demesne. A farmer employed his workers, both full-time servants hired by the year and labourers who worked by the day.

The farmer was expected to pay rents in instalments at set times through the year, without delaying for more than a month. Lords reserved the right to distrain if rent was owed, and to re-enter the land, that is, to terminate the lease, if there were serious delays in payment. Farmers were often prevented from subletting the land, except with the lord's permission. The farmer in most cases was a free man, who developed a relationship with the lord on the basis of the mutual advantages of the contract. Lords had no legal superiority over the farmers of the kind that they enjoyed over their customary tenants. Indeed, the lords' bargaining position was rather weak, as they had abandoned direct management because their demesnes made such meagre profits, and they had no wish to take them back in hand.

[67] e.g. Worcester Cathedral Library, Register A6, fo. 4; R. I. Jack (ed.), *The Grey of Ruthin Valor*, Bedfordshire Historical Record Society, 46 (1965), 18; Michelmore (ed.), *Fountains Abbey, passim*.

[68] Norfolk Record Office, National Register of Archives report on the records of the Earl of Kimberley, part 3, 121 (MTD/N/36, a lease of Barnham, Norfolk, in 1451).

Farmers were sometimes hard to find. The Paston letters describe the hunt on their Norfolk manors for suitable tenants, many of whom expressed considerable reluctance. One excused himself on the grounds that he wished to continue to live with his father-in-law.[69] The main reason for their lack of enthusiasm lay in the doubts among the potential tenants about the profitability of the land. In 1460 Richard Calle, the bailiff, reported that he had difficulties in finding a tenant for the close of Mautby, which had evidently been allowed to run down. Three men offered to take it, but only if John Paston would pay £6 for the initial cleaning and ploughing of the land. They would accept a term of seven years, and would pay a rent of 12*d.* per acre, but only if they were allowed to have it for no rent at all for the first two years.[70] The lords reassured candidates for leases that they would benefit from the land. One was told by the bailiff that a previous farmer of a piece of land 'has bought a fair place since he was your farmer, and paid therefore', in other words, had been able to invest his profits in a freeholding.[71] The Pastons on their side were looking out for 'able' farmers who would pay rents promptly and look after the land and buildings.

The arrangements for leasing the demesne was clearly part of a market system, in which lessor and lessee bargained over the terms, and the farmer depended on the market to sell his produce, hire labour, and buy equipment and building materials. If he wished to improve the land with enclosures or marling, he would have to bear the cost. Woods would need careful protection with secure fences, and in marshlands the farmer might well be expected to maintain the sea walls, drains, and other defences. The farmers needed capital, especially in the majority of cases in which no livestock or implements came with the lease. One imagines the difficulty facing a new farmer, beginning a lease at Michaelmas (29 September), who would not be able to begin effective cultivation on even a small demesne of 200 acres without an immediate expenditure of £15 or £20 on seed, oxen, horses, ploughs and carts, harness, and within a short time a flock of sheep. Peasants might hope to be helped by their relatives, like Geoffrey Atgor of Brantham in Suffolk, who in 1454 held land in three villages and left his son, 'for the increase of his farm', 40 quarters of grain, thirty-one cattle, 200 sheep, and other animals.[72] If help was not available from their families, the new farmers presumably raised funds by means of loans, not just at the beginning of the lease but throughout, assuring the lenders that they had assets as security and the prospect of a substantial income for twenty years or more, depending on the length of the lease.

[69] N. Davis (ed.), *Paston Letters and Papers of the Fifteenth Century,* 2 vols. (Oxford, 1971 and 1976), ii. 81–2.
[70] Ibid. 217–18.   [71] Ibid. 81–2.
[72] Suffolk Record Office, Ipswich Branch, J421/1, fo. 119.

Farmers who combined their tenure of a large demesne with a mercantile role were able to use their trading profits to fund the stocking and equipping of their land. Emmota Richards, as the daughter-in-law of Henry Richards, woolman, was the heiress of a large wool-trading business, with land in five places in south-west Oxfordshire. She owned, when she died in 1501, wool worth £610 and good debts totalling more than £1,000, so the cost of maintaining her flocks, sheepcotes, the enclosures of the pastures, and equipment for arable cultivation would have posed no great problems.[73]

The negotiations between the lord and the farmer did not stop once the indenture had been written. Circumstances changed, especially in the course of a long lease. It seems that adjustments made in the terms and conditions reflected the tenant's increasing confidence, sometimes expressed in grumbling, as the changes were usually made in the farmer's favour. For example, even when the indenture gave the farmer the responsibility for repairs, lords were persuaded to carry out building work. Alternatively, farmers would pay for the repairs but obtain compensation in the form of a temporary cessation in rent payment or a rent reduction.[74] The indentures agreed between lords and farmers sometimes ruled out the subletting of land, but again, if such an arrangement suited the farmer lords were willing to accept the reality, and even to receive rent payments direct from the subtenant or under-farmer.

Farmers who found themselves committed to paying an annual rent in years of depressed prices failed to pay in full, or even paid nothing at all. John Benet, farmer of Sir John Fastolf in his manor of Saxthorpe in Norfolk, was supposed to pay £20 per annum, but by the late 1450s had built up a debt of £45.[75] Tenants who persistently failed to keep up rent payments may have had genuine difficulties in raising the money, but they were also using their non-payment to bring pressure to bear on the lord to make permanent reductions. According to the indenture, the lord was entitled to distrain the tenant after a month or two. Farmers sometimes entered into a bond which could be used by the lord to obtain money if the rent was not paid.[76] These sanctions were often not applied, as lords were forced to tolerate slow payment in order to keep a tenant.

The length of the term was as variable as the rent, and could be adjusted in the light of the demand for land. Generalization over the whole country is difficult, but usually the relatively short terms of seven to ten years which were commonly agreed in the first generations of leases gave way to twenty,

[73] J. R. H. Weaver and A. Beardwood (eds.), *Oxfordshire Wills, 1393–1510*, Oxfordshire Record Society, 39 (1958), 26–7, 37, 70–1; TNA: PRO, PROB 2/465.

[74] F. W. B. Charles, *The Great Barn of Bredon: Its Fire and Rebuilding* (Oxford, 1997), 28.

[75] Davis (ed.), *Paston Letters*, ii. 191–2.

[76] York Minster Library, M2/5, fos. 349–350, a lease of Newthorp, Yorkshire, of 1494, in which the farmer entered into a £40 bond.

thirty, or forty years in the mid- and late fifteenth century. The long leases persisted after 1500, though it is sometimes possible to find farmers competing over short leases. When the tithe corn of Crosthwaite in Cumberland was leased for seven years in 1508, within a year another would-be tenant had negotiated to take it on a twelve-year term from 1515, whereupon the first farmer arranged to acquire the lease on the expiry of that term.[77] Rarely, the lord's patience was tested to its limit by an awkward farmer who broke his contract, and the tenancy was terminated or the lease was bought out from the tenant. Sometimes the farmer gave up before the completion of the term. If the tenancy was working well the farmer would stay without a formal renewal, and a twenty-year term would stretch out to its twenty-fifth or thirtieth year. Farmers complained about their rent and the cost of repairs. One of the Paston letters records that one farmer 'cursyth the time that he ever came in the farm of Oxnead'.[78] Of course that cursing may have been entirely justified, or it may have been part of a bargaining strategy. For all of their show of reluctance, a farm rarely lay untenanted, and farmers were often willing to stay for a second term, arrange for their son to take over the lease, and indicate by their actions that they really regarded the lease as a valuable asset.

The level of rent reflected market conditions, often being set in the early stages of leasing in relation to the profits that had been achieved under direct management. Leasehold rents for complete arable demesnes tended to begin at quite a high rate around 1400, declined in the middle of the fifteenth century, and then levelled off or increased a little at the end of the century and after 1500. Pasture rents, in Derbyshire for example, rose decisively in the late fifteenth century.[79]

The rent tells us something about the internal management of the land under the farmers. They were contracted to pay, and in most cases did pay, substantial sums of money, from £4 for a small demesne up to £20 or £30. As the demesne consisted of a package of assets, including access to pasture and woods which were shared with tenants, the sum cannot easily be reduced to a rent per acre, but occasionally this can be calculated. In Essex, for example, demesne arable in the mid-fifteenth century was rented for 6d.–7d. per acre, and in Norfolk 7d.–8d. was being paid around 1500.[80] These sums could represent a good return for the lord, who was sometimes in despair at making

[77] Michelmore (ed.), *Fountains Abbey*, 10–11.

[78] Davis (ed.), *Paston Letters*, i. 666.

[79] I. S. W. Blanchard (ed.), *The Duchy of Lancaster's Estates in Derbyshire 1485–1540*, Derbyshire Archaeological Society Record Series, 3 (1971), 1–13.

[80] L. R. Poos, *A Rural Society After the Black Death: Essex 1350–1525* (Cambridge, 1991), 49–51; Whittle, *Agrarian Capitalism*, 69.

any profit from arable cultivation in the last years of direct management, as we have seen in the case of the Duchy of Lancaster's manors in Northamptonshire (pp. 195–6). If we compare the profits obtained by the lord at Plympton and Sampford Courtney in Devon in 1382–3 with the leasehold rent in 1421–2, the lord had gained extra income, and also had the advantage of stability, as the farmer was expected to pay the same amount each year regardless of the changing agricultural conditions.[81]

Once leased, each demesne was contributing to the maintenance of two large households: that of the lord, who drew his rent to pay for the food, servants, and buildings that had always been funded from that land; and the farmer's more modest establishment. Most farmers would be attempting to squeeze £5 or £10 out of a demesne for their own income. Production must have been conducted with great efficiency, and costs would have been cut. Lords' reeves could be very sensitive in adjusting the crops sown in relation to movements in prices, and in selling in the best markets, but reeves did not have the same incentives as the farmers to maximize their profits.[82] Farmers needed to keep a very close eye on the movements in price in the most advantageous markets. Tenants of demesne farms within the hinterland of Stratford-upon-Avon, like Richard Hogges of Bourton-on-the-Hill, Robert Otehull of Blockley, and Richard Stowte of Sutton-under-Brailes—all near neighbours—joined the town's fraternity of the Holy Cross in the middle years of the fifteenth century, presumably helping to forge links with a local market centre.[83] Large-scale farmers looked further afield for the best opportunities for sales, like John Spencer from east Warwickshire, who in his will of 1496 left money to mend the roads around Banbury, where one of the premier livestock fairs in the midlands was held. Or the farmer would acquire a house in an appropriate town, like Richard Scrase of Hangleton in Sussex, who owned property in Chichester in 1487.[84]

Farmers, under the stimulus of the market, changed the management of land to enable them to pay rent and to reward themselves. The slavish continuation of the old demesne agriculture, which Winchcombe Abbey attempted to impose on Thomas Jannes, was not an option. Farmers negotiated with lords to obtain the size and shape of holding that suited their needs. Cistercian granges, for example, had been established in the twelfth and thirteenth centuries when the most efficient unit amounted to 300 or

---

[81] *AHEW* iii. 581.

[82] D. Stone, 'Medieval Farm Management and Technological Mentalities: Hinderclay Before the Black Death', *Ec.HR* 54 (2001), 612–38.

[83] J. H. Bloom (ed.), *The Register of the Gild of the Holy Cross, the Blessed Mary and St. John the Baptist of Stratford-upon-Avon* (London, 1907), 98, 99, 127; Harvey, 'Abbot of Westminster's Demesnes', 21, 24; Dyer, *Lords and Peasants*, 212.

[84] TNA: PRO, PROB 11/11, fo. 39; 11/8, fo. 41.

400 acres. Farmers evidently preferred rather smaller acreages, and when they were leased out they were often split into two parts.[85] Similarly, when a more conventional demesne had been developed in a number of separate blocks of land, these might be leased on their own, and new farmhouses built in the midst of the fields.[86] In other circumstances, in pursuit of holdings of moderate size or compactness the farmers might increase their initial lease-hold, like the farmer of Bishop Burton rectory in Yorkshire, Henry Sperk, who added to the glebe by renting 6 oxgangs (90 acres) in the village.[87]

Some leaseholds provided the farmer with linked assets inherited from the former estate management. For example, when Richard Cokkis took on Abload in the Severn valley in 1504 from Gloucester Abbey, he acquired access to hill pasture at Coberley in the Cotswolds 12 miles to the east.[88] This was an old transhumance connection forged in the days when the abbey's sheep flocks were driven on to the hills for summer pasture. More commonly, these traditional estate arrangements broke down as each manor was leased separately to a different farmer, or in the first half of the fifteenth century the arable lands would be leased and the pastures retained under the lord's management. The leaseholders formed new groupings of land as the more ambitious farmers acquired a number of holdings, often rented from differ-ent lords.

The farmer's aim could have been directly opposite to those of the creators of the old estate groupings. When the great church estates were formed in the early middle ages, their founders deliberately sought out a mixed estate that would give access to complementary types of land, so that the household could be self-sufficient in food, fuel, and building materials; in the event of drought, flood, or animal disease, not all production would be lost. The farmers, in contrast, built up specialized estates, most strikingly those con-sisting almost entirely of pastures. In other words, their primary concern was to respond to current market demand. The Mervyn family of Warwickshire lived on the mixed arable and pasture farm of Church Lawford, which supplied their household and enabled them to sell surplus grain in nearby Coventry (Fig. 5.1). They had acquired by 1494, at some distance, two pasture farms, at Poultney in Leicestershire and Westcote in Warwickshire, which were worth the inconvenience of travel because they were large and compact, and gave the opportunity for seriously profitable livestock produc-

---

[85] J. S. Donnelly, 'Changes in the Grange Economy of English and Welsh Cistercian Abbeys, 1300–1540', *Traditio*, 10 (1954), 399–458.

[86] C. Dyer, 'Peasants and Farmers: Rural Settlements and Landscapes in an Age of Transition', in D. Gaimster and P. Stamper (eds.), *The Age of Transition: The Archaeology of English Culture 1400–1600*, Society For Medieval Archaeology Monograph, 15 (1997), 69–70.

[87] Borthwick Institute of Historical Research, York, D. and C. wills, 1522, Sperk.

[88] Gloucester Cathedral Library, Register C, 108–11.

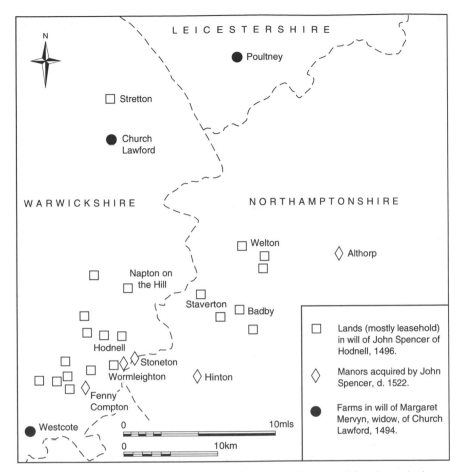

Fig. 5.1. Estates of the Spencer and Mervyn families, 1494–1522. This shows the lease-hold lands mentioned in the will of Margaret Mervyn, widow, of Church Lawford (War.), 1494, and those mentioned in John Spencer of Hodnell's will in 1496. In addition the manors acquired by John Spencer, nephew of the earlier John Spencer, who died in 1522, are shown.

Sources: TNA: PRO, PROB 11/10, fo. 199; PROB 11/11, fo. 39; see n. 96.

tion which was lacking at Lawford.[89] A more extensive example of one of these groupings is the leasehold estate created by the Spencers of Hodnell at the end of the fifteenth century, which by 1500 extended over a dozen Warwickshire parishes within a few miles of Hodnell and into adjacent Northamptonshire. A high proportion of the land consisted of pastures

---

[89] TNA: PRO, PROB 11/10, fo. 199; Magdalen College, Oxford, Westcote 17.

previously occupied by villages and their fields. The holdings of John Sadyler of Kirby le Soken on the Essex coast, who died in 1493, consisted of land at Moze, Oakley, and Wrabness, up to 10 miles away, suggesting that he sought to specialize in pastures on the salt marshes.[90]

We often find that farmers responded to the market by increasing the area under grass, and therefore gaining the benefit of low labour costs and better prices for livestock and their products. The lords were clearly attempting to prevent this when they occasionally put clauses into their leases requiring that fields be ploughed and manured, and that barns for storing corn should be kept in repair. A lord might even encourage a farmer to remove bushes to improve the land, and make the resumption of cultivation possible.[91] Farmers' inventories show that on occasion they made drastic changes to traditional balanced husbandry practices. Thomas Vicars of Strensall near York leased two demesnes in 1451. He kept two ploughs at work, but his main profits came from 799 sheep, 198 cattle, and ninety-two horses. He was fattening young beef cattle for the York market, and breeding horses, both draught animals for farm use and valuable riding animals. Even more tilted towards pasture was John Sadyler's enterprise on the east Essex coast, with its 30 acres under the plough and 800 sheep and fifty-three cattle. Richard Scrase, exploiting two abandoned village sites on the Sussex coast in 1486 kept 4,366 sheep, the profits of which must have left him with a large surplus beyond the £20 annual rent that he paid for the parish of Hangleton.[92]

The shift in the balance of agricultural production was accompanied by changes in the organization of land and the techniques of exploitation of a familiar kind. By taking over previously separate holdings, both as leaseholds or copyholds, commonly known as engrossing, the area of the farm would be increased and the parcels rationalized into a compact territory that could be managed as a single unit. The erection of fences and hedges would replace the old pattern of arable strips and furlongs, or areas of open common grazing, with convenient pasture closes. New buildings, such as sheepcotes, would be erected. The most drastic changes along these lines could only be contemplated in collaboration with the lord. This can be seen at Burton Dassett in Warwickshire, where Roger Heritage had run a mixed farm, with a strong bias

---

[90] H. Thorpe, 'The Lord and the Landscape, Illustrated Through the Changing Fortunes of a Warwickshire Parish, Wormleighton', *Transactions of the Birmingham Archaeological Society*, 80 (1962), 58; TNA: PRO, PROB 11/10, fo. 89; PROB 2/64.

[91] Examples of leases with husbandry clauses are found in those for the archbishopric of Canterbury's manors: F. R. H. Du Boulay (ed.), 'Calendar of the Demesne Leases Made by Archbishop Warham (1503–32)', in id. (ed.), *Documents Illustrative of Medieval Kentish Society*, Kent Records, 18 (1964), 275, 277.

[92] J. Raine (ed.), *Testamenta Eboracensia*, 3, Surtees Society, 45 (1864), 118–24; TNA: PRO, PROB 2/64; PROB 11/8, fo. 41; Northamptonshire Record Office, Spencer 159.

towards pastoral farming. He died in 1495, and his son John took over. Within three years he co-operated with the new lord, Edward Belknap, to enclose the land, force out the remaining tenants, and convert the whole township into a specialist pasture.[93] By using the techniques of landscape history we can reconstruct the transformation brought to such a township, as at Lark Stoke in Warwickshire (Fig. 1.1), where irregular enclosures were created often by setting new hedges along the old headlands of the defunct open-field system. The organizers of this may well have been the Colchester family, members of which held leases there in the late fifteenth and early sixteenth centuries.[94]

Only rarely are we given a glimpse of farmers' performance as producers, and the few figures available, even if they are an untypically small sample, are still worth some attention. At Hackford in Norfolk in 1468–9, for two years some of the land was let for the third sheaf. In one year the lord received $10\frac{1}{2}$ quarters of oats from 13 acres, and in another 10 quarters of the same grain from $11\frac{1}{2}$ acres, which implies yields of 19.4 bushels and 20.9 bushels per acre, when lords running demesnes in the county under direct management in the early fifteenth century harvested between 5.5 and 16.4 bushels of oats per acre, with mean yields in the region of 14 bushels.[95] This suggests that farmers could achieve excellent results, presumably motivated by the need to make a reasonable surplus for themselves after the rent had been deducted.

Farmers cannot be easily fitted into conventional social categories, and as we have seen, Edmund Dudley saw them as a separate group, linked significantly with graziers. Those who came from the gentry acquired their status from their freehold land and manorial lordships, and engaged in leasing as a source of financial profit. The farmers who lived on leasehold land alone could not aspire to rise into the gentry until they acquired land of a more permanent and prestigious kind, and so although the Spencers gained enormous wealth from the exploitation of land held on lease, they were accounted gentlemen and granted arms only in 1504, and their claim to gentility was really secure only after they acquired the lordship of the manors of Fenny Compton and Wormleighton in 1506 and of Althorp in Northamptonshire in 1508 (Fig. 5.1).[96]

---

[93] C. Dyer, 'Were There Any Capitalists in Fifteenth-Century England?', in J. Kermode (ed.), *Enterprise and Individuals in Fifteenth-Century England* (Stroud, 1991), 15–16.

[94] Warwickshire County Record Office, CR 1911/13; Bloom (ed.), *Register*, 187; R. Hoyle (ed.), *The Military Survey of Gloucestershire, 1522*, Gloucestershire Records Series, 6 (1993), 221.

[95] Norfolk Record Office, Aylsham 733 TI 89B; B. M. S. Campbell, 'Land, Labour, Livestock, and Productivity Trends in English Seignorial Agriculture, 1208–1450', in id. and M. Overton (eds.), *Land, Labour and Livestock: Historical Studies in European Agricultural Productivity* (Manchester, 1991), 175–82.

[96] Thorpe, 'Lord and the Landscape', 57; M. Finch, *The Wealth of Five Northamptonshire Families 1540–1640*, Northamptonshire Record Society, 19 (1956), 58–9.

A few farmers were clergymen, but the great bulk of them came from the laity. Some of them reveal in their wills that they owned books, and their sons who went to school sometimes embarked on careers in the church, like Roger Heritage's son, who became a fellow of Oriel College, Oxford.[97]

The farmers who were also heavily involved in commercial activity gained their status and social links through the merchant class. William Bradwey of Chipping Campden was a large-scale agricultural producer, with a thousand sheep, fifty-two cattle, and 200 acres under the plough. But his social position was defined by his role as a wool merchant and dealer in cloth, which also provided him with the bulk of his wealth, judging from the £1,925 owed to him by three Londoners at his death in 1488.[98]

The lessees of the demesne were necessarily drawn into relations with the local peasant community. Many of them were of peasant origin, and in legal records were identified by the familiar 'peasant' titles of 'husbandman' and 'yeoman'. When the demesne was split up among many tenants the leasehold-ers were simply better-provided peasants alongside poorer neighbours, but not always with great disparities of wealth. A gulf was, however, formed between the farmer of a large demesne and the villagers when he had ten times more land than they, and therefore had different interests in relation to production, marketing, and the employment of labour. Such a farmer, like Robert Parman of Chevington in Suffolk between 1440 and 1475, appears in the manorial court as a juror and in other official capacities, and might sometimes be amerced for offences against the manorial disciplines. His wife was a regular brewer of ale, and was therefore presented for breaking the assize. He sup-ported the parish church and the local fraternity, leaving them generous bequests in his will. But although he interacted with his neighbours in these activities, he must have been regarded as a dominating figure, acquiring tenant holdings, encouraging his numerous children to take on land and official positions, and arranging for one son to be appointed as rector of the parish church.[99] The social and economic inequalities can be appreciated from the tax assessments of farmers recorded in the lay subsidy of 1524–5, which were often in the region of £20 to £100. In most villages the majority of the taxpayers had their goods or wages valued at £1 or £2, and these would have included some of the labourers employed by the farmers to work on the demesnes. The most substantial villagers had their goods or lands assessed at between £3 and £12, which was well below the wealth of many farmers (Table 5.3).

[97] Dyer, 'Were There Any Capitalists?', 14; a Yorkshire farmer owned a primer: Borthwick Institute of Historical Research, York, Register 2, fos. 449–450.

[98] TNA: PRO, PROB 11/8, fo. 120; PROB 2/21; P. C. Rushen, *The History and Antiquities of Chipping Campden* (London, n.d.), 23, 25.

[99] Suffolk Record Office, Bury St Edmunds Branch, IC500/2/11, fos. 92–93; E3/15.3/1.35; 2.35–42.

Table 5.3. Some examples of farmers in the lay subsidies of 1524 and 1525.

Village	Farmer	Leasehold rent	Farmer's assessment (goods)	Villagers' assessment (goods or wages)
Gloucestershire				
Abload	Richard Cokkis	£18	£18	24 @ £1; 10 @ £2; 9 @ £3–£12.
Aldsworth	Richard Lysholy	£4. 13s. 4d.	£20	7 @ £1; 2 @ £2; 7 @ £3–£14; 2 @ £30
Bibury	Richard Bagot	£12	£100	7 @ £1; 3 @ £2 6 @ £4–£18
Brookthorpe	Andrew Nyblet	£12. 13s. 4d.	£60	4 @ £1; 5 @ £2; 11 @ £3–£16
Coln St Aldwyn	John Spenser	£4. 13s. 4d.	£73	3 @ £2; 5 @ £3–£26
Duntisbourne Abbots	John Turnor	£3. 6s. 8d.	£13	1 @ £1; 1 @ £2 6 @ £3–£8
Sussex				
Bersted	John Cokwell	£32	£100	7 @ £1; 20 @ £2; 6 @ £2–£8; 1 @ £15
East Lavant	John Standen	£32	£100	14 @ £1; 5 @ £2; 10 @ £3–£14; 8 @ £15–33
Nytimber	Robert Sandam	£15 6s. 8d.	£20	6 @ £1; 5 @ £2; 3 @ £4–£8; 1 @ £10.
Stonham	Robert Aborough	£44	£50	43 @ £1; 20 @ £2; 17 @ £2. 13s. 4d.– £13. 6s. 8d.; 2 @ £20
Tarring	Edward Weston	£18	£33	6s.8d. 14 @ £1; 5 @ £2; 10 @ £3. 6s. 8d.; 8 @ £15–£33.
Worcestershire				
Blockley*	John Freman	£9 10s. 0d.	£40	7 @ £1; 9 @ £2; 6 @ £3–£7; 1 @ £12
Hanbury	William Hunte	£10 10s. 0d.	£20	7 @ £1; 13 @ £2; 23 @ £3–£8.
Pensham	John Smyth	£8	£15	10 @ £3–£8

Note:* now in Gloucestershire. Freman was joint lessee.
Sources: Glos.: TNA: PRO, E179/113/213; E179/113/189; Gloucester Cathedral Library, Register C; *Sussex*: J. Cornwall (ed.), *The Lay Subsidy Rolls for the County of Sussex, 1524–5*, Sussex Record Society, 56 (1957); Du Boulay (ed.), 'Calendar of the Demesne Leases' ; *Worcs.*: M. Faraday (ed.), *Worcestershire Taxes in the 1520s*, Worcestershire Historical Society, NS, 19 (2003); Worcestershire Record Office, ref. 009: 1, BA 2636/37 (iii), 43806, fo. 23; TNA: PRO, SC6 Henry VIII, 7444; B. Harvey, 'The Leasing of the Abbot of Westminster's Demesnes in the Later Middle Ages', *Ec.HR*, 2nd ser., 22 (1969), 23.

Farmers were major employers of labour, and many of them took on a group of servants as well as hiring part-time labourers by the day. In most villages they were the main source of employment for cottagers and the younger people dependent on wages. This dimension will be explored in Chapter 6.

Conclusion

The period between the Black Death and the Reformation, and particularly between 1375 and 1520, was a hard one for producers. In some respects they were forced to pull back from the market, but in general exchange relationships survived, and the network of towns and markets functioned and adapted. In some ways the commercial framework was becoming more sophisticated. Farmers came into being because prices and profits were so low, in order to make a better fist of managing declining assets—a point which their modern successors appreciate with irony. They were by no means all successful. We find John Yorke of Etwall in Derbyshire concerned, when he made his will in 1497, that after his debts had been paid he would not have enough in his estate to provide legacies both for pious works and for his relatives. Roger Smethe of South Elmham in Suffolk in 1465 had an obligation to pay £72. 13s. 4d. to a relative, which left him with little to bequeath to others.[100] In times of difficulty the farmers went in for a great deal of restructuring, and the more enterprising and successful of them profitably reorganized the countryside. This would not be the first time that the harsh discipline of recession forced people to change their ways, and their successors after the mid-sixteenth century reaped much greater rewards.

[100] TNA: PRO, PROB 11/11, fo. 118; Norfolk Record Office, NCC wills, 2, 3 Cobald.

6

Work and Leisure

This final chapter explores the nature of work, and especially employment, at the end of the middle ages. It will address the question, central to the 'transition from feudalism to capitalism' debate, about the existence of a proletariat, and about the increase in the number of wage-earners in the long term. The discussion will be extended to consider attitudes to work, leisure, and charity, with the aim of understanding the 'work ethic'.

The Nature of Employment

Historians have come to emphasize the number of wage-earners in pre-industrial English society. For example, Hoskins, writing about the early sixteenth century, stated that two-thirds of the population 'consisted of wage-earners and their dependants'.[1] He exaggerated, but more recent estimates show that both before 1500 as well as after that date wage-earning provided a majority of the population with a significant part of their living.

We have the means for observing and counting wage-earners over many parts of the country from the records of the military survey of 1522 and the subsidies of 1524 and 1525, which either identified people as labourers and servants, or assessed their taxes on the basis of their wages, or credited them with such a modest quantity of goods that they must be judged to have depended mainly on wages.[2] This has perhaps given the impression that the large body of wage-earners in the 1520s was a relatively new development, but of course workers had been employed to labour for others for centuries.

[1] W. G. Hoskins, *The Age of Plunder: The England of Henry VIII, 1500–1547* (London, 1976), 105.
[2] J. C. K. Cornwall, *Wealth and Society in Early Sixteenth Century England* (London, 1988), 198–216.

To underline the deep roots of wage-earning, or at least the ancestry of systems of work in return for some material reward, not necessarily in cash, we can go back to the eleventh century. The descriptions of demesnes in Domesday Book imply a hidden servant population, as we are told of many demesnes with slave ploughmen, with two for each plough, but these were not accompanied in the description by other specialist workers such as shepherds and swineherds. We know that these specialists commonly existed, as they and their duties were described in other eleventh-century texts.[3] In those parts of the country where slaves were few, and on those numerous manors without slaves, a permanent staff of ploughmen and other farm servants must have existed, but are not mentioned in the survey. With the end of slavery in the twelfth century much routine agricultural work on demesnes was carried out by servants, and we discover in the following century that even a small demesne employed at least four *famuli*, and some had more than a dozen.[4] The peasant communities of the eleventh century, with their tenants of large and small holdings living as neighbours, can only have functioned through the employment of the cottars and bordars by those with larger quantities of land. As in later centuries, many of the villeins, for example, those with 30 acres, who through infertility, infant mortality, or the accident of the birth of females needed extra labour to work their holdings, would have employed a full-time servant. In the same period we presume that many people in towns, as they did later, worked as servants in households and workshops, and were hired in a less continuous way for employment in crafts and to provide services such as transport. A rough estimate of the number of servants in 1086, allowing for agricultural servants on demesnes and larger peasant holdings, and servants in towns and in aristocratic households, comes to 150,000 people. Combined with the 100,000 households of smallholding peasants, who are likely to have worked for others part-time, the employed population accounts for a significant proportion of the total of about 2.5 million.[5]

The economic growth of the twelfth and thirteenth centuries was accompanied by a great expansion in wage labour, as most lords' demesnes used wage labour rather than labour services, the number of smallholdings multi-

---

[3] D. C. Douglas and G. W. Greenaway, *English Historical Documents*, Vol. II, *1042–1189*, 2nd edn. (London, 1981), 875–9.

[4] F. M. Page, *The Estates of Crowland Abbey* (Cambridge, 1934), 227, 230, 234; R. A. L. Smith, *Canterbury Cathedral Priory: A Study in Monastic Administration* (Cambridge, 1943), 124–5.

[5] The calculations use figures in H. C. Darby, *Domesday England* (Cambridge, 1977), 337, 364–8; J. Moore, ' "Quot homines?" The Population of Domesday England', *Anglo-Norman Studies*, 19 (1996), 307–34; J. J. N. Palmer, 'The Wealth of the Secular Aristocracy in 1086', *Anglo-Norman Studies*, 22 (1999), 279–91.

plied, agriculture became more intensive and responsive to commerce, and migrants crowded into towns, both old and new.

Attitudes towards labour adapted to new circumstances during the middle ages. The negative view embedded in patristic theology persisted, that work was a punishment for sin, imposed on Adam and Eve after the Fall. Those who spent their lives in physical labour could be depicted as ugly and malevolent.[6] A more favourable view of work was expressed by the monks who embraced physical labour as part of their routine. Writers from the twelfth century began to refer to God the creator as an artisan. They said that work could be 'sweet and delightful', and an antidote to sin.[7] Among those who revived the idea of the three orders in the fourteenth century, the workers, personified usually as peasants, were idealized as unselfish contributors to the material well-being of the clergy and aristocracy. In the Luttrell Psalter, illuminated just before the Black Death, workers are portrayed as worthily employed, supporting the knight who commissioned the manuscript, and in harmony with the divine order celebrated in the texts for which they provide marginal illustrations.[8]

The ploughmen and harvesters of the Luttrell Psalter may have been conceived by the artist and those who admired his illustrations as doing services on the lord's demesne, or cultivating their own land. But many of those who worked on Geoffrey Luttrell's real manors did so as his employees. Labour for wages could be regarded as virtuous; even the author of *Piers Plowman*, writing in the 1370s, who was heavily critical of the greed and idleness of labourers and servants, could still at one point in his allegory depict Piers working as an honest servant in husbandry, ploughing the fields of his employer, Truth.[9]

Work for wages was a well-established and integral part of the medieval economy, both as it was lived and as it was depicted. No proletariat, however, existed in the middle ages. In contrast with modern industrial society, a great body of workers did not depend on wages for all of their income for the whole of their lives, and workers were not usually to be found in large numbers in one

---

[6] P. Freedman, *Images of the Medieval Peasant* (Stanford, 1999), 15–20; D. Wood, *Medieval Economic Thought* (Cambridge, 2002), 52–3; M. van den Hoven, *Work in Ancient and Medieval Thought* (Leiden, 1996), 245–55.

[7] G. Ovitt, *The Restoration of Perfection: Labour and Technology in Medieval Culture* (New Brunswick, 1987), esp. 58–70.

[8] M. Camille, 'Labouring For the Lord: The Ploughman and the Social Order in the Luttrell Psalter', *Art History*, 10 (1987), 423–54; R. K. Emmerson and P. J. P. Goldberg, ' "The Lord Geoffrey had me made": Lordship and Labour in the Luttrell Psalter', in J. Bothwell, P. J. P. Goldberg, and W. M. Ormrod (eds.), *The Problem of Labour in Fourteenth-Century England* (Woodbridge, 2000), 60–1.

[9] G. Kane and E. Talbot (eds.), *Piers Plowman: The B Version* (London, 1975), 340–1 (ll. 537–55).

place, such as a factory, in the employ of a single person or institution. Very many people expected to be employees during an episode of their lives, above all in their youth as servants in households large and small, in workshops and warehouses, and in agriculture. The servant labour force in pre-industrial society has been characterized as consisting mainly of unmarried persons, working in their teens and early twenties. They would live in their employers' houses, receiving bed, board, and clothing and a small amount of cash, and would gain experience and training in preparation for independent adult life. They would ideally serve an annual contract, beginning at Michaelmas (29 September) in the south or Martinmas (11 November) and at Whitsun (Pentecost) in the north. 'Life-cycle' servants can be found in manorial court rolls, when their rewards were regulated by the court, and when they were accused of petty crime, raised the hue and cry, or figured in litigation. In the poll tax of 1381 they could be listed along with their employers, and sons and daughters could be described as servants in their own parents' household. In church court proceedings they would be expected to provide evidence about the intimate lives of their employers and fellow servants, underlining the close relationship that existed within the household.[10]

The evidence suggests many departures from the 'life-cycle servant' ideal. Pleas in manorial courts would arise from the alleged failure of employers to reward them with the agreed food, clothing, and money. In some circumstances servants resented their conditions: under the labour laws enforced with particular vigour in the forty or fifty years after the Black Death individuals would refuse to accept annual contracts because they preferred the freedom and better rewards of short-term work.[11] We can find servants living independently in cottages, and they could be of all ages.[12] They were paid in a variety of ways: they might be rewarded primarily in cash—40s. per annum, together with food, is sometimes mentioned as a servant's pay in the fifteenth century—or with a share of the product, like the eight pairs of shoes allowed to cordwainers' servants in Bristol in 1364, and shepherds could be allowed to keep and feed a certain number of their own sheep along with their master's flock.[13]

[10] R. H. Hilton, *The English Peasantry in the Later Middle Ages* (Oxford, 1975), 30–6, 51–2; P. J. P. Goldberg, *Women, Work and Life Cycle in a Medieval Economy: Women in York and Yorkshire c.1300–1520* (Oxford, 1992), 175–80, 217–32.

[11] S. Penn and C. Dyer, 'Wages and Earnings in Late Medieval England: Evidence From the Enforcement of the Labour Laws', *Ec.HR*, 2nd ser., 43 (1990), 356–76.

[12] B. Dodds, 'Workers On the Pittington Demesne in the Later Middle Ages', *Archaeologia Aeliana*, 5th ser., 28 (2000), 155–7; C. Dyer, *Standards of Living in the Later Middle Ages: Social Change in England c.1200–1520*, revised edn. (Cambridge, 1998), 212.

[13] Dyer, *Standards of Living*, 196; F. B. Bickley (ed.), *The Little Red Book of Bristol*, 2 vols. (Bristol and London, 1900), i. 41–4; C. Dyer, *Warwickshire Farming 1349–c.1520: Preparations for Agricultural Revolution*, Dugdale Society Occasional Papers, 27 (1981), 21.

Servants could come from every section of society, from the sons and daughters of the poorest cottagers who went to work for neighbouring peasants and artisans, to gentlemen servants in aristocratic households. Servants, therefore, did not belong to an employed class, and many of them progressed in their twenties from their state of dependence through the acquisition of land or a workshop. Servants lived close to their employers, and to some degree formed part of their family. At the same time, households observed a hierarchy and the servants received instruction. An insight into the relationship comes from a witness's evidence in a tithe dispute in north Worcestershire in about 1530. At issue was the payment of tithes from two fields at Holeway on the boundary between the parishes of Hanbury and Bradley. Thomas Horooth of Berrow, aged 43, recalled that he worked as a servant for Robert Hunt, a farmer of Holeway, for six years, probably around 1500. He said that 'Robert Hunt his master would divers times say to him, "Thomas good boy, take heed what lambs and calves be born in Colmons and Badgers [the disputed fields], for we must pay tithe for them to the parson of Bradley" ', while animals elsewhere on the farm were exempt from tithe. Thomas said that he would ask his master 'why so?', and Robert would explain the location of the parish boundary and the local rules about tithe exemption and liability. We may doubt whether Horooth could accurately recall the precise words used in a conversation almost thirty years before, and as always in legal proceedings the evidence is likely to have been improved and clarified by the lawyers. We can believe, however, that he reported words that his listeners would regard as credible, and he and they clearly expected employers of servants to adopt an avuncular and didactic manner, while the good servant was ever eager to learn: hence the question 'why so?'[14]

Another large section of society throughout their lives worked occasionally and spasmodically for wages. These were the labourers or cottagers who, in the country, held and cultivated at least a small amount of land, and who therefore earned wages to supplement the produce from their holdings, often for a few days at a time. In the towns the labourers could be householders, who were again engaged by the day. People of many ranks would be involved in short-term employment, including those who were adding wages to already adequate sources of income. For example, a substantial peasant of Navestock (James Ford's parish), John Convers junior, in 1533 carted timber from the woods of the canons of St Paul's to the bank of the Thames.[15] The payment to him is expressed as a wage, but he could be seen as a contractor, using his own horses and cart, which few cottagers would have owned.

[14] TNA: PRO, E 328/25/1, 2, 3, 6, 7.
[15] Guildhall Library, Corporation of London, Ms. 25191.

Similarly, many building workers, who were paid by the day or week and appear in the employers' records as wage-earners, in some ways again resemble modern contractors or 'self employed' workers, as they supplied their own tools, were sometimes in a position to provide materials, and could be assisted by servants and apprentices.[16] In Durham city between 1495 and 1516 the priory, the biggest local employer, paid 10*s.* per annum to a smith, William Ranaldson, as a retainer, and 2*d.* per stone for any iron that he worked.[17] This would bring this artisan a considerable sum from the priory each year, up to £7, but he was also working on his own account from his shop in the town, so he was both a wage-earner and a businessman. He was also an employer, as his heavy work-load would keep a number of workers busy.

Just as the servants and part-time workers belonged to no single class or social rank, so the employers were very varied. They included, in addition to the lords and institutions, and the merchants, artisans, and more substantial tenants, people of modest means who needed labour, for example, those who lacked sons, or who were too old or ill to manage land, craft, or a business unaided. Widows who were continuing to make their livelihood from a holding, even one of moderate size, would need the help of a servant. Take the Rutland village of Brooke, where in 1522 the military survey records six servants.[18] Two of them were employed by rich landowners, the prior of Brooke Abbey and John Harrington esquire. Three others had quite well-heeled husbandmen and a prosperous widow as their employers, and one worked for another widow, Ellen Wilcokes, whose goods were valued at a not very high figure of £3. Servants were an especially important part of the urban workforce, and a high proportion of households included servants. For example, at Coventry in the 1520s no less than 39 per cent of the households included servants, so servants were by no means confined to the houses of the rich.[19] Finally, an important group of employers were wage-earners themselves, because many jobs requiring a team would be contracted between the employer and a leader for a price, and then the contractor would assemble the workers and pay their wages. Prosecutions under the Statute of Labourers in Essex in 1378 included men like John Rande, labourer, of Finchingfield who had 'retained' mowers of hay and paid them above the statute rate as part of a

[16] D. Woodward, *Men at Work: Labourers and Building Craftsmen in the Towns of Northern England, 1450–1750* (Cambridge, 1995), 25–6, 35–40.

[17] C. M. Newman, 'Employment On the Estates of the Priory of Durham, 1494–1519: The Priory As an Employer', *Northern History*, 36 (2000), 51, 52.

[18] J. Cornwall (ed.), *The County Community under Henry VIII*, Rutland Record Society, 1 (1980), 73.

[19] C. Phythian-Adams, *Desolation of a City: Coventry and the Urban Crisis of the Late Middle Ages* (Cambridge, 1979), 204.

gang.[20] Subcontracted employment of this kind could be on a large scale. For example, in 1469 William Fyssher, labourer of Coventry, agreed in an indentured contract with the lord of the manor of Chesterton in Warwickshire, John Peyto esquire, to dig an enlarged moat around his manor house for a price of £5. 6s. 8d. The job would evidently take some months, as the money was to be paid in quarterly instalments. The scale of the work can be judged from Peyto's agreement to allow eight oxen hauling loads of earth to feed on his grass. Fyssher would have been employing at least two assistants on this work.[21]

The conclusion, therefore, is that neither employees nor employers belonged to a homogeneous class, and that a sharp dividing-line cannot be drawn between those who paid wages and those who earned them. The term 'proletariat' suggests an impersonal employment structure, in which the work force would be separated from employers by a social gulf. Hiring fairs, recorded as early as 1351, where those in search of work and employers could meet, indicate that the two groups could be strangers to one another, and that they needed some institutionalized meeting point.[22] A similar conclusion can be drawn from the complaints voiced during the enforcement of the Statute of Labourers in the late fourteenth century, that in a large town such as Lincoln employment agents would put those seeking workers in touch with potential employees.[23]

On the other hand, many employers made contact with workers through personal links, based on kinship, tenancy, neighbourhood, and friendship. Churchwardens who were employing workers to build or repair a church would often take on parishioners.[24] Work was often carried out in the household, or in premises attached to the house, and most employees operated in an intimate group of two, three, or four, with members of the family and the employees working side by side. A Canterbury fuller, John Munde, was listed in the poll tax of 1381 with Alice his wife and three servants, Christina, Elena, and Richard.[25] Discipline would have been imposed informally, and arrangements for rewarding workers could have been

---

[20] E. C. Furber (ed.), *Essex Sessions of the Peace 1351, 1377–9*, Essex Archaeological Society, Occasional Publications, 3 (1953), 158.

[21] Shakespeare Birthplace Trust Records Office, Stratford-upon-Avon, DR98/514 (indenture in the Willoughby de Broke collection).

[22] Penn and Dyer, 'Wages and Earnings', 365.

[23] Ibid. 365–6.

[24] e.g. at Ashburton in Devon the smith who was employed on the ironwork of the church served his term as churchwarden: A. Hanham (ed.), *Churchwardens' Accounts of Ashburton, 1479–1580*, Devon and Cornwall Record Society, NS, 15 (1970), 24, 29.

[25] Goldberg, *Women, Work, and Life Cycle*, 158–202; C. C. Fenwick (ed.), *The Poll Taxes of 1377, 1379 and 1381*, part 1, British Academy Records of Social and Economic History, NS, 27 (1998), 421.

irregular, with delays in payment. Goods might be substituted for cash. Extra payments might be made, especially in an atmosphere of competition between employers for scarce workers, when gifts and favours would help to secure the employee's loyalty. Such informality provided plenty of opportunity for misunderstandings and ultimately for disputes, but gave little scope for the type of fundamental alienation associated with large groups of workers in modern factories or firms. Evidence for the contrary is provided by the many wills in which employers remembered servants with affection, left them money and goods, and even bequeathed property, workshops, or the tools of trade. Some of them were effectively making the servant their heir.

Numbers of Wage-Earners

Did the 'age of transition' see an increase in the number or at least the proportion of those working for wages? We have an opportunity to compare the numbers of employees, both servants, labourers, and other receiving wages, from records of the poll taxes of 1377–81, especially those of 1381, and the lists compiled for the military survey and lay subsidies of the early 1520s.

In fact an exact and fully convincing comparison is almost impossible to achieve. In the poll taxes people are identified as labourers, *servientes*, and *famuli*. They included the occasional 'son and servant' or 'daughter and servant' of the head of the household, so one might hope that a document which identified intimate working relationships within the family was providing a comprehensive census. But the lists which purport to give us the most precise occupational descriptions are those compiled for various counties in 1381, when evasions and concealments multiplied alarmingly, which is almost as disconcerting for historians as for the tax-gathering officials at the time.[26] Records occasionally survive of the reassessment of that year, when officials, dissatisfied with the sudden reduction in the number of taxpayers, went back to investigate the omissions. The supplementary lists consist mainly of wage-earners, so this was the group which was systematically undercounted in the first round of collection. The first assessment of the Gloucestershire village of Bibury collected money from forty-seven people, among whom women were severely underrepresented, with only twenty of them, and where the nine servants and labourers also seem to be suspiciously few in number. When the tax assessors visited the village again they added five

---

[26] Fenwick (ed.), *Poll Taxes*, part 1, pp. xiii–xxxix, for the official procedures.

more labourers and servants, four of them female.[27] In most counties, where there are no supplementary lists we have unconvincing depictions of communities which consisted mainly of adults, with dozens of married couples but very few young people or servants, even though the tax net included everyone aged 15 and over. Women, including young women, were all supposed to pay the poll tax, yet the whole country was apparently suffering from a severe gender imbalance, with an especially suspicious shortage of females in their late teens and early twenties. In addition to these problems of illicit omission, the official regulations of the poll tax allowed the exemption of the very poor, which was interpreted to include indigent householders, who are likely to have earned wages occasionally.[28]

In the 1520s, as most of the taxpayers were paying on valuations of their lands and goods, a large number of the less affluent, most of them wage-earners, were omitted from the tax, and many evaded payment.[29] The tax officials were inconsistent in their application of the rules, sometimes assessing large numbers of people on their wages, and sometimes including them among those paying on small quantities of goods, valued at a pound or two. Occupational descriptions were given inconsistently, and the majority of names were not assigned a status or trade at all. The basis on which the 1522 military survey was conducted and the taxes of 1524 and 1525 assessed was completely different from that used for the poll taxes, and we cannot make direct comparisons between them.

Having made these reservations, the unreliable figures that can be compiled for these two periods 144 years apart suggest that wage-earning had not changed fundamentally. In 1381 the percentage of people described as labourers and servants could be as low as 18 per cent in Staffordshire, rising to about 30 per cent in Leicestershire and 40 per cent in Gloucestershire.[30] In Essex, where 52 per cent of the households were headed by labourers, the mean holding of land by a labourer has been calculated at about 4 acres, which would have compelled members of the household, in order to feed a family of four, to seek at least eighty days of paid work each year. Similarly high proportions of labourers, and also many servants, were recorded in Suffolk.[31]

[27] R. H. Hilton, 'Some Social and Economic Evidence in Late Medieval English Tax Returns', in id., *Class Conflict and the Crisis of Feudalism* (London, 1985), 261–3; id., *English Peasantry*, 32; Fenwick (ed.), *Poll Taxes*, part 1, 294, 312.

[28] C. C. Fenwick, 'The English Poll Taxes of 1377, 1379 and 1381', University of London, Ph.D. thesis (1983), 113–14, 176–8.

[29] Some of the problems of this tax are rehearsed in A. Dyer, ' "Urban Decline" in England, 1377–1525', in T. R. Slater (ed.), *Towns in Decline* AD *100–1600* (Aldershot, 2000), 267–72.

[30] Dyer, *Standards of Living*, 213.

[31] L. R. Poos, *A Rural Society After the Black Death: Essex 1300–1525* (Cambridge, 1991), 22–7, 183–7; R. H. Hilton, *Bond Man Made Free: Medieval Peasant Movements and the English Rising of 1381* (London, 1973), 171.

In the early 1520s the wage-earning population has been estimated in different counties at between 32 and 41 per cent.[32] In Essex 43 per cent of taxpayers were assessed on wages, or their goods were valued at below 40*s*. Labourers were often assessed on 20*s*. in goods. In parts of Norfolk, using the assumption that those with goods worth less than 40*s*. were labourers, the proportion of wage-earners could have been as high as 54 per cent or 59 per cent.[33]

Bearing in mind the tendency for the poor, young, and female sections of the population to be undercounted, we could estimate that both in 1381 and in 1522–5 those who depended on wages for most of their income accounted for a little below half of the population in most of the country, but more than half in the eastern counties, from Kent to Lincolnshire.

If we wish to put these figures into a longer historical perspective by turning to an earlier period, no documents give direct indications of the numbers of wage-earners in whole communities in about 1300. We should bear in mind that near to a fifth of the population lived in towns, and a majority of them depended on wages. In the countryside two-fifths of tenants, and four-fifths in much of eastern England, were smallholders, unable to grow all of their food needs; and in the west lists of *garciones* on the manors of Glastonbury Abbey show that these landless unmarried workers could be as numerous as the householders.[34] Surveys and court rolls, without sufficient precision to allow an accurate count, hint at the existence of hidden groups of subtenants, lodgers, landless workers, wanderers, and others on the fringes of society, all of whom would have worked for wages when opportunity arose.[35] Wage-earners must have been at least as plentiful in 1300 as in 1381 and the 1520s. There can be no basis for an argument that wage-earning increased in importance in the economy as a whole in the later middle ages, and it may even have diminished during the fourteenth century, as the cottagers were reduced more drastically in number than other tenants, and the ranks of the landless were much eroded after the Black Death.

This suggestion of a 'steady state' in the wage-earning section of the economy over more than two centuries should not be taken to mean that the world of employment did not go through important changes. If we concentrate on the period between 1381 and 1524, we can identify some

[32] J. Yang, 'Wage-Earners in Early Sixteenth-Century England', University of Birmingham, Ph.D. thesis (1986).

[33] Poos, *Rural Society*, 30; J. Whittle, *The Development of Agrarian Capitalism: Land and Labour in Norfolk 1440–1580* (Oxford, 2000), 227–37.

[34] H. S. A. Fox, 'Exploitation of the Landless By Lords and Tenants in Early Medieval England', in Z. Razi and R. Smith (eds.), *Medieval Society and the Manor Court* (Oxford, 1996), 539–41.

[35] Ibid. 522–6; G. C. Homans, *English Villagers of the Thirteenth Century* (Cambridge, Mass., 1941), 136–9.

tendencies which diminished the extent of wage-earning and others which led to its expansion. To begin with the negative influences, the supply of potential employees was reduced by the shortage of young people, evident from the small family sizes—the result of endemic disease in one view, or late marriage in another, or perhaps both factors working together.[36] The landless workers either fell victim to the plagues or found some better employment: the Somerset *garciones* melted away.[37] Land was more easily available, which reduced the amount of wage work which cottars and smallholders needed to take, as they could add to their acres. The demand for labour in towns was reduced by the long-term decline of some industries, such as cloth-making in York.[38] Some of the largest units of employment, the big demesnes, were occasionally broken up, distributed among peasants, and reduced to such a size that they could be worked mainly by family labour. As land was converted from arable to pasture, both in peasant holdings and former demesnes, the amount of labour needed to produce from each acre was reduced. Patterns of employment changed locally, as some pastoral farmers hoped to engage herdsmen who could look after animals throughout the year, and required fewer weeders, threshers, and harvesters who worked for a few days or weeks each year, usually within the confines of an appropriate season. Women were in demand for occasional tasks such as weeding and harvesting, but did not usually work as shepherds, though they were still needed as dairymaids. In the regions of the most radical change from arable to pasture, such as the midland champion country, the opportunities for female short-term employment probably declined.

Long-term changes created more employment. The rising rate of pay is a well-attested feature of the period, and can be interpreted in a number of ways. Workers received greater rewards for each day or each task completed. A carpenter was paid 3*d.* per day in southern England just before the Black Death, 4*d.* in the late fourteenth century, and 6*d.* in the late fifteenth. The piece rate for threshing and winnowing 3 quarters of grain rose over the same period from 5*d.* to 8*d.* and then to 11*d.*[39] Such a rise in pay is not just evidence of fewer workers. The population was certainly falling in the late fourteenth century, but seems to have levelled off around 1400, yet wages continued to rise. The shortage of bullion in the early and mid-fifteenth

[36] R. M. Smith, 'Human Resources', in G. Astill and A. Grant (eds.), *The Countryside of Medieval England* (Oxford, 1988), 208–11; M. Bailey, 'Demographic Decline in Late Medieval England: Some Thoughts on Recent Research'. *Ec.HR* 49 (1996), 1–19.

[37] M. Ecclestone, 'Mortality of Rural Landless Men Before the Black Death: The Glastonbury Head-Tax Lists', *Local Population Studies*, 63 (1999), 6–29.

[38] J. Kermode, *Medieval Merchants: York, Beverley and Hull in the Later Middle Ages* (Cambridge, 1998), 202–5.

[39] *AHEW* iii. 471.

century should have had a depressive impact on wage rates, and there was a period of slight decline in money wages, in the 1410s and 1420s, but this effect was only temporary. The rising rates of pay must reflect the sustained demand for labour, relative to the population. There were more jobs, and carpenters, labourers, and all the others were being offered more work and longer periods of work. No longer would labourers have suffered, as they must have done in *c*.1300, from a lack of opportunities for employment.

The supply of workers was helped by the enlistment of more women, children, and old men into the work-force. They were tempted to seek work by the higher level of wages, and employers forgot the prejudices that had previously prevented women from carrying out 'men's work'—either heavy or more skilled tasks.[40] The contemporary claim of widespread idleness and vagrancy has to be treated sceptically. There must have been vagabonds and beggars, and workers took breaks to play games and drink ale, but we cannot be sure that this was a serious economic problem. The source of the complaints should be seen as reflecting the indignation among employers, who reacted to any lack of industry and diligence at a time when labour was hard to find and cost, in their eyes, too much money.[41]

The demand for workers greatly increased in the industrial sector, especially in rural cloth-making. This was more than enough to offset the decline in urban industry. The mechanization (which we examined under the heading of investment in chapter 4) did not reduce employment drastically, and some mills, such as those powering Sussex blast furnaces, created new labour demands in such ancillary activities as cutting and carrying fuel. Many of the former lords' demesnes under the leaseholders continued to need hired labour, and the rising number of tenant holdings with more than 30 acres were competing with the farmers for both servants and labourers. The amount of unpaid work was reduced, as the last vestiges of lords' labour services were removed by about 1400. The much greater quantity of labour which was not directly rewarded was that done within the family or household, and that also diminished. As well as the many households which lacked sons through demographic factors, those peasants and farmers who had successfully brought up a son who could help on the land found that these ungrateful offspring preferred to leave home and seek land and independence

[40] Goldberg, *Women, Work and Life-Cycle*, 101–4, 127–37.

[41] For these complaints, M. K. McIntosh, *Controlling Misbehavior in England, 1370–1600* (Cambridge, 1998); for a sceptical interpretation of the prohibitions on sports, C. Dyer, 'Leisure Among the Peasantry in the Later Middle Ages', in S. Cavaciocchi (ed.), *Il Tempo Libero. Economia e Societa*, Istituto Internazionale di Storia Economica 'F. Datini', Prato, 26 (1994), 291–306; they are given more credence in J. Hatcher, 'Labour, Leisure and Economic Thought Before the Nineteenth Century', *P&P* 160 (1998), 64–115.

elsewhere. Wives and daughters, judging from the numbers found employed in the harvest field or in service in towns, also spent less time working at home. The head of the household would sometimes have taken on workers to substitute for these losses.

We can draw the conclusion that while the proportion of servants, labourers, and other employees was neither increasing nor declining very much throughout the period 1300–1525, the pattern of employment altered, so that workers were redistributed and their experience of work was changed. I propose to explore some of those developments, first in the employment relationship, secondly in the role of wage-earners in particular communities and enterprises, and thirdly in attitudes towards work, leisure, and social security.

Changing Working Patterns

Relationships Between Employers and Employees

From 1349 work and labour relations were the subject of a mass of regulation and legislation. Before the Black Death there had been moves to regularize the number and frequency of holidays, and village communities sought to prevent potential harvest workers moving out of the village, or gleaning rather than accepting paid work in the harvest field.[42] The Ordinance and Statute of Labourers set rates of pay, enforced employment contracts, which should ideally have lasted a year, and restricted the mobility of workers. Legislation with similar aims was revised and reiterated, most elaborately in the Statute of Cambridge in 1388 and in laws that were repeated or rephrased through the fifteenth and sixteenth centuries.[43] The villages occasionally reiterated their rules about harvest workers, but also sought to introduce other controls, for example, by forbidding illicit games and setting a curfew. At Elmley Castle in Worcestershire in 1451 the steward ordered that no one should be awake and walking about after the hour of nine at night.[44] In the towns the craft guilds or fraternities issued sets of rules which governed rates of pay, working hours, length of apprenticeship, and other employment matters. In the case of the Bristol cordwainers, masters' wives were forbidden to offer extra gifts to workers. Often masters were forbidden to poach journeymen. The urban authorities refused to allow less skilled workers,

---

[42] W. O. Ault, *Open-Field Farming in Medieval England* (London, 1972), 27–34.
[43] E. Clark, 'Medieval Labor Law and English Local Courts', *American Journal of Legal History*, 27 (1983), 330–53; C. Given-Wilson, 'The Problem of Labour in the Context of English Government, c.1350–1450', in Bothwell *et al.* (eds.), *Problem of Labour*, 85–100.
[44] Ault, *Open-Field Farming*, 129.

such as daubers, to form fraternities, and journeymen's associations were sometimes dissolved as they were seen as conspiracies to raise wages.[45] The towns installed clocks in the fourteenth and fifteenth centuries. Their initial purpose was to indicate the times of religious services, and they became symbols of civic pride, but eventually they were used to signal the beginning and end of the working day.[46]

The church courts had a role in regulating labour, above all by enforcing the observance of holidays and Sundays as non-working days, and their concern for sexual morality had implications for relations between employers and employees, as fornication and adultery between male householders or their sons and female servants were common causes of scandal.[47]

The impression given is that working life was being conducted within a framework, even a straitjacket, of regulations. But were these restrictions obeyed? There is no shortage of evidence for the enforcement of these laws. Numerous prosecutions were mounted under the Statute of Labourers in the late fourteenth century, and methods were found to enlist the support of communities and to encourage informers. For example, the fines collected could be used to offset the tax payments of the village, or the informer might even receive a proportion of the offender's fine.[48] Although the vigour of enforcement was relaxed after the 1370s, the laws did not lapse, and as late as the 1560s workers in Norfolk were being taken to court under the Statute of Labourers.[49] Workers were most likely to have felt the force of the law in small units of government where their activities were observed and the authorities especially vigilant, as in the case of the urban craft fraternities. In villages the constables had been given the role of enforcing the statute in 1351, and this could have persisted long after the Justices of the Peace had ceased to hear hundreds of cases of breaches of the labour laws.[50]

Perhaps the most effective coercion that was brought to bear on workers, for example, to force them to agree to annual contracts of employment or to accept pay below the going rate, came from informal pressure from individ-

[45] H. Swanson, 'The Illusion of Economic Structure: Craft Guilds in Late Medieval English Towns, *P&P* 121 (1998), 29–48; G. Rosser, 'Crafts, Guilds and the Negotiation of Work in the Medieval Town', *P&P* 154 (1997), 3–31; S. Rees Jones, 'Household, Work and the Problem of Mobile Labour: The Regulation of Labour in Medieval English Towns', in Bothwell *et al.* (eds.), *Problem of Labour*, 133–53.

[46] C. M. Cipolla, *European Culture and Overseas Expansion* (Harmondsworth, 1970), 114–28; an example of its use to fix working hours is the regulation of the journeymen cappers of Coventry, who went to work from 6 'of the clock' in the morning until 6 at night: M. D. Harris (ed.), *The Coventry Leet Book*, Early English Text Society, os, 134, 135, 138, 146 (1907–13), 574.

[47] Goldberg, *Women, Work and Life Cycle*, 184.

[48] L. Poos, 'The Social Context of Statute of Labourers Enforcement', *Law and History Review*, 1 (1983), 27–52.

[49] Whittle, *Agrarian Capitalism*, 288–95.

[50] Ibid. 295, 297.

ual employers or from the local community. In the late fourteenth century we find lords granting holdings of land in exchange for a promise to accept offers of paid work at 'reasonable' (a code-word for low) wages.[51] In the fifteenth and early sixteenth centuries ordinary countrymen and townsmen were included in the affinities of the local gentry, and in such circumstances might have found it difficult to refuse employment for 'reasonable' pay. For example, people in Bromsgrove in Worcestershire belonged to the affinity of the Staffords of Grafton, a local gentry family, and in 1454–5 John Bochour from the town slaughtered animals for the household of Humphrey Stafford. Was his reward of 11*d.* fixed according to the prevailing market rate, or was he expected to do the job at a cheap price in return for past or future 'good lordship'?[52]

Patronage networks operated among the peasantry, by which better-off families acted as protectors of cottagers, standing surety for them and no doubt lending them money in hard times. After the Black Death many tenants who were accumulating holdings took on cottages along with larger tenements. In the Devon village of Stokenham the more substantial tenants by 1390 had an average of 45 acres, and many had acquired cottages.[53] They could then have been sublet to workers who were under some obligation to accept employment, no doubt for such favours as reduced rents and access to grazing. The tied cottage had probably originated at an earlier period when villages contained subtenants, but they were much more necessary at a time of labour shortage. In towns the master of an artisan household expected to exercise discipline over his household. John Bown, a York cordwainer, felt responsible for the conduct of his servants and, when in 1417 he discovered that under his roof John Waryngton had seduced Margaret Barker, pressured them into marrying, which Waryngton later regretted.[54] This episode suggests that if a master could exercise such influence over his servants, he could also have imposed on them employment conditions convenient for him.

The balance of probability must be against the overall effectiveness of regulation. Even in the 1350s, when the Justices of Labourers were numerous and especially zealous in pursuit of a new danger armed with a new law, wages

[51] C. Dyer, 'The Social and Economic Background to the Rural Revolt of 1381', in R. H. Hilton and T. Aston (eds.), *The English Rising of 1381* (Cambridge, 1984), 25–6.

[52] C. Dyer, *Bromsgrove: A Small Town in Worcestershire in the Middle Ages*, Worcestershire Historical Society Occasional Publications, 9 (2000), 45, 58–9; British Library Add. Roll 74174.

[53] H. S. A. Fox, 'Servants, Cottagers and Tied Cottages During the Later Middle Ages: Towards a Regional Dimension', *Rural History*, 6 (1995), 125–54.

[54] P. J. P. Goldberg (ed.), *Women in England c.1275–1525* (Manchester, 1995), 110–14; id., 'Masters and Men in Medieval England', in D. M. Hadley (ed.), *Masculinity in Medieval Europe* (Harlow, 1999), 56–70.

were commonly being paid above the limit. The subsequent repetition of legislation is surely a good indication that it was not being observed. Servants were most likely to have worked in a structured and disciplined environment, and a very high proportion of work was carried out by those paid by the day. The daily or piece rates meant that earnings could be much higher than for annual contracts, if enough days could be worked. A fully employed carpenter in the late fifteenth century on 6*d*. per day could have earned £6 annually, when 'gentlemen' were attempting to keep up their status on as little as £10 per annum. Whenever employment records survive, the importance of these short-term, transient, or episodic employment arrangements is all too clear. On the farm at Stebbing in Essex in 1483–4 the majority of workers were employed for between one and thirty days. Two-thirds of those working for Durham Priory in 1495–6 were earning 10*s*. or less, again suggesting that most of them were employed for no more than thirty days.[55] Employers tended to offer a series of small jobs, and the workers probably derived some satisfaction from working for a succession of employers and thereby retaining some independence. The authorities complained about their wandering, and found it difficult to distinguish a vagabond from a worker moving from one employer to another.

Many of those who worked for wages moved frequently, both in the sense of travelling some distance each day to the place of work, and also in changing their residence. Their mobility was only part of a general tendency. When people gave evidence to church courts they gave their place of birth and dwelling-place, and in Essex in 1467–97 only 24 per cent can be described 'life-time stayers' who were still living in the parish of their birth.[56] Similarly, in the tithe dispute about land at Holeway in Worcestershire already mentioned (p. 215 above), a wide variety of people—farmers, tenants of smaller holdings, labourers, and servants—reported their movements.[57] John Woodward, for example, had been born in Salwarpe, and had lived in Hanbury for sixteen years, but at the time of the hearing had moved to Abberton. These places are only 7 and 4 miles from Holeway respectively, and of the twenty-three witnesses nine had moved quite short distances, but another five had travelled into the area from Oxfordshire, Shropshire, Staffordshire, and other relatively remote places.

Labour seems sometimes to have flowed almost at random, as if movement occurred for its own sake and with no overall effect on population density. But sometimes we can see that labour migrated in distinct patterns. In the

---

[55] Poos, *Rural Society*, 213–16; Newman, 'Employment on the Estates of the Priory of Durham', 50.

[56] Poos, *Rural Society*, 159–79.

[57] TNA: PRO, E328/25/1, 2, 3, 6, 7.

country as a whole the density of people had risen remarkably in the south-west between the fourteenth and the sixteenth centuries, with some concentration in western Somerset and Devon by the 1520s, reflecting the rising fortunes of the cloth industry.[58] By contrast, the mainly agrarian east midland counties, which had seemed relatively thickly peopled in 1377, had sunk back by the early sixteenth century. Within individual counties some districts advanced while others stagnated or declined. Population density in north-west Warwickshire rose, reflecting the liveliness of its pastoral and industrial economy, while the south and east of the county, which before 1350 specialized in cereal cultivation and had supported a dense population, suffered losses through migration.[59]

On a more local level a common story was of rural depopulation and the shrinkage of villages, with pockets where desertion of a number of contiguous villages and severe shrinkage left districts severely deprived of people. Parts of eastern Leicestershire or southern Warwickshire fall into this category.[60] This abandonment of settlements is a well-known feature of the period between 1320 and 1520, with a period of most intense depopulation in the early and middle years of the fifteenth century. Yet simultaneously settlements grew and new houses were built. In woodland parishes cottages were sited on commons in such places as Sedgley in Staffordshire, where the growth can be connected with employment in local industries such as ironworking and coal-mining.[61] On a less intense scale, new cottages were being built in many places, only one or two at a time, but cumulatively amounting to a significant trend.[62] New hamlets were founded, and existing settlements expanded in the cloth-making areas, such as the Stour valley on the border of Essex and Suffolk, where the timber-framed buildings constructed at that time still survive to remind us that this was a period of settlement growth. Elsewhere, such as in the valleys around Stroud and Bisley in Gloucestershire, dozens of new cottages for cloth-workers were built around the fulling mills and clothiers' houses, but the continued development of the industry in subsequent centuries has left few physical reminders of the early phases of that rural

[58] R. M. Smith, 'Human Resources', 198–202.

[59] M. J. Stanley, 'Medieval Tax Returns as Source Material', in T. R. Slater and P. J. Jarvis (eds.), *Field and Forest: An Historical Geography of Warwickshire and Worcestershire* (Norwich, 1982), 231–56.

[60] C. Lewis, P. Mitchell-Fox, and C. Dyer, *Village, Hamlet and Field: Changing Medieval Settlements in Central England*, 2nd edn. (Macclesfield, 2001), 123–31; C. J. Bond, 'Deserted Medieval Villages in Warwickshire and Worcestershire', in Slater and Jarvis (eds.), *Field and Forest*, 147–71.

[61] *AHEW* iii. 85.

[62] C. Dyer, 'Peasants and Farmers: Rural Settlements and Landscapes in an Age of Transition', in D. Gaimster and P. Stamper (eds.), *The Age of Transition: The Archaeology of English Culture 1400–1600*, Society for Medieval Archaeology Monographs, 15 (1997), 70–1.

expansion.[63] On the Devon coast, where fishing had traditionally been conducted from temporary shelters near the beach by part-time, seasonal fishermen who lived in villages inland, new permanently occupied fishing villages grew in the late fifteenth and early sixteenth centuries. The three coastal hamlets called Cockwoods which appeared in Dawlish parish by 1513 contained a total of twenty cottages.[64]

An often repeated cliché about this period emphasizes the movement of labour into the towns. This receives some justification from attempts by the authorities, acting in the interests of rural landlords, in 1388 and 1406 to restrict young people from the country taking up apprenticeships.[65] Although this was not in general a period of urban growth, and most towns, like most villages, became smaller, there were exceptions, especially in the cloth-making districts, so that places such as Exeter and Tiverton in Devon were increased in size between the 1370s and the 1520s.[66] A handful of places grew into urban centres at this time, in the clothing districts, for example, Pensford in Somerset.[67] Even those towns which persisted with a population lower than they had supported around 1300 were still receiving immigrants, which were necessary to replace those moving on to other towns or returning to villages, or simply to step into the places of those who had died. Of the seventy or so families living at Bromsgrove in Worcestershire in 1470, about 90 per cent had moved into the town in the previous century. Permanent residents were in a distinct minority.[68]

To sum up, the authorities, especially after the Black Death, attempted to restrict and control the market for labour, and succeeded only to a limited extent. What appears to have been an age of regulation was really one of growing opportunity and freedom for workers. The rewards for work increased, and the employees chose short-term contracts, movement between employers, and flexible working patterns. The work-force achieved such levels of mobility that the distribution of the population, both regionally and locally, was changed significantly. The legislation is of most value to us in indicating some of the trends observed by contemporaries which they sought ineffectively, to prevent.

---

[63] C. Dyer, 'Villages and Non-villages in the Medieval Cotswolds', *Transactions of the Bristol and Gloucestershire Archaeological Society,* 120 (2002), 32.

[64] H. Fox, *The Evolution of the Fishing Village: Landscape and Society Along the South Devon Coast, 1086–1550* (Oxford, 2001), 146–9.

[65] *Statutes of the Realm,* Record Commission (1810–28), ii. 57, 157.

[66] *CUHB* i. 605–6.

[67] Ibid. 537, 638; C. Dyer, 'Small Places With Large Consequences: The Importance of Small Towns in England, 1000–1540', *Historical Research,* 75 (2002), 23.

[68] Dyer, *Bromsgrove,* 52–4.

Work in Specific Communities and Enterprises

Given the difficulties in using the various tax lists to provide us with a comprehensive census of wage-earners, an alternative approach to assessing trends in employment is to examine individual employers, and specific communities, especially those where additional evidence helps us to interpret the tax records. In the late fourteenth century demesnes under the direct management of lords employed the largest concentration of workers, full- and part-time, in the countryside. A large manor often provided work for between four and ten full-time farm servants, together with a dozen or two of day labourers. In the towns of that period quite large groups of employees can be found in a small minority of households. For example, in Colchester in 1377 among a thousand households there were six which employed as many as six, seven, and eight servants, but the largest of all contained eleven, that of John Reek.[69] The trades of these taxpayers are not given, but at Chipping Campden in 1381, when each householder's occupation is identified, a wool merchant, William Grevil, and a smith, Robert Mors, each employed six servants.[70] The largest non-agricultural employers were merchants, who needed hands to pack and carry goods, and also factors and agents to travel with commodities and make deals. Among artisans, the metalworkers needed much labour for hammering or casting, making moulds, organizing fuel, and working bellows.

To some extent this pattern continued in the next century-and-a-half. Small-scale employment persisted. Perhaps a higher proportion of peasants hired servants, or needed day labourers at harvest time. The demesnes were still the source of much employment, whether they continued in the management of the lords, or if they had been leased out to farmers. Some factors reduced the size of the labour force employed by individuals, such as the division of large demesnes into two or more farms and the scaling down of the cultivated area. Farmers were still major employers, like Roger Heritage of Burton Dassett in 1495, who seems to have had work for a large number: he accommodated six living-in servants, and probably employed six other full- timers who had their own houses, while part-timers would have come on to the farm to perform seasonal tasks.[71] Unlike the absentee lord who had managed the demesne in the previous century, Heritage lived in a farmhouse at the centre of the manor, so his work-force included both farmhands and domestic servants.

---

[69] Fenwick (ed.), *Poll Taxes*, part 1, 194–205.
[70] Ibid. 284.
[71] TNA: PRO, PROB 2/457.

In the towns again we find concentrations of servants in the households of merchants. At Coventry, according to a listing of 1523, the very wealthy Richard Marler, a mercer, employed fourteen servants, followed by two drapers, John Bond and Julian Nethermyll, each with ten.[72] The largest known medieval manufacturing enterprise, that of the London pewterer Thomas Dounton, in 1457 employed eighteen servants and apprentices. Typically, he worked metal, though he was also a mercer.[73] In brewing the nature of employment changed, especially in the larger towns, with the decline of the independent, self-employed ale-wives, and their replacement by large breweries, producing a thousand gallons at a time, often of beer rather than ale. The beer brewers could employ as many as eleven servants, usually male.[74] Clothiers are also found with many servants and apprentices, and they, like the brewers, represent an emergent group of employers. A clothier appears in the 1523 census at Coventry, with seven servants, but clothing had fallen on hard times in that city.[75] In the more active centres we find people like John Briggs of Salisbury in 1491, and John Benett of Cirencester in 1497, each with thirteen servants and apprentices.[76]

A great extension in the dependency of workers came about with the development of the putting-out system, often associated with proto-industrialization, when rural and small-town industry developed in a special-ized way, orchestrated by entrepreneurs who supplied international markets. Apparently in Essex in the late fourteenth century the artisans who carried out the various stages of cloth-making co-ordinated their activities without a clothier sitting at the centre of the operation. A hundred years later the clothiers were leaving money in their wills to all of their spinners, implying that their workers had fallen into a more subordinate relationship. John Golding of Glemsford in Suffolk in 1495 had seven servants, and left 12*d.* to each of his spinners, both in and out of the town, and one suspects very numerous.[77] The impression is given that these workers had by that date been drawn into a system which limited their independence and their earnings. Weavers in the military survey of 1522 in Suffolk could include people of sufficient substance to have their goods valued at £8 or £10, who presumably employed assistants, but many were sometimes too poor to be assessed, and

---

[72] M. H. M. Hulton (ed.), *Coventry and Its People in the 1520s*, Dugdale Society, 38 (1999), 145, 148.

[73] R. F. Homer, 'Tin, Lead and Pewter', in J. Blair and N. Ramsay (eds.), *English Medieval Industries, Craftsmen, Techniques, Products* (London, 1991), 71.

[74] J. M. Bennett, *Ale, Beer, and Brewsters in England: Women's Work in a Changing World, 1300–1600* (New York, 1996), 48–50; 83.

[75] Hulton (ed.), *Coventry and Its People*, 141 (Henry Wall).

[76] TNA: PRO, PROB 11/9, fo. 5; 11/11, fo. 90.

[77] Ibid., PROB 11/11, fo. 110.

in Worcestershire in 1525 weavers and other clothing artisans had their goods valued for tax at the lowest assessment of 20*s*., just like labourers.[78]

Wage-earning expanded in the textile-making districts, not just because of the activities of the clothiers, but also because fullers and other artisans needed employees, as did the other tradesmen, such as bakers and brewers, who sold their products to the textile workers. The village of Bisley, which included a number of hamlets in south Gloucestershire in 1381, seems to have been primarily agricultural, and most of the taxpayers were called 'cultivators', or as we would say, peasants, and a handful of labourers. By 1524, after a period of growth in cloth-making in the district made famous by the 'Stroudwater' name, 46 per cent of the taxpayers were assessed on wages, one of the highest proportions in the county.[79] A similar proportion of people assessed on wages (with a few people paying tax on goods valued at 20*s*., who are presumed to have depended on earnings), 44 per cent, is found in the textile town of Kidderminster in Worcestershire.[80] This is a much higher proportion of wage assessments than is found in Pershore, a market town in the country which lacked industrial specialisms.[81] In the Worcestershire countryside, in those villages where the peasantry persisted, like Claines and Kempsey on the outskirts of the county town, the percentage of those assessed on wages seems comparatively low, at 18 per cent and 7 per cent respectively.[82] No doubt many of the holders of 6 or 12 or even 24 acres who lived in those villages earned wages part-time, but they were sufficiently endowed with goods for the tax assessors to use those assets as the basis of their taxation.

A very high proportion of wage-earners is found in three types of rural economy. First, the villages which had been abandoned and replaced by a large pasture farm left the tax administrators with the task of assessing a single wealthy lord or lessee, and a group of servants who worked as herdsmen. At Lasborough in Gloucestershire, for example, in 1381 the place was reported as uninhabited. In 1524 William Hobyn was assessed at £40 on goods, and two men were taxed on wages.[83] At Compton Verney in Warwickshire, which had been finally abandoned in the 1460s and 1470s, by 1525 the taxpayers were Richard Verney esquire and four wage-earners.[84] The second type were

---

[78] J. Pound (ed.), *The Military Survey of 1522 For Babergh Hundred*, Suffolk Records Society, 28 (1986), 24, 27, 31, 33; M. Faraday (ed.), *Worcestershire Taxes in the 1520s*, Worcestershire Historical Society, NS, 19 (2003), 176, 179.

[79] Fenwick (ed.), *Poll Taxes*, part 1, 285; TNA: PRO, E 179/113/213 (I owe this transcript to Professor Jei Yang).

[80] Faraday (ed.), *Worcestershire Taxes*, 143–5, 240.

[81] Ibid. 115–16.   [82] Ibid. 96–7.

[83] Fenwick (ed.), *Poll Taxes*, part 1, 303; TNA: PRO, E 179/113/213 (from Professor Jei Yang).

[84] TNA: PRO, E 179/192/135; for the village's history, see pp. 70–1 above.

villages that shrank rather than being deserted, concentrating land in the hands of the few, who then needed labour. At Hazleton in the Gloucestershire Cotswolds there had been forty peasant holdings before the Black Death and twenty after the plague in 1355. By 1540 only four tenants remained, two with about 400 acres each, one with 200, and one with 120. The rector had a large glebe. The 1524 tax assessment reflects this distribution of land almost exactly, with five people paying on substantial amounts of goods, with one assessed on 40s. of goods, and six wage-earners who presumably worked for this handful of cultivators.[85]

Finally, settlements involved in industry—not just cloth, but often metal-working—and commercial centres in the countryside might have a high proportion of wage-earners. At Cradley in Worcestershire, the scene of early ironworking, 45 per cent of taxpayers in 1524 paid on wages, and at Redditch in the same county the 40 per cent of taxpayers assessed on wages owed something to its position as an informal centre of trade, with inns and woodland industries.[86] Our sources are very fallible, and the omission of all but a small minority of servants from the records of the 1520s means that we cannot know how many servants were employed, for example in pastoral husbandry. Most of the figures for individual settlements calculated here are based on the numbers paying on wages. If those assessed on goods worth 20s. or 40s. were included, the percentage of those whose incomes included a high proportion of wages would rise considerably.

Changes in the pattern of production encouraged shifts in the distribution of labour. There was no wholesale increase in the wage-earning workforce, but local economic changes created pockets of demand for wage labour, and so we find groups of wage-earners in particular places and employed in specific enterprises.

Changing Attitudes to Work

If the terms of employment, mobility of labour, and distribution of employees changed, was there also any development in attitudes towards work? There is a well-rehearsed argument that workers, given higher daily rates of pay, would have earned until they had enough to satisfy the basic necessities of life, and then stopped.[87] This limited their earnings, and they were unlikely to have achieved high levels of productivity. This is supported by

---

[85] The changes from the 1340s can be traced in Gloucestershire Record Office, D678, Safe 3, fos. 21–2; TNA: PRO, SC2/175/1, fo. 32; E179/113/213.

[86] Faraday (ed.), *Worcestershire Taxes*, 133, 138.

[87] I. Blanchard, 'Introduction', in I. S. W. Blanchard (ed.), *Labour and Leisure in Historical Perspective: Thirteenth to Twentieth Centuries* (Stuttgart, 1994), 9–38.

numerous contemporary comments on the fecklessness of servants and labourers, their fondness for playing disorderly and time-wasting games, and their refusal to work diligently or for long hours.

There are various reasons for doubting that this should be regarded as the universal reaction of workers to the better wages and working conditions of the period. First, the criticisms are those that we would expect from employers experiencing 'the servant problem', and should be treated with scepticism. Secondly, the evidence for expanding consumption at the lower end of society of food, clothing, and other goods suggests that wage-earners may have wished to maximize their earnings, and not always to opt for leisure (see pp. 128–32). Thirdly, the increase in the participation of women in paid work in the generations after the Black Death suggests a desire to increase household incomes, and again not to choose leisure.[88] Fourthly, the argument that people worked as little as possible is related to the idea that servants, labourers, and part-time workers were held in low regard, and indeed had such a low level of self esteem that they had no incentive to work to better themselves. There is plenty of evidence for insulting and contemptuous attitudes towards wage-earners, from the nicknames given to the Somerset *garciones* such as 'pig' and 'skinhead', through the condemnation of the 'wasters' in *Piers Plowman*, to the assumption by the London authorities in 1419, in setting out the procedures for holding courts in the wards of the city, that the inhabitants could be divided between respectable householders and the less trustworthy 'hired servants'.[89]

Workers, however, could be highly regarded. Some employers in their wills expressed affectionate attitudes to servants, who were clearly appreciated by them as reliable, honest, and admirable. Humphrey Newton, a Cheshire landed gentleman, used to have his deeds witnessed by his employees.[90] His servants were trusted to visit markets and trade on their employer's behalf. In towns servants were given considerable responsibilities in running their master's affairs, particularly in the sale of goods. In the borough court at Andover in Hampshire in the late fourteenth century a number of servants were named, either alone or together with their masters, in pleas of debt, almost as if they were regarded as business partners, and in some cases they may have been trading on their own account. William, servant of John Estbury, in 1387 was fined for making a false claim against John More, but he successfully brought a plea against William Cosham, and recovered a debt

---

[88] Goldberg, *Women, Work, and Life Cycle*, 82–157.
[89] Rees Jones, 'Regulation of Labour', 134–5.
[90] D. Youngs, 'Servants and Labourers on a Late Medieval Demesne: The Case of Newton, Cheshire, 1498–1520', *Ag.HR* 47 (1999), 152.

of 5s.[91] There were clearly some workers who expected to improve themselves; for example, those who worked as artisans in towns hoped to start their own workshop, and we can sometimes observe in wills their diligence rewarded when their employer bequeathed his equipment to them (see p. 120).

Resolving the dilemma about attitudes to work would be helped by better evidence for productivity. Total output after 1349 must have fallen with the drastic reduction in the number of producers and consumers, and the shrinkage in the area under cultivation. The yield per acre of demesnes tended to fall, and peasants would have had problems in maintaining yields on their land, as they could not afford the labour for intensive husbandry, such as repeated ploughing and weeding. Production per worker increased, in that large quantities of tin and iron were extracted by a depleted workforce. The number of bushels of grain and pounds of wool produced by individual workers must have risen. As a crude indication of this, fewer ploughmen were employed on demesnes after the Black Death, without a comparable decrease in the cultivated area. Shepherds were expected to look after larger flocks—on the Winchester estate the number of sheep per man increased from 300 to 340 during the fourteenth century.[92]

For more precise measures of productivity, we need figures for individual enterprises which can be compared with those for earlier or later periods. In the building trades practices and materials have not changed as much as in mechanized manufacturing, so that a comparison can be made between the performances of late medieval and modern workers. A Hull tiler in the late fifteenth century could fix 300 tiles on a roof in a day.[93] His modern equivalent boasts of laying a thousand, but we do not know enough about the work to be sure that the tasks were similar: the medieval tiler may have been nailing on the laths as well as carrying the tiles up a ladder and setting them in place; tiles vary in size; and so on. In the north-eastern coal-mines of Whickham and Railey, in 1500 and 1460 respectively, the output was in the range of 1.2 to 2 tons per man per day, which can be compared with 1–1.5 tons in the early nineteenth century.[94] The coal-mines are a good example of a medieval industry which attracted capital for such work as drainage, and where the labour force had the same specialized roles as in later mining— there were hewers, barrowmen, winders, and a banksman. These calculations

---

[91] Hampshire Record Office, 37 M85 2/HC/14.

[92] D. Farmer, 'The *famuli* in the Later Middle Ages', in R. Britnell and J. Hatcher (eds.), *Progress and Problems in Medieval England: Essays in Honour of Edward Miller* (Cambridge, 1996), 221.

[93] Woodward, *Men at Work*, 129–30.

[94] J. Hatcher, *The History of the British Coal Industry*, Vol. I, *Before 1700: Towards the Age of Coal* (Oxford, 1993), 345–6.

suggest that we should not underestimate the productivity of late medieval labour.

Venetian ambassadors in the early and mid-sixteenth century reported that the English were lazy, and that they failed to exploit vigorously their country's resources.[95] This comment must have reflected the low density of population compared with northern Italy. English population began to recover from its stagnation after the Black Death in about 1540, while in France and Italy numbers had been climbing rapidly for almost a century (see pp. 156–7). The visitors would have been struck by the amount of pasture, and the easy life of those who looked after animals, compared with the intensive labour of the Italian countryside. A symptom of the contrast is apparent in the quantities of vegetables and horticultural produce imported into England. Continental peasants were putting a great deal of effort into growing cabbages, onions, garlic, and hops, as well as plants such as woad and madder for dyes and teasels for the finishing of woollen textiles. These were labour-intensive activities with low financial rewards, which were evidently practised on the continent but not to the same degree in England.[96] The English could apparently afford to buy these commodities out of the profits of selling livestock, wool, and other animal products. The English passion for gardening seems to have been a modern development.

In general, a case can be made for the strengthening of a work ethic in the period between the Black Death and the Reformation. Such a statement is, of course, in direct contradiction to the view that workers were encouraged by high pay to be idle, and to the picture of workers without commitment which emerges from the pens of legislators, preachers, and moralists. It is also inconsistent with the view that the work ethic was an invention of the early modern period, and in particular that it was a concept devised by Protestants.

One approach to the problem is to look at the history of leisure—the opposite of work. It is said that the strict division between work and leisure is a modern invention.[97] Medieval aristocrats imagined that hunting animals was a useful task. Medieval workers often combined work with play or ritual, for example, when the labour service of haymaking was rewarded with the quantity of grass that could be lifted on the scythe of the mower. Work tended to be a collective act, where individual effort was not so important. Work was

---

[95] Hoskins, *Age of Plunder*, 105–6; C. A. Sneyd (ed.), *A Relation or Rather a True Account of the Island of England*, Camden Society, 37 (1847), 10, 31.

[96] e.g. W. R. Childs (ed.), *The Customs Accounts of Hull 1453–1490*, Yorkshire Archaeological Society Record Series, 144 (1986), 2–7, 12–13, 30–2, 46–8, 50–6.

[97] K. Thomas, 'Work and Leisure in Pre-industrial Society', *P&P* 29 (1964), 50–66; P. Burke, 'The Invention of Leisure in Early Modern Europe', *P&P* 146 (1995), 136–50; the latter work has attracted criticism in J.-L. Marfany, 'Debate: The Invention of Leisure in Early Modern Europe', *P&P* 156 (1997), 174–91.

done in order to complete a task, and workers were not conscious of the discipline of time. Leisure was irrationally conceived, as the rhythms and routines of the year were not dominated entirely by the work of planting and harvest: the church's calendar was based on otherworldly priorities, which enforced holidays on the faithful, often at impractical times during the spring planting or the corn harvest. It is often imagined that medieval people had a great deal of time to kill. Attitudes changed in the early modern period, when traditional sports and games were denounced as disorderly and immoral, and more-refined leisure pursuits were advocated in books such as those on how to play chess. Modern production, and especially factory work, was strictly governed by precise measurement of time. Ultimately, in the nineteenth century sports were codified, sanitized, and organized to give the workers an outlet under the control of their masters.[98]

The contrast between medieval and modern attitudes to leisure cannot be sustained, however. Elite writers in the fifteenth and early sixteenth centuries, like Edmund Dudley, denounced games and alehouses.[99] Humanists before the Reformation, like Erasmus, criticized time-wasting, and equated hard work with the godly life.[100] These views were not confined to the intellectual elite—fifteenth-century wills (see above, p. 124) showed a belief in self-discipline, moderation, and sober and responsible behaviour. Local by-laws periodically prohibited illicit sports, such as football and dice, which wasted time and threatened public order. Archery was encouraged officially because it trained young men in military skills useful to the state. The aristocracy may have had difficulty in distinguishing between their hours devoted to work and leisure, but for those who made their living from physical work the difference must have been only too clear. Work occupied people for many days and long hours. Contrary to the belief that the farming seasons left many of those working with time on their hands, current estimates suggest that a tenant of a 20-acre holding would be occupied for 260 days of the year.[101] In towns the twelve-hour days specified in the ordinances of craft fraternities may not always have been worked in full, but if people in practice spent an hour or two less in work per day, it still occupied a very high proportion of their lives.

Medieval work could be arduous and repetitive. If people sang as they toiled it was not because they were mixing leisure with their tasks: it just made the drudgery bearable. Nor was it possible to lose the effort of the individual

---

[98] R. W. Malcolmson, *Popular Recreation in English Society, 1700–1850* (Cambridge, 1973); J. Clarke and C. Critcher, *The Devil Makes Work: Leisure in Capitalist Britain* (Basingstoke, 1985).

[99] D. M. Brodie (ed.), *The Tree of Commonwealth: A Treatise Written by Edmund Dudley* (Cambridge, 1948), 39, 45–6, 48.

[100] R. Iliffe, 'Working Bodies: Protestantism, the Productive Individual, and the Politics of Idleness', in P. Gouk (ed.), *Wellsprings of Achievement* (Aldershot, 1995), 135–58, esp. 136–7.

[101] Fox, 'Exploitation of the Landless', 544–9.

in the collective process. In the desperate labour shortage of the period everyone's contribution counted, and most work groups consisted of only two or three individuals. Slacking or incompetence would quickly be noticed by workmates as well as by supervisors and employers. Humphrey Newton of Cheshire, for example, noted in his commonplace book around 1500 when Ellen Porter spoiled the ale and missed work for four weeks while apparently feigning illness.[102] The harvest field would contain the largest work gangs, but everyone was identified as an individual, as some fifteenth-century manorial accounts list the workers by name, which rarely occurred before 1350.[103] The gangs of labourers who dug ditches and ponds did so for a fixed price, and the whole group would have lost earnings if any individual failed to pull his weight.

The cessation of work was often occasioned by religious festivals, but they still gave the workers the opportunity to pursue leisure. A good example of the combination of the religious and secular are the associations of young men, young women, wives, and other groups based on age and gender who in the south-west held social events, centred on dancing, play-acting, and no doubt ale-drinking. This was pleasure with a purpose, as it also generated some money for parish funds.[104] We know most about the illicit games of football, tennis, bowls, cards, dice, and other forms of gambling precisely because they were prohibited, which shows that a strong body of opinion expected that a distinction should be drawn between harmful and divisive pastimes and wholesome, useful, and socially cohesive activities such as archery practice and the summer games and Rogation processions.[105]

Work and leisure were separated in medieval practice. Working hours and working days were defined quite precisely. The working lives of individuals were structured, beginning with a period when young people acquired skills and experience, and ending with forms of retirement, though this was easier to achieve for those with land or property that could be traded for a promise of maintenance.

In such a context the work ethic could develop. It was expressed in village by-laws before 1349, when the able-bodied were forbidden to glean in the harvest field or to leave the village for higher pay. They were supposed to join

---

[102] Youngs, 'Servants and Labourers', 156.

[103] e.g. the account of Richard Best, supervisor of the lord's husbandry at Methley in Yorkshire names most of those working on the demesne: 'To Agnes Webster labouring in hay for 14 days . . .' In all 31 harvest workers, mostly women, were named: West Yorkshire Archive Service, Leeds, MX/M6/3/10.

[104] K. L. French, *The People of the Parish: Community Life in a Late Medieval Diocese* (Philadelphia, 2001), 127.

[105] McIntosh, *Controlling Misbehavior*, 96–107; C. Dyer, 'The Political Life of the Fifteenth-Century English Village', *The Fifteenth Century*, 4 (2004), 135–57.

in the harvest for a 'reasonable' wage.[106] Those attitudes were strengthened
after the Black Death, when Piers Plowman expresses the exasperation
of peasant employers faced with lazy employees, who would be disciplined
by Hunger, as if the author welcomed the restraints made necessary in times
of hardship.[107] These views were not confined to a moralistic poet's
imagining a peasant's reactions to the labour problem—although the labour
laws provoked general resentment, the appearance of so many workers in
the courts in the late fourteenth century must have resulted from information provided by peasant and artisan employers.[108] Employers subscribed
to the work ethic, and so did wage-earners, as the prospect of increased
spending power and promotion into a position of greater economic independence as a landholder or self-employed artisan gave then a strong motiv-
ation.[109]

Social Security

The problem of work and leisure is closely connected with questions of
welfare and social security. Those who did not work would have to be
supported by their neighbours. Attitudes to charity and its implementation
changed perceptibly within our period. The first prohibition on begging by
the able-bodied in national legislation was included in the Ordinance of
Labourers in 1349. The sudden shortage of labour made voluntary idleness
especially repugnant. Expressions of the need for discrimination in charity,
and moves against beggars, continued for the next century-and-a-half, and
were then renewed with vigour at the end of the fifteenth and in the early
sixteenth centuries. 'Idle and suspect persons, living suspiciously' reappear
regularly in the proclamations of Henry VII and Henry VIII, and were
associated with other social evils—crime and disorder, Scottish immigration
into the north of England, the decay of tillage, and unlawful games.[110]

The varied measures used to combat poverty and vagrancy amount to a
new dimension in social policy. The more punitive measures, such as the
orders to expel vagrants from towns, or the growing number of by-laws in
villages and small towns which forbad the harbouring of suspicious strangers,

---

[106] Ault, *Open-Field Farming*, 32–4.
[107] Kane and Talbot (eds.), *Piers Plowman*, 358–68 (ll. 172–331).
[108] Poos, 'Statute of Labourers Enforcement'.
[109] C. Dyer, 'Work Ethics in the Fourteenth Century', in Bothwell *et al.* (eds.), *Problem of Labour*, 21–41.
[110] P. L. Hughes and J. F. Larkin (eds.), *Tudor Royal Proclamations*, Vol. I, *The Early Tudors* (New Haven and London 1964), 17, 23, 32–3, 85–93, 127. On the general context of social policy, P. Slack, *From Reformation to Improvement: Public Welfare in Early Modern England* (Oxford, 1999), 14–21.

were entirely consistent with the more positive steps taken to look after the 'deserving poor'. A characteristic phrase in wills urged that alms should go to those 'in greatest need'. Around 1400, parliament was concerned with the decline in parochial charity and the decay of hospitals.[111] By about 1500 some of the old hospital foundations had degenerated into rest homes for a very small number of wealthy pensioners, but there were also new foundations reflecting a fresh concern with the relief of genuine poverty, from the huge Savoy in London, based on Italian models, to the small but quite numerous almshouses, often founded by fraternities. There were twenty *maisondieus* in York alone by 1500.[112] The care given to the inmates of these institutions varied with the wealth of the endowment. Some could not afford to feed the old people, but this gave private donors—in life presumably, as well as on their deathbeds when they dictated their wills—the chance to give money purposefully. Bequests of sums varying between 2*d.* and 6*d.* for each poor person in an almshouse would feed the inmates for a few days, and the testators would know that their money was going to relieve those regarded as in genuine need, as only the deserving poor would be admitted to an almshouse. Almshouse founders often reflected trends in thinking about care for the poor. John Greenway, the rich clothier from Tiverton in Devon, had an almshouse built in his home town in the early sixteenth century which advertised his generosity and piety with coats of arms, merchant marks, and improving inscriptions. Instead of leading the collective life favoured by the older hospitals, each pauper had separate accommodation ('a several house and chamber') and a very generous 18*d.* per week.[113]

Some of the traditional sources of support for the poor declined. Those who retired could not count on the help of children, as there were more childless couples, and sons and daughters were more likely to move from their native village or town and have no need for the family holding or house. The emphasis shifted from family to community support. Some people making their wills reveal that a poor person was lodging in their house, or refer to individuals by name, like 'a certain pauper called Poor John', a familiar figure, perhaps, in the streets of Cirencester, who was bequeathed 20*d.* by John Benett, the Gloucestershire clothier, in 1497.[114] Neighbourly help could involve informal fund-raising, like the 'help ales' held in the Yorkshire

---

[111] *Statutes of the Realm*, 2, 80, 136–7, 175.

[112] P. Cullum and P. J. P. Goldberg, 'Charitable Provision in Late Medieval York: "to the praise of God and the use of the poor" ', *Northern History*, 29 (1993), 24–39.

[113] A. E. Welsford, *John Greenway, 1460–1529: Merchant of Tiverton and London: A Devon Worthy* (Tiverton, 1984), 15–16.

[114] TNA: PRO, PROB 11/11, fo. 90.

manor of Wakefield, where the profit from communal brewing and selling of a batch of ale would be given to some local unfortunate.[115] In villages the charitable arrangements became increasingly formal, as the money collected for the payment of the lay subsidy was linked with funds for the relief of the poor. Those making their wills would leave money to the 'common box', to pay the penny or two that the poor were expected to contribute to the tax. From the tiny number of communities where evidence survives of the mechanics of tax collection, the sum collected exceeded the quota of taxation which each vill was supposed to pay, so a surplus in the common box would have been available for distribution to the needy.[116] Wealthy villagers would leave land, the income from which would be used to pay the subsidy, but as the tax was not levied every year, the rent income could then be used for poor relief. Funds were also held by fraternities, the many functions of which included the relief of poverty.[117] Parishes in the fifteenth century were also building poorhouses. When the state legislated for relief of the poor in 1536 and ruled that each parish should have a common box and accept responsibility for the poor, it was building on existing practice in many villages and towns.

All of these social-security arrangements are closely connected with the work ethic. Charity was focused on those who could not work rather than on the voluntarily idle. The parishioners who contributed to the common box became ever more concerned that their money should not go to vagrants and beggars, and they would support discriminatory measures against the work-shy. There was a stronger sense of individual responsibility, and the poor were not seen as part of a crowd scrambling for bread at a monastery gate or for pennies at a funeral. Anyone who relied entirely on wages lacked the safety-net of even a small amount of land from which they could gain support in the event of unemployment, illness, and old age. The interests of employers as well as workers were served by the existence of a systematic parochial arrangement which would assure those mainly dependent on wages that they would not starve in their old age.[118]

---

[115] J. M. Bennett, 'Conviviality and Charity in Medieval and Early Modern England', *P&P* 134 (1992), 19–41; M. Moisa and J. M. Bennett, 'Debate: Conviviality and Charity in Medieval and Early Modern England', *P&P* 154 (1997), 223–42.

[116] C. Dyer, 'The English Medieval Village Community and Its Decline', *Journal of British Studies*, 33 (1994), 415–16; id., 'Taxation and Communities in Late Medieval England', in Britnell and Hatcher (eds.), *Progress and Problems*, 187.

[117] K. Farnhill, *Guilds and the Parish Community in Late Medieval East Anglia, c.1470–1550* (York, 2001), 74–7.

[118] P. M. Solar, 'Poor Relief and English Economic Development Before the Industrial Revolution', *Ec.HR* 48 (1995), 1–22.

Conclusion

Although the proletariat was not born in the later middle ages, and the proportion of people earning wages may not have changed greatly in the period 1300–1525, the nature of employment shifted in important ways. Although many attempts were made to regulate and control wage-earning, these measures were largely ineffective, and labour flowed into the places and activities where work was in greatest demand. The acute shortage of labour encouraged the development of a work ethic among employers, but it can also be detected among wage-earners, who could hope to better themselves. 'Modern' attitudes towards leisure and social security, which are so often thought to have developed under Protestant influence, were emerging in association with the work ethic. The early sixteenth century in the country-side saw the beginnings of a process which would lead to an increase in landless wage-earners. Tenants hung on to their large holdings, so the increased numbers in successive generations could not acquire land easily, and had to accept wage-earning as their principal source of income.

Conclusion

At the end of the middle ages much of our evidence comes from the estate records of the aristocracy and church institutions. They are useful sources of information, but they should not be allowed to dominate our historical interpretation, particularly as the people for whom they were written were playing a less decisive role in the economy. If we put too much reliance on the documents produced by the great estates, we are given an overwhelmingly picture of decayed rents, ruinous buildings, and declining wealth. Another story, more interesting and more positive, can be told from new sources, or rather sources that were being preserved for the first time, such as wills.

A good example of the dilemmas created by the evidence from the old institutions lies in the mass of regulation and legislation produced in the period 1349–1520. If we were to believe that these rules were obeyed, then no one received a wage increase, no one kept more than a fixed quota of animals on the common, no serfs left their lord's manor, country boys did not become artisans in towns, no lower-class person wore expensive clothing, everyone ground their corn at their lord's mill, grain was not bought by middlemen and then sold at a higher price, and in some villages no one played football.

The new world was informal, and much of its business was conducted by word of mouth, but much of the 'hidden trade', 'hidden investment', and concealed economy is known only from hints in documents, or accidental survivals of written or material evidence.

The people we have been investigating seem as 'unofficial' as their documents. Contemporaries referred to an ideal version of their society, which consisted of the three orders of knights, clergy, and peasants. They also used a more specific and detailed hierarchy of dukes, earls, barons, knights, esquires, gentlemen, yeomen, and so on. The clergy could be similarly assembled into ranks, from archbishops to chaplains and clerks. We have our own sociological classification for the middle ages, consisting of lords, peasants, wage-earners, and various categories of townspeople. Many of the people with whom this book has been concerned do not fit easily into either the orders and ranks devised in the middle ages or the classes and groups used by modern historians. Rural artisans and entrepreneurs, middlemen of various kinds, farmers and graziers who fall somewhere between gentlemen and yeomen, clergy who lent money, servants who traded on their own account, artisans who received wages and in turn employed others, all pose problems for those searching for the correct pigeon-hole. But this should not be surprising, because the classifications belong to a traditional society that was concerned with preserving as much as it could of privileges and social distinctions, but initiatives were coming from previously underprivileged groups. Engrossing of holdings, conversion of arable to pasture, and enclosure, the actions which paved the way for larger and more efficient units of agrarian production, were organized by peasants in more cases than they were imposed by lords. Women crossed barriers and took up trades that would once have been thought unsuitable.

In the same way, the old institutional and territorial divisions were losing their significance. Property was acquired in a number of villages and manors, and it was common to have interests in both town and country. Individuals held land by a number of different tenures. They pursued a number of occupations, both agricultural and commercial. People belonged to particular villages and towns, though they had often taken up residence there a few years earlier, and they had an awareness of wider horizons. This lack of fixed attachments to place can be traced back to before 1300, but probably became more marked in the succeeding two centuries.

Those who lived through the late middle ages experienced hard times. Many people died young, not just in the first major plague epidemic of 1348–9, but in frequent subsequent lesser epidemics and from endemic infections. Society was diminished in size: the population was halved, and obstinately failed to recover. The whole economy shrank. Labour was scarce, and prices of many primary commodities were reduced, creating many difficulties for producers. The cultivators, miners, and manufacturers were tested, and many failed. The lords, recognizing that they faced a struggle to make profits, gave up direct management of agriculture. The new men who continued production are often to be found grumbling and complaining. Everyone with an interest in the land despaired of the low price of cereals. Farmers told their lords that they could not pay their rents. Peasants, gathered at an ale-house, were amazed if one of their number could display a purse containing coins worth more than a few shillings. Estate administrators gloomily compared rents before the Black Death with the miserable sums that were being paid by the 1450s. Even the reduced rents were not paid in full or on time, and estate officials counted the accumulated arrears.

Merchants bemoaned foreign competition, crises of supply, high taxes, and the insecurity of war and piracy. Those with patience, talent, and cunning could do well in these difficult circumstances, but only with considerable effort.

Much of the debate about the 'transition' hinges on chronology. This book argues that the supposed turning-point around 1500 has been given excessive importance, as many of the features of the early modern period can be observed well before 1500 and even before 1300. The campaign of moral 'improvement', involving such notions as the deserving poor and discrimination in charity against sturdy beggars, usually associated with 'puritans', appears to have begun soon after 1350. The conception of economic 'improvement' was current among both lords and peasants before the Black Death. Some of the features of a 'consumer society' can be traced back to the fourteenth century, if not earlier. The occupational structure in which a substantial proportion (40 per cent) of the English population was not employed primarily in agriculture was emerging well before the late sixteenth century. 'Turning-points' are useful for organizing our ideas and make us aware of chronological benchmarks. Significant dates include the inflation around 1200, which helped to trigger commercial growth in the thirteenth century. The end of that era of expansion lay somewhere between the troubled 1290s and the Black Death of 1348–9. The year 1375 saw the end of an era of high corn prices, and ushered in a period of rising real wages and difficulty for lords, and the revolt of 1381 indicated a landmark in peasant self-confidence and independence. The 1430s saw bad harvests and the beginnings of the great depression in trade which lasted for three decades. In the 1470s recovery was promised, and rents and land values rose, but the beginnings of a population increase was not sustained. The inflation after 1518 and the sustained population growth from about 1540 mark major departures from the previous two centuries.

A search for significant dates has the danger that the statistical series of prices, wages, rents, and grain yields dominates our thinking, whereas they provide the background for the really important structural changes. The developments that have been investigated in these lectures did not occur overnight, but were the subject of constant negotiation. Private property and common rights were repeatedly defined and redefined over a period of at least five centuries. The enclosure movement of the thirteenth century probably planted more miles of hedges than that of the fifteenth. Individual interests did not always triumph over those of the collective groups in a one-way movement. Individuals freed themselves from family control, sometimes as late as the 1430s, but then became tied up in the constraints of inheritance around 1500. The village community entered a new phase of vitality in the fifteenth and early sixteenth centuries. On close examination, the 'community' could mean a privileged elite defending its interests. We have seen an example of a village where the 'community' consisted of six rather wealthy individuals. In the same way, the building of roads and bridges, which we call public works, benefited from charitable bequests by those who sought to save their individual souls.

If our chronology dissolves into a series of significant dates spread over many centuries, and the supposed rise of the individual and private property rights seems not to follow a straightforward path, can we talk about 'an age of transition' at all? The thirteenth century, it is true, looks less rigid and backward than it was once thought, and emerges as an era of commercial growth, technical adaptation, mobility, urbanization, informality, competitiveness, and flexibility. But much was to change subsequently.

After 1400, the aristocracy were weakened by their loss of direct management of agriculture, and let the economic initiative pass to their social inferiors. Most of the gentry lived on rents, and only a minority embraced the possibilities of transforming their lands into productive enterprises. Sections of the countryside were converted from villages of middling peasants practising open-field agriculture to specialist pasture farms producing wool, meat, and dairy produce for the market. Peasants in the villages which persisted were building up larger holdings and forging stronger relations with the market. The farmers who managed the largest units of production were often recruited from the upper ranks of the peasantry. The farms can be numbered among the new enterprises of the period, together with the new mills, especially those devoted to industry, the new clothiers' businesses, and the first large-scale breweries.

From 1375 the threat of bad harvests receded, and as well as a better diet ordinary people could afford to buy more manufactured goods. At the depth of the fifteenth-century recession houses were being built in country and town in larger numbers. The material symptoms of these changes included the new settlements, such as farmhouses in the midst of their fields, the cloth villages, the cottages for industrial workers, and the new towns, often in the industrial districts. Two-storey houses without halls mark a stage in the emergence of private domestic space. A new combination of ideas helped to change attitudes towards work and social security. Work ethics put a high value on labour, and workers were encouraged to greater efforts by the possibility of a better standard of consumption. The poor were supported by public welfare, but only those who merited charitable donations.

If we recognize all of these changes, that does not mean that by the mid-sixteenth century England had become a modern capitalist economy. The 'steady state' in the wage-earning sector gives one piece of compelling evidence for the survival of elements of the old world. The transition was for the long term, and it should not be a cause of surprise or disappointment that such a momentous historical episode began before 1300 and was complete only after 1800. We should rather be impressed by the ability of men and women to endure arduous times, gain a good living, and achieve structural change.

Bibliography

Unprinted primary sources

Birmingham City Archives
  Erdington Court Rolls
Bodleian Library, Oxford
  Suffolk Rolls
Borthwick Institute of Historical Research, York
  Dean and Chapter Wills
  Will Registers
British Library, London
  Additional MSS.
  Additional Rolls
  Althorp papers
  Harleian Rolls
Cambridge University Library
  Ely Diocesan Records
Centre for Kentish Studies, Maidstone
  Rochester Consistory Court Will Registers
Corpus Christi College, Oxford
  Temple Guiting Records
Cumbria Record Office, Carlisle
  Diocesan Records (Carlisle)
  Pennington Family Archives
Devon Record Office, Exeter
  DD Collection (formerly Exeter City Library)
  Fortescue of Castle Hill Archive
Dorset Record Office, Dorchester
  Sherborne Almshouse Archive
  Weld of Lulworth Collection
Gloucester Cathedral Library
  Lease Register
Gloucestershire Record Office, Gloucester
  Dean and Chapter of Gloucester Records
  Sherborne Estate Records
Guildhall Library, Corporation of London
  Dean and Chapter of St Paul's MSS.
Hereford Record Office
  Arkwright Family Collection

John Rylands Library, Manchester
  Phillipps Charters
Lincolnshire Archives, Lincoln
  Lindsey Manorial Rolls
Magdalen College, Oxford
  Court Books
  Quinton MSS.
  Westcote MSS.
New College, Oxford
  Great Horwood Court Rolls
Norfolk Record Office, Norwich
  Aylsham Collection
  Bradfer Lawrence Collection
  Hare of Stow Bardolph Collection
  Norfolk Record Society Collection
  Norwich Consistory Court Will Registers
  Norwich Diocesan Archives
  Townshend MSS.
Northamptonshire Record Office, Northampton
  Archdeaconry of Northampton Will Register
  Spencer Rolls
Shakespeare Birthplace Trust Records Office, Stratford-upon-Avon
  Archer of Tanworth Collection
  Stratford Borough Records: Records of the Guild of the Holy Cross
  Throckmorton of Coughton Collection
  Verney (Lord Willoughby de Broke) of Compton Verney Collection
Somerset Archive and Record Service, Taunton
  Trevelyan Family of Nettlecombe Collection
Staffordshire Record Office, Stafford
  Lord Stafford's MSS.
Suffolk Record Office (Bury St Edmund's Branch)
  Archdeaconry of Sudbury Will Registers
  Hengrave Hall Collection
Suffolk Record Office (Ipswich Branch)
  Archdeaconry of Suffolk Will Registers
  Dennington Parish Records
  Elveden Hall, Iveagh Cornwallis MSS.
  Iveagh (Phillipps) Suffolk MSS.
The National Archives, Public Record Office, London
  C131 (Extents for Debt)
  E101 (Accounts Various)
  E164 (King's Remembrancer, Miscellaneous Books)
  E179 (Lay Subsidies)
  E357 (LTR Escheators' Accounts)

PROB 2 and PROB 11 (Probate Records of the Prerogative Court of Canterbury)
REQ 2 (Court of Requests)
SC2 (Court Rolls)
SC6 (Ministers' Accounts)
Warwickshire County Record Office, Warwick
Bishopton and Palmer Family Collection
Westminster Abbey
Westminster Abbey Muniments
West Yorkshire Archive Service, Leeds
Earls of Mexborough Family and Estate Archive
Gascoigne of Parlington Family and Estate Archive
West Yorkshire Archive Service, Yorkshire Archaeological Society, Leeds
Ripley Castle MSS.
Worcester Cathedral Library
Court Rolls
Priory Registers
Worcestershire Record Office
Bishops' Registers
Bishopric of Worcester Records (Church Commissioners)
Diocesan Registry Records
York Minster Library
Will Registers

Printed Primary Sources

ANON. (ed.), 'Rotuli collectorum subsidii regi a laiciis anno secundo concessi in Westrythyngo in comitatu Eboraci', *Yorkshire Archaeological and Topographical Journal*, 5 (1879).

BAILEY, M., *The English Manor c.1200–c.1500* (Manchester, 2002).

BEARMAN, R. (ed.), *Miscellany I*, Dugdale Society, 31 (1977).

BENSON, L. D. (ed.), *The Riverside Chaucer* (Oxford, 1988).

BICKLEY, F. B. (ed.), *The Little Red Book of Bristol*, 2 vols. (Bristol and London, 1900).

BIRRELL, J. R. (ed.), 'The *Status Maneriorum* of John Catesby, 1385 and 1386', in R. BEARMAN (ed.), *Miscellany I*, Dugdale Society, 31 (1977).

BLANCHARD, I. S. W. (ed.), *The Duchy of Lancaster's Estates in Derbyshire 1485–1540*, Derbyshire Archaeological Society Record Series, 3 (1971).

BLOOM, J. H. (ed.), *The Register of the Gild of the Holy Cross, the Blessed Mary and St. John the Baptist of Stratford-upon-Avon* (London, 1907).

BRADLEY, H. (ed.), *Dialogues in French and English by William Caxton*, Early English Text Society, extra ser., 79 (1900).

BRODIE, D. M. (ed.), *The Tree of Commonwealth: A Treatise Written by Edmund Dudley* (Cambridge, 1948).

Calendar of Patent Rolls, 52 vols. (Public Record Office, 1891–1916).

CHAMBERS, R. W. (ed.), *A Fifteenth-Century Courtesy Book*, Early English Text Society, OS, 148 (1914).

CHILDS, W. R., *The Customs Accounts of Hull 1453–1490*, Yorkshire Archaeological Society Record Series, 144 (1986).

CLARKE, A. (ed.), *The English Register of Godstow Nunnery, near Oxford*, Early English Text Society, OS, 129, 130, 142 (1905–11).

CORNWALL, J. (ed.), *The Lay Subsidy Rolls for the County of Sussex, 1524–5*, Sussex Record Society, 56 (1957).

—— (ed.), *The County Community under Henry VIII*, Rutland Record Society, 1 (1980).

DAVIS, N. (ed.), *Paston Letters and Papers of the Fifteenth Century*, 2 vols. (Oxford, 1971 and 1976).

DOUGLAS, D. C. and GREENAWAY, G. W., *English Historical Documents*, Vol. II, *1042–1189*, 2nd edn. (London, 1981).

DU BOULAY, F. R. H. (ed.), 'Calendar of the Demesne Leases Made by Archbishop Warham (1503–32)', in id. (ed.), *Documents Illustrative of Medieval Kentish Society*, Kent Records, 18 (1964).

FARADAY, M. A. (ed.), *Worcestershire Taxes in the 1520s*, Worcestershire Historical Society, NS, 19 (2003).

FENWICK, C. C. (ed.), *The Poll Taxes of 1377, 1379 and 1381, Part 1*, British Academy Records of Social and Economic History, NS, 27 (1998); *Part 2*, NS, 29 (2001).

FRANKLIN, P. (ed.), *The Tax Payers of Medieval Gloucestershire* (Stroud, 1993).

FURBER, E. C. (ed.), *Essex Sessions of the Peace 1351, 1377–9*, Essex Archaeological Society, Occasional Publication, 3 (1953).

GALBRAITH, V. H. (ed.), *The Anonimalle Chronicle 1333–1381* (Manchester, 1970).

HALE, W. H. (ed.), *The Domesday of St. Paul's*, Camden Society, 69 (1858).

HANHAM, A. (ed.), *Churchwardens' Accounts of Ashburton, 1479–1580*, Devon and Cornwall Record Society, NS, 15 (1970).

HARDING, A. (ed.), *The Roll of the Shropshire Eyre of 1256*, Selden Society, 96 (1980).

HARDY, W. J. (ed.), *Stratford-on-Avon Corporation Records: The Guild Accounts* (Stratford-upon-Avon, 1880).

HARRIS, M. D. (ed.), *The Coventry Leet Book*, Early English Text Society, OS, 134, 135, 138, 146 (1907–13).

HARRIS, M. (ed.), 'The Account of the Great Household of Humphrey, First Duke of Buckingham, for the Year 1452–3', *Camden Miscellany XXVIII*, Camden Society, 4th ser., 29 (1984).

HAZLITT, W. (ed.), *Early Popular Poetry of England*, 4 vols. (London, 1866).

H[ERVEY], S. H. A. (ed.), *Suffolk in 1524: Being the Return for a Subsidy Granted in 1523*, Suffolk Green Books, 10 (Woodbridge, 1910).

HIEATT, C. B. and BUTLER, S. (eds.), *Curye on Inglysch: English Culinary Manuscripts of the Fourteenth Century*, Early English Text Society, special ser., 8 (1985).

HOBHOUSE, E. (ed.), *Church-wardens Accounts*, Somerset Record Society, 4 (1890).

HOLLINGS, M. (ed.), *The Red Book of Worcester*, Worcestershire Historical Society (1934–50).

HOYLE, R. (ed.), *The Military Survey of Gloucestershire, 1522*, Gloucestershire Records Series, 6 (1993).

HUGHES, P. L. and LARKIN, J. F. (eds.), *Tudor Royal Proclamations*, vol. I, *The Early Tudors* (New Haven and London, 1964).

HULTON, M. H. M. (ed.), *Coventry and its People in the 1520s*, Dugdale Society, 38 (1999).

JACK, R. I. (ed.), *The Grey of Ruthin Valor*, Bedfordshire Historical Record Society, 46 (1965).

JAMES, T. B. (ed.), *The Port Book of Southampton 1509–10*, Southampton Records Series, 32 (1990).

KANE, G. (ed.), *Piers Plowman: The A Version. Will's Visions of Piers Plowman and Do-Well* (London, 1960).

—— and TALBOT, E. (eds.), *Piers Plowman: The B Version* (London, 1975).

LEADAM, I. S. (ed.), *The Domesday of Inclosures 1517–1518*, Royal Historical Society (1897).

LISTER, J. (ed.), *Court Rolls of the Manor of Wakefield*, Vol. IV, *1315–1317*, Yorkshire Archaeological Society Record Series, 78 (1930).

LOCK, R. (ed.), *The Court Rolls of Walsham le Willows 1303–1350*, Suffolk Records Society, 41 (1998).

MAITLAND, F. W. (ed.), *Select Pleas in Manorial and other Seignorial Courts*, Selden Society, 2 (1888).

MANDER, G. P. (ed.), *History of the Wolseley Charters*, Collections For a History of Staffordshire, 3rd ser. (1934).

MICHELMORE, D. J. H. (ed.), *The Fountains Abbey Lease Book*, Yorkshire Archaeological Society Record Series, 140 (1981).

NELSON, W. (ed.), *A Fifteenth Century School Book* (Oxford, 1956).

NORTHEAST, P. (ed.), *Wills of the Archdeaconry of Sudbury 1439–1474, Part 1*, Suffolk Records Society, 44 (2001).

OSCHINSKY, D. (ed.), *Walter of Henley and Other Treatises on Estate Management and Accounting* (Oxford, 1971).

POOS, L. R. (ed.), *Lower Ecclesiastical Jurisdiction in Late-Medieval England*, British Academy Records of Social and Economic History, NS, 32 (2001).

—— and BONFIELD, L. (eds.), *Select Cases in Manorial Courts 1250–1550: Property and Family Law*, Selden Society, 114 (1997).

POUND, J. (ed.), *The Military Survey of 1522 for Babergh Hundred*, Suffolk Records Society, 28 (1986).

PUGH, T. B. (ed.), *The Marcher Lordships of South Wales, 1415–1536: Select Documents* (Cardiff, 1963).

RAINE, J. (ed.), *Testamenta Eboracensia*, 4 vols., Surtees Society, 4, 30, 45, 53 (1836, 1855, 1864, 1868).

ROBERTS, E. and PARKER, K. (eds.), *Southampton Probate Inventories 1447–1575*, Southampton Records Series, 34 (1992).

Royal Commission on Historical Manuscripts, *Ninth Report*, part 1 (1883).

SALTER, H. E. (ed.), *Eynsham Cartulary*, 2 vols., Oxford Historical Society, 49, 51 (1907–8).

SNEYD, C. A. (ed.), *A Relation or Rather a True Account of the Island of England*, Camden Society, 37 (1847).

Statutes of the Realm, 11 vols., Record Commission (1810–28).

STENTON, D. M. (ed.), *Rolls of the Justices in Eyre, being the Rolls of Pleas and Assizes for Lincolnshire and Worcestershire 1221*, Selden Society, 53 (1934).

STOCKTON, E. W. (ed.), *The Major Latin Works of John Gower* (Seattle, 1962).

TOOMEY, J. P. (ed.), *Records of Hanley Castle Worcestershire, c.1147–1547*, Worcestershire Historical Society, NS, 18 (2001).

TRIGG, S. (ed.), *Wynnere and Wastoure*, Early English Text Society, 297 (1990).

TOULMIN SMITH, L. (ed.), *Leland's Itinerary in England and Wales* (London, 1906).

Valor Ecclesiasticus, 6 vols., Record Commission (1810–34).

WALKER, S. S. (ed.), *The Court Rolls of the Manor of Wakefield from October 1331 to September 1333*, Wakefield Court Roll Series of the Yorkshire Archaeological Society, 3 (1982).

WEAVER, F. W. (ed.), *Somerset Medieval Wills (1383–1500)*, Somerset Record Society, 16 (1901).

WEAVER, J. R. H. and BEARDWOOD, A. (eds.), *Oxfordshire Wills, 1393–1510*, Oxfordshire Record Society, 39 (1958).

WILLIS BUND, J. W. and AMPHLETT, J. (eds.), *Lay Subsidy Roll for the County of Worcester circa 1280 [recte 1275]*, Worcestershire Historical Society (1893).

WILSON, R. A. (ed.), *The Register of Walter Reynolds, Bishop of Worcester 1308–1313*, Dugdale Society, 9 (1928).

—— (ed.), *Court Rolls of the Manor of Hales*, part 3, Worcestershire Historical Society (1933).

WROTTESLEY, G. (ed.), *Extracts from the Plea Rolls of the Reigns of Henry V and Henry VI*, Collections for a History of Staffordshire, 17 (1896).

—— (ed.), *Extracts from the Plea Rolls, temp. Edward IV, Edward V and Richard III*, Collections for a History of Staffordshire, NS, 6, part 1 (1903).

Secondary Works

ABU LUGHOD, J., *Before European Hegemony: The World System, A.D. 1250–1350* (New York, 1989).

ACHESON, E., *A Gentry Community: Leicestershire in the Fifteenth Century, c.1422–c.1485* (Cambridge, 1992).

ALBARELLA, U. and DAVIS, S. J. M., 'Mammals and Birds from Launceston Castle, Cornwall: Decline in Status and the Rise of Agriculture', *Circaea. The Journal of the Association of Environmental Archaeology*, 12 (1996 for 1994).

ALCOCK, N. W., 'The Medieval Cottages of Bishop's Clyst, Devon', *MA* 9 (1965).

—— 'Enclosure and Depopulation in Burton Dassett: A Sixteenth Century View', *Warwickshire History*, 3 (1977).

ALLEN, M., 'The Volume of the English Currency, 1158–1470', *Ec.HR* 54 (2001).

ALLEN, R. C., *Enclosure and the Yeoman* (Oxford, 1992).

ALLISON, K. J., 'Flock Management in the Sixteenth and Seventeenth Centuries', *Ec.HR*, 2nd ser., 11 (1958).

ALLMAND, C. (ed.), *The New Cambridge Medieval History*, Vol. VII, *1415–1500* (Cambridge, 1998).

ALMOND, R. and POLLARD, A. J., 'The Yeomanry of Robin Hood and Social Terminology in Fifteenth-Century England', *P&P* 170 (2001).

ANDREWS, D. D. and MILNE, G. (eds.), *Wharram: A Study of Settlement on the Yorkshire Wolds*, Society for Medieval Archaeology Monograph, 8 (1979).

APPLEBY, A. B., 'Agrarian Capitalism or Seigneural Reaction? The Northwest of England, 1500–1700, *American Historical Review*, 80 (1975).

—— *Famine in Tudor and Stuart England* (Stanford, 1978).

ARKELL, T., EVANS, N., and GOOSE, N. (eds.), *When Death Us Do Part: Understanding and Interpreting the Probate Records of Early Modern England* (Oxford, 2000).

ASTILL, G., 'Economic Change in Later Medieval England: An Archaeological Review', in T. H. ASTON, *et al.* (eds.), *Social Relations and Ideas: Essays in Honour of R. H. Hilton* (Cambridge, 1983).

ASTILL, G. G., 'Rural Settlement: The Toft and the Croft', in G. ASTILL and A. GRANT (eds.), *The Countryside of Medieval England* (Oxford, 1988).

—— *A Medieval Industrial Complex and its Landscape: The Metal-Working Watermill and Workshops at Bordesley Abbey*, Council for British Archaeology Research Report, 92 (1993).

—— and GRANT, A. (eds.), *The Countryside of Medieval England* (Oxford, 1988).

—— and LANGDON, J. (eds.), *Medieval Farming and Technology: The Impact of Agricultural Change in Northwest Europe* (Leiden, 1997).

ASTON, M., *Interpreting the Landscape: Landscape Archaeology in Local Studies* (London, 1985).

—— (ed.), *Medieval Fish, Fisheries and Fishponds in England*, British Archaeological Reports, British Ser., 182 (1988).

ASTON, T. H. (ed.), *Landlords, Peasants and Politics in Medieval England* (Cambridge, 1987).

—— and PHILPIN, C. H. E. (eds.), *The Brenner Debate: Agrarian Class Structure and Economic Development in Pre-Industrial Europe* (Cambridge, 1985).

—— COSS, P. R., DYER, C., and THIRSK, J. (eds.), *Social Relations and Ideas: Essays in Honour of R. H. Hilton* (Cambridge, 1983).

AULT, W. O., *Open-Field Farming in Medieval England* (London, 1972).

AUSTIN, D., 'Excavations at Okehampton Deer Park, Devon, 1976–1978', *Proceedings of the Devon Archaeological Society*, 36 (1978).

—— GERRARD, G. A. M., and GREAVES, T. A. P., 'Tin and Agriculture in the Middle Ages and Beyond: Landscape Archaeology in St. Neot Parish, Cornwall', *Cornish Archaeology*, 28 (1989).

BAECHLER, J., *The Origins of Capitalism* (Oxford, 1975).

BAILEY, M., 'The Rabbit and the Medieval East Anglian Economy', *Ag.HR* 36 (1988).

BAILEY, M., *A Marginal Economy? East Anglian Breckland in the Later Middle Ages* (Cambridge, 1989).

—— 'Demographic Decline in Late Medieval England: Some Thoughts on Recent Research', *Ec.HR* 49 (1996).

—— 'Peasant Welfare in England, 1290–1348', *Ec.HR* 51 (1998).

BAINBRIDGE, V., *Gilds in the Medieval Countryside: Social and Religious Change in Cambridgeshire c.1350–1558* (Woodbridge, 1996).

BAKER, J. H., *The Oxford History of the Laws of England*, Vol. VI, *1483–1558* (Oxford, 2003).

BALESTRACCI, D., *The Renaissance in the Fields* (Philadelphia, 1999).

BARLEY, M., *Houses and History* (London, 1986).

BARNWELL, P. S. and ADAMS, A. T., *The House Within: Interpreting Medieval Houses in Kent*, Royal Commission on the Historical Monuments of England (1994).

BARRON, C. M., 'Johanna Hill (d. 1441) and Johanna Sturdy (d. *c.*1460), Bell-founders', in C. M. BARRON and A. F. SUTTON (eds.), *Medieval London Widows, 1300–1500* (London, 1994).

—— and SUTTON, A. F. (eds.), *Medieval London Widows, 1300–1500* (London, 1994).

BARRY, J. and BROOKES, C. (eds.), *The Middling Sort of People: Culture, Society and Politics in England, 1550–1800* (London, 1994).

BATESON, M., 'The Laws of Breteuil', *English Historical Review*, 16 (1901).

BEAN, J. M. W., *The Estates of the Percy Family, 1416–1537* (Oxford, 1958).

BEARMAN, R. (ed.), *The History of an English Borough: Stratford-upon-Avon 1196–1996* (Stratford-upon-Avon, 1997).

—— (ed.), *Compton Verney: A History of the House and its Owners* (Stratford-upon-Avon, 2000).

BELL, C. and DURHAM, B., 'Archaeological Excavations at Lawn Farm, Bulkington, 1994', *Wiltshire Archaeological and Natural History Magazine*, 90 (1997).

BELLAMY, J. G., *Bastard Feudalism and the Law* (London, 1989).

BENNETT, J. M., 'Conviviality and Charity in Medieval and Early Modern England', *P&P* 134 (1992).

—— *Ale, Beer, and Brewsters in England: Women's Work in a Changing World, 1300–1600* (New York, 1996).

BERESFORD, G., 'The Medieval Manor of Penhallam, Jacobstow, Cornwall, *MA* 18 (1974).

BERESFORD, M. W., 'A Review of Historical Research (to 1968)', in M. W. Beresford and J. G. Hurst (eds.), *Deserted Medieval Villages: Studies* (London, 1971).

—— and HURST, J. G. (eds.), *Deserted Medieval Villages: Studies* (London, 1971).

BETTERTON, A. and DYMOND, D., *Lavenham: Industrial Town* (Lavenham, 1989).

BIRRELL, J. R., 'Peasant Craftsmen in the Medieval Forest', *Ag.HR* 17 (1969).

—— 'Medieval Agriculture', *VCH Staffordshire*, Vol. VI (1979).

—— 'Common Rights in the Medieval Forest: Disputes and Conflicts in the Thirteenth Century', *P&P* 117 (1987).

BLACKBURN, M. A. S. and DUMVILLE, D. N. (eds.), *Kings, Currency and Alliances: History and Coinage of Southern England in the Ninth Century* (Woodbridge, 1998).

BLAIR, J., 'Hall and Chamber: English Domestic Planning 1000–1250', in G. Meirion-Jones and M. Jones (eds.), *Manorial Domestic Building in England and Northern France*, Society of Antiquaries Occasional Papers, 15 (1993).

—— and RAMSAY, N. (eds.), *English Medieval Industries: Craftsmen, Techniques, Products* (London, 1991).

BLANCHARD, I. S. W., 'Seigneurial Entrepreneurship: The Bishops of Durham and the Weardale Lead Industry 1406–1529', *Business History*, 15 (1973).

—— 'Introduction', in I. S. W. BLANCHARD (ed.), *Labour and Leisure in Historical Perspective: Thirteenth to Twentieth Centuries* (Stuttgart, 1994).

—— (ed.), *Labour and Leisure in Historical Perspective: Thirteenth to Twentieth Centuries* (Stuttgart, 1994).

BOIS, G., *The Crisis of Feudalism: Economy and Society in Eastern Normandy c.1300–1550* (Cambridge, 1984).

—— *La Grande Dépression médiévale: XIVe–XVe siècles. Le précédent d'une crise systémique* (Paris, 2000).

BOLTON, J. L., *The Medieval English Economy 1150–1500* (London, 1980).

BOND, C. J., 'Deserted Medieval Villages in Warwickshire and Worcestershire', in T. R. Slater and P. J. Jarvis (eds.), *Field and Forest: An Historical Geography of Warwickshire and Worcestershire* (Norwich, 1982).

BOND, J. and LEWIS, C., 'The Earthworks of Hawling', *Transactions of the Bristol and Gloucestershire Archaeological Society*, 109 (1991).

BONFIELD, L. and POOS, L. R., 'The Development of the Deathbed Transfer in Medieval English Manor Courts', *Cambridge Law Journal*, 47 (1988).

—— SMITH, R. M., and WRIGHTSON, K. (eds.), *The World We Have Gained: Histories of Population and Social Structure* (Oxford, 1986).

BOSERUP, E., *The Conditions of Agricultural Growth* (London, 1965).

BOTHWELL, J., GOLDBERG, P. J. P., and ORMROD, W. M. (eds.), *The Problem of Labour in Fourteenth-Century England* (Woodbridge, 2000).

BRAUDEL, F., *Civilization and Capitalism, 15th–18th Century*, 3 vols. (New York, 1981–4).

BRAUNSTEIN, P., 'Innovation in Mining and Metal Production in Europe in the Late Middle Ages', *Journal of European Economic History*, 12 (1983).

BRENNER, R., 'Agrarian Class Structure and Economic Development in Pre-industrial Europe', *P&P* 70 (1976).

—— 'The Origins of Capitalist Development: A Critique of Neo-Smithian Marxism', *New Left Review*, 104 (1977).

BREWER, J. and PORTER, R. (eds.), *Consumption and the World of Goods* (London, 1993).

BRIDBURY, A. R., *Economic Growth: England in the Later Middle Ages* (London, 1962).

—— 'The Black Death', *Ec.HR*, 2nd ser., 26 (1973).

—— 'English Provincial Towns in the Later Middle Ages', *Ec.HR*, 2nd ser., 34 (1981).

BRIGGS, C., 'Creditors and Debtors and Their Relationships at Oakington, Cottenham and Dry Drayton (Cambridgeshire), 1291–1350', in P. R. Schofield and N. J. Mayhew (eds.), *Credit and Debt in Medieval England c.1180–c.1350* (Oxford, 2002).

BRITNELL, R. H., 'Minor Landlords in England and Medieval Agrarian Capitalism', in T. H. Aston (ed.), *Landlords, Peasants and Politics in Medieval England* (Cambridge, 1987).

—— 'The Pastons and their Norfolk', *Ag.HR* 36 (1988).

—— 'The Towns of England and Northern Italy in the Early Fourteenth Century', *Ec.HR* 44 (1991).

—— *The Commercialisation of English Society 1000–1500* (Cambridge, 1993).

—— 'Commerce and Capitalism in Late Medieval England: Problems of Description and Theory', *Journal of Historical Sociology,* 6 (1993).

—— *The Closing of the Middle Ages? England, 1471–1519* (Oxford, 1997).

—— 'The English Economy and the Government, 1450–1550', in J. L. Watts (ed.), *The End of the Middle Ages? England in the Fifteenth and Sixteenth Centuries* (Stroud, 1998).

—— 'Specialization of Work in England, 1100–1300', *Ec.HR* 54 (2001).

—— and CAMPBELL, B. M. S. (eds.), *A Commercialising Economy: England 1086–c.1300* (Manchester, 1995).

—— and HATCHER, J. (eds.), *Progress and Problems in Medieval England: Essays in Honour of Edward Miller* (Cambridge, 1996).

BRITNELL, W. J. and SUGGETT, R., 'A Sixteenth Century Hallhouse in Powys: Survey and Excavation of Tyddyn Llwydion, Pennant Melangell, Montgomeryshire', *Archaeological Journal,* 159 (2002).

BROOKS, C. W., *Pettyfoggers and Vipers of the Commonwealth: The 'Lower Branch' of the Legal Profession in Early Modern England* (Cambridge, 1986).

BROWN, A. (ed.), *The Rows of Chester,* English Heritage Archaeological Report, 16 (1999).

BURKE, P., 'The Invention of Leisure in Early Modern Europe', *P&P* 146 (1995).

BUSH, M. L. (ed.), *Serfdom and Slavery: Studies in Legal Bondage* (Harlow, 1996).

BUTCHER, A. F., 'The Economy of Exeter College, 1400–1500', *Oxoniensia,* 44 (1979).

CAM, H. M., 'The Decline and Fall of English Feudalism', *History,* 25 (1940).

CAMILLE, M., 'Labouring For the Lord: The Ploughman and the Social Order in the Luttrell Psalter', *Art History,* 10 (1987).

CAMPBELL, B. M. S., 'Agricultural Progress in Medieval England: Some Evidence from Eastern Norfolk', *Ec.HR,* 2nd ser., 36 (1983).

—— 'Population Pressure, Inheritance and the Land Market in a Fourteenth-Century Peasant Community', in R. M. Smith (ed.), *Land, Kinship and Life-cycle* (Cambridge, 1984).

—— 'Land, Labour, Livestock, and Productivity Trends in English Seignorial Agriculture, 1208–1450', in B. M. S. Campbell and M. Overton (eds.), *Land, Labour and Livestock: Historical Studies in European Agricultural Productivity* (Manchester, 1991).

—— 'Matching Supply to Demand: Crop Production and Disposal by English Demesnes in the Century of the Black Death', *Journal of Economic History*, 57 (1997).

—— *English Seigniorial Agriculture, 1250–1450* (Cambridge, 2000).

—— (ed.), *Before the Black Death: Studies in the 'Crisis' of the Early Fourteenth Century* (Manchester, 1991).

—— and OVERTON, M. (eds.), *Land, Labour and Livestock: Historical Studies in European Agricultural Productivity* (Manchester, 1991).

—— —— 'A New Perspective on Medieval and Early Modern Agriculture: Six Centuries of Norfolk Farming *c*.1250–*c*.1850', *P&P* 141 (1994).

—— GALLOWAY, J. A., KEENE, D., and MURPHY, M., *A Medieval Capital and its Grain Supply: Agrarian Production and Distribution in the London Region c.1300*, Historical Geography Research Series, 30 (1993).

CARLIN, M. and ROSENTHAL, J. T. (eds.), *Food and Eating in Medieval Europe* (London, 1998).

CARPENTER, C., *Locality and Polity: A Study of Warwickshire Landed Society, 1401–1499* (Cambridge, 1992).

—— *The Wars of the Roses: Politics and the Constitution in England, c.1437–1509* (Cambridge, 1997).

CARUS-WILSON, E. M., *Medieval Merchant Venturers: Collected Studies* (London, 1954).

—— 'Evidences of Industrial Growth on Some Fifteenth-Century Manors', *Ec.HR*, 2nd ser., 12 (1959).

—— 'The Woollen Industry', in M. M. Postan and E. Miller (eds.), *The Cambridge Economic History of Europe*. Vol. II, 2nd edn. (Cambridge, 1987).

—— and COLEMAN, O., *England's Export Trade 1275–1547* (Oxford, 1963).

CAVACIOCCHI, S. (ed.), *Il Tempo Libero. Economia e Societa*, Istituto Internazionale di Storia Economica 'F. Datini', Prato, 26 (1994).

—— (ed.), *Economia e Energia, Secc. XIII–XVIII*, Istituto Internazionale di Storia Economica 'F. Datini', Prato, 34 (2002).

CHARLES, F. W. B., *The Great Barn of Bredon: Its Fire and Rebuilding* (Oxford, 1997).

CHARTRES, J., *Internal Trade in England 1500–1700*, Economic History Society, (1977).

—— and HEY, D. (eds.), *English Rural Society, 1500–1800: Essays in Honour of Joan Thirsk* (Cambridge, 1990).

CHEYNEY, E. P., 'The Disappearance of English Serfdom', *English Historical Review*, 15 (1900).

CHILDS, W., 'The English Export Trade in Cloth in the Fourteenth Century', in R. Britnell and J. Hatcher (eds.), *Progress and Problems in Medieval England* (Cambridge, 1996).

CHORLEY, P., 'The Evolution of the Woollen, 1300–1700', in N. B. Harte (ed.), *The New Draperies in the Low Countries and England, 1300–1800* (Oxford, 1997).

CIPOLLA, C. M., *European Culture and Overseas Expansion* (Harmondsworth, 1970).

CLARK, E., 'Charitable Bequests, Deathbed Land Sales, and the Manor Court in Later Medieval England', in Z. Razi and R. Smith (eds.), *Medieval Society and the Manor Court* (Oxford, 1996).

—— 'Medieval Labor Law and English Local Courts', *American Journal of Legal History*, 27 (1983).

CLARK, P. (ed.), *Cambridge Urban History of Britain*, Vol. II, *1540–1840* (Cambridge, 2000).

CLARKE, J. and CRITCHER, C., *The Devil Makes Work: Leisure in Capitalist Britain* (Basingstoke, 1985).

CLARKSON, L. A., *Proto-Industrialization: The First Phase of Industrialization?* (London, 1985).

CLAYTON, M., *Catalogue of Rubbings of Brasses and Incised Slabs* (London, 1968).

CLEERE, H. and CROSSLEY, D., *The Iron Industry of the Weald* (Leicester, 1985).

CLOUGH, C. H. (ed.), *Profession, Vocation and Culture in Later Medieval England* (Liverpool, 1982).

COBB, H. S., 'Textile Imports in the Fifteenth Century: The Evidence of Customs' Accounts', *Costume*, 29 (1995).

CONTAMINE, P., et al., *L'Économie médiévale* (Paris, 1993).

CORNWALL, J. C. K., *Wealth and Society in Early Sixteenth Century England* (London, 1988).

COSS, P. R., 'Literature and Social Terminology: The Vavasour in England', in T. H. Aston *et al.* (eds.), *Social Relations and Ideas: Essays in Honour of R. H. Hilton* (Cambridge, 1983).

—— and KEEN, M. (eds.), *Heraldry, Pageantry and Social Display in Medieval England* (Woodbridge, 2002).

COWGILL, J., DE NEERGAARD, M., and GRIFFITHS, N., *Knives and Scabbards*, Medieval Finds From Excavations in London, 1 (1987).

CRESSY, D., 'Kinship and Kin Interaction in Early Modern England', *P&P* 113 (1986).

CROOK, D., 'Freedom, Villeinage and Legal Process: The Dispute Between the Abbot of Burton and his Tenants of Mickleover, 1280', *Nottingham Medieval Studies*, 44 (2000).

CROSS, C., LOADES, D., and SCARISBRICK, J. (eds.), *Law and Government Under the Tudors* (Cambridge, 1988).

CROWFOOT, E., PRITCHARD, F., and STANILAND, K., *Textiles and Clothing c.1150–c.1450*, Medieval Finds From Excavations in London, 4 (1992).

CULLUM, P. and GOLDBERG, P. J. P., 'Charitable Provision in Late Medieval York: "to the praise of God and the use of the poor" ', *Northern History*, 29 (1993).

CURRIE, C. R. J., 'Larger Medieval Houses in the Vale of White Horse', *Oxoniensia*, 57 (1992).

DARBY, H. C., *Domesday England* (Cambridge, 1977).

DAVENPORT, F. G., 'The Decay of Villeinage in East Anglia', *Transactions of the Royal Historical Society*, NS, 14 (1900).

DAY, J., *The Medieval Market Economy* (Oxford, 1987).

DE VRIES, J., 'Between Purchasing Power and the World of Goods: Understanding the Household Economy in Early Modern Europe', in J. Brewer and R. Porter (eds.), *Consumption and the World of Goods* (London, 1993).

DIMMOCK, S., 'English Small Towns and the Emergence of Capitalist Relations, c.1450–1550', *Urban History*, 28 (2001).

DOBSON, R. B., *The Peasants' Revolt of 1381* (London, 1970).

DODDS, B., 'Workers on the Pittington Demesne in the Later Middle Ages', *Archaeologia Aeliana*, 5th ser., 28 (2000).

DONKIN, R. A., *The Cistercians: Studies in the Geography of Medieval England and Wales* (Toronto, 1978).

DONNELLY, J. S., 'Changes in the Grange Economy of English and Welsh Cistercian Abbeys, 1300–1540', *Traditio*, 10 (1954).

DOUGLAS, M. and ISHERWOOD, B., *The World of Goods: Towards an Anthropology of Consumption* (London, 1996).

DRAPER, G., 'The Farmers of Canterbury Cathedral Priory and All Souls College on Romney Marsh c.1443–1545', in J. Eddison, M. Gardiner, and A. Long (eds.), *Romney Marsh: Environmental Change and Human Occupation in a Coastal Lowland*, Oxford University Committee For Archaeology Monographs, 46 (1998).

DU BOULAY, F. R. H., 'Who Were Farming the English Demesnes at the End of the Middle Ages?', *Ec.HR*, 2nd ser., 17 (1965).

DUPLESSIS, R. S., *Transition to Capitalism in Early Modern Europe* (Cambridge, 1997).

DUVOSQUEL, J.-M. and THOEN, E. (eds.), *Peasants and Townsmen in Medieval Europe: Studies in Honorem Adriaan Verhulst* (Ghent, 1995).

DYER, A. D., *Decline and Growth in English Towns 1400–1640* (Cambridge, 1995).

—— ' "Urban decline" in England, 1377–1525', in T. R. Slater (ed.), *Towns in Decline AD 100–1600* (Aldershot, 2000).

DYER, C., 'A Small Landowner in the Fifteenth Century', *Midland History*, 1 (1972).

—— *Lords and Peasants in a Changing Society: The Estates of the Bishopric of Worcester, 680–1540* (Cambridge, 1980).

—— *Warwickshire Farming 1349–c.1520: Preparations for Agricultural Revolution*, Dugdale Society Occasional Papers, 27 (1981).

DYER, C., 'The Social and Economic Background to the Rural Revolt of 1381', in R. H. Hilton and T. H. Aston (eds.), *The English Rising of 1381* (Cambridge, 1984).

—— 'English Peasant Buildings in the Later Middle Ages (1200–1500)', *MA* 30 (1986).

—— 'The Hidden Trade of the Middle Ages: Evidence From the West Midlands', *Journal of Historical Geography*, 18 (1992).

—— 'Leisure Among the Peasantry in the Later Middle Ages', in S. Cavaciocchi (ed.), *Il Tempo Libero. Economia e Societa*, Istituto Internazionale di Storia Economica 'F. Datini', Prato, 26 (1994).

—— 'Gardens and Orchards in Medieval England', in C. Dyer, *Everyday Life in Medieval England* (London, 1994).

—— 'Were There Any Capitalists in Fifteenth-Century England?', in C. Dyer, *Everyday Life in Medieval England* (London, 1994).

—— 'The Consumer and the Market in the Later Middle Ages', in C. Dyer, *Everyday Life in Medieval England* (London, 1994).

—— *Everyday Life in Medieval England* (London, 1994).

—— 'The English Medieval Village Community and its Decline', *Journal of British Studies*, 33 (1994).

—— 'How Urbanised Was Medieval England?', in J.-M. Duvosquel and E. Thoen (eds.), *Peasants and Townsmen in Medieval Europe: Studies in Honorem Adriaan Verhulst* (Ghent, 1995).

—— 'Sheepcotes: Evidence for Medieval Sheep Farming', *MA* 34 (1995).

—— 'Market Towns and the Countryside in Late Medieval England', *Canadian Journal of History*, 31 (1996).

—— 'Memories of Freedom: Attitudes Towards Serfdom in England, 1200–1350', in M. L. Bush (ed.), *Serfdom and Slavery: Studies in Legal Bondage* (Harlow, 1996).

—— 'Taxation and Communities in Late Medieval England', in R. Britnell and J. Hatcher (eds.), *Progress and Problems in Medieval England: Essays in Honour of Edward Miller* (Cambridge, 1996).

—— 'Medieval Stratford: A Successful Small Town', in R. Bearman (ed.), *The History of an English Borough: Stratford-upon-Avon 1196–1996* (Stroud and Stratford-upon-Avon, 1997).

—— 'Peasants and Farmers: Rural Settlements in an Age of Transition', in D. Gaimster and P. Stamper (eds.), *The Age of Transition: The Archaeology of English Culture 1400–1600*, Society For Medieval Archaeology Monographs, 15 (1997).

—— 'Did the Peasants Really Starve in Medieval England?', in M. Carlin and J. T. Rosenthal (eds.), *Food and Eating in Medieval Europe* (London, 1998).

—— 'Rural Europe', in C. Allmand (ed.), *The New Cambridge Medieval History*, Vol. VII, *1415–1500* (Cambridge, 1998).

—— *Standards of Living in the Later Middle Ages: Social Change in England c.1200–1520*, revised edn. (Cambridge, 1998).

—— *Bromsgrove: A Small Town in Worcestershire in the Middle Ages*, Worcestershire Historical Society, Occasional Publications, 9 (2000).

—— 'Compton Verney: Landscape and People in the Middle Ages', in R. Bearman (ed.), *Compton Verney: A History of the House and its Owners* (Stratford-upon-Avon, 2000).

—— 'Work Ethics in the Fourteenth Century', in J. Bothwell, P. J. P. Goldberg, and W. M. Ormrod (eds.), *The Problem of Labour in Fourteenth-Century England* (Woodbridge, 2000).

—— 'Small Places With Large Consequences: The Importance of Small Towns in England, 1000–1540', *Historical Research*, 75 (2002).

—— 'The Urbanizing of Staffordshire: The First Phases', *Staffordshire Studies*, 14 (2002).

—— 'Villages and Non-villages in the Medieval Cotswolds', *Transactions of the Bristol and Gloucestershire Archaeological Society*, 120 (2002).

—— 'The Archaeology of Medieval Small Towns', *MA* 47 (2003).

—— 'The Political Life of the Fifteenth-Century English Village', *The Fifteenth Century*, 4 (2004).

—— 'Seignorial Profits on the Landmarket in Late Medieval England', in L. Feller (ed.), *Le Marché de la terre au moyen âge* (Paris, 2004).

ECCLESTONE, M., 'Mortality of Rural Landless Men Before the Black Death: The Glastonbury Head-Tax Lists', *Local Population Studies*, 63 (1999).

EDDISON, J., GARDINER, M., and LONG, A. (eds.), *Romney Marsh: Environmental Change and Human Occupation in a Coastal Lowland*, Oxford University Committee for Archaeology Monographs, 46 (1998).

EGAN, G., 'Industry and Economics on the Medieval and Later London Waterfront', in G. L. Good, R. H. Jones, and M. W. Ponsford (eds.), *Waterfront Archaeology: Proceedings of the Third International Conference*, Council for British Archaeology Research Report, 74 (1991).

—— *Playthings from the Past* (London, 1996).

—— and PRITCHARD, F., *Dress Accessories, c.1150–c.1450*, Medieval Finds From Excavations in London, 3 (1991).

ELIASSEN, F.-E. and ERSLAND, G. A. (eds.), *Power, Profit and Urban Land: Landownership in Medieval and Early Modern Northern European Towns* (Aldershot, 1996).

EMERY, A., *Greater Medieval Houses of England and Wales 1300–1500*, Vol. II (Cambridge 2000).

EMMERSON, R. K. and GOLDBERG, P. J. P., ' "The Lord Geoffrey had me made": Lordship and Labour in the Luttrell Psalter', in J. Bothwell, P. J. P. Goldberg, and W. M. Ormrod (eds.), *The Problem of Labour in Fourteenth-Century England* (Woodbridge, 2000).

ENRIGHT, D. and WATTS, M., *A Romano-British and Medieval Settlement Site at Stoke Road, Bishop's Cleeve, Gloucestershire*, Cotswold Archaeology: Bristol and Gloucestershire Archaeological Reports, 1 (2002).

EPSTEIN, S. R., *An Island for Itself: Economic Development and Social Change in Late Medieval Sicily* (Cambridge, 1992).

—— *Freedom and Growth: The Rise of States and Markets in Europe, 1300–1750* (London, 2000).

—— (ed.), *Town and Country in Europe, 1300–1800* (Cambridge, 2001).

EVERSON, P. L., TAYLOR, C. C., and DUNN, C. J., *Changes and Continuity: Rural Settlement in North-West Lincolnshire*, Royal Commission on the Historical Monuments of England (1991).

FAITH, R. J., 'Berkshire: Fourteenth and Fifteenth Centuries', in P. D. A. Harvey (ed.), *The Peasant Land Market in Medieval England* (Oxford, 1984).

FARMER, D., 'The *Famuli* in the Later Middle Ages', in R. Britnell and J. Hatcher (eds.), *Progress and Problems in Medieval England: Essays in Honour of Edward Miller* (Cambridge, 1996).

FARNHILL, K., *Guilds and the Parish Community in Late Medieval East Anglia, c.1470–1550* (York, 2001).

FAULKNER, P. A., 'Medieval Undercrofts and Town Houses', *Archaeological Journal*, 123 (1966).

FELLER, L. (ed.), *Le Marché de la terre au moyen âge* (Paris, 2004).

FIELD, P. J. C., 'Thomas Malory and the Warwick Retinue Roll', *Midland History*, 5 (1979–80).

FIELD, R. K., 'Worcestershire Peasant Buildings, Household Goods and Farming Equipment in the Later Middle Ages', *MA* 9 (1965).

FINCH, M., *The Wealth of Five Northamptonshire Families 1540–1640* Northamptonshire Record Society, 19, (1956).

FINE, B. and LEOPOLD, E., *The World of Consumption* (London, 1993).

FOX, H. S. A., 'The Chronology of Enclosure and Economic Development in Medieval Devon', *Ec.HR*, 2nd ser., 28 (1975).

—— 'The Alleged Transformation from Two-field to Three-field Systems in Medieval England', *Ec.HR*, 2nd ser., 39 (1986).

—— 'Servants, Cottagers and Tied Cottages During the Later Middle Ages: Towards a Regional Dimension', *Rural History*, 6 (1995).

—— 'Exploitation of the Landless By Lords and Tenants in Early Medieval England', in Z. Razi and R. Smith (eds.), *Medieval Society and the Manor Court* (Oxford, 1996).

FOX, H., *The Evolution of the Fishing Village: Landscape and Society Along the South Devon Coast, 1086–1550* (Oxford, 2001).

FREEDMAN, P., *Images of the Medieval Peasant* (Stanford, 1999).

FRENCH, K. L., *The People of the Parish: Community Life in a Late Medieval Diocese* (Philadelphia, 2001).

GAIMSTER, D. and NENK, B., 'English Households in Transition c.1450–1550: The Ceramic Evidence', in D. Gaimster and P. Stamper (eds.), *The Age of Transition: The Archaeology of English Culture 1400–1600*, Society for Medieval Archaeology Monographs, 15 (1997).

—— and Stamper, P. (eds.), *The Age of Transition: The Archaeology of English Culture 1400–1600*, Society for Medieval Archaeology Monographs, 15 (1997).

Galloway, J. A., 'Driven By Drink? Ale Consumption and the Agrarian Economy of the London Region, *c.*1300–1400', in M. Carlin and J. T. Rosenthal (eds.), *Food and Eating in Medieval Europe* (London, 1998).

—— 'One Market or Many? London and the Grain Trade of England', in J. A. Galloway (ed.), *Trade, Urban Hinterlands and Market Integration c.1300–1600*, Centre for Metropolitan History Working Paper Series, 3 (2000).

—— (ed.), *Trade, Urban Hinterlands and Market Integration c.1300–1600*, Centre for Metropolitan History Working Papers Series, 3 (2000).

—— Keene, D., and Murphy, M., 'Fuelling the city: Production and Distribution of Firewood and Fuel in London's Region, 1290–1400', *Ec.HR*, 49 (1996).

Gardiner, M., 'Settlement Change on Denge and Walland Marshes, 1400–1550', in J. Eddison, M. Gardiner, and A. Long (eds.), *Romney Marsh: Environmental Change and Human Occupation in a Coastal Lowland*, Oxford University Committee for Archaeology Monographs, 46 (1998).

—— 'Vernacular Buildings and the Development of the Late Medieval Domestic Plan in England', *MA* 44 (2000).

Gerrard, S., *The Early British Tin Industry* (Stroud, 2000).

Giles, K. and Dyer, C. (eds.), *Town and Country in the Middle Ages: Contrasts, Contacts and Interconnections, 1100–1500*, Society for Medieval Archaeology Monographs, 22 (2005).

Girouard, M., *Life in the English Country House: A Social and Architectural History* (New Haven, 1978).

Given-Wilson, C., 'Wealth and Credit, Public and Private: The Earls of Arundel, 1306–1397', *English Historical Review*, 106 (1991).

—— 'The Problem of Labour in the Context of English Government, *c.*1350–1450', in J. Bothwell, P. J. P. Goldberg, and W. M. Ormrod (eds.), *The Problem of Labour in Fourteenth-Century England* (Woodbridge, 2000).

Glennie, P., 'In Search of Agrarian Capitalism: Manorial Land Markets and the Acquisition of Land in the Lea Valley *c.*1450–*c.*1560', *Continuity and Change*, 3 (1988).

Glick, T. F., *Irrigation and Society in Medieval Valencia* (Cambridge, Mass., 1970).

Goldberg, P. J. P., *Women, Work, and Life Cycle in a Medieval Economy: Women in York and Yorkshire c.1300–1520* (Oxford, 1992).

—— 'Masters and Men in Medieval England', in D. M. Hadley (ed.), *Masculinity in Medieval Europe* (Harlow, 1999).

—— (ed.), *Women in England c.1275–1525* (Manchester, 1995).

Good, G. L., Jones, R. H., and Ponsford, M. W. (eds.), *Waterfront Archaeology: Proceedings of the Third International Conference*, Council for British Archaeology Research Reports, 74 (1991).

Goodman, A. E., *The Wars of the Roses: Military Activity and English Society, 1452–97* (London, 1981).

GOUK, P. (ed.), *Wellsprings of Achievement* (Aldershot, 1995).

GRANT, L., (ed.), *Medieval Art, Architecture and Archaeology in London*, British Archaeological Association (1990).

GRASSBY, R., *The Idea of Capitalism Before the Industrial Revolution* (Lanham, Md., 1999).

GRAY, C. M., *Copyhold, Equity, and the Common Law* (Cambridge, Mass., 1963).

GRAY, E. F., 'Inclosures in England in the Sixteenth Century', *Quarterly Journal of Economics*, 17 (1903).

GRAY, I., 'A Gloucestershire Postscript to the "Domesday of Inclosures" ', *Transactions of the Bristol and Gloucestershire Archaeological Society*, 94 (1976).

GREENFIELD, L., *The Spirit of Capitalism* (Cambridge, Mass., 2001).

GRENVILLE, J., *Medieval Housing* (London, 1997).

GREW, F. and DE NEERGAARD, M., *Shoes and Pattens*, Medieval Finds From Excavations in London, 2 (1988).

HADLEY, D. M. (ed.), *Masculinity in Medieval Europe* (Harlow, 1999).

HALL, J. A., *Power and Liberties: The Causes and Consequences of the Rise of the West* (Oxford, 1985).

HALLAM, H. E. (ed.), *Agrarian History of England and Wales*, Vol. II, *1042–1350* (Cambridge, 1988).

HANHAM, A., *The Celys and their World: An English Merchant Family of the Fifteenth Century* (Cambridge, 1985).

HARDING, A., 'Political Liberty in the Middle Ages', *Speculum*, 55 (1980).

HARE, J. N., 'The Demesne Lessees of Fifteenth-Century Wiltshire', *Ag.HR* 29 (1981).

HARGREAVES, P., 'Seignorial Reaction and Peasant Responses: Worcester Priory and its Peasants After the Black Death', *Midland History*, 24 (1999).

HARRISON, B. and HUTTON, B., *Vernacular Houses in North Yorkshire and Cleveland* (Edinburgh, 1984).

HARRISON, D. F., 'Bridges and Economic Development, 1300–1800', *Ec.HR* 45 (1992).

HARRISS, G. L., 'Political Society and the Growth of Government in Late Medieval England', *P&P* 138 (1993).

HARTE, N. B. (ed.), *The New Draperies in the Low Countries and England, 1300–1800* (Oxford, 1997).

HARTLEY, R., 'Coleorton', *Current Archaeology*, 134 (1993).

HARVEY, B., 'The Leasing of the Abbot of Westminster's Demesnes in the Later Middle Ages', *Ec.HR*, 2nd ser., 22 (1969).

—— *Westminster Abbey and its Estates in the Middle Ages* (Oxford, 1977).

—— *Living and Dying in England 1100–1540: The Monastic Experience* (Oxford, 1993).

HARVEY, I. M. W., *Jack Cade's Rebellion of 1450* (Oxford, 1991).

HARVEY, P. D. A., *A Medieval Oxfordshire Village: Cuxham, 1240–1400* (Oxford, 1965).

—— (ed.), *The Peasant Land Market in Medieval England* (Oxford, 1984).

HATCHER, J., *Rural Economy and Society in the Duchy of Cornwall 1300–1500* (Cambridge, 1970)

—— *English Tin Production and Trade Before 1550* (Oxford, 1973).

—— 'Mortality in the Fifteenth Century: Some New Evidence', *Ec.HR*, 2nd ser., 39 (1986).

—— 'English Serfdom and Villeinage: Towards a Reassessment', in T. H. Aston (ed.), *Landlords, Peasants and Politics in Medieval England* (Cambridge, 1987).

—— *The History of the British Coal Industry*, Vol. I, *Before 1700: Towards the Age of Coal* (Oxford, 1993).

—— 'England in the Aftermath of the Black Death', *P&P* 144 (1994).

—— 'The Great Slump of the Mid-Fifteenth Century', in R. Britnell and J. Hatcher (eds.), *Progress and Problems in Medieval England: Essays in Honour of Edward Miller* (Cambridge, 1996).

—— 'Labour, Leisure and Economic Thought Before the Nineteenth Century', *P&P* 160 (1998).

—— and BAILEY, M., *Modelling the Middle Ages: The History and Theory of England's Economic Development* (Oxford, 2001).

—— and BARKER, T. C., *A History of British Pewter* (London, 1974).

HILL, N. and MILES, D., 'The Royal George, Cottingham, Northamptonshire: An Early Cruck Building', *Vernacular Architecture*, 32 (2001).

HILTON, R. H., 'Capitalism—What's In a Name?', *P&P* 1 (1952).

—— 'Freedom and Villeinage in England', *P&P* 31 (1965).

—— *The Decline of Serfdom in Medieval England*, Economic History Society (1969).

—— *Bond Man Made Free: Medieval Peasant Movements and the English Rising of 1381* (London, 1973).

—— 'Gloucester Abbey Leases of the Late Thirteenth Century', in R. H. Hilton, *The English Peasantry in the Later Middle Ages* (Oxford, 1975).

—— 'Rent and Capital Formation in Feudal Society', in R. H. Hilton, *The English Peasantry in the Later Middle Ages* (Oxford, 1975).

—— *The English Peasantry in the Later Middle Ages* (Oxford, 1975).

—— *A Medieval Society: The West Midlands at the End of the Thirteenth Century*, 2nd edn. (Cambridge, 1983).

—— 'Ideology and the Social Order in Late Medieval England', in R. H. Hilton, *Class Conflict and the Crisis of Feudalism* (London, 1985).

—— 'The Small Town and Urbanisation—Evesham in the Middle Ages', in R. H. Hilton, *Class Conflict and the Crisis of Feudalism* (London, 1985).

—— 'Some Social and Economic Evidence in Late Medieval English Tax Returns', in R. H. Hilton, *Class Conflict and the Crisis of Feudalism* (London, 1985).

—— 'Women Traders in Medieval England', in R. H. Hilton, *Class Conflict and the Crisis of Feudalism* (London, 1985).

—— *Class Conflict and the Crisis of Feudalism* (London, 1985).

HILTON, R. H., *English and French Towns in Feudal Society: A Comparative Study* (Cambridge, 1992).

—— (ed.), *Peasants, Knights and Heretics* (Cambridge, 1976).

—— (ed.), *The Transition from Feudalism to Capitalism* (London, 1976).

—— and ASTON, T. H. (eds.), *The English Rising of 1381* (Cambridge, 1984).

HINTON, D. A., *Archaeology, Economy and Society: England from the Fifth to the Fifteenth Century* (London, 1990).

HODGES, R., *The Anglo-Saxon Achievement: Archaeology and the Beginnings of English Society* (London, 1989).

HOFFMAN, P. T., *Growth in a Traditional Society: The French Countryside 1450–1815* (Princeton, 1996).

HOLMES, G. A., *The Estates of the Higher Nobility in Fourteenth-Century England* (Cambridge, 1957).

HOLT, R., *The Early History of the Town of Birmingham 1166 to 1600*, Dugdale Society Occasional Papers, 30 (1985).

—— 'Whose Were the Profits of Corn Milling? An Aspect of the Changing Relationship Between the Abbots of Glastonbury and Their Tenants, 1086–1350', *P&P* 116 (1987).

—— *The Mills of Medieval England* (Oxford, 1988).

HOLTON, R. J., *The Transition from Feudalism to Capitalism* (London, 1985).

HOMANS, G. C., *English Villagers of the Thirteenth Century* (Cambridge, Mass., 1941).

HOMER, R. F., 'Tin, Lead and Pewter', in J. Blair and N. Ramsey (eds.), *English Medieval Industries: Craftsmen, Techniques, Products* (London, 1991).

HOOKE, D., *The Landscape of Anglo-Saxon England* (London, 1998).

HOSKINS, W. G., *The Age of Plunder: The England of Henry VIII, 1500–1547* (London, 1976).

—— 'English Provincial Towns in the Early Sixteenth Century', in W. G. Hoskins, *Provincial England* (London, 1963).

—— *Provincial England* (London, 1963).

—— *The Making of the English Landscape*, revised edn. (London, 1988).

HOULBROOKE, R., *The English Family, 1450–1700* (London, 1984).

HOYLE, R. W., 'Tenure and the Land Market in Early Modern England: Or a Late Contribution to the Brenner Debate', *Ec.HR*, 2nd ser., 43 (1990).

HURST, J. D., 'A Medieval Ceramic Production Site and Other Medieval Sites in the Parish of Hanley Castle: Results of Fieldwork in 1987–92', *Transactions of the Worcestershire Archaeological Society*, 3rd ser., 14 (1994).

HYAMS, P. R., *Kings, Lords and Peasants in Medieval England: The Common Law of Villeinage in the Twelfth and Thirteenth Centuries* (Oxford, 1980).

—— 'What Did Edwardian Villagers Understand By "Law"?', in Z. Razi and R. M. Smith (eds.), *Medieval Society and the Manor Court* (Oxford, 1996).

ILIFFE, R., 'Working Bodies: Protestantism, the Productive Individual, and the Politics of Idleness', in P. Gouk (ed.), *Wellsprings of Achievement* (Aldershot, 1995).

IVES, E. W., *The Common Lawyers of Pre-Reformation England: Thomas Kebell: A Case Study* (Cambridge, 1983).

JERVOISE, E., *The Ancient Bridges of the North of England* (London, 1931).

JOHNSON, M., *Housing Culture: Traditional Architecture in an English Landscape* (London, 1993).

—— *The Archaeology of Capitalism* (Oxford, 1996).

—— *Behind the Castle Gate: From Medieval to Renaissance* (London, 2002).

JONES, E. L., *The European Miracle* (Cambridge, 1981).

JONES, E., 'River Navigation in Medieval England', *Journal of Historical Geography*, 26 (2000).

JONES, N., *God and the Moneylenders: Usury and Law in Early Modern England* (Oxford, 1989).

JOPE, E. M. (ed.), *Studies in Building History: Essays in Recognition of the Work of B. H. St. J. O'Neil* (London, 1961).

KAYE, J., *Economy and Nature in the Fourteenth Century* (Cambridge, 1998).

KEENE, D., 'Shops and Shopping in Medieval London', in L. Grant (ed.), *Medieval Art, Architecture and Archaeology in London*, British Archaeological Association (1990).

—— 'Small Towns and the Metropolis: The Experience of Medieval England', in J.-M. Duvosquel and E. Thoen (eds.), *Peasants and Townsmen in Medieval Europe: Studies in Honorem Adriaan Verhulst* (Ghent, 1995).

—— 'Landlords, the Property Market and Urban Development in Medieval England', in F.-E. Eliassen and G.A. Ersland (eds.), *Power, Profit and Urban Land: Landownership in Medieval and Early Modern Northern European Towns* (Aldershot, 1996).

—— 'Changes in London's Economic Hinterland as Indicated by Debt Cases in the Court of Common Pleas', in J. Galloway (ed.), *Trade, Urban Hinterlands and Market Integration c. 1300–1600*, Centre for Metropolitan History Working Paper Series, 3 (2000).

KERMODE, J. I., 'Money and Credit in the Fifteenth Century: Some Lessons From Yorkshire', *Business History Review*, 65 (1991).

—— *Medieval Merchants: York, Beverley and Hull in the Later Middle Ages* (Cambridge, 1998).

—— (ed.), *Enterprise and Individuals in Fifteenth-Century England* (Stroud, 1991).

KERSHAW, I., *Bolton Priory: The Economy of a Northern Monastery 1286–1325* (Oxford, 1973).

KING, E., *Peterborough Abbey 1086–1310: A Study in the Land Market* (Cambridge, 1973).

KOSMINSKY, E. A., *Studies in the Agrarian History of England in the Thirteenth Century* (Oxford, 1956).

KOWALESKI, M., *Local Markets and Regional Trade in Medieval Exeter* (Cambridge, 1995).

KÜMIN, B., *The Shaping of a Community: The Rise and Reformation of the English Parish c.1400–1560* (Aldershot, 1996).

LACHAUD, F., 'Dress and Social Status in England Before the Sumptuary Laws', in P. Coss and M. Keen (eds.), *Heraldry, Pageantry and Social Display in Medieval England* (Woodbridge, 2002).

LANGDON, J., 'The Economics of Horses and Oxen in Medieval England', *Ag.HR* 30 (1982).

—— 'Horse Hauling: A Revolution in Vehicle Transport in Twelfth- and Thirteenth-Century England', in T. H. Aston (ed.), *Landlords, Peasants and Politics in Medieval England* (Cambridge, 1987).

—— 'Watermills and Windmills in the West Midlands, 1086–1500', *Ec.HR* 44 (1991).

—— 'Lordship and Peasant Consumerism in the Milling Industry of Early Fourteenth-Century England', *P&P* 145 (1994).

—— 'Was England a Technological Backwater in the Middle Ages?', in G. G. Astill and J. Langdon (eds.), *Medieval Farming and Technology: The Impact of Agricultural Change in Northwest Europe* (Leiden, 1997).

—— 'Inland Water Transport in Medieval England—The View From the Mill', *Journal of Historical Geography*, 26 (2000).

—— *Mills in the Medieval Economy: England 1300–1540* (Oxford, 2004).

LANGHOLM, O., *Economics in the Medieval Schools: Wealth, Exchange, Value, Money and Usury according to the Paris Theological Tradition, 1200–1350* (Leiden, 1992).

LAPSLEY, G. T., 'The Account Roll of a Fifteenth-century Iron Master', *English Historical Review*, 14 (1899).

LAUGHTON, J. and DYER, C., 'Seasonal Patterns of Trade in the Later Middle Ages: Buying and Selling at Melton Mowbray, Leicestershire, 1400–1520', *Nottingham Medieval Studies*, 46 (2002).

—— JONES, E. and DYER, C., 'The Urban Hierarchy in the Later Middle Ages: A Study of the East Midlands', *Urban History*, 28 (2001).

LENNARD, R., *Rural England, 1086–1135: A Study of Social and Agrarian Conditions* (Oxford, 1959).

LE PATOUREL, H. E. J., 'Documentary Evidence and the Medieval Pottery Industry', *MA* 12 (1968).

LEWIS, C., MITCHELL-FOX, P., and DYER, C., *Village, Hamlet and Field: Changing Medieval Settlements in Central England*, 2nd edn. (Macclesfield, 2001).

LINEHAN, C. D., 'Deserted Sites and Rabbit-Warrens on Dartmoor, Devon', *MA* 10 (1966).

LIPSON, E., *The Economic History of England* (London, 1915).

—— *The History of the Woollen and Worsted Industries* (London, 1921).

LLOYD, T. H., *Some Aspects of the Building Industry in Medieval Stratford-upon-Avon*, Dugdale Society Occasional Papers, 14 (1961).

—— *The English Wool Trade in the Middle Ages* (Cambridge, 1977).

LOMAS, R. A., 'The Priory of Durham and its Demesnes in the Fourteenth and Fifteenth Centuries', *Ec.HR*, 2nd ser., 31 (1978).

MCCLURE, P., 'Patterns of Migration in the Late Middle Ages: The Evidence of English Place-Name Surnames', *Ec.HR*, 2nd ser., 32 (1979).

McCracken, G., *Culture and Consumption: New Approaches to the Symbolic Character of Consumer Goods and Activities* (Bloomington and Indianapolis, 1990).

MacCulloch, D., 'Bondmen Under the Tudors', in C. Cross, D. Loades, and J. Scarisbrick (eds.), *Law and Government Under the Tudors* (Cambridge, 1988).

MacFarlane, A., *The Origins of English Individualism* (Oxford, 1978).

McFarlane, K. B., 'William Worcester, a Preliminary Survey', in K. B. McFarlane, *England in the Fifteenth Century* (London, 1981).

—— 'The Investment of Sir John Fastolf's Profits of War', in K. B. McFarlane, *England in the Fifteenth Century* (London, 1981).

—— *England in the Fifteenth Century* (London, 1981).

McIntosh, M. K., *Controlling Misbehavior in England, 1370–1600* (Cambridge, 1998).

McKendrick, N., Brewer, J., and Plumb, J. H., *The Birth of a Consumer Society: The Consumer in Eighteenth-Century England* (London, 1982).

McRae, A., *God Speed the Plough: The Representation of Agrarian England, 1500–1660* (Cambridge, 1996).

Maddern, P. C., *Violence and Social Order: East Anglia 1422–1442* (Oxford, 1992).

Maddicott, J. R., *The English Peasantry and the Demands of the Crown, 1294–1341*, *P&P* supplement, 1 (1975).

Malcolmson, R. W., *Popular Recreation in English Society, 1700–1850* (Cambridge, 1973).

Mann, J., *Chaucer and Medieval Estates Satire: The Literature of Social Classes and the General Prologue to the Canterbury Tales* (Cambridge, 1973).

Mann, M., *The Sources of Social Power*, Vol. I, *A History of Power from the Beginning of A.D. 1760* (Cambridge, 1986).

Marfany, J.-L., 'Debate: The Invention of Leisure in Early Modern Europe', *P&P* 156 (1997).

Martin, D., 'The Configuration of Inner Rooms and Chambers in the Transitional Houses of Eastern Sussex', *Vernacular Architecture*, 34 (2003).

Martin, J., 'Sheep and Enclosure in Sixteenth-Century Northamptonshire', *Ag.HR* 36 (1988).

Masschaele, J., 'Transport Costs in Medieval England', *Ec.HR* 46 (1993).

—— 'The Multiplicity of Medieval Markets Reconsidered', *Journal of Historical Geography*, 20 (1994).

—— *Peasants, Merchants, and Markets: Inland Trade in Medieval England, 1150–1350* (New York, 1997).

Mate, M., 'Profit and Productivity on the Estates of Isabella de Forz (1260–92)', *Ec.HR*, 2nd ser., 33 (1980).

—— 'The Agrarian Economy of South-East England Before the Black Death: Depressed or Buoyant?', in B. M. S. Campbell (ed.), *Before the Black Death: Studies in the 'Crisis' of the Early Fourteenth Century* (Manchester, 1991).

—— 'The East Sussex Land Market and Agrarian Class Structure in the Late Middle Ages', *P&P* 139 (1993).

MATE, M., *Daughters, Wives and Widows After the Black Death: Women in Sussex, 1350–1535* (Woodbridge, 1998).

MAYHEW, N. J., 'Modelling Medieval Monetisation', in R. H. Britnell and B. M. S. Campbell (eds.), *A Commercialising Economy: England 1086–c.1300* (Manchester, 1995).

—— 'Population, Money Supply, and the Velocity of Circulation in England, 1300–1700', *Ec.HR* 48 (1995).

MEIRION-JONES, G. and JONES, M. (eds.), *Manorial Domestic Building in England and Northern France*, Society of Antiquaries Occasional Papers, 15 (1993).

MELLOR, M., 'A Synthesis of Middle and Late Saxon, Medieval and Early Post-Medieval Pottery in the Oxford Region', *Oxoniensia*, 59 (1994).

MENJOT, D. (ed.), *Manger et boire au moyen âge*, 2 vols. (Nice, 1984).

METCALF, D. M., 'The Prosperity of North-Western Europe in the Eighth and Ninth Centuries', *Ec.HR*, 2nd ser., 20 (1967).

—— 'The Monetary Economy of Ninth-Tenth Century England South of the Humber: A Topographical Analysis', in M. A. S. Blackburn and D. N. Dumville (eds.), *Kings, Currency and Alliances: History and Coinage of Southern England in the Ninth Century* (Woodbridge, 1998).

MILLER, D., *Material Culture and Mass Consumption* (Oxford, 1987).

—— (ed.), *Acknowledging Consumption* (London, 1990).

MILLER, E., *The Abbey and Bishopric of Ely* (Cambridge, 1951).

—— 'The Fortunes of the English Textile Industry During the Thirteenth Century', *Ec.HR*, 2nd ser., 18 (1965).

—— (ed.), *Agrarian History of England and Wales*, Vol. III, *1348–1500* (Cambridge, 1991).

—— and HATCHER, J., *Medieval England: Rural Society and Economic Change, 1086–1348* (London, 1978).

—— —— *Medieval England: Towns, Commerce and Crafts, 1086–1348* (Harlow, 1995).

MILNE, G., *The Port of Medieval London* (Stroud, 2003).

MOISA, M. and BENNETT, J. M., 'Debate: Conviviality and Charity in Medieval and Early Modern England', *P&P* 154 (1997).

MOORE, J., ' "Quot homines?" The Population of Domesday England', *Anglo-Norman Studies*, 19 (1996).

MORAN, M., *Vernacular Buildings of Shropshire* (Almeley, Hereford., 2003).

MORETON, C. E., *The Townshends and their World: Gentry, Law and Land in Norfolk c.1450–1551* (Oxford, 1992).

—— and RICHMOND, C., ' "Beware of grazing on foul mornings": A Gentleman's Husbandry Notes', *Norfolk Archaeology*, 43 (2000).

MORRIS, J. E., *The Welsh Wars of Edward I* (Oxford, 1901).

MULDREW, C., *The Economy of Obligation: The Culture of Credit and Social Relations in Early Modern England* (London, 1998).

MÜLLER, M., 'The Function and Evasion of Marriage Fines on a Fourteenth-Century English Manor', *Continuity and Change*, 14 (1999).

—— 'The Aims and Organisation of a Peasant Revolt in Early Fourteenth-Century Wiltshire', *Rural History. Economy, Society, Culture*, 14 (2003).

MUNRO, J. H., 'Industrial Transformation in the North-West European Textile Trades, *c*.1290–*c*.1340: Economic Progress or Economic Crisis?' in B. M. S. Campbell (ed.), *Before the Black Death* (Manchester, 1991).

—— 'Textile Technology in the Middle Ages', in J. H. Munro, *Textiles, Towns and Trade* (Aldershot, 1994).

—— *Textiles, Towns and Trade* (Aldershot, 1994).

—— 'The "Industrial Crisis" of the English Textile Towns, *c*.1290–*c*.1330', *Thirteenth Century England*, 7 (1997).

—— 'Industrial Energy from Water-Mills in the European Economy, 5th to 18th Centuries: The Limitations of Power', in S. Cavaciocchi (ed.), *Economia e Energia, Secc. XIII–XVIII*, Istituto Internazionale di Storia Economica 'F. Datini', Prato, 34 (2002).

MUSSON, A., *Medieval Law in Context: The Growth of Legal Consciousness from Magna Carta to the Peasants' Revolt* (Manchester, 2001).

MYNARD, D. C., ZEEPVAT, R. J., and WILLIAMS, R. J., *Excavations at Great Linford, 1974–80*, Buckinghamshire Archaeological Society Monograph Series, 3 (1991).

NEWMAN, C. M., 'Employment on the Estates of the Priory of Durham, 1494–1519: The Priory As an Employer', *Northern History*, 36 (2000).

NEWTON, S. M., *Fashion in the Age of the Black Prince* (Woodbridge, 1980).

NICHOLAS, D. M., 'Economic Reorientation and Social Change in Fourteenth-Century Flanders', *P&P* 70 (1976).

NIGHTINGALE, P., 'Monetary Contraction and Mercantile Credit in Later Medieval England', *Ec.HR*, 2nd ser., 43 (1990).

—— *A Medieval Mercantile Community: The Grocers' Company and the Politics and Trade of London 1000–1485* (New Haven and London, 1995).

—— 'Knights and Merchants: Trade, Politics and the Gentry in Late Medieval England', *P&P* 169 (2000).

NOONAN, J. T., *The Scholastic Analysis of Usury* (Cambridge, Mass., 1957).

NORRIS, M., *Monumental Brasses: The Memorials* (London, 1977).

OGILVIE, S. and CERMAN, M., *European Proto-Industrialization* (Cambridge, 1996).

O'BRIEN, P. K. and HUNT, P. A., 'England, 1485–1815', in R. Bonney (ed.), *The Rise of the Fiscal State in Europe, c.1200–1815* (Oxford, 1999).

OEXLE, O. G., 'The Middle Ages Through Modern Eyes: A Historical Problem', *Transactions of the Royal Historical Society*, 6th ser., 9 (1999).

ORME, N., *Medieval Children* (New Haven and London, 2001).

OVERTON, M., *Agricultural Revolution in England: The Transformation of the Agrarian Economy, 1500–1850* (Cambridge, 1996).

OVITT, G., *The Restoration of Perfection: Labour and Technology in Medieval Culture* (New Brunswick, 1987).

PAGE, F. M., *The Estates of Crowland Abbey* (Cambridge, 1934).

PALLISER, D., *The Staffordshire Landscape* (London, 1976).

PALLISER, D., (ed.), *The Cambridge Urban History of Britain*, Vol. I, *c.600–1540* (Cambridge, 2000).

PALMER, J. J. N., 'The Wealth of the Secular Aristocracy in 1086', *Anglo-Norman Studies*, 22 (1999).

PANTIN, W. A., 'Medieval Inns', in E. M. Jope (ed.), *Studies in Building History: Essays in Recognition of the Work of B. H. St. J. O'Neil* (London, 1961).

PATTEN, J., 'Village and Town: An Occupational Study', *Ag.HR* 20 (1972).

PEACOCK, D. P. S. (ed.), *Pottery and Early Commerce* (London, 1977).

PEARSON, S., *The Medieval Houses of Kent: An Historical Analysis*, Royal Commission on the Historical Monuments of England (1994).

—— 'The Chronological Distribution of Tree-ring Dates, 1980–2001: An Update", *Vernacular Architecture*, 32 (2001).

—— 'Rural and Urban Houses 1100–1500: "Urban Adaptation" Reconsidered', in K. Giles and C. Dyer (eds.), *Town and Country in the Middle Ages: Contrasts, Contacts and Interconnections, 1100–1500*, Society for Medieval Archaeology Monographs, 22 (2005).

PELLING, M. and SMITH, R. M. (eds.), *Life, Death and the Elderly* (London, 1991).

PENN, S. and DYER, C., 'Wages and Earnings in Late Medieval England: Evidence from the Enforcement of the Labour Laws', *Ec.HR*, 2nd ser., 43 (1990).

PERSSON, G., 'Consumption, Labour and Leisure in the Late Middle Ages', in D. Menjot (ed.), *Manger et boire au moyen âge*, 2 vols. (Nice, 1984).

PHYTHIAN-ADAMS, C., *Desolation of a City: Coventry and the Urban Crisis of the Late Middle Ages* (Cambridge, 1979).

PIPONNIER, F. and MANE, P., *Dress in the Middle Ages* (New Haven and London, 1997).

POLLARD, A., 'The North-Eastern Economy and the Agrarian Crisis of 1438–40', *Northern History*, 25 (1989).

POLLOCK, F. and MAITLAND, F., *The History of English Law Before the Time of Edward I*, new edn. (Cambridge, 1968).

POMERANZ, K., *The Great Divergence: Europe, China and the Making of the Modern World Economy* (Princeton, 2000).

POOS, L., 'The Social Context of Statute of Labourers Enforcement', *Law and History Review*, 1 (1983).

—— 'Population Turnover in Medieval Essex', in L. Bonfield, R. M. Smith, and K. Wrightson (eds.), *The World We Have Gained: Histories of Population and Social Structure* (Oxford, 1986).

—— *A Rural Society after the Black Death: Essex 1350–1525* (Cambridge, 1991).

POSTAN, M. M., 'Agricultural Problems of Under-developed Countries in the Light of European Agrarian History', in *Second International Conference of Economic History, Aix en Provence, 1962* (Paris, 1965).

—— 'Medieval Agrarian Society in its Prime: England', in M. M. Postan (ed.), *The Cambridge Economic History of Europe*, Vol. I, *The Agrarian Life of the Middle Ages*, 2nd edn. (Cambridge, 1966).

—— 'Investment in Medieval Agriculture', *Journal of Economic History*, 27 (1967).

—— *The Medieval Economy and Society: An Economic History of Britain 1100–1500* (London, 1972).

—— *Essays on Medieval Agriculture and General Problems of the Medieval Economy* (Cambridge, 1973).

—— (ed.), *The Cambridge Economic History of Europe*, Vol. I, *The Agrarian Life of the Middle Ages*, 2nd edn. (Cambridge, 1966).

—— and MILLER, E. (eds.), *The Cambridge Economic History of Europe*, Vol. II, 2nd edn. (Cambridge, 1987).

POUND, J. F., 'The Social and Trade Structure of Norwich, 1525–1575', *P&P* 34 (1966).

POWER, E., 'The Wool Trade in the Fifteenth Century', in E. Power and M. M. Postan (eds.), *Studies in English Trade in the Fifteenth Century* (London, 1933).

—— and POSTAN, M. M. (eds.), *Studies in English Trade in the Fifteenth Century* (London, 1933).

RACKHAM, O., *Ancient Woodland* (London, 1980).

RAFTIS, J. A., *The Estates of Ramsey Abbey* (Toronto, 1957).

—— *Tenure and Mobility* (Toronto, 1964).

RAMSAY, N., 'Alabaster', in J. Blair and N. Ramsay (eds.), *English Medieval Industries: Craftsmen, Techniques, Products* (London, 1991).

RAPPAPORT, S., *Worlds Within Worlds: Structures of Life in Sixteenth-Century London* (Cambridge, 1989).

RAVEN, J. J., 'Extracts From the Parish Book of Dennington, Co. Suffolk', *The East Anglian or Notes and Queries etc.*, NS, 3 (1889–90).

RAWCLIFFE, C., *The Staffords, Earls of Stafford and Dukes of Buckingham 1394–1521* (Cambridge, 1978).

RAZI, Z., 'Family, Land and the Village Community in Later Medieval England', in T. H. Aston (ed.), *Landlords, Peasants and Politics in Medieval England* (Cambridge, 1987).

—— 'The Myth of the Immutable English Family', *P&P* 140 (1993).

—— and SMITH, R. M., 'The Origins of the English Manorial Court Rolls as a Written Record: A Puzzle', in Z. Razi and R. M. Smith (eds.), *Medieval Society and the Manor Court* (Oxford, 1996).

—— —— and Smith, R. (eds.), *Medieval Society and the Manor Court* (Oxford, 1996).

REES JONES, S., 'Household, Work and the Problem of Mobile Labour: The Regulation of Labour in Medieval English Towns', in J. Bothwell, P. J. P. Goldberg, and W. M. Ormrod (eds.), *The Problem of Labour in Fourteenth Century England* (Woodbridge, 2000).

RICHARDS, J., *Viking Age England* (London, 1991).

RICHMOND, C., *John Hopton: A Fifteenth Century Suffolk Gentleman* (Cambridge, 1981).

—— 'The Transition From Feudalism To Capitalism in the Archives of Magdalen College', *History Workshop Journal*, 37 (1994).

RIGBY, S. H., *English Society in the Later Middle Ages: Class, Status and Gender* (Basingstoke, 1995).

ROBERTS, E., 'Overton Court Farm and the Late-Medieval Farmhouses of Demesne Lessees in Hampshire', *Proceedings of the Hampshire Field Club*, 51 (1996).

—— *Hampshire Houses 1250–1700: Their Dating and Development* (Winchester, 2003).

ROSKELL, J. S., 'William Catesby, Counsellor to Richard III', *Bulletin of the John Rylands Library*, 42 (1959).

ROSSER, G., 'Going to the Fraternity Feast: Commensality and Social Relations in Late Medieval England', *Journal of British Studies*, 33 (1994).

—— 'Crafts, Guilds and the Negotiation of Work in the Medieval Town, *P&P* 154 (1997).

ROSTOW, W. W., *How It All Began: Origins of the Modern Economy* (London, 1975).

RUSHEN, P. C., *The History and Antiquities of Chipping Campden* (London, n.d.).

SALZMAN, L. F., *Building in England: Down to 1540*, 2nd edn. (Oxford, 1967).

SAUL, N., *Knights and Esquires: The Gloucestershire Gentry in the Fourteenth Century* (Oxford, 1981).

—— 'The Social Status of Chaucer's Franklin: A Reconsideration', *Medium Aevum*, 52 (1983).

SCHOFIELD, P. R., 'Dearth, Debt and the Local Land Market in a Late Thirteenth-century Village Community', *Ag.HR* 45 (1997).

—— '*Extranei* and the Market for Customary Land on a Westminster Abbey Manor in the Fifteenth Century', *Ag.HR* 49 (2001).

—— 'Access to Credit in the Early Fourteenth-Century English Countryside', in P. R. Schofield and N. J. Mayhew (eds.), *Credit and Debt in Medieval England c.1180–c.1350* (Oxford, 2002).

—— *Peasant and Community in Medieval England 1200–1500* (Basingstoke, 2003).

—— and MAYHEW, N. J. (eds.), *Credit and Debt in Medieval England c.1180–c.1350* (Oxford, 2002).

SCHUBERT, H. R., *History of the British Iron and Steel Industry from c.450 B.C. to A.D. 1775* (London, 1957).

SCOTT, T., *Freiburg and the Breisgau: Town–Country Relations in the Age of Reformation and Peasants' War* (Oxford, 1986).

—— *Regional Identity and Economic Change: The Upper Rhine, 1450–1600* (Oxford, 1997).

—— (ed.), *The Peasantries of Europe from the Fourteenth to the Eighteenth Centuries* (Harlow, 1998).

SEABOURNE, G., *Royal Regulation of Loans and Sales in Medieval England: 'Monkish Superstition and Civil Tyranny'* (Woodbridge, 2003).

SHAMMAS, C., *The Preindustrial Consumer in England and America* (Oxford, 1990).

SIMCO, A. and McKEAGUE, P., *Bridges of Bedfordshire*, Bedfordshire Archaeology Occasional Monograph Series, 2 (1997).

SKIPP, V., *Medieval Yardley* (London, 1970).

SLACK, P., *Poverty and Policy in Tudor and Stuart England* (London, 1988).

—— *From Reformation to Improvement: Public Welfare in Early Modern England* (Oxford, 1999).

SLATER, T., 'Domesday Village to Medieval Town: The Topography of Medieval Stratford-upon-Avon', in R. Bearman (ed.), *The History of an English Borough: Stratford-upon-Avon 1196–1996* (Stroud, 1997).

—— (ed.), *Towns in Decline AD 100–1600* (Aldershot, 2000).

—— and JARVIS, P. J. (eds.), *Field and Forest: An Historical Geography of Warwickshire and Worcestershire* (Norwich, 1982).

SMITH, R. A. L., *Canterbury Cathedral Priory: A Study in Monastic Administration* (Cambridge, 1943).

SMITH, R. M., 'Rooms, Relatives and Residential Arrangements: Some Evidence in Manor Court Rolls 1250–1500', *Medieval Village Research Group Annual Report*, 30 (1982).

—— 'Some Thoughts on "Hereditary" and "Proprietary" Rights in Land Under Customary Law in Thirteenth and Fourteenth Century England', *Law and History Review*, 1 (1983).

—— 'Families and Their Land in an Area of Partible Inheritance: Redgrave, Suffolk 1260–1320', in R. M. Smith (ed.), *Land, Kinship and Life-Cycle* (Cambridge, 1984).

—— (ed.), *Land, Kinship and Life-Cycle* (Cambridge, 1984).

—— 'Human Resources', in G. Astill and A. Grant (eds.), *The Countryside of Medieval England* (Oxford, 1988).

—— 'The Manorial Court and the Elderly Tenant in Late Medieval England', in M. Pelling and R. M. Smith (eds.), *Life, Death and the Elderly* (London, 1991).

—— 'The English Peasantry, 1250–1650', in T. Scott (ed.), *The Peasantries of Europe from the Fourteenth to the Eighteenth Centuries* (Harlow, 1998).

SOLAR, P. M., 'Poor Relief and English Economic Development Before the Industrial Revolution', *Ec.HR* 48 (1995).

SOMBART, W., *The Quintessence of Capitalism* (New York, 1967).

SPENCER, B., *Pilgrim Souvenirs and Secular Badges*, Salisbury Museum Medieval Catalogue, 2 (1990).

SPUFFORD, M., *Contrasting Communities: English Villagers in the Sixteenth and Seventeenth Centuries* (Cambridge, 1974).

—— 'The Limitations of the Probate Inventory', in J. Chartres and D. Hey (eds.), *English Rural Society, 1500–1800: Essays in Honour of Joan Thirsk* (Cambridge, 1990).

SPUFFORD, P., *Money and its Use in Medieval Europe* (Cambridge, 1988).

—— *Power and Profit: The Merchant in Medieval Europe* (London, 2002).

STANLEY, M. J., 'Medieval Tax Returns as Source Material', in T. R. Slater and P. J. Jarvis (eds.), *Field and Forest: An Historical Geography of Warwickshire and Worcestershire* (Norwich, 1982).

STEPHENSON, M., 'Wool Yields in the Medieval Economy', *Ec.HR*, 2nd ser., 41 (1988).

STINSON, M., 'Assarting and Poverty in Early Fourteenth-Century West Yorkshire', *Landscape History*, 5 (1983).

STONE, D., 'Farm Management and Agricultural Mentalities on the Demesne of Wisbech Barton in the Fourteenth and Early Fifteenth Centuries', in Economic History Society, *New Researchers' Papers* (Oxford, 1999).

—— 'Medieval Farm Management and Technological Mentalities: Hinderclay Before the Black Death', *Ec.HR* 54 (2001).

STONE, E. L. G., 'Profit and Loss Accountancy at Norwich Cathedral Priory', *Transactions of the Royal Historical Society*, 5th ser., 12 (1962).

STOREY, R. L., 'Gentlemen-Bureaucrats', in C. H. Clough (ed.), *Profession, Vocation and Culture in Later Medieval England* (Liverpool, 1982).

SUGGETT, R., 'The Chronology of Late-Medieval Timber Houses in Wales', *Vernacular Architecture*, 27 (1996).

SUTTON, A. F., 'Mercery Through Four Centuries, 1130–c.1500', *Nottingham Medieval Studies*, 41 (1997).

—— 'Some Aspects of the Linen Trade, c.1130 to 1500, and the Part Played by the Mercers of London', *Textile History*, 30 (1999).

—— 'The Merchant Adventurers of England: Their Origins and the Mercers' Company of London', *Historical Research*, 75 (2002).

SWANSON, H., 'The Illusion of Economic Structure: Craft Guilds in Late Medieval English Towns', *P&P* 121 (1988).

SWANSON, H., *Medieval Artisans: An Urban Class in Late Medieval England* (Oxford, 1989).

SWANSON, R. N., *Church and Society in Late Medieval England* (Oxford, 1989).

SWEEZY, P., 'A Critique', in R. Hilton (ed.), *The Transition from Feudalism to Capitalism* (London, 1976).

TAYLOR, C., *Roads and Tracks of Britain* (London, 1979).

TAYLOR, C. C., *Village and Farmstead: A History of Rural Settlement in England* (London, 1983).

TAWNEY, R. H., *The Agrarian Problem in the Sixteenth Century* (London, 1912).

THIRSK, J., 'The Common Fields', in R. H. Hilton (ed.), *Peasants, Knights and Heretics* (Cambridge, 1976).

—— *Economic Policy and Projects: The Development of a Consumer Society in Early Modern England* (Oxford, 1978).

—— *Agrarian Regions and Agrarian History in England, 1500–1750* (London and Basingstoke, 1987).

—— *Alternative Agriculture: A History* (Oxford, 1997).

—— (ed.), *The English Rural Landscape* (Oxford, 2000).

THOMAS, K., 'Work and Leisure in Pre-industrial Society', *P&P* 29 (1964).

THOMPSON, M. W., *The Decline of the Castle* (Cambridge, 1987).

THORNTON, T. (ed.), *Social Attitudes and Political Structures in the Fifteenth Century* (Stroud, 2000).

THORPE, H., 'The Lord and the Landscape, Illustrated Through the Changing Fortunes of a Warwickshire Parish, Wormleighton', *Transactions of the Birmingham Archaeological Society*, 80 (1962).

THRELFALL-HOLMES, M., 'Late Medieval Iron Production and Trade in the Northeast', *Archaeologia Aeliana*, 5th ser., 27 (1999).

THRUPP, S., *Merchant Class of Medieval London (1300–1500)* (Ann Arbor, 1948).

TITOW, J. Z., *English Rural Society 1200–1350* (London, 1969).

TITS-DIEUAIDE, M.-J., *La Formation des prix céréalières en Brabant et en Flandre au XVe siècle* (Brussels, 1975).

TRIBE, K., *Genealogies of Capitalism* (London, 1981).

UNGER, R. W., 'Technical Change in the Brewing Industry in Germany, the Low Countries and England in the Late Middle Ages', *Journal of European Economic History*, 21 (1992).

VAN DEN HOVEN, M., *Work in Ancient and Medieval Thought* (Leiden, 1996).

VEALE, E., *The English Fur Trade in the Later Middle Ages* (Oxford, 1966).

Victoria County Histories, Cheshire, Essex, Oxfordshire, Staffordshire, Warwickshire.

VINCE, A., 'The Medieval and Post-medieval Ceramic Industry of the Malvern Region: The Study of a Ware and its Distribution', in D. P. S. Peacock (ed.), *Pottery and Early Commerce* (London, 1977).

VINOGRADOFF, P., *Villainage in England* (Oxford, 1892).

WALLERSTEIN, I., *The Modern World System: Capitalist Agriculture and the Origins of the European World-Economy in the Sixteenth Century* (New York, 1974).

WATKINS, A., 'Cattle Grazing in the Forest of Arden in the Later Middle Ages', *Ag.HR* 37 (1989).

—— 'The Woodland Economy of the Forest of Arden in the Later Middle Ages', *Midland History*, 18 (1993).

—— 'Landowners and Their Estates in the Forest of Arden in the Fifteenth Century', *Ag.HR*, 45 (1997).

WATTS, J. L. (ed.), *The End of the Middle Ages? England in the Fifteenth and Sixteenth Centuries* (Stroud, 1998).

WEATHERILL, L., *Consumer Behaviour and Material Culture in Britain, 1660–1760* (London, 1988).

WEDDELL, P. J. and REED, S. J., 'Observations at Sourton Down, Okehampton, 1986–1991: Roman Road, Deserted Medieval Hamlet and Other Landscape Features', *Devon Archaeological Society Proceedings*, 55 (1997).

WELCH, C., 'Ralph Wolseley, a Fifteenth-Century Capitalist', *Staffordshire Archaeological and Historical Society Transactions*, 39 (2001).

WELSFORD, A. E., *John Greenway, 1460–1529: Merchant of Tiverton and London: A Devon Worthy* (Tiverton, 1984).

WHITE, W. J., *Skeletal Remains from the Cemetery of St. Nicholas Shambles, City of London*, London and Middlesex Archaeological Society, Special Paper 9 (1988).

WHITTLE, J., *The Development of Agrarian Capitalism: Land and Labour in Norfolk 1440–1580* (Oxford, 2000).

WILLIAMS, E. H. D., 'Church Houses in Somerset', *Vernacular Architecture*, 23 (1992).

WILLIAMSON, J. A., *The Cabot Voyages and Bristol Discovery Under Henry VII*, Hakluyt Society, 2nd ser., 120 (1962).

WOOD, D., *Medieval Economic Thought* (Cambridge, 2002).

WOODWARD, D., *Men at Work: Labourers and Building Craftsmen in the Towns of Northern England, 1450–1750* (Cambridge, 1995).

WOOLGAR, C. M., *The Great Household in Late Medieval England* (New Haven and London, 1999).

WORDIE, J. R., 'The Chronology of English Enclosure, 1500–1914', *Ec.HR*, 2nd ser., 36 (1983).

WRIGHT, S. M., *The Derbyshire Gentry in the Fifteenth Century*, Derbyshire Record Society, 8 (1983).

WRIGHTSON, K., ' "Sorts of people" in Tudor and Stuart England', in J.Barry and C. Brookes (eds.), *The Middling Sort of People: Culture, Society and Politics in England, 1550–1800* (London, 1994).

WRIGHTSON, K., *Earthly Necessities. Economic Lives in Early Modern Britain* (New Haven and London, 2000).

WRIGHTSON, K. and Levine, D., *Poverty and Piety in an English Village, Terling, 1525–1700* (New York, 1979).

WRIGLEY, E.A., 'A Simple Model of London's Importance in Changing English Society and Eeconomy, 1650–1750', *P&P* 37 (1967).

WRIGLEY, E.A., 'Urban Growth and Agricultural Change: England and the Continent in the Early Modern Period', *Journal of Interdisciplinary History*, 15 (1985).

WRIGLEY, E.A., 'Country and Town: the Primary, Secondary and Tertiary Peopling of England in the Early Modern Period', in P. Slack and R. Ward (eds.), *The Peopling of Britain: The Shaping of a Human Landscape. The Linacre Lectures 1999* (Oxford, 2002).

WRIGLEY, E. A. and Schofield, R.S., *The Population History of England, 1541–1872: a Reconstruction* (London, 1981).

YATES, M., 'Watermills in the Local Economy of a Late Medieval Manor in Berkshire', in T. Thornton (ed.), *Social Attitudes and Political Structures in the Fifteenth Century* (Stroud, 2000).

YELLING, J., *Common Field and Enclosure in England, 1450–1850* (London, 1977).

YOUNGS, D., 'Servants and Labourers on a Late Medieval Demesne: the Case of Newton, Cheshire, 1498–1520', *Ag.HR* 47 (1999).

YOUNGS, D., 'Estate Management, Investment and the Gentleman Landlord in Later Medieval England', *Historical Research*, 73 (2000).

ZELL, M., 'Fifteenth- and Sixteenth-Century Wills as Historical Sources', *Archives*, 14 (1979).

—— *Industry in the Countryside: Wealden Society in the Sixteenth Century* (Cambridge, 1994).

Theses

CARLIN, M. N., 'Christ Church, Canterbury and its Lands, from the Beginning of the Priorate of Thomas Chillenden to the Dissolution (1391–1540)', University of Oxford, B.Litt. thesis (1970).

FENWICK, C. C., 'The English Poll Taxes of 1377, 1379 and 1381', University of London, Ph.D. thesis (1983).

LLOYD, T. H., 'The Medieval Gilds of Stratford-upon-Avon and the Timber-Framed Building Industry', University of Birmingham, MA thesis (1961).

THOMAS, R., 'Animals, Economy and Status: The Integration of Historical and Zooarchaeological Evidence in the Study of a Medieval Castle', University of Birmingham, Ph.D. thesis (2003).

YANG, J., 'Wage-Earners in Early Sixteenth-Century England', University of Birmingham, Ph.D thesis (1986).

Index

Note: Places are identified by the counties as they existed in 1931–74